Texts in Comp

Volume 20

An Introduction to
Ontology Engineering

Texts in Computing Series Editor
Ian Mackie

mackie@lix.polytechnique.

An Introduction to Ontology Engineering

C. Maria Keet

© Individual author and College Publications 2018. All rights reserved.

ISBN 978-1-84890-295-4

College Publications
Scientific Director: Dov Gabbay
Managing Director: Jane Spurr

http://www.collegepublications.co.uk

Cover produced by Laraine Welch
Frontcover image made using htmlgraph

Printed by Lightning Source, Milton Keynes, UK

Contents

Preface

This book is my attempt at providing the first textbook for an introduction in ontology engineering. Indeed, there are books about ontology engineering, but they either promote one specific ontology or methodology only, are handbooks, or are conference proceedings. There have been collaborative initiatives that aimed for a generic introduction, yet they have not made it to the writing stage. Problems to overcome with such an endeavour—aside from the difficult task of finding time to write it—are, mainly, to answer the questions of 1) *which topics should an introductory textbook on ontology engineering cover?* and 2) *how comprehensive should an introduction be?* The answer to the first question is different for the different audiences, in particular with respect to emphases of one topic or another and the order of things. The intended audience for this textbook are people at the level of advanced undergraduate and early postgraduate studies in computer science. This entails, for instance, that I assume the reader will know what UML class diagrams and databases are. As computing degrees seem to have a tendency to have become less theoretical, a solid background in logic, reasoning, and computational complexity is not expected, so a gentle introduction (or recap, as it may be) of the core concepts is provided. There are no lengthy philosophical debates in any of the chapters, but philosophical aspects are presented and discussed mainly only insofar as they are known to affect the engineering side. There still will be sections of interest for philosophers and domain experts, but they may prefer to work through the chapters in a different order (see 'how to use the book').

As to how comprehensive an introduction to ontology engineering should be, there is no good answer. At least for this first version, the aim is for a semester-long course, where each chapter can be covered in a week and does not require too much reading of core material, with the core material being the contents of the chapter. For an introductory course at undergraduate level, the citations in the text may be ignored, but it serves to read 1-3 scientific papers per chapter for more detail, especially if this book is used in a postgraduate course. This makes also sense in the light that ontology engineering is still an active field of research—hence, some basics may change still—and it allows for flexibility in a course programme so as to emphasise one topic more than another, as the lecturer may prefer. The in-text references also may help students to start reading scientific papers when they are working on their assignments, as a place to start the consultation of the literature.

I hope I have succeeded in striking a good balance on topics & depth in the first two blocks of the textbook. Suggestions for improvement are welcome. (Knowing that ontologists can be a quite critical group, perhaps I should add to that: *antes de criticarme, intenta superarme*, i.e., before you criticise me, try to do a better job at writing an ontology engineering textbook than me.)

The contents of the textbook was written by gradually improving, extending, and further updating material that started with blog posts in 2009 for the European Masters in Computational Logic's Semantic Web Technologies course I taught at the Free University of Bozen-Bolzano, Italy, in 2009/2010, with the hope of generating and facilitating online discussions. That failed miserably, but the posts were visited often. The blogposts were reworked into short syllabi for the Ontology Engineering courses at the University of Havana and University of Computer Science, Cuba, in 2010 and at the Masters Ontology Winter School 2010 in South Africa, which, in turn, were reworked into the COMP718/720 lecture notes at the University of KwaZulu-Natal and the Ontology Engineering honours course lecture notes at the University of Cape Town, South Africa, of which the latest version was in 2015. All those chapters have been updated for this textbook, new material added, and course-specific data has been removed. I had put a CC BY-NC-SA licence on those 2015 lecture notes, so therefore this book has that Creative Commons licence as well. If you think this sounds problematic: it probably is not; if in doubt, please contact me.

Some contents of this book or associated exercises are adapted from slides or tutorials made by other people, and I would like to thank them for having made that material available for use and reuse. They are (in alphabetic order) Jos de Bruijn, Diego Calvanese, Nicola Guarino, Matthew Horridge, Ian Horrocks, Markus Krötzsch, Tommie Meyer, Mariano Rodríguez-Muro, František Simančík, Umberto Straccia, and David Toman. I also would like to thank the students who were enrolled in any of the aforementioned courses, who provided feedback on the blog posts and lecture notes, and assisted me in fine-tuning where more or less explanations and exercises were deemed useful.

For the rest, it was a lot of hard work, with a few encouragements by some academics who appreciated sections of the lecture notes (thank you!) and some I-ignore-that-advice by others who told me it's a waste of time because one cannot score brownie points with a textbook anyway. The most enjoyable of all the sessions of updating the contents was the increment from the 2015 lecture notes to the first full draft of the textbook, which was at Consuelo's *casa particular* in La Habana in June 2018 and interspersed with a few casino (salsa) lessons to stretch the legs and get-togethers with acquaintances and colleagues.

Cape Town, South Africa   C. Maria Keet
October, 2018

How to use the book

0.1 Aims and Synopsis

The principal aim of this textbook is to provide the student with a comprehensive introductory overview of ontology engineering. A secondary aim is to provide hands-on experience in ontology development that illustrate the theory, such as language features, automated reasoning, and top-down and bottom-up ontology development with methods and methodologies.

This textbook covers material such that, upon completion, the student:

(i) has a general understanding of the notion of what ontologies and knowledge bases are, what they can be used for, how, and when not;

(ii) has obtained an understanding of the, currently, main ontology languages—OWL and its underlying Description Logics languages—in order to represent the knowledge in ontologies formally and to reason over them, and have a basic understanding of what an automated reasoner does;

(iii) can confidently use an Ontology Development Environment;

(iv) can confidently use methods and methodologies to develop ontologies, including the top-down approach with foundational ontologies and bottom-up using non-ontological resources such as relational databases, natural language or thesauri; and

(v) has become acquainted with several major applications and application scenarios, such as the Semantic Web Technologies for ontologies, and has had a taste of the research trends in the field.

Interwoven in the aims is skills development for a 4th year/honours project or masters dissertation. The students will become familiar with reading scientific literature and will gain experience in report writing and presenting their work to their peers, in particular when carrying out the two suggested assignments.

0.2 Content at a glance

The chapters are structured such that one could cover one chapter per week for a semester-long course with, depending on one's interest, e.g., to spread Chapter 6 over two lectures or elaborate more on Chapter 5.

1. *Chapter 1: Introduction.* The introductory chapter addresses differences between databases and knowledge bases, conceptual data models and ontologies, what an ontology is (and is not), and takes a sampling of application areas, such as the Semantic Web and data integration.

2. **Block 1: Logic foundations for ontologies**

   (a) *Chapter 2: First order logic and automated reasoning.* This chapter provides a recap of the basics of first order predicate logic, including the notion of model-theoretic semantics. The second part introduces the principles of reasoning over a logical theory, and tableau reasoning in particular.

   (b) *Chapter 3: Description Logics.* This chapter is devoted to a gentle introduction to the basics of Description Logics, which are a family of languages that are decidable fragments of FOL and lie at the basis of most 'species' of the World Wide Web consortium's standardised Web Ontology Language OWL. Tableau reasoning returns and is adapted to the DL setting.

   (c) *Chapter 4: The web ontology language OWL and Automated Reasoning.* The chapter starts with a few historical notes to put the language(s) into context, and proceeds with OWL 2 and its computationally better behaved profiles. In addition, we take a look at the principal automated reasoning services for (OWL) ontologies, such as satisfiability checking and classification and how this works in the currently available software. It has a short recap on computational complexity to appreciate the trade-offs between language features and scalable applications, and closes with a note on the broader context of the Semantic Web on the one hand, and more expressive logics on the other.

3. **Block 2: Developing good ontologies**

   (a) *Chapter 5: Methods and Methodologies.* This chapter starts with a sampling of methodologies to structure the process of actually developing an ontology. Drilling down into some detail, this also requires several methods to improve an ontology's quality, which, to some extent, use the automated reasoner to the developer's benefit as well as some philosophical notions.

   (b) *Chapter 6: Top-down Ontology Development.* One step of ontology development is the use of foundational ontologies and their formalisations. We shall have a look at some typical content of foundational ontologies and look at how they represent things differently from conceptual modelling practice so as to foster interoperability. Several foundational ontologies will pass the revue. As part-whole relations are deemed very important in ontology development, both its foundations as well as some practical guidance on its use as discussed.

   (c) *Chapter 7: Bottom-up Ontology Development.* In addition to starting from 'above' with a foundational ontology, one can reuse legacy material to generate candidate classes and relations to speed up populating an ontology. In particular, we will look at relational databases, thesauri (including SKOS), spreadsheets, and natural language processing. It also introduces ontology design patterns.

4. **Block 3: Advanced Topics**

   This block contains a (small) selection of advanced topics.

   (a) *Chapter 8: Ontology-Based Data Access.* Due to various usage scenarios, there is a need to maintain the link between the data and the knowledge, such as in scientific workflows

or *in silico* biology and enhanced user and content management in e-learning applications. For scalability purposes, one
connects a database to an ontology so that one can query the
database 'intelligently' through the ontology. The chapter
starts with a motivation and design choices and then proceeds to one such instantiation with (roughly) OWL 2 QL, a
mapping layer, and a relational database.

(b) *Chapter 9: Ontologies and natural language.* This chapter
considers two principal interactions between ontologies and
natural language: dealing with the internationalisation and
localisation of ontologies, and a natural language interface to
ontology by means of a controlled natural language to render
the axioms readable for domain experts.

(c) *Chapter 10: Advanced modelling with additional language
features.* There are various extensions to the 'basic' ontology languages and reasoning services to cater for additional
knowledge that needs to be represented, such as vagueness,
uncertainty, and temporal aspects of a subject domain. The
chapter touches upon fuzzy and rough ontologies and considers briefly a temporal DL that, albeit impractical at present,
does solve a range of modelling issues.

While the textbook is aimed at advanced undergraduate/early postgraduate level for people studying for a degree in, or with a background
in, computer science, it can be used differently. For instance, one may
be a logician and wonder what those philosophers are going on about,
or are unfamiliar with the 'hands in the mud' of some bio-ontologies
project and wants to gain an appreciation of those efforts. In that case,
it would be better to commence with Block II and just consult Block I
as/if the need arise. Conversely, if one has tried to develop an ontology
and 'fights' with the reasoner or cannot represent the things one would
like, then commence with Block I, which will provide some answers to
solve such issues. In any case, both the material of Block I and Block II
are prerequisites for the advanced topics in Block III. The three chapters
in Block III can be done in order of preference, or just a subset thereof.

Finally, additional materials are available online at the book's webpage at `http://www.meteck.org/teaching/OEbook/`. These materials

consist mainly of supporting material for the exercises.

0.3 Assessment

There are review questions at the end of each chapter, whose answers can be found in the text of that chapter. Exercises are intended to obtain practical hands-on experiences and sometimes challenge the student. A selection of the exercises' answers is included in the appendix. Assignments require the student to integrate the material and, especially for the mini project, delve deeper into a specific sub-topic.

There can be several assessment modes for a final mark of a course. I have used mainly the following format, but one can choose differently:

- A test (exam) at the end of the course [50%]
- A practical assignment due some time half-way the course duration [15%]
- Mini-project due at the end of the course [30%]

Students had to submit something for each component in order to have a chance to pass the course.

Chapter 1

Introduction

This chapter introduces ontologies: what they are (roughly), what they are used for, and describes a few success stories where they have been instrumental at solving problems. Where and how an ontology can solve problems is not of the variety "when you have only a hammer, everything looks like a nail", but where the use of an ontology was *the* solution to a particular problem, or at least an essential ingredient of it. To place "ontologies" in its right context, the first two questions one has to ask and answer are:

- What is an ontology?

- What is it good for? (or: what problems does it solve?)

A very short and informal way of clarifying what "an ontology" in computing is, is that it is a text file containing structured knowledge about a particular subject domain, and this file is used as a component of a so-called 'intelligent' information system. Fancy marketing talk may speak of some of those **ontology-driven information systems** as "like a database, *on steroids!*" and similar. Ontologies have been, and are being, used to solve data integration problems by providing the *common, agreed-upon vocabulary* which is then used in a way so that the software understands that, say, an entity Student of a relational database DB_1 actually means the same thing as AdvancedLearners in some application software OO_2. Tools can then be developed to link up those two applications and exchange information smoothly thanks to the shared vocabulary. Over time, people figured out other ways to use ontologies and contribute to solving entirely different problems. For instance, a question-answering system that lets the scientist chat with a library chatterbot to more easily find relevant literature (compared to string and keyword matching), automatically find a few theoretically feasible candidate rubber molecules out of very many (compared to painstaking trial-and-error work in the laboratory), and automated discovery of a new enzyme (outperforming the human experts!).

In the next section (Section 1.1), we have a quick peek at what an ontology—the artefact—looks like, and proceed to the more and less pedantic viewpoints of defining what an ontology is (Section 1.2). We will then look at the original motivations why ontologies were taken up in computing & IT and look at a few examples of other uses and what may be considered as some of the success stories (Section 1.3). Lots of new terms are introduced in this chapter that are fleshed out in much more detail in subsequent chapters. Therefore, it is probably useful to revisit this chapter later on—and don't be put off if it is not all clear immediately and raises many questions now! In fact, it should raise questions, which hopefully will motivate you to want to have them answered, which indeed will be in the subsequent chapters.

1.1   What does an ontology look like?

Most of you may only vaguely have heard of 'ontologies', or not at all. Instead of delving into the theory straight away, we'll have a quick look at the artefact, to show that, practically in computing and intelligent software development, it is an object one can play with and manipulate. The actual artefact can appear in multiple formats that are tailored to the intended user, but at the heart of it, there is a logic-based representation that the computer can process. Let us take as example the African Wildlife Ontology (AWO), which is a so-called 'tutorial ontology' that will return in the exercises. The AWO contains knowledge about wildlife, such as that giraffes eat leaves and twigs, that they are herbivores, that herbivores are animals, and so on. A mathematician may prefer to represent such knowledge with first order predicate logic.

For instance:

$$\forall x(Lion(x) \to \forall y(eats(x,y) \to Herbivore(y)) \wedge$$
$$\exists z(eats(x,z) \wedge Impala(z))) \qquad (1.1)$$

that states that "all lions eat herbivores, and they also eat some impalas". This axiom may be one of the axioms in the ontology. One can represent the same knowledge also in logics other than plain vanilla first order logic. For instance, in a **Description Logic** language, we have the same knowledge formally represented as:

$$Lion \sqsubseteq \forall eats.Herbivore \sqcap \exists eats.Impala \qquad (1.2)$$

A domain expert, however, typically will prefer a more user-friendly rendering, such as an automatically generated (pseudo-)natural language rendering, e.g.:

Each **lion** *eats* only **herbivore** and *eats* some **Impala**

where the first "∀" in equation 2.4 is verbalised as Each and the second one as only, the "∧" as and, and the "∃" as some. Another option is to use a graphical language that is more or less precise in showing the knowledge, as shown in Figure 1.1.

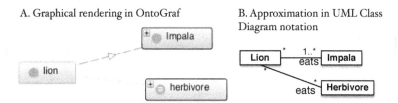

Figure 1.1: Two graphical rendering of lions eating only herbivores and at least some impala, with the OntoGraf plugin in the Protégé 4.x ontology development environment (A) and in UML class diagram style notation (B).

Considering all those different renderings of the same knowledge, remember that an ontology is an engineering artefact that has to have a machine-processable format that faithfully adheres to the logic. None of these aforementioned representations are easily computer-processable, however. To this end, there are **serialisations** of the ontology into a text file that are easily computer-processable. The most widely-used one is the **Web Ontology language OWL**. The required format is called the RDF/XML format, so then a machine-processable version of the class lion in the RDF/XML format looks as follows:

```
<owl:Class rdf:about="&AWO;lion">
   <rdfs:subClassOf rdf:resource="&AWO;animal"/>
   <rdfs:subClassOf>
      <owl:Restriction>
        <owl:onProperty rdf:resource="&AWO;eats"/>
        <owl:someValuesFrom rdf:resource="&AWO.owl;Impala"/>
      </owl:Restriction>
   </rdfs:subClassOf>
   <rdfs:subClassOf>
      <owl:Restriction>
        <owl:onProperty rdf:resource="&AWO;eats"/>
        <owl:allValuesFrom rdf:resource="&AWO;herbivore"/>
      </owl:Restriction>
   </rdfs:subClassOf>
   <rdfs:comment>Lions are animals that eat only herbivores.
   </rdfs:comment>
</owl:Class>
```

where the "$\forall$" from equation 2.4 is serialised as `owl:allValuesFrom`, the "$\exists$" is serialised as `owl:someValuesFrom`, and the subclassing ("$\rightarrow$" and "$\sqsubseteq$" in Eqs 2.4 and 1.2, respectively) as `rdfs:subClassOf`. You typically will not have to write an ontology in this RDF/XML format. As a computer scientist, you may design tools that will have to process or modify such machine-processable ontology files, though even there, there are tool development toolkits and APIs that cover many tasks. For the authoring of an ontology, there are **ontology development environments** (ODEs) that render the ontology graphically, textually, or with a logic view. A screenshot of one such tool, Protégé, is included in Figure 1.2.

1.2   What is an ontology?

Note: You may prefer to read this section again later on in the course, when we are well into Block II. Try to read it now anyway, but if it's not clear upon the first read, then don't worry, as it will become clearer as we go along.

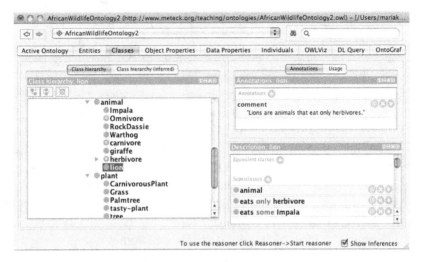

Figure 1.2: Screenshot of the lion eating only herbivores and at least some impala in the Protégé ontology development environment.

1.2.1 The definition game

To arrive at some answer(s) as to what an ontology is, let us first compare it with some artefacts you are already familiar with: relational databases and conceptual data models such as EER and UML. An important distinction between conceptual data models and ontologies is that a conceptual data model provides an *application-specific* implementation-independent representation of the data that will be handled by the prospective application, whereas (domain) ontologies provide an *application-independent* representation of a specific subject domain, i.e., in principle, regardless the particular application, or, phrased positively: (re)usable by multiple applications. From this distinction follow further differences regarding their contents—in theory at least—to which we shall return to in Block II. Looking at actual ontologies and conceptual data models, the former is normally formalised in a logic language, whereas conceptual modelling is more about drawing the boxes and lines informally[1], and they are used differently and serve different purposes.

A comparison between relational databases and ontologies as **knowledge bases** reveals that, unlike RDBMSs, ontologies (knowledge bases)

---

[1]though one surely can provide them with logic-based reconstructions (e.g., [ACK+07, BCDG05, Kee13])

include the *representation of the knowledge explicitly*, by having rules included, by using *automated reasoning* (beyond plain queries) *to infer implicit knowledge and detect inconsistencies* of the knowledge base, and they usually operate under the Open World Assumption[2].

This informal brief comparison gives a vague idea of what an ontology might be, or at least what it is not, but it does not get us closer to a definition of what an ontology is. An approach to the issue of definitions was taken in the 2007 Ontolog Communiqué[3], where its participants and authors made a collection of things drawn into a diagram to express 'things that have to do with an ontology'; this is depicted in Figure 1.3. It is intended as a "Template for discourse" about ontologies, which has a brief[4] and longer[5] explanation of the text in the labeled ovals. The "semantic" side has to do with the meaning represented in the ontology and the "pragmatic" side has to do with the practicalities of using ontologies.

Let us now look at attempts to put that into words into a definition. Intuitively it is known by the ontologists what an ontology is, but putting that into words such that it also can survive philosophers' scrutiny is no trivial matter. The consequence is that, at the time of writing, there is no unanimously agreed-upon definition what an ontology is. The descriptions have been improving over the past 20 years, though. We mention them here, as some are better than others, and you may come across this in the scientific literature. The most quoted (but problematic!) definition is the following one by Tom Gruber:

Definition 1.1 ([Gru93]). *An ontology is a specification of a conceptualization.*

You may see this quote especially in older scientific literature on ontologies, but it has been superseded by other, more precise ones, for Gruber's definition is unsatisfactory for several reasons: what is a "conceptualization" exactly, and what is a "specification"? Using two nebulous terms

---

[2]vs. Closed World Assumption in a relational database setting. We return to the OWA and CWA in a later chapter.

[3]http://ontolog.cim3.net/cgi-bin/wiki.pl?OntologySummit2007_Communique

[4]http://ontolog.cim3.net/cgi-bin/wiki.pl?OntologySummit2007_FrameworksForConsideration/DimensionsMap

[5]http://ontolog.cim3.net/cgi-bin/wiki.pl?OntologySummit2007_Communique

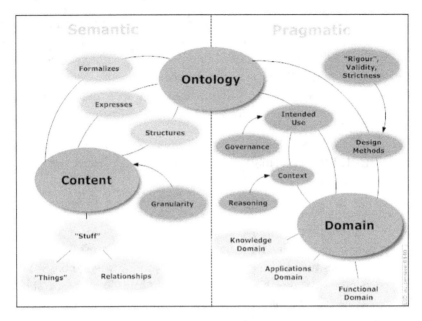

Figure 1.3: The OntologySummit2007's "Dimension map".

to describe a third one does not clarify matters. A proposed refinement to address these two questions is the following one:

Definition 1.2 ([SBF98]). *An ontology is a formal, explicit specification of a shared conceptualization.*

However, this still leaves us with the questions as to what a "conceptualization" is and what a "formal, explicit specification" is, and why and how "shared"? Is it shared enough when, say, you and I agree on the knowledge represented in the ontology, or do we need a third one or a whole group to support it? A comprehensive definition is given in Guarino's landmark paper on ontologies [Gua98] (revisited in [GOS09]):

Definition 1.3 ([Gua98]). *An ontology is a logical theory accounting for the* intended meaning *of a formal vocabulary, i.e. its ontological commitment* to a particular *conceptualization of the world. The intended models of a logical language using such a vocabulary are constrained by its ontological commitment. An ontology indirectly reflects this commitment (and the underlying conceptualization) by approximating these intended models.*

A broader scope is also described in [Gua09], and a more recent overview about definitions of "an ontology" versus Ontology in philosophy can be found in [GOS09], which refines in a step-wise and more precise fashion Definitions 1.2 and 1.3. It is still not free of debate [Neu17], though, and it is a bit of a mouthful as definition. A simpler definition is given by the developers of the World Wide Web Consortium's standardised ontology language OWL[6]:

Definition 1.4 ([HPSvH03]). *An ontology being equivalent to a Description Logic knowledge base.*

That last definition has a different issue, and is unduly restrictive, because 1) it surely is possible to have an ontology that is represented in another logic language (OBO format, Common Logic, etc.) and 2) then formalising a thesaurus as a "Description Logic knowledge base" (or: in OWL) also ends up as a simple 'light-weight ontology' (e.g., the NCI thesaurus as cancer 'ontology') and a conceptual data model in EER or UML that is translated into OWL becomes an 'application ontology' or 'operational ontology' by virtue of it being formalised in OWL. But, as we saw above, there are differences between the two.

   For better or worse, currently, and in the context of the most prominent application area of ontologies—the **Semantic Web**—the tendency is toward it being equivalent to a logical theory, and a Description Logics knowledge base in particular (Definition 1.4). Ontologists at least frown when someone calls 'a thesaurus in OWL' or 'an ER diagram in OWL' ontologies, but even aside from that: the blurring of the distinctions between the different artefacts is problematic for various reasons (discussed in later chapters), and one should note the fact that just because something is represented in OWL does not make it an ontology, just like that something that is represented in a language other than OWL may well be an ontology.

1.2.2   Some philosophical notes on ontologies

The previous section mentioned that the definition would have to survive the philosophers' scrutiny. But why so? The reason for that is that 'ontologies' in computer science did not come out of nowhere. Philosophers

---

[6]Note: we will go into some detail of OWL, Description Logics, and knowledge bases in Chapters 3 and 4.

are in the picture because the term 'ontology' is taken from philosophy, where it has a millennia-old history, and one uses insights emanating from philosophy when developing good ontologies. When we refer to that philosophical notion, we use **Ontology**, with a capital 'O', and it does not have a plural. Orthogonal to the definition game, there are discussions about what is actually represented in an ontology, i.e., its contents, from a philosophical perspective.

One debate is about ontology as a representation of a conceptualisation—roughly: things you are thinking of—and as a representation of reality. Practically, whether that is a relevant topic may depend on the subject domain for which you would be developing an ontology. If you represent formally the knowledge about, say, malaria infections, you would better represent the (best approximation of) reality, being the current state of scientific knowledge, not some divergent political or religious opinion about it, because the wrong representation can lead to wrong inferences, and therewith wrong treatments that are either ineffective or even harmful. Conversely, there are subject domains where it does not really matter much whether you represent reality or a conceptualisation thereof, or something independent of whether that exists in reality or not, or even certainly does not exist in reality. Such discussions were commonplace in computing and applications of ontologies some 10-15 years ago, but have quieted down in recent years. One such debate can be found in writing in [Mer10a, Mer10b, SC10]. Merrill [Mer10a] provides several useful clarifications. First, there is an *"Empiricist Doctrine"* where "the terms of science... are to be taken to refer to actually existing entities in the real world", such as Jacaranda tree, HIV infection and so forth, which are considered mind-independent, because HIV infections occurred also without humans thinking of it, knowing how it worked, and naming those events HIV infections. This is in contrast with the "conceptualist view according to which such terms refer to concepts (which are taken to be psychological or abstract formal entities of one sort or another)", with concepts considered to be mind-dependent entities; prototypical examples of such mind-dependent entities are Phlogiston and Unicorn—there are no objects in the world as we know it that are phlogiston or unicorns, only our outdated theories and fairy tale stories, respectively, about them. Second, the *"Universalist Doctrine"*, which asserts "that the so-called "general terms" of science" (HIV infection etc.) "are to be understood as *referring directly to universals"*, with universals being "a class of mind independent entities, usually contrasted with individuals, postulated to ground and explain relations of qualitative identity and resemblance among individuals. Individuals are said to be similar in virtue of sharing universals." [MR05]. However, philosophers do not agree on the point whether universals exist, and even if they exist, what kind of things they are. This brings the inquiring person to metaphysics, which, perhaps, is not necessarily crucial in building ontologies that are to serve information systems; e.g., it need not be relevant for developing an ontology about viruses whilst adhering to the empiricist doctrine. The philosophically inclined reader may wish to go a step further and read about interactions between Ontology and metaphysics by, e.g., [Var12].

There are other aspects of philosophy that can have an effect on what is represented in an ontology and how. For instance, it can help during the modelling stage, like that there's a difference between what you are vs. the role(s) you play and between participating in an event vs. being part of an event, and help clarifying assumptions you may have about the world that may trickle into the ontology, like whether you're convinced that the vase and the clay it is made of are the same thing or two different things. We will return to this topic in Chapter 6.

1.2.3   Good, not so good, and bad ontologies

Just like one can write good and bad code, one can have good and bad ontologies. Their goodness, or badness, is a bit more elaborate than with software code, however. Bad software code can be unmaintainable spaghetti code or have bugs or not even compile. For ontologies, the equivalent to 'not compile' is when there is a violation of the syntax. We'll get into the syntax in Block I. The equivalent to 'bugs' is two-fold, as it is for software code: there can be errors in the sense that, say, a class cannot have any instances due to conflicting constraints and there can be semantic errors in that what has been represented is logically correct, but entirely unintended. For instance, that a class, say, Student somehow turns up as a subclass of Table, which it obviously should not.

There are further intricate issues that make one ontology better than another. Some structuring choices are excluded because of ontological constraints. Let us take the example of green apples. One could formalise it as that we have apples that have the attribute green or say there are green objects that have an apple-shape. Logic does not care about this distinction, but, at least intuitively, somehow, objects having the colour green seems more reasonable than green objects having an apple-shape. There are reasons for that: Apple carries an identity condition, so one can identify the object (it is a 'sortal'), whereas Green does not (it is a value of the attribute hasColor that a thing has). Ontology helps explaining such distinctions, as we shall see in Chapter 6.

Finally, with the interplay between the logic one uses to represent the knowledge in an ontology and the meaning of the entities in the subject domain, we can show schematically a notion of good and bad ontologies. Consider Figure 1.4. We have a *good ontology* when what we want to represent has been represented in the ontology, yet what is actually represented is very close and only slightly more than the intention; that is, we have a high precision and maximum coverage. We have a *less good ontology* when the ontology represents quite a bit more than what it should; that is, we have a low precision and maximum coverage. Things can go wrong when we have a maximum precision, but only limited coverage, or: the ontology does not contain all that it should, hence, would be a *bad ontology* when it can't do what it should in our ontology-driven information system. Things are even worse if we have both a low precision and limited coverage: then it contains stuff we don't want in there and does not contain stuff that should be in there.

The interplay between precision and coverage have to do both with the language one uses for the ontology and with good modelling. This will be addressed in Block I and Block II, respectively.

1.3 What is the usefulness of an ontology?

Now that we have some idea of ontologies, let us have a look at where they are being used. Ontologies for information systems were first proposed to contribute to solving the issues with **data integration**: an ontology provides the common vocabulary for the applications that is at one level of abstraction higher up than conceptual data models such as EER diagrams and UML Class Diagrams. Over the years, it has been used also for other purposes. We start with two distinct scenarios of data integration where ontologies play a central role, and subsequently describe other scenarios where ontologies are an important part of the solution.

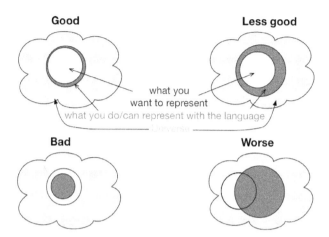

Figure 1.4: Good, less good, bad, and even worse ontologies. The white circle denotes the subject domain (say, African Wildlife), the dark grey circle denotes what's in the ontology (say, the AWO).

1.3.1   Data and information system integration

Figure 1.5 sketches the idea of the ontology-driven *schema-based data integration* and Figure 1.6 further below shows an example of *data-based data integration* that we shall elaborate on in the next two subsections.

Integrating legacy systems

In the setting of ontology-driven schema-based (and conceptual data model-based) data integration, a typical situation is as follows. You have several databases containing data on the same topic. For instance, two universities join forces into one: each university had its own database with information about students, yet, as the new mega-university, there has to be one single database to manage the data of all students. This means that the two databases have to be integrated somehow. A similar situation occurs oftentimes in industry, especially due to mergers and acquisitions, in government due to the drive for e-Government services to the citizens of the country, or attempting to develop a software system for integrated service delivery, as well as in healthcare due to a drive for electronic health records that need to combine various systems, say, a laboratory database with the doctor's database, among other scenarios.

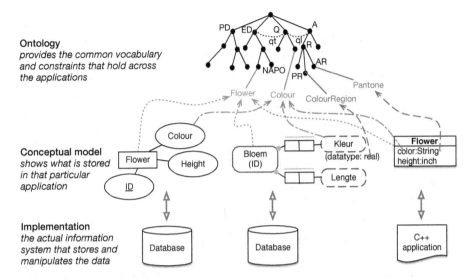

Figure 1.5: Sketch of an ontology-based application integration scenario. Bottom: different implementations, such as relational databases and OO software; Centre: conceptual data models tailored to the application (a section of an EER, ORM, and UML diagram, respectively); Top: an ontology that provides a shared common vocabulary for interoperability among the applications. See text for explanation.

While the topic of data integration deserves its own textbook[7], we focus here only on the ontology-driven aspect. Let us assume we have the relational databases and therewith at least their respective physical schemas, and possibly also the relational model and even the respective conceptual models, and also some object-oriented application software on top of the relational database. Their corresponding conceptual data models are tailored to the RDBMS/OO application and may or may not be modelled in the same conceptual data modelling language; e.g., one could be in EER, another in ORM, in UML and so forth. The example in Figure 1.5 is a sketch of such a situation about information systems of flower shops, where at the bottom of the figure we have two databases and one application that has been coded in C++. In the layer above that, there is a section of their respective conceptual data models: we have one in EER with bubble-notation, one in ORM, and one UML Class Diagram. Each conceptual data model has "Flower" and

---

[7]the 'principles of...' series may be a good start; e.g., [DHI12].

"Colour" included in some way: in the UML Class diagram, the colour is an attribute of the flower, i.e., Color $\mapsto$ Flower $\times$ String (that actually uses only the values of the Pantone System) and similarly in the EER diagram (but then without the data type), and in the ORM diagram the colour is a value type (unary predicate) Kleur with an additional relation to the associated datatype `colour region` in the spectrum with as data type `real`. Clearly, the notion of the flower and its colour is the same throughout, even though it is represented differently in the conceptual data models and in the implementations. It is here that the ontology comes into play, for it is *the* place to assert exactly that underlying, agreed-upon notion. It enables one to assert that:

- EER's and UML diagram's Flower and ORM's Bloem 'means' *Flower* in the domain ontology[8], which is indicated with the (red) short-dashed arrows.
- EER's Colour, ORM's Kleur and UML's Color denote the same kind of thing, albeit at one time it is represented as a unary predicate (in ORM) and other times it is a binary relation with a data type, i.e., an attribute. Their 'mappings' to the entity in the ontology ((green) short-long dashed arrows), *Colour*, indicates that agreement.
- There is no agreement among the conceptual models when it comes to the data type used in the application, yet they may be mapped into their respective notion in an ontology ((purple) long-dashed arrows); e.g., the *ColourRegion* for the values of the colour(s) in the colour spectrum is a *PhysicalRegion*, and one might say that the *PantoneSystem* of colour encoding is an *AbstractRegion*.

The figure does not include names of relationships in the conceptual data model, but they obviously can be named at will; e.g., heeftKleur ('hasColour') in the ORM diagram. Either way, there is, from an ontological perspective, a specific type of relation between the class and its attribute: one of dependency or inherence, i.e., that specific colour instance depends on the existence of the flower, for if that particular flower does not exist, then that specific instance of colour does not exist either. An ontology can provide those generic relations, too. In the sketch, this happens to be the *qt* relationship between enduring objects (like flowers) and the qualities they have (like their colour), and from

---

[8]that in this case is linked to a *foundational ontology*, DOLCE, and there it is a subclass of a Non-Agentive Physical Object; we return to this in Block II

the quality to the value regions (more precisely: qualia), the relation is called *ql* in Figure 1.5.

Although having established such links does not complete the data integration, it is the crucial step—the rest has become, by now, largely an engineering exercise.

Data-level data integration

While in computer science the aforementioned approach to data integration was under investigation, domain experts in molecular biology needed a quick and practical solution to the data integration problem, urgently. Having noticed the idea of ontologies, they came up with another approach, being interoperability at the instance-level, tuple-by-tuple, or even cell-by-cell, and that with multiple databases over the Internet instead of the typical scenario of RDBMSs within an organisation. This can be achieved with lightweight ontologies, or **structured controlled vocabularies**.

The basic idea is illustrated in Figure 1.6. There are multiple databases, which in the figure are the KEGG and InterPro databases. In the KEGG database, there is a tuple with as key K01834 and it has several attributes (columns in the table in the relational database), such as the name (gpmA), and further down in the display there is an attribute Other DBs, which has as entry GO:0004619; i.e., there is a tuple in the table along the line of ⟨K01834, ..., GO:0004619⟩. In the InterPro database, we have a similar story but then for the entity with the key IPR005995, where there is a section "GO Term Annotation" with an attribute function that has GO:0004619; i.e., a tuple ⟨IPR005995, ..., GO:0004619⟩. That is, they are clearly distinct tuples—each with their separate identifier from a different identifier scheme, with different attributes, one physically stored in a database in Japan and the other in the USA—yet they actually talk about the same thing: GO:0004619, which is the identifier for Phosphoglycerate Mutase Activity.

The "GO:0004619" is an identifier for a third artefact: a class in the Gene Ontology (GO) [Gen00]. The GO is a structured controlled vocabulary that contains the concepts and their relationship that the domain experts agree upon to annotate genes with; the GO contains over 40000 concepts by now. The curators of the two databases each annotated their entity with a term from the GO, and thereby they assert they have to do with that same thing, and therewith have created an

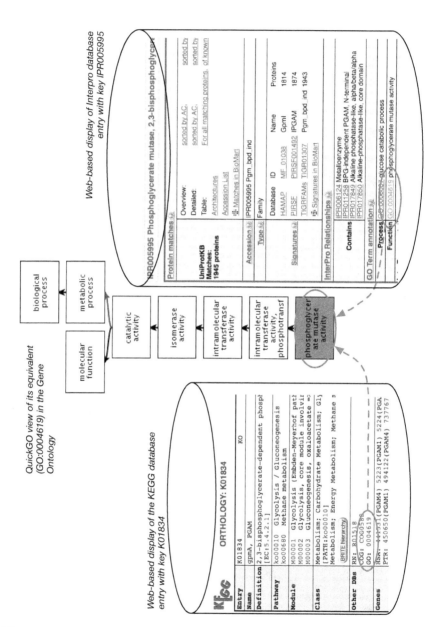

Figure 1.6: Illustration of ontology-based data-level integration: two databases, the KEGG and InterPro, with a web-based front-end, and each database has its data (each tuple in the database, where possible) annotated with a term from the Gene Ontology.

entity-level linking and interoperability through the GO. Practically, on top of that, these fields are hyperlinked (in the soft copy: blue text in KEGG and green underlined text in the screenshot of the InterPro entry), so that a vast network of data-level interlinked databases has been created. Also, the GO term is hyperlinked to the GO file online, and in this way, you can browse from database to database availing of the terms in the ontology without actually realising they are wholly different databases. Instead, they appear like one vast network of knowledge.

There are many more such ontologies, and several thousand databases that are connected in this way, not only thanks to ontologies, but where the ontology serves as the essential ingredient to the data integration. Some scientific journals require the authors to use those terms from the ontologies when they write about their discoveries, so that one more easily can find papers about the same entity[9].

Trying to prevent interoperability problems

A related topic in the data integration scenarios, is trying to *prevent* the integration problems form happening in the first place. This may be done though generating conceptual models for related new applications based on the knowledge represented in the ontology [EGOMA06, JDM03, SS06]. This is a bit alike the Enterprise Models you may have come across in information system design. In this way, interoperability is guaranteed upfront because the elements in the new conceptual data models are already shared thanks to the link with the same ontology. For instance, some relation R between A and B, as is depicted in Figure 1.7 (e.g., an enrols relation between Student and Course), is reused across the conceptual data models, yet each model may have its own additional constraints and data types for attributes. For instance, in one university (hence, student information management system), students may not register for more than six courses and have to be registered for at least one to count as student, whereas at another university, a student may well decide not to be registered for any course at a particular time during the year and still count as a registered student. Whichever rules

---

[9]It used to be a sport among geneticists to come up with cool names for the genes they discovered (e.g., "Sonic hedgehog"); when a gene was independently recovered, each research team typically had given the gene a different name, which can end up as a Tower of Babel of its own that hampered progress in science. The GO and similar ontologies resolve that issue.

there may be at each individual university, the systems do agree on the notions of **Student**, **Course**, and **enrols**. Thus, the ontology provides the shared common vocabulary for interoperability among the applications.

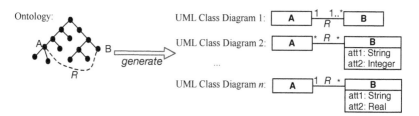

Figure 1.7: Basic illustration of taking information from an ontology and using it for several conceptual data models (here: UML Class Diagrams), where the constraints may be refined or attributes added, yet sharing the semantics of A, B, and R.

1.3.2   Ontologies as part of a solution to other problems

Over the years, ontologies have been shown to be useful in a myriad of other application scenarios; among others, negotiation between software services, mediation between software agents, bringing more quality criteria into conceptual data modelling to develop a better model (hence, a better quality software system), orchestrating the components in semantic scientific workflows, e-learning, ontology-based data access, information retrieval, management of digital libraries, improving the accuracy of question answering systems, and annotation and analysis of electronic health records, to name but a few. Four of them are briefly illustrated in this section.

e-Learning

The 'old-fashioned' way of e-learning is a so-called content-push: the lecturer sends out softcopies of the notes, slides, answers to the solutions, and perhaps the video recordings of the lectures, and the student consumes it. This is a one-size-fits-all approach regardless the student's background with acquired knowledge and skills, and learning preferences and habits, which cannot be assumed to be homogeneous in an e-learning setting, or at least much less so than with respect to your fellow students in the ontology engineering class. A more sophisticated way for e-learning is *adaptive e-learning*, which tailors the contents to the student based on prior knowledge and learning habits. To be able to automatically tailor the offering to the student, one has to develop a 'smart' e-learning application that can figure out what kind of student is enrolled. Put differently: students have certain properties (part-time/full-time student, age, undergraduate degree, etc.), the learning objects have to be annotated (by skill level and topic), and user logs have to be categorised according to type of learning pattern, and based on that the material and presentation can be adjusted, like skipping the section on first order logic and delve deeper into, or spend more time on, ontology engineering and modelling if you have a mathematics background, whereas a philosopher may crave for more content about foundational ontologies but skip reverse engineering of relational databases, or offer a student more exercises on a topic s/he had difficulties with. This requires **knowledge representation**—of the study material, questions, answers, students' attributes, learning approaches—and **automated reasoning** to classify usage pattern and student, and annotated content, i.e., using ontologies and knowledge bases to make it work solidly and in a repeatable way. See, e.g., [HDN04] as a start for more details on this topic.

Deep question answering with Watson

Watson[10] is a sophisticated question answering engine that finds answers to trivia/general knowledge questions for the *Jeopardy!* TV quiz that, in the end, did consistently outperform the human experts of the game. For instance, a question could be "who is the president of South Africa?": we need algorithms to parse the question, such as that 'who' indicates the answer has to be a person and a named entity, it needs to be capable to detect that South Africa is a country and what a country is, and so on, and then have some kind of a look-up service in knowledge bases and/or natural language documents to somehow find the answer by relating 'president', 'South Africa' and 'Cyril Ramaphosa' and that he is the current president of the country. An ontology can then be used in the algorithms of both the understanding of the question and finding the right answer[11] and integrating data sources and knowledge, alongside

---

[10]http://en.wikipedia.org/wiki/Watson_(computer)

[11]On a much more modest scale, as well as easier accessible and shorter to read, Vila and Ferrández describe this principle and demonstrated benefits for their Spanish

natural language processing, statistical analysis and so on, comprising more than 100 different techniques[12]. Thus, a key aspect of the system's development was that one cannot go in a linear fashion from natural language to knowledge management, but have to use an integration of various technologies, including ontologies, to make a successful tool.

Digital humanities

Some historians and anthropologists in the humanities try to investigate what happened in the Mediterranean basin some 2000 years ago, aiming to understand food distribution systems. Food was stored in pots (more precisely: an amphora) that had engravings on it with text about who, what, where etc. and a lot of that has been investigated, documented, and stored in multiple resources, such as in databases. None of the resources cover all data points, but to advance research and understanding about it and food trading systems in general, it has to be combined and made easily accessible to the domain experts. That is, essentially it is an instance of a data access and integration problem. Also, humanities researchers are not at all familiar with writing SQL queries, so that would need to be resolved as well, and in a flexible way so that they would not have to be dependent on the availability of a system administrator.

A recent approach, of which the technologies have been maturing, is Ontology-Based Data Access (OBDA). The general idea of OBDA applied to the Roman Empire Food system is shown in Figure 1.8. There are the data sources, which are federated (one 'middle layer', though still at the implementation level). The federated interface has mapping assertions to elements in the ontology. The user then can use the terms of the ontology (classes and their relations and attributes) to query the data, without having to know about how the data is stored and without having to write page-long SQL queries. For instance, a query "retrieve inscriptions on amphorae found in the city of 'Mainz' containing the text 'PNN'" would use just the terms in the ontology, say, Inscription, Amphora, City, found in, and inscribed on, and any value constraint added (like the PNN), and the OBDA system takes care of the rest to return the answer.

---

language based question-answering system in the agricultural domain [VF09].

[12]ftp://public.dhe.ibm.com/common/ssi/ecm/en/pow03061usen/ POW03061USEN.PDF

More high-level details of the system are described in [CLM+16] and we will look at its technicalities in Chapter 8.

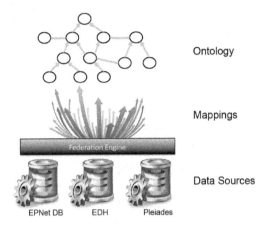

Figure 1.8: OBDA in the EPnet system (Source: [CLM+16])

Semantic scientific workflows

Due to the increase in a variety of equipment, their speed, and decreasing price, scientists are generating more data than ever, and are collaborating more. This data has to be analysed and managed. In the early days, and, to some extent, to this day, many one-off little tools were developed, or simply scripted together with PERL, Ruby on Rails, or Python, used once or a few times and then left for what it was. This greatly hampers repeatability of experiments, insight in the provenance of the data, and does not quite follow a methodological approach for so-called *in silico* biology research. Over the past 10 years, comprehensive software and hardware infrastructures have been, and are being, built to fix these and related problems. Those IT 'workbenches' (as opposed to the physical ones in the labs) are realised in *semantic scientific workflow systems*. An example of a virtual bench is Taverna [GWG+07], which in the meantime has gone 'mainstream' as a project within the Apache Software Foundation[13] [WHF+13]. This, in turn can be extended further; e.g., to incorporate data mining in the workflow to go with the times of Big Data, as depicted in Figure 1.9. This contains ontologies of both the

---

[13]https://taverna.incubator.apache.org/

subject domain where it is used as well as ontologies about data mining itself that serve to find appropriate models, algorithms, datasets, and tools for the task at hand, depicted in Figure 1.10. Thus, we have a large software system—the virtual workbench—to facilitate scientists to do their work, and some of the components are ontologies for integration and data analysis across the pipeline.

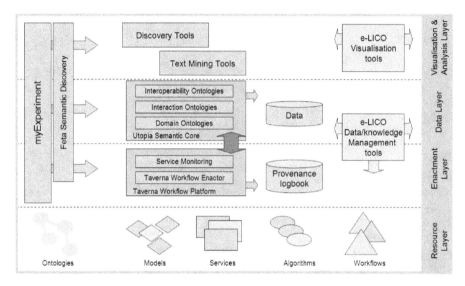

Figure 1.9: Overview of the architecture of the e-Laboratory for Interdisciplinary Collaborative Data Mining (Source: originally retrieved from http://www.e-lico.eu/?q=node/17).

Now that we have seen some diverse examples, this does not mean that ontologies are the panacea for everything, and some ontologies are better suitable to solve one or some of the problems, but not others. Put differently, it is prudent to keep one's approach to engineering: conduct a problem analysis first, collect the requirements and goals, and then assess if an ontology indeed is part of the solution or not. If it is part of the solution, then we enter in the area of **ontology engineering**.

1.3.3   Success stories

To be able to talk about successes of ontologies, and its incarnation with Semantic Web Technologies in particular, one first needs to establish

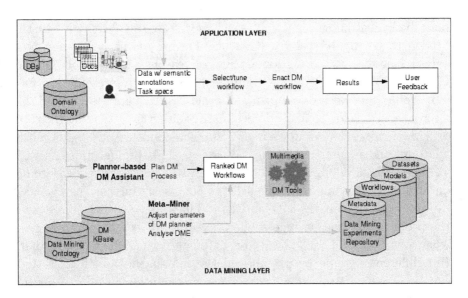

Figure 1.10: The data mining and application layers of the e-Laboratory for Interdisciplinary Collaborative Data Mining (Source: originally retrieved from http://www.e-lico.eu/?q=node/17).

when something can be deemed a success, when it is a challenge, and when it is an outright failure. Such measures can be devised in an absolute sense—compare technology x with an ontology-mediated one: does it outperform on measure y?—and relative—to whom is technology x deemed successful?

A major success story of the development and use of ontologies for data linking and integration is the Gene Ontology [Gen00], its offspring, and subsequent coordinated evolution of ontologies [SAR+07]. These frontrunners from the Gene Ontology Consortium[14] and their colleagues in bioinformatics were adopters of some of the Semantic Web ideas even before Berners-Lee, Hendler, and Lassila wrote their Scientific American paper in 2001 [BLHL01], even though they did not formulate their needs and intentions in the same terminology: they did want to have shared, controlled vocabularies with the same syntax to facilitate data integration—or at least interoperability—across Web-accessible databases, have a common space for identifiers, it needing to be a dynamic, changing system, to organize and query incom-

---

[14]http://www.geneontology.org/

plete biological knowledge, and, albeit not stated explicitly, it all still needed to be highly scalable [Gen00]. The results exceeded anyone's expectations in its success for a range of reasons. Many tools for the Gene Ontology (GO) and its common Knowledge Representation format, .obo, have been developed, and other research groups adopted the approach to develop controlled vocabularies either by extending the GO, e.g., rice traits, or adding their own subject domain, such as zebrafish anatomy and mouse developmental stages. This proliferation, as well as the OWL development and standardisation process that was going on at about the same time, pushed the goal posts further: new expectations were put on the GO and its siblings and on their tools, and the proliferation had become a bit too wieldy to keep a good overview what was going on and how those ontologies would be put together. Put differently, some people noticed the inferencing possibilities that can be obtained from moving from a representation in obo to one in OWL and others thought that some coordination among all those obo bio-ontologies would be advantageous given that post-hoc integration of ontologies of related and overlapping subject domains is not easy. Thus came into being the OBO Foundry to solve such issues, proposing an approach for coordinated evolution of ontologies to support biomedical data integration [SAR+07] within the OBO Foundry Project[15].

People in related disciplines, such as ecology, have taken on board experiences of these very early adopters, and instead decided to jump on board after the OWL standardization. They, however, were not only motivated by data(base) integration. Referring to Madin et al's paper [MBSJ08], I highlight three points they made:

  - "terminological ambiguity slows scientific progress, leads to redundant research efforts, and ultimately impedes advances towards a unified foundation for ecological science", i.e., identification of some serious problems they have in ecological research;
  - "Formal ontologies provide a mechanism to address the drawbacks of terminological ambiguity in ecology", i.e., what they expect that ontologies will solve for them (disambiguation); and
  - "fill an important gap in the management of ecological data by facilitating powerful data discovery based on rigorously defined, scientifically meaningful terms", i.e., for what purpose they want to use ontologies and any associated computation (discovery using

---

[15]http://www.obofoundry.org/

automated reasoning).

That is, ontologies not as a—one of many possible—'*tool*' in the engineering infrastructure, but as a *required part of a method* in the scientific investigation that aims to discover new information and knowledge about nature (i.e., in answering the who, what, where, when, and how things are the way they are in nature). Success in inferring novel biological knowledge has been achieved with classification of protein phosphatases [WSH07], precisely thanks to the expressive ontology and its automated reasoning services.

Good quality ontologies have to built and maintained, though, and there needs to be working infrastructure for it. This textbook hopefully will help you with that.

1.4 Outline and usage of the book

The preceding sections already indicated that several aspects would return 'later in the course'. The order that will be followed in this book, is to commence with a recap (or brief introduction, as may be the case) of First Order Predicate Logic regarding the formalisation with syntax, semantics (what it all 'means', formally), and principles of automated reasoning. Full FOL is undecidable, but there are less expressive languages, i.e., fragments of FOL, that are decidable for a set of important problems in computing in the area of ontologies and knowledge bases. One such family of languages is the Description Logics (DL) family of languages. These two topics are covered in Chapter 2 and Chapter 3, respectively. Several DLs, in turn, form the basis of the W3C standardised Web Ontology Language OWL (actually, a family of languages, too). OWL specifies a computer-processable serialisation of the ontology and knowledge base, and interacts with the automated reasoners for OWL. OWL and the so-called standard reasoning services are summarised in Chapter 4.

After these logic foundations in Block I, we shall look at how one can develop an ontology. The first approach is a so-called 'top-down' approach, where we use foundational ontologies with the high-level categories and relationship to get us started with the principal choices and the modelling so that a modeller does not have to reinvent the wheel; this is covered in Chapter 6. However, designing an ontology from scratch is rather cumbersome, and much information already has been represented in various ways—natural language, conceptual data models, etc.—so, one can speed up ontology development also by somehow reusing those 'legacy' sources, which is described in Chapter 7. Both approaches, however, are just that—not a 'cookbook recipe' for ontology development— and there exist interdependencies, methods, tools, and methodologies that help structure and carry out the activities, which is described in Chapter 5. One could go through Block II either in the order of Chapters 6, 7, and 5, or first Chapter 5 and then 6 and 7.

Blocks I and II form the foundations of ontology engineering at an introductory level, and the topics that follow afterward deepen and extend that material. Block III contains a few short chapters that introduce various subtopics, which is far from exhaustive and the block is intended mainly to illustrate that there is a range of themes within ontology engineering. In one direction, you may wish to explore further some quite involved theory and technology to realise a practical ontology-driven information system, being querying databases by means of an ontology, which is the topic of Chapter 8. Ontologies are used throughout the world, and not all systems are in English, therefore we will look at the interaction of natural language with ontologies in Chapter 9. There are extensions to the standard ontology languages, because it is perceived to be needed to be more precise in representing the subject domain. Chapter 10 touches upon the temporal, uncertain, and vague dimension.

Depending on one's background, one can study Block I after Block II—unless one's knowledge of logic is a bit rusty or limited. In any case, both the material of Block I and Block II are prerequisites for Block III, advanced topics. Within Block III, the chapters can be done in order of preference, or just a subset thereof.

This is the first version of the textbook, but essentially the fourth version of prior lecture notes, and due to time constraints, perhaps not everything that should have been in the book made it into the book. Also, because it is of an introductory nature and a reader may be interested more in one sub-topic than another, it is liberally referenced, so you more easily can look up further details. There are many references in the bibliography. You are not expected to read all of them; instead, each chapter has a "Literature and reference material" section with a small selection of recommended reading. The large reference list may be useful especially for the practical assignment (Appendix A.1) and the mini-project assignment (Appendix A.2): there are *very* many more references in computer science conference proceedings and journals, but the ones listed, first, in the "literature and reference material" and, second, in the bibliography, will give you a useful 'entry point' or may even suffice, depending on the chosen topics.

Exercises are structured along the line of review questions and then either practical exercises or further analysis questions. Some exercises refer to particular ontologies, which can be found at the book's webpage at `http://www.meteck.org/teaching/OEbook/` or the URL provided. The answers to the review questions can be found in the respective chapter. A selection of answers to the exercises is included in Appendix D.

1.5 Exercises

Review question 1.1. There are several terms in the preceding sections that were highlighted in bold in the text. Find them, and try to describe them in your own words, in particular: ontology-driven information system, Ontology, ontology, and ontology engineering.

Review question 1.2. List several uses of ontologies.

Review question 1.3. Describe the difference between schema vs. instance-level data integration.

Exercise 1.1. You may like to get a practical 'feel' of ontologies and how they look like in an ontology development environment. To this end, install an ODE, such as Protégé, load the `AfricanWildlifeOntology1.owl` from the book's supplementary material page at `http://www.meteck. org/teaching/OEbook/` in the tool and browse around. Download the `AfricanWildlifeOntology1.owl` file (right-click, save as) and open it in your text editor, such as notepad.

Exercise 1.2. Having inspected the `AfricanWildlifeOntology1.owl`, is it a good, less good, bad, or even worse ontology? Why?

1.6 Literature and reference material

1. Berners-Lee, Tim; James Hendler and Ora Lassila. The Semantic Web. *Scientific American Magazine*, May 17, 2001. `http://www.`

sciam.com/article.cfm?id=the-semantic-web&print=true

2. Nicola Guarino, Daniel Oberle, and Steffen Staab. What Is An Ontology? In: S. Staab and R. Studer, *Handbook on Ontologies*, Chapter 6. Springer. 2009. pp1-17.

Part I

Logic foundations for ontologies

Chapter 2

First order logic and automated reasoning in a nutshell

Perhaps more foundations in modelling may be useful before delving into how to represent what you want to represent, but at the same time, one also needs to understand the language to model in. In this case, this means obtaining a basic grasp of logic-based ontology languages, which will help understanding the ontologies and ontology engineering better, and how to formalise the things one wants to represent. Therefore, we shall refresh the basics of first order logic in Section 2.1 (comprehensive introductions can be found elsewhere, e.g., [Hed04]), which is followed by a general idea of (automated) reasoning and two examples of tableau reasoning in Section 2.2. If you have had a basic course in logic from a mathematics department, you may wish to just skim over Section 2.1; my experience is that automated reasoning is typically not covered in such a mathematics or standard basic course in logic and you should therefore still engage with Section 2.2.

2.1 First order logic syntax and semantics

Observe first that logic is not the study of truth, but of the *relationship between the truth of one statement and that of another*. That is, in logic, we do not care whether a statement like "If angels exist then necessarily all of them fit on the head of a needle" (suitably formalised) is indeed true in reality[1], but if the if-part were true (resp., false), then what does that say about the truth value of the then-part of the statement? And likewise for a whole bunch of such sentences. Others do care what is represented formally with such a logic language, but we will defer that to Block II.

To be able to study those aspects of logic, we need a language that is unambiguous; natural language is not. You may have encountered propositional logic already, and first order predicate logic (FOL) is an extension of that, which enables us to represent more knowledge in more detail. Here, I will give only a brief glimpse of it. Eventually, you will need to be able to recognise, understand, and be able to formalise at least a little bit in FOL. Of all the definitions that will follow shortly, there are four important ideas to grasp: the *syntax* of a language, the *model-theoretic semantics* of a language, what a *theory* means in the context of logic, and the notion of *deduction* where we apply some rules to what has been represented explicitly so as to derive knowledge that was represented only implicitly. We will address each in turn.

First, there are two principal components to consider for the language:

- **Syntax** has to do with what 'things' (symbols, notations) one is allowed to use in the language and in what way; there is/are a(n):
  - Alphabet
  - Language constructs
  - Sentences to assert knowledge
- **Semantics**
  - Formal meaning, which has to do what those sentences with the alphabet and constructs are supposed to mean.

Their details are presented in the remainder of this section.

2.1.1 Syntax

The lexicon of a first order language contains the following:

- Connectives and Parentheses: $\neg$, $\rightarrow$, $\leftrightarrow$, $\wedge$, $\vee$, (and);
- Quantifiers: $\forall$ (universal) and $\exists$ (existential);
- Variables: $x, y, z, ...$ ranging over particulars (individual objects);
- Constants: $a, b, c, ...$ representing a specific element;
- Functions: $f, g, h, ...$, with arguments listed as $f(x_1, ...x_n)$;

---

[1]or, for that matter, whether there is a reality and whether we have access to it

- Relations: $R, S, ...$ with an associated arity.

There is an (countably infinite) supply of *symbols* (signature): variables, functions, constants, and relations.

In other words: we can use these things to create 'sentences', like we have in natural language, but then controlled and with a few extra figurines. Let us look first at how we can formalise a natural language sentence into first order logic.

Example 2.1. *From Natural Language to First order logic (or vv.).* Consider the following three sentences:
- "Each animal is an organism"
- "All animals are organisms"
- "If it is an animal then it is an organism"

This can be formalised as:

$$\forall x(Animal(x) \rightarrow Organism(x)) \qquad (2.1)$$

Observe the underlined words in the natural language sentences: 'each' and 'all' are different ways to say "$\forall$" and the 'is a' and 'are' in the first two sentences match the "$\rightarrow$", and the combination of the "$\forall$" and "$\rightarrow$" in this particular construction can be put into natural language as 'if ... then'.

Instead of talking about all objects of a particular type, one also can assert there are at least some of them; e.g.,
- "Aliens exist"

could be formalised as

$$\exists x \; Alien(x) \qquad (2.2)$$

with the 'exist' matching the $\exists$, and
- "There are books that are heavy"

(well, at least one of them is) as:

$$\exists x(Book(x) \wedge heavy(x)) \qquad (2.3)$$

where the 'there are' is another way to talk about "$\exists$" and the 'that' hides (linguistically) the "$\wedge$". A formulation like "There is at least one book, and it is heavy" is a natural language rendering that is closer to the structure of the axiom.

A sentence—or, more precisely, its precise meaning—such as "Each student must be registered for a degree programme" requires a bit more consideration. There are at least two ways to say the same thing in the way the sentence is formulated (we leave the arguments for and against each option for another time):

   i) $\forall x, y(registered\_for(x, y) \rightarrow Student(x) \wedge DegreeProgramme(y))$
      "if there is a *registered_for* relation, then the first object is a student and the second one a degree programme"
      $\forall x(Student(x) \rightarrow \exists y \; registered\_for(x, y))$
      "Each student is registered for at least one y", where the y is a degree programme (taken from the first axiom)

   ii) $\forall x(Student(x) \quad \rightarrow \quad \exists y(registered\_for(x, y) \wedge DegreePro\-gramme(y)))$
      "Each student is registered for at least one degree programme"

But all this is still just syntax (it does not say what it really means), and it looks like a 'free for all' on how we can use these symbols. This is, in fact, not the case, and the remainder of the definitions will make this more precise, which will be illustrated in Example 2.2 afterward. ◇

    There is a systematic to the axioms in the examples, with the brackets, arrows, etc. Let us put this more precisely now. We start from the basic elements and gradually build it up to more complex things.

Definition 2.1. (Term) *A term is inductively defined by two rules, being:*
- *Every variable and constant is a term.*
- *if f is a m-ary function and $t_1, \ldots t_m$ are terms, then $f(t_1, \ldots, t_m)$ is also a term.*

Definition 2.2. (Atomic formula) *An* atomic formula *is a formula that has the form $t_1 = t_2$ or $R(t_1, ..., t_n)$ where R is an n-ary relation and $t_1, ..., t_n$ are terms.*

Definition 2.3. (Formula) *A string of symbols is a formula of FOL if and only if it is constructed from atomic formulas by repeated applications of rules R1, R2, and R3.*
  R1. If ϕ is a formula then so is $\neg\phi$.
  R2. If ϕ and ψ are formulas then so is $\phi \wedge \psi$.
  R3. If ϕ is a formula then so is $\exists x\phi$ for any variable x.

A *free variable* of a formula ϕ is that variable occurring in ϕ that is not quantified. For instance, if $\phi = \forall x(Loves(x,y))$, then y is the free variable, as it is not bound to a quantifier. We now can introduce the definition of *sentence*.

Definition 2.4. (Sentence) *A sentence of FOL is a formula having no free variables.*

Check that there are no free variables in the axioms in Example 2.1, i.e., they are all sentences.

Up to this point, we have seen only a few examples with going back-and-forth between sentences in natural language and in FOL. This is by no means to only option. One can also formalise diagrams and provide logic-based reconstructions of, say, UML class diagrams in order to be precise. We can already do this with syntax introduced so far. Let's consider again the lion eating impalas and herbivores, as was shown in Figure 1.1-B in Chapter 1. First, we 'bump up' the **eats** association end to the name of the binary relation, *eats*. Second, noting that UML uses look-across notation for its associations, the 1..* 'at least one' amounts to an existential quantification for the impalas, and the * 'zero or more' to a universal quantification for the herbivores. This brings us back to Eq. 2.4 from Chapter 1:

$$\forall x(Lion(x) \rightarrow \forall y(eats(x,y) \rightarrow Herbivore(y))\wedge$$
$$\exists z(eats(x,z) \wedge Impala(z))) \tag{2.4}$$

Another example with different constraints is shown in Figure 2.1, which could be the start of a UML class diagram (but incomplete; notably because it has no attributes and no methods) or an abuse of notation, in that an ontology is shown diagrammatically in UML class diagram notation, as there is no official graphical language to depict ontologies. Either way, syntactically, also here the UML classes can be converted into unary predicates in FOL, the association is translated into a binary relation, and the multiplicity constraint turns into an existential quantification that is restricted to exactly 4 limbs[2]. In the interest of

---

[2]There are animals that indeed do not have 4 limbs (e.g., the sirens and the Mexican mole lizard have only two limbs and the millipede *Illacme plenipes* has 750 (the most), and there are animals with specific numbers of limbs in between, but that is beside the point as it would not change much the features used in the formalisation, just become more cluttered.

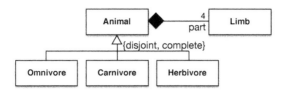

Figure 2.1: A UML model that can be formally represented in FOL; see text for details.

succinctness and convention, the latter is permitted to be abbreviated as $\exists^{=4}$. The corresponding sentence in FOL is listed in Eq. 2.5. One can dwell on the composite aggregation (the black diamond), and we will do so in a later chapter. Here, it is left as an association with an 'at most one' constraint on the whole side (Eq. 2.6), or: "if there's a limb related to two animal instances through *whole*, then those two instances must be the same object".

$$\forall x(Animal(x) \rightarrow \exists^{=4}y(part(x,y) \wedge Limb(y))) \qquad (2.5)$$

$$\forall x, y, z(Limb(x) \wedge whole(x,y) \wedge whole(x,z) \wedge Animal(y)\wedge$$
$$Animal(z) \rightarrow y = z) \qquad (2.6)$$

That is, indeed, literally talking of two references to one object.

The 'new' constraints that we have not translated before yet, are the subclassing, the disjointness, and the completeness. Subclassing is the same as in Eq. 2.1, hence, we obtain Eqs. 2.7-2.9.

$$\forall x(Omnivore(x) \rightarrow Animal(x)) \qquad (2.7)$$

$$\forall x(Herbivore(x) \rightarrow Animal(x)) \qquad (2.8)$$

$$\forall x(Carnivore(x) \rightarrow Animal(x)) \qquad (2.9)$$

Disjoint means that the intersection is empty, so it has the pattern $\forall x(A(x) \wedge B(x) \rightarrow \bot)$, where "$\bot$" is the bottom concept/unary predicate that is always false; hence, Eq. 2.10 for the sample classes of Figure 2.1.

Completeness over the specialisation means that all the instances of the superclass must be an instance of either of the subclasses; hence Eq. 2.11.

$$\forall x(Omnivore(x) \wedge Herbivore(x) \wedge Carnivore(x) \rightarrow \bot) \qquad (2.10)$$

$$\forall x (Animal(x) \rightarrow Omnivore(x) \vee Herbivore(x) \vee Carnivore(x)) \quad (2.11)$$

These are all syntactic transformations, both by example and that informally some translation rules and a general pattern (like for disjointness) have been noted. From a software engineering viewpoint, this can be seen as a step toward a logic-based reconstruction of UML class diagrams. From a logic viewpoint, the diagram can be seen as 'syntactic sugar' for the axioms, which is more accessible to domain experts (non-logicians) than logic.

This playing with syntax, however, does not say what it all *means*. How do these sentences in FOL map to the objects in, say, the Java application (if it were a UML diagram intended as such) or to some domain of objects wherever that is represented somehow (if it were a UML diagram depicting an ontology)? And can the latter be specified a bit more precise? We shall see the theoretical answers to such question in the next section.

2.1.2 Semantics

Whether a sentence is true or not depends on the underlying set and the interpretation of the function, constant, and relation symbols. To this end, we have structures: a *structure* consists of an *underlying set* together with an *interpretation* of functions, constants, and relations. Given a sentence ϕ and a structure M, M *models* ϕ means that the sentence ϕ is true with respect to M. More precisely, through the following set of definitions (which will be illustrated afterward):

Definition 2.5. (Vocabulary) *A vocabulary $\mathcal{V}$ is a set of function, relation, and constant symbols.*

Definition 2.6. ($\mathcal{V}$-structure) *A $\mathcal{V}$-structure consists of a non-empty underlying set Δ along with an interpretation of $\mathcal{V}$. An interpretation of $\mathcal{V}$ assigns an element of Δ to each constant in $\mathcal{V}$, a function from Δ^n to Δ to each n-ary function in $\mathcal{V}$, and a subset of Δ^n to each n-ary relation in $\mathcal{V}$. We say M is a structure if it is a $\mathcal{V}$-structure of some vocabulary $\mathcal{V}$.*

Definition 2.7. ($\mathcal{V}$-formula) *Let $\mathcal{V}$ be a vocabulary. A $\mathcal{V}$-formula is a formula in which every function, relation, and constant is in $\mathcal{V}$. A $\mathcal{V}$-sentence is a $\mathcal{V}$-formula that is a sentence.*

When we say that M *models* ϕ, denoted with $M \models \phi$, this is with respect to M being a $\mathcal{V}$-structure and $\mathcal{V}$-sentence ϕ is true in M.

Model theory is about the interplay between M and a set of first-order sentences $\mathcal{T}(M)$, which is called the *theory of* M, and its 'inverse' from a set of sentences Γ to a class of structures.

Definition 2.8. (Theory of M) *For any $\mathcal{V}$-structure M, the theory of M, denoted with $\mathcal{T}(M)$, is the set of all $\mathcal{V}$-sentences ϕ such that $M \models \phi$.*

Definition 2.9. (Model) *For any set of $\mathcal{V}$-sentences, a model of Γ is a $\mathcal{V}$-structure that models each sentence in Γ. The class of all models of Γ is denoted by $\mathcal{M}(\Gamma)$.*

Now we can go to the interesting notions: *theory* in the context of logic:

Definition 2.10. (Complete $\mathcal{V}$-theory) *Let Γ be a set of $\mathcal{V}$-sentences. Then Γ is a* complete *$\mathcal{V}$-theory if, for any $\mathcal{V}$-sentence ϕ either ϕ or $\neg\phi$ is in Γ and it is not the case that both ϕ and $\neg\phi$ are in Γ.*

It can then be shown that for any $\mathcal{V}$-structure M, $\mathcal{T}(M)$ is a complete $\mathcal{V}$-theory (for proof, see, e.g., [Hed04], p90).

Definition 2.11. *A set of sentences Γ is said to be* consistent *if no contradiction can be derived from Γ.*

Definition 2.12. (Theory) *A* theory *is a consistent set of sentences.*

The latter two definitions are particularly relevant later on when we look at the typical reasoning services for ontologies.

Example 2.2. *How does all this work out in practice? Let us take something quasi-familiar: a conceptual data model in Object-Role Modeling notation, depicted in the middle part of Figure 2.2, with the top-half its 'verbalisation' in a controlled natural language, and in the bottom-part some sample objects and the relations between them.*

First, we consider it as a theory, creating a logical reconstruction of the icons in the figure. There is one binary predicate, attends*, and there are two unary predicates,* Student *and* DegreeProgramme*. The binary predicate is typed, i.e., its domain and range are defined to be those two entity types, hence:*

$$\forall x, y(attends(x, y) \rightarrow Student(x) \wedge DegreeProgramme(y)) \quad (2.12)$$

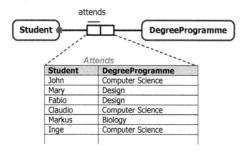

Student **is an entity type.**
DegreeProgramme **is an entity type.**
Student attends DegreeProgramme.

Each Student attends **exactly one** DegreeProgramme.
It is possible that more than one Student attends **the same** DegreeProgramme.
OR, in the negative:
For each Student, **it is impossible that that** Student attends **more than one**
DegreeProgramme.
It is impossible that any Student attends **no** DegreeProgramme.

Figure 2.2: A theory denoted in ORM notation, ORM verbalization, and some data in the database. See Example 2.2 for details.

Note that x and y quantify over the whole axiom (thanks to the brackets), hence, there are no free variables, hence, it is a sentence. There are two constraints in the figure: the blob and the line over part of the rectangle, and, textually, "Each Student attends exactly one DegreePro-gramme" and "It is possible that more than one Student attends the same DegreeProgramme". The first constraint can be formalised (in short-hand notation):

$$\forall x(Student(x) \rightarrow \exists^{=1} y \; attends(x, y)) \qquad (2.13)$$

The second one is already covered with Eq. 2.12 (it does not introduce a new constraint). So, our vocabulary is {$attends, Student, DegreePro-gramme$}, and we have two sentences (Eq. 2.12 and Eq. 2.13). The sentences form the theory, as they are not contradicting and admit a model.

Let us now consider the structure. We have a non-empty underlying set of objects: $\Delta = \{John, Mary, Fabio, Claudia, Markus, Inge, Compu-terScience, Biology, Design\}$. The interpretation then maps the instances in Δ with the elements in our vocabulary; that is, we end up with $\{John, Mary, Fabio, Claudia, Markus, Inge\}$ as instances of $Student$, and similarly for $DegreeProgramme$ and the binary $attends$. Observe

that this structure does not contradict the constraints of our sentences.
$\Diamond$

Equivalences

With the syntax and semantics, several equivalencies between formulae can be proven. We list them for easy reference, with a few 'informal readings' for illustration. ϕ, ψ, and χ are formulas.

- Commutativity:

  $\phi \wedge \psi \equiv \psi \wedge \phi$

  $\phi \vee \psi \equiv \psi \vee \phi$

  $\phi \leftrightarrow \psi \equiv \psi \leftrightarrow \phi$

- Associativity:

  $(\phi \wedge \psi) \wedge \chi \equiv \phi \wedge (\psi \wedge \chi)$

  $(\phi \vee \psi) \vee \chi \equiv \phi \vee (\psi \vee \chi)$

- Idempotence:

  $\phi \wedge \phi \equiv \phi$

  $\phi \vee \phi \equiv \phi$ *//'itself or itself is itself'*

- Absorption:

  $\phi \wedge (\phi \vee \psi) \equiv \phi$

  $\phi \vee (\phi \wedge \psi) \equiv \phi$

- Distributivity:

  $(\phi \vee (\psi \wedge \chi)) \equiv (\phi \vee \psi) \wedge (\phi \vee \chi)$

  $(\phi \wedge (\psi \vee \chi)) \equiv (\phi \wedge \psi) \vee (\phi \wedge \chi)$

- Double negation:

  $\neg\neg\phi \equiv \phi$

- De Morgan:

  $\neg(\phi \wedge \psi) \equiv \neg\phi \vee \neg\psi$

  $\neg(\phi \vee \psi) \equiv \neg\phi \wedge \neg\psi$ *//'negation of a disjunction implies the negation of each of the disjuncts'*

- Implication:

  $\phi \rightarrow \psi \equiv \neg\phi \vee \psi$

- Tautology:

  $\phi \vee \top \equiv \top$

- Unsatisfiability:

  $\phi \wedge \bot \equiv \bot$

- Negation:

  $\phi \wedge \neg\phi \equiv \bot$ *//something cannot be both true and false*

  $\phi \vee \neg\phi \equiv \top$

- Neutrality:

$\phi \wedge \top \equiv \phi$

$\phi \vee \bot \equiv \phi$

- Quantifiers:

$\neg \forall x.\phi \equiv \exists x.\neg \phi$

$\neg \exists x.\phi \equiv \forall x.\neg \phi$ //*'if there does not exist some, then there's always none'*

$\forall x.\phi \wedge \forall x.\psi \equiv \forall x.(\phi \wedge \psi)$

$\exists x.\phi \vee \exists x.\psi \equiv \exists x.(\phi \vee \psi)$

$(\forall x.\phi) \wedge \psi \equiv \forall x.(\phi \wedge \psi)$ if x is not free in ψ

$(\forall x.\phi) \vee \psi \equiv \forall x.(\phi \vee \psi)$ if x is not free in ψ

$(\exists x.\phi) \wedge \psi \equiv \exists x.(\phi \wedge \psi)$ if x is not free in ψ

$(\exists x.\phi) \vee \psi \equiv \exists x.(\phi \vee \psi)$ if x is not free in ψ

Note: The ones up to (but excluding) the quantifiers hold for both propositional logic and first order predicate logic.

2.2 Reasoning

Having a logic language with a semantics is one thing, but it may be only a means to an end rather than an end in itself. From the computational angle—especially from a logician's perspective—the really interesting aspect of having such a language and (someone else) having put in the effort to formalise some subject domain, is to reason over it to infer implicit knowledge. Here, we are not talking about making a truth table, which is computationally way too costly when one has to analyse many sentences, but deploying other techniques so that it can be scaled up compared to the manual efforts. Automated reasoning, then, concerns computing systems that automate the ability to make inferences by designing a formal language in which a problem's assumptions and conclusion can be written and providing correct algorithms to solve the problem with a computer in an efficient way.

How does one find out whether a formula is valid or not? How do we find out whether our knowledge base is satisfiable? The main proof technique for DL-based ontologies is tableaux, although there are several others[3]. The following subsections first provide a general introduc-

---

[3]The remainder of Section 2.2 consists of amended versions of my "Reasoning, automated" essay and related definitions that have been published in Springer's Encyclopedia of Systems Biology.

tion (Section 2.2.1), the essential ingredients for automated reasoning (Section 2.2.2), and then describes deduction, abduction, and induction (Section 2.2.3).

2.2.1   Introduction

Characteristics

People employ reasoning informally by taking a set of premises and somehow arriving at a conclusion, i.e., it is *entailed by* the premises (deduction), arriving at a hypothesis (abduction), or generalizing from facts to an assumption (induction). Mathematicians and computer scientists developed ways to capture this formally with logic languages to represent the knowledge and rules that may be applied to the axioms so that one can construct a *formal proof* that the conclusion can be derived from the premises. This can be done by hand [Sol05] for small theories, but that does not scale up when one has, say, 80 or more axioms even though there are much larger theories that require a formal analysis, such as checking that the theory can indeed have a model and thus does not contradict itself. To this end, much work has gone into automating reasoning. The remainder of this section introduces briefly several of the many purposes and usages of automated reasoning, its limitations, and types of automated reasoners.

Purposes

Automated reasoning, and deduction in particular, has found applications in 'every day life'. A notable example is hardware and (critical) software verification, which gained prominence after Intel had shipped its Pentium processors with a floating point unit error in 1994 that lost the company about $500 million. Since then, chips are routinely automatically proven to function correctly according to specification before taken into production. A different scenario is scheduling problems at schools to find an optimal combination of course, lecturer, and timing for the class or degree program, which used to take a summer to do manually, but can now be computed in a fraction of it using constraint programming. In addition to such general application domains, it is also used for specific scenarios, such as the demonstration of discovering (more precisely: deriving) novel knowledge about protein phosphatases [WSH07]. They represented the knowledge about the subject domain of protein phosphatases in humans in a formal bio-ontology and classified the enzymes of both human and the fungus *Aspergillus fumigatus* using an automated reasoner, which showed that (i) the reasoner was as good as human expert classification, (ii) it identified additional p-domains (an aspect of the phosphatases) so that the human-originated classification could be refined, and (iii) it identified a novel type of calcineurin phosphatase like in other pathogenic fungi. The fact that one can use an automated reasoner (in this case: deduction, using a Description Logics knowledge base) as a viable method in science is an encouragement to explore such avenues further.

Limitations

While many advances have been made in specific application areas, the main limitation of the implementations are due to the computational complexity of the chosen representation language and the desired automated reasoning services. This is being addressed by implementations of optimisations of the algorithms or by limiting the expressiveness of the language, or both. One family of logics that focus principally on 'computationally well-behaved' languages is Description Logics, which are decidable fragments of first order logic [BCM+08]; that is, they are languages such that the corresponding reasoning services are guaranteed to terminate with an answer. Description Logics form the basis of most of the Web Ontology Languages OWL and OWL 2 and are gaining increasing importance in the Semantic Web applications area. Giving up expressiveness, however, does lead to criticism from the modellers' community, as a computationally nice language may not have the features deemed necessary to represent the subject domain adequately.

Tools

There are many tools for automated reasoning, which differ in which language they accept, the reasoning services they provide, and, with that, the purpose they aim to serve.

There are, among others, generic first- and higher order logic theorem provers (e.g., Prover9, MACE4, Vampire, HOL4), SAT solvers that compute if there is a model for the formal theory (e.g., GRASP, Satz), Constraint Satisfaction Programming for solving, e.g., scheduling problems and reasoning with soft constraints (e.g., Eclipse), DL reasoners that are used for reasoning over OWL ontologies using deductive reasoning to compute satisfiability, consistency, and perform taxonomic and instance classification (e.g., Fact++, RacerPro, Hermit, CEL, QuOnto), and inductive logic programming tools (e.g., PROGOL and Aleph).

2.2.2   Basic idea

Essential to automated reasoning are:

1. *The choice of the class of problems the software program has to solve*, such as checking the consistency of a theory (i.e., whether there are no contradictions) or computing a classification hierarchy of concepts subsuming one another based on the properties represented in the logical theory;

2. *The formal language in which to represent the problems*, which may have more or less features to represent the subject domain knowledge, such as cardinality constraints (e.g., that spiders have as part exactly eight legs), probabilities, or temporal knowledge (e.g., that a butterfly is a transformation of a caterpillar);

3. *The way how the program has to compute the solution*, such as using natural deduction or resolution; and

4. *How to do this efficiently*, be this achieved through constraining the language into one of low complexity, or optimising the algorithms to compute the solution, or both.

Concerning the first item, with a *problem* being, e.g., "is my theory is consistent?", then the *problem's assumptions* are the axioms in the logical theory and the *problem's conclusion* that is computed by the automated reasoner is a "yes" or a "no" (provided the language in which the assumptions are represented is decidable and thus guaranteed to terminate with an answer). With respect to how this is done (item iii), two properties are important for the calculus used: soundness and completeness. To define them, note/recall that "⊢" means 'derivable with a set of inference rules' and "⊨" denotes 'implies', i.e., every truth assignment that satisfies Γ also satisfies ϕ. The two properties are defined as follows:

- Completeness: if $\Gamma \models \phi$ then $\Gamma \vdash \phi$
- Soundness: if $\Gamma \vdash \phi$ then $\Gamma \models \phi$

If the algorithm it is incomplete, then there exist entailments that cannot be computed (hence, 'missing' some results), if it is unsound then false conclusions can be derived from true premises, which is even more undesirable.

An example is included in Section 2.2.4, once the other ingredients have been introduced as well: proving the validity of a formula (the class of the problem) in propositional logic (the formal language) using tableau reasoning (the way how to compute the solution) with the Tree Proof Generator[4] (the automated reasoner); more detail, with reflection and other techniques, can be found in [Por10] among others.

2.2.3   Deduction, abduction, and induction

There are three principle ways of making the inferences—deduction, abduction, and induction—that are described now.

Deduction

Deduction is a way to ascertain if a theory T represented in a logic language entails an axiom α that is not explicitly asserted in T (written as $T \models \alpha$), i.e., whether α can be *derived* from the premises through repeated application of *deduction rules*. For instance, a theory that states that "each Arachnid has as part exactly 8 legs" and "each Tarantula is an Arachnid" then one can deduce—it is entailed in the theory—that "Each Tarantula has as part 8 legs". An example is included further below (after having introduced a reasoning technique), which formally demonstrates that a formula is entailed in a theory T using said rules.

Thus, strictly speaking, a deduction does not reveal *novel* knowledge, but only that what was already represented implicitly in the theory. Nevertheless, with large theories, it is often difficult to oversee all implications of the represented knowledge and, hence, the deductions may be perceived as novel from a domain expert perspective, such as with the example about the protein phosphatases. (This is in contrast to Abduction and Induction, where the reasoner 'guesses' knowledge that is not already entailed in the theory; see below).

There are various ways how to ascertain $T \models \alpha$, be it manually or automatically. One can construct a step-by-step proof 'forward' from the premises by applying the deduction rules or prove it indirectly such

---

[4]http://www.umsu.de/logik/trees/

that $T \cup \{\neg\alpha\}$ must lead to a contradiction. The former approach is called *natural deduction*, whereas the latter is based on techniques such as resolution, matrix connection methods, and sequent deduction (which includes *tableaux*). How exactly that is done for tableau is described in Section 2.2.4.

Abduction

One tries to infer a as an explanation of b. That is, we have a set of observations, a theory of the domain of the observations, and a set of (possible, hypothesised) explanations that one would hope to find. For each explanation, it should be the case that the set of observations follows from the combination of the theory and the set of explanations, noting that the combination of the theory and the set of explanation has to be consistent. One can add additional machinery to these basics to, e.g., find out which of the explanations are the most interesting.

Compared to deduction, there is less permeation of automated reasoning for abduction. From a scientist's perspective, automation of abduction may seem appealing, because it would help one to generate a hypothesis based on the facts put into the reasoner [Ali04]. Practically, it has been used for, for instance, fault detection: given the knowledge about a system and the observed defective state, find the likely fault in the system. To formally capture theory with assumptions and facts and find the conclusion, several approaches have been proposed, each with their specific application areas; for instance, sequent calculus, belief revision, probabilistic abductive reasoning, and Bayesian networks.

Induction

With induction, one generalises toward a conclusion based on a set of individuals. However, the conclusion is *not* a logical consequence of the premise. Thus, it allows one to arrive at a conclusion that actually may be false even though the premises are true. The premises provide a *degree of support* so as to infer a as an explanation of b. Such a 'degree' can be based on probabilities (a statistical syllogism) or analogy. For instance, we have a premise that "The proportion of bacteria that acquire genes through horizontal gene transfer is 95%" and the fact that "*Staphylococcus aureus* is a bacterium", then we induce that the probability that *S. aureus* acquires genes through horizontal gene transfer is

95%.

Induction by analogy is weaker version of reasoning, in particular in logic-based systems, and yields very different answers than deduction. For instance, let us encode that some instance, Tibbles, is a cat and we know that all cats have the properties of having a tail and four legs and that they are furry. When we encode that another animal, Tib, who happens to have four legs and is also furry, then by inductive reasoning by analogy, we conclude that Tib is also a cat, even though in reality it may well be an instance of cheetah. On the other hand, by deductive reasoning, Tib will not be classified as being an instance of cat (but may be an instance of a superclass of cats (e.g., still within the suborder *Feliformia*), provided that the superclass has declared that all instances have four legs and are furry. Given that humans do perform such reasoning, there are attempts to mimic this process in software applications, most notably in the area of machine learning and inductive logic programming. The principal approach with inductive logic programming is to take as input positive examples + negative examples + background knowledge and then derive a hypothesised logic program that entails all the positive and none of the negative examples.

2.2.4 Proofs with tableaux

Simply put, a proof is a convincing argument expressed in the language of mathematics. The steps in the process of the (automated) reasoning provide a proof. Several outcomes are possible for a given formula:

- A formula is *valid* if it holds under *every* assignment[5]; this is denoted as "$\models \phi$". A valid formula is called a *tautology*.
- A formula is *satisfiable* if it holds under *some* assignment.
- A formula is *unsatisfiable* if it holds under *no* assignment. An unsatisfiable formula is called a *contradiction*.

The questions that need to be answered to realise the next step are:

- *How* do we find out whether a formula is valid or not?
- *How* do we find out whether our theory is satisfiable?

A rather unpractical approach is truth tables, which may be fine in a paper-based logic course, but won't do for computing. While there are several tools with several techniques, we will look at one that is, at the

---

[5]typically, the assignments are 'true' and 'false', but there are also other logics that allow more/other assignments

time of writing, the 'winner' in the realm of ontologies: *tableaux-based reasoning*, which is also the principal approach for DL reasoners and the OWL tools. A tableau provides a sound and complete procedure that decides satisfiability by checking the existence of a model[6]. It exhaustively looks at all the possibilities, so that it can eventually prove that no model could be found for unsatisfiable formulas. That is:

- $\phi \models \psi$ iff $\phi \wedge \neg\psi$ is NOT satisfiable—if it is satisfiable, we have found a counterexample

It does this by decomposing the formula in top-down fashion. Tableaux calculus works only if the formula has been translated into *Negation Normal Form*, however, so the first step in the process is:

(1.) Push the negations inside to convert a sentence into Negation Normal Form, if applicable.

We use the aforementioned equivalences for that, which were listed on page 40. For instance, one of the De Morgan rules is $\neg(\phi\wedge\psi) \equiv \neg\phi\vee\neg\psi$, where the 'outer' negation outside the brackets is pushed inside right in front of the formula, which can be done likewise with the quantifiers, such as substituting $\neg\forall x.\phi$ with $\exists x.\neg\phi$.

Now it is ready to enter the tableau. Use any or all of the following rules, as applicable (in a 'smart' order):

(2a.) If a model satisfies a *conjunction*, then it also satisfies each of the conjuncts:
$$\frac{\phi \wedge \psi}{\substack{\phi \\ \psi}}$$

(2b.) If a model satisfies a *disjunction*, then it also satisfies one of the disjuncts (which is non-deterministic):
$$\frac{\phi \vee \psi}{\phi \mid \psi}$$

(2c.) If a model satisfies a universally quantified formula ($\forall$), then it also satisfies the formula where the quantified variable has been substituted with some term (and the prescription is to use all the

---

[6]model in the sense of logic (recall Definition 2.9), not in the sense of 'conceptual data model' like a UML class diagram.

terms which appear in the tableaux),

$$\frac{\forall x.\phi}{\phi\{X/t\}}$$
$$\forall x.\phi$$

(2d.) For an existentially quantified formula, if a model satisfies it, then it also satisfies the formula where the quantified variable has been substituted with a new Skolem constant,

$$\frac{\exists x.\phi}{\phi\{X/a\}}$$

To complete the proof:

(3.) Apply the completion rules 2a-d until either:

 (a) an explicit contradiction is generated in each branch due to the presence of two opposite literals in a node (called a *clash*), or

 (b) there is a completed branch where no more rule is applicable.

(4.) Determine the outcome:

 (a) If *all* branches result in clashes, i.e., there is no completed branch, then $\phi \wedge \neg\psi$ is NOT satisfiable, which makes the original one, $\phi \models \psi$, satisfiable.

 (b) If there is *a completed* branch, then we have found a model for $\phi \wedge \neg\psi$, hence, have found a counterexample for some assignments of the original $\phi \models \psi$, hence $\phi \nvDash \psi$.

This completes the procedure.

One can also do the above for individual formulas and not bother with the negation at the start and then simply check if one can find a model for some formula; i.e., 'try to build a model' (to see if everything can be instantiated) with the completion rules cf. the 'check there is no model (when negated)' of the tableau procedure above. In that case, the conclusions one should draw are the opposite, i.e., then if there's a completed branch it means that that formula is satisfiable for it has found a model, and if there are only clashes, the tableau cannot find a model so there's some contradiction in the formula. For instance, the formula $\exists x(p(x) \wedge \neg q(x)) \wedge \forall y(\neg p(y) \vee q(y))$ is unsatisfiable.

Let's have a look at how to apply all this, which is depicted in Figure 2.3 and described in the example below.

Example 2.3. *Let us take some arbitrary theory T that contains two axioms stating that relation R is reflexive (i.e., $\forall x(R(x,x))$, a thing relates to itself) and asymmetric (i.e., $\forall x, y(R(x,y) \to \neg R(y,x))$, if a thing a relates to b through relation R, then b does not relate back to a). We then can deduce, among others, that $T \cup \{\neg \forall x, y(R(x,y))\}$ is satisfiable. We do this by demonstrating that the negation of the axiom is unsatisfiable.*

To enter the tableau, we first rewrite the asymmetry into a disjunction using equivalences, i.e., $\forall x, y(R(x,y) \to \neg R(y,x))$ is equivalent to $\forall x, y(\neg R(x,y) \lor R(y,x))$, thanks to applying the implication rule from page 40. Then add a negation to $\{\neg \forall x, y(R(x,y))\}$, which thus becomes $\forall x, y(R(x,y))$. So, to start the tableau, we have three axioms (1, 2, 3), and subsequently the full tableau as in Figure 2.3. ◇

Number	Tableau	Explanation
1	$\forall x.R(x,x)$	Reflexivity axiom in the original theory T
2	$\forall x,y.\ \neg R(x,y) \lor \neg R(y,x)$	Asymmetry axiom in the original theory T
3	$\forall x,y.R(x,y)$	The negated axiom added to theory T
4		Substitute x for term a in 1,2,3
5	$R(a,a)$	
6	$\forall y.\ \neg R(a,y) \lor \neg R(y,a)$	
7	$\forall y.R(a,y)$	
8		Substitute y for term a in 2 and 3
9	$R(a,a)$	
10	$\neg R(a,a) \lor \neg R(a,a)$	
11	$R(a,a)$	
12		Split the disjunction of 10
13	$\neg R(a,a)$ $\neg R(a,a)$	Which each generate a clash with 9 and 11, hence, $\neg \forall x,y.R(x,y)$ is entailed by T.

Figure 2.3: Tableau example (using notation with a "." not the brackets).

This is a fairly simple example that uses rules 2d and 2b and only a few steps. It can quickly get more elaborate even for simpler languages such as propositional logic. If you have not seen propositional logic, you are free to skip the following example; else you may want to read through it: all the 19 (!) steps use only rules 2a and 2b (as propositional logic does not have the variables and quantifiers).

Example 2.4. *A sample computation to prove automatically whether the propositional formula* $((p \vee (q \wedge r)) \to ((p \vee q) \wedge (p \vee r)))$ *is valid or not is included in Figure 2.4 and Figure 2.5, using tableau reasoning (see Deduction, Section 2.2.3). The tableau method is a decision procedure that checks the existence of a model (i.e., that it can be instantiated). It exhaustively looks at all the possibilities, so that it can eventually prove that no model could be found for unsatisfiable formulas (if it is satisfiable, we have found a counterexample). This is done by decomposing the formula in top-down fashion after it has been translated into Negation Normal Form (i.e., all the negations have been pushed inside), which can be achieved using equivalences. Further, if a model satisfies a conjunction, then it also satisfies each of the conjuncts ("$\wedge$"), and if a model satisfies a disjunction ("$\vee$"), then it also satisfies one of the disjuncts (this is a non-deterministic rule and it generates two alternative branches). Last, one has to apply these completion rules until either (a) an explicit contradiction is obtained due to the presence of two opposite literals in a node (a clash) is generated in each branch, or (b) there is a completed branch where no more rule is applicable.* ◊

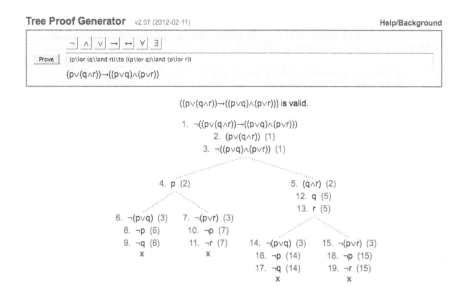

Figure 2.4: Sample computation using semantic tableau proving that the propositional formula is valid; see Figure 2.5 for an explanation.

Axiom Number	Explanation
Start	The aim is to prove that ((p ∨ (q ∧ r)) →((p ∨ q) ∧ (p ∨ r)) is valid
1	This we approach by demonstrating that its *negation* (¬((p ∨ (q ∧ r)) → ((p ∨ q) ∧ (p ∨ r))) leads to a *contradiction*
1a	The implication (→) is rewritten following the rule that φ → φ equals ¬φ ∨ φ, so that we obtain ¬(¬(p ∨ (q ∧ r)) ∨ ((p ∨ q) ∧(p ∨ r))
1b	The result of 1a is rewritten to push the negation inside using the equivalence that ¬(φ ∨ φ) ≡ ¬φ ∧ ¬φ, so that we obtain ¬¬(p ∨ (q ∧ r)) ∧ ¬((p ∨ q) ∧ (p ∨ r))
1c	Double negation is the same as positive, hence we obtain ((p ∨ (q ∧ r)) ∧ ¬((p ∨ q) ∧ (p ∨ r)) that continues in the tableau
2, 3	For a conjunction (1c), both parts, being ((p ∨ (q ∧ r)) and ((p ∨ q) ∧ (p ∨ r)), must hold; hence, the axiom is split into those two part, numbered 2 and 3
4, 5	Starting with 2, it has a disjunction that is split into p and (q ∧ r)
4a	The negation in 3 is pushed inside following the rule that ¬(φ ∧ φ) ≡ ¬φ ∨ ¬φ, hence we obtain ¬(p ∨ q) ∨ ¬(p ∨ r)
6, 7	The result of 4a is disjunction and thus generates two branches that we append to 4
8, 9	Rewriting 6 by pushing negation inside generates a conjunction so that both parts must hold. However, with 9 we obtain ¬p whereas from 4 we know that p must hold, hence, a contradiction
10, 11	Analogously, rewriting 7 by pushing negation inside generates a conjunction so that both parts must hold, where we have again ¬p that contradicts p of 4
	Given that these two branches are exhausted, we continue with 5
12, 13	The conjunction of 5 means that both p and r
14, 15	Like with 6, 7, also here we must generate two branches to deal with ¬(p ∨ q) ∨ ¬(p ∨ r)
16, 17	The same procedure as with 8,9 is repeated here, which also generates a contradiction, between 12 and 17
18, 19	Unfolding the last branch (like in 10, 11) we arrive at a contradiction between 13 and 19
End	Given that all branches of the negated original formula lead to a contradiction, we have proven that the original formula is valid

Figure 2.5: Explanation of the tableaux in Figure 2.4.

2.3 Exercises

Review question 2.1. What is the difference between syntax and semantics for a logic?

Review question 2.2. What is a theory?

Review question 2.3. Name the four core components for automated reasoning.

Review question 2.4. Describe the procedure for tableau reasoning in four shorts sentences.

Exercise 2.1. Write in one natural language sentence what the following sentences in First-Order Logic state.
   a. $\forall x(Lion(x) \rightarrow Mammal(x))$

b. $\forall x(PC(x) \rightarrow \exists y, z(hasPart(x,y) \land connected(x,z) \land CPU(y) \land Monitor(z)))$

c. $\forall x, y(hasProperPart(x,y) \rightarrow \neg hasProperPart(y,x))$

Exercise 2.2. Formalise the following natural language sentence into First-Order Logic.

a. Each car is a vehicle.

b. Every human parent has at least one human child.

c. Any person cannot be both a lecturer and a student editor of the same course.

Exercise 2.3. Consider the structures in Figure 2.6, which are graphs.

a. Figures 2.6-A and B are different depictions, but have the same descriptions w.r.t. the vertices and edges. Check this.

b. C has a property that A and B do not have. Represent this in a first-order sentence.

c. Find a suitable first-order language for A (/B), and formulate at least two properties of the graph using quantifiers.

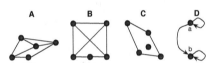

Figure 2.6: Graphs for Exercise 2.3 (figures A-C) and Exercise 2.4 (figure D).

Exercise 2.4. Consider the graph in Figure 2.6, and first-order language $\mathcal{L} = \langle R \rangle$, with R being a binary relation symbol (edge).

a. Formalise the following properties of the graph as $\mathcal{L}$-sentences: (i) (a,a) and (b,b) are edges of the graph; (ii) (a,b) is an edge of the graph; (iii) (b,a) is not an edge of the graph. Let T stand for the resulting set of sentences.

b. Prove that $T \cup \{\forall x \forall y R(x,y)\}$ is unsatisfiable using tableaux calculus.

Exercise 2.5. Let us have a logical theory Θ with the following sentences:

- $\forall x Pizza(x)$, $\forall x PizzaT(x)$, $\forall x PizzaB(x)$, which are disjoint
- $\forall x(Pizza(x) \rightarrow \neg PizzaT(x))$,
- $\forall x(Pizza(x) \rightarrow \neg PizzaB(x))$,

- $\forall x(PizzaT(x) \rightarrow \neg PizzaB(x))$,
- $\forall x, y(hasT(x, y) \rightarrow Pizza(x) \wedge PizzaT(y))$,
- $\forall x, y(hasB(x, y) \rightarrow Pizza(x) \wedge PizzaB(y))$,
- $\forall x(ITPizza(x) \rightarrow Pizza(x))$, and
- $\forall x(ITPizza(x) \rightarrow \neg \exists y(hasT(x, y) \wedge FruitT(y)))$, where
- $\forall x(VegeT(x) \rightarrow PizzaT(x))$ and
- $\forall x(FruitT(x) \rightarrow PizzaT(x))$.

Task (read in full first before attempting it):

a. A Pizza margherita has the necessary and sufficient conditions that it has mozzarella, tomato, basilicum and oil as toppings and has a pizza base. Add this to Θ.

Annotate you commitments: what have you added to Θ and how? Hint: fruits are not vegetables, categorise the toppings, and "necessary and sufficient" is denoted with $\leftrightarrow$.

b. We want to merge our new Θ with some other theory Γ that has knowledge about fruits and vegetables. Γ contains, among other formulas, $\forall x(Tomato(x) \rightarrow Fruit(x))$. What happens? Represent the scenario formally, and prove your answer.

Actually, this is not easy to figure out manually, and there are ways to automate this, which you will do later in Chapter 4.

2.4 Literature and reference material

The following literature is optional for the scope of ontology engineering, but you may find of interest if you would like to design your own logic, for instance.

1. Hedman, S. *A first course in logic—an introduction to model theory, proof theory, computability, and complexity.* Oxford: Oxford University Press. 2004.
2. Solow, D. *How to read and do proofs.* 4th Ed. Wiley. 2005.

Chapter 3

Description Logics

A Description Logic (DL) is a structured fragment of FOL; more precisely: any (basic) Description Logic language is a subset of $\mathcal{L}_3$, i.e., the function-free FOL using only at most three variable names. Its representation is at the predicate level: no variables are present in the formalism. DLs provide a logical reconstruction and (claimed to be a) unifying formalism for other knowledge representation languages, such as frames-based systems, object-oriented modelling, Semantic data models, etc. They provide the language to formulate theories and systems declaratively *expressing structured knowledge* and for *accessing* it and *reasoning* with it, and they are used for, among others, terminologies and ontologies, logic-based conceptual data modelling, and information integration.

Figure 3.1 shows a basic overview of the principal components of a DL knowledge base, with the so-called *TBox* containing the knowledge at the class-level and the *ABox* containing the data (individuals). Sometimes you will see added to the figure an *RBox*, which is used to make explicit there are relationships and the axioms that hold for them.

The remainder of this section contains, first, a general introduction to DL (Section 3.1), which are the first five sections of the DL Primer [KSH12], and is reproduced here with permission of its authors Markus Krötzsch, František Simančík, and Ian Horrocks[1]. (Slightly more de-

---

[1]I harmonised the terminology so as to use the same terms throughout the book, cf. adding synonyms at this stage, and added a few references to other sections in this book to integrate the text better. Also, I moved their $\mathcal{SROIQ}$ section into

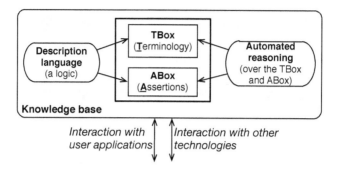

Figure 3.1: A Description Logic knowledge base. Sometimes you will see a similar picture extended with an "RBox", which denotes the DL roles and their axioms.

tailed introductory notes with examples can be found in the first 8 pages of [Tur10] and the first 10 pages of [Sat07]; a DL textbook is in the pipeline). We then proceed to several important DLs out of the very many DLs investigated, being $\mathcal{ALC}$ and $\mathcal{SROIQ}$, in Section 3.2. We then proceed to describing and illustrating the standard reasoning services for DLs in Section 3.3, which essentially applies and extends the tableau reasoning of the previous chapter. Note that DLs and its reasoning services return in Chapter 4 about OWL 2, building upon the theoretical foundations introduced in this chapter.

3.1   DL primer

Description logics (DLs) are a family of knowledge representation languages that are widely used in ontology development. An important practical reason for this is that they provide one of the main underpinnings for the Web Ontology Language OWL as standardised by the World Wide Web Consortium (W3C). However, DLs have been used in knowledge representation long before the advent of ontologies in the context of the Semantic Web, tracing back to first DL modelling languages in the mid 1980s.

As their name suggests, DLs are logics (in fact they are decidable fragments of first-order logic), and as such they are equipped with a *for-*

Section 3.2 and inserted $\mathcal{ALC}$ there, and made the family composition examples more inclusive.

mal semantics: a precise specification of the meaning of DL ontologies. This formal semantics allows humans and computer systems to exchange DL ontologies without ambiguity as to their intended meaning, and also makes it possible to use logical deduction to *infer* additional information from the facts stated explicitly in an ontology – an important feature that distinguishes DLs from other modelling languages such as UML.

The capability of inferring additional knowledge increases the modelling power of DLs but it also requires some understanding on the side of the modeller and, above all, good tool support for computing the conclusions. The computation of inferences is called *reasoning* and an important goal of DL language design has been to ensure that reasoning algorithms of good performance are available. This is one of the reasons why there is not just a single description logic: the best balance between expressivity of the language and complexity of reasoning depends on the intended application.

We provide a self-contained first introduction to Description Logics. We start by explaining the basic way in which knowledge is modelled in DLs in Section 3.1.1 and continue with an intuitive introduction to the most important DL modelling features in Section 3.1.2. In Section 3.1.3, we explain the underlying ideas of DL semantics. Then a common starting point of DLs is introduced, being $\mathcal{ALC}$, and subsequently the rather expressive DL called $\mathcal{SROIQ}$ (summarised in Section 3.2.2), which forms the basis of the OWL 2 DL language. Many DLs can be obtained by omitting some features of $\mathcal{SROIQ}$ and in Section 3.2.3 we review some of the most important DLs obtained in this way. In particular, this includes various light-weight description logics that allow for particularly efficient reasoning and are also standardised, as fragments of OWL.

3.1.1 Basic building blocks of DL ontologies

Description logics (DLs) provide means to model the relationships between entities in a domain of interest. In DLs there are three kinds of entities: concepts, roles and individual names. Concepts denote sets of individuals, roles denote sets of binary relations between the individuals[2], and individual names denote single individuals in the domain.

---

[2]There are a few DLs that permit *n*-aries, which are the $\mathcal{DLR}$ and $\mathcal{CFD}$ families of logics that were inspired by conceptual data modelling and relational models.

Readers familiar with first-order logic will recognise these as unary predicates, binary predicates and constants.

For example, an ontology representing the domain of people and their family relationships might use concepts such as Parent to denote the set of all parents and Female to represent the set of all female individuals, roles such as parentOf to denote the (binary) relationship between parents and their children, and individual names such as julia and john to denote the individuals Julia and John.

Unlike a database, a DL ontology does not fully describe a particular situation or "state of the world"; rather it consists of a set of statements, called axioms, each of which must be true in the situation described. These axioms typically capture only partial knowledge about the situation that the ontology is describing, and there may be many different states of the world that are consistent with the ontology. Although, from the point of view of logic, there is no principal difference between different types of axioms, it is customary to separate them into three groups: assertional (ABox) axioms, terminological (TBox) axioms and relational (RBox) axioms.

Asserting Facts with ABox Axioms   ABox axioms capture knowledge about named individuals, i.e., the concepts to which they belong and how they are related to each other. The most common ABox axioms are *concept assertions* such as

$$\text{Mother(julia)} \tag{3.1}$$

which asserts that Julia is a mother or, more precisely, that the individual named julia is an *instance* of the concept Mother.

Role assertions describe relations between named individuals. The assertion

$$\text{parentOf(julia, john)} \tag{3.2}$$

for example, states that Julia is a parent of John or, more precisely, that the individual named julia is in the relation that is denoted by parentOf to the individual named john. The previous sentence shows that it can be rather cumbersome to explicitly point out that the relationships expressed by an axiom are really relationships between the individuals, sets and relations that are denoted by the respective individual names, concepts and roles. Assuming that this subtle distinction between syntactic identifiers and semantic entities is understood, we will thus often adopt a more sloppy and readable formulation. Section 3.1.3 below explains the underlying semantics with greater precision[3].

Although it is intuitively clear that Julia and John are different individuals, this fact does not logically follow from what we have stated so far. DLs may or may not make the *unique name assumption*, so different names might refer to the same individual unless explicitly stated otherwise[4]. The *individual inequality* assertion

$$\text{julia} \not\approx \text{john} \tag{3.3}$$

is used to assert that Julia and John are actually different individuals. On the other hand, an *individual equality* assertion, such as

$$\text{john} \approx \text{johnny} \tag{3.4}$$

states that two different names are known to refer to the same individual. Such situations can arise, for example, when combining knowledge about the same domain from several different sources, a task that is known as *ontology alignment.*

Expressing Terminological Knowledge with TBox Axioms TBox axioms describe relationships between concepts. For example, the fact that all mothers are parents is expressed by the *concept inclusion*

$$\text{Mother} \sqsubseteq \text{Parent} \tag{3.5}$$

in which case we say that the concept Mother is *subsumed* by the concept Parent. Such knowledge can be used to infer further facts about individuals. For example, (3.1) and (3.5) together imply that Julia is a parent.

Concept equivalence asserts that two concepts have the same instances, as in

$$\text{Person} \equiv \text{Human} \tag{3.6}$$

---

[3]It is the same as the model-theoretic semantics we have seen in Section 2.1.2, but then restated for DLs.

[4]i.e., the unique name assumption (UNA) means that different names refer to different individuals, as is customary in the database world. There are consequences for UNA/no-UNA both regarding computational complexity and automated reasoners: no-UNA is more costly and the deductions are different when reasoning with UNA or not. We will see the effects of especially the latter in the exercises of Chapter 4.

While synonyms may be perceived to be an obvious example of equivalent concepts, in practice one uses concept equivalence to give a name to complex expressions as introduced in Section 3.1.2 below and put real synonyms in the annotations or extra labels in the ontology file. Furthermore, such additional concept expressions can be combined with equivalence and inclusion to describe more complex situations such as the disjointness of concepts, which asserts that two concepts do not share any instances.

Modelling Relationships between Roles with RBox Axioms
RBox axioms refer to properties of roles. As for concepts, DLs support *role inclusion* and *role equivalence* axioms. For example, the inclusion

$$\mathsf{parentOf} \sqsubseteq \mathsf{ancestorOf} \tag{3.7}$$

states that parentOf is a *subrole* of ancestorOf, i.e., every pair of individuals related by parentOf is also related by ancestorOf. Thus (3.2) and (3.7) together imply that Julia is an ancestor of John.

In role inclusion axioms, *role composition* can be used to describe roles such as uncleOf. Intuitively, if Charles is a brother of Julia and Julia is a parent of John, then Charles is an uncle of John. This kind of relationship between the roles brotherOf, parentOf and uncleOf is captured by the *complex role inclusion* axiom

$$\mathsf{brotherOf} \circ \mathsf{parentOf} \sqsubseteq \mathsf{uncleOf} \tag{3.8}$$

Note that role composition can only appear on the left-hand side of complex role inclusions. Furthermore, in order to retain decidability of reasoning (see Appendix C for a recap on complexity and decidability), their use is restricted by additional structural restrictions that specify whether or not a collection of such axioms can be used together in one ontology.

Nobody can be both a parent and a child of the same individual, so the two roles parentOf and childOf are disjoint. In DLs we can write *disjoint roles* as follows:

$$Disjoint(\mathsf{parentOf}, \mathsf{childOf}) \tag{3.9}$$

Further RBox axioms include *role characteristics* such as reflexivity, symmetry and transitivity of roles. These are closely related to a number of other DL features and we will discuss them again in more detail in Section 3.1.2.

3.1.2 Constructors for concepts and roles

The basic types of axioms introduced in Section 3.1.1 are rather limited for accurate modelling. To describe more complex situations, DLs allow new concepts and roles to be built using a variety of different constructors. We distinguish concept and role constructors depending on whether concept or role expressions are constructed. In the case of concepts, one can further separate basic Boolean constructors, role restrictions and nominals/enumerations. At the end of this section, we revisit the additional kinds of RBox axioms that have been omitted in Section 3.1.1.

Boolean Concept Constructors   Boolean concept constructors provide basic Boolean operations that are closely related to the familiar operations of intersection, union and complement of sets, or to conjunction, disjunction and negation of logical expressions.

For example, concept inclusions allow us to state that all mothers are female and that all mothers are parents, but what we really mean is that mothers are *exactly* the female parents. DLs support such statements by allowing us to form complex concepts such as the *intersection* (also called *conjunction*)

$$\text{Female} \sqcap \text{Parent} \tag{3.10}$$

which denotes the set of individuals that are both female and parents. A complex concept can be used in axioms in exactly the same way as an atomic concept, e.g., in the equivalence Mother $\equiv$ Female $\sqcap$ Parent.

Union (also called *disjunction*) is the dual of intersection. For example, the concept

$$\text{Father} \sqcup \text{Mother} \tag{3.11}$$

describes those individuals that are either (biological) fathers or mothers. Again, it can be used in an axiom such as Parent $\equiv$ Father $\sqcup$ Mother, which states that a parent is either a father or a mother (and vice versa). One can extend this further, of course, by stating, e.g., that a parent is equivalent to father or mother or guardian: Parent $\equiv$ Father $\sqcup$ Mother $\sqcup$ Guardian.

Sometimes we are interested in individuals that do *not* belong to a certain concept, e.g., in women who are not married. These could be described by the complex concept

$$\text{Female} \sqcap \neg\text{Married} \tag{3.12}$$

where the *complement* (also called *negation*) ¬Married denotes the set of all individuals that are not married.

It is sometimes useful to be able to make a statement about every individual, e.g., to say that everybody is either male or female. This can be accomplished by the axiom

$$\top \sqsubseteq \mathsf{Male} \sqcup \mathsf{Female} \tag{3.13}$$

where the *top concept* $\top$ is a special concept with every individual as an instance; it can be viewed as an abbreviation for $C \sqcup \neg C$ for an arbitrary concept C. Note that this modelling is rather coarse as it presupposes that *every* individual has a gender, which may not be reasonable, especially for instances of a concept such as Computer. We will see more useful applications for $\top$ later on.

To express that, for the purposes of our modelling, nobody can be both a parent and childless at the same time, we can declare the set of parents and the set of childless individuals to be disjoint. While ontology languages like OWL provide a basic constructor for disjointness, it is naturally captured in DLs with the axiom

$$\mathsf{Parent} \sqcap \mathsf{Childless} \sqsubseteq \bot \tag{3.14}$$

where the *bottom concept* $\bot$ is the dual of $\top$, that is the special concept with no individuals as instances; it can be seen as an abbreviation for $C \sqcap \neg C$ for an arbitrary concept C. The above axiom thus says that the intersection of the two concepts is empty.

Role Restrictions   So far we have seen how to use TBox and RBox axioms to express relationships between concepts and roles, respectively. The most interesting feature of DLs, however, is their ability to form statements that link concepts and roles together. For example, there is an obvious relationship between the concept Parent and the role parentOf, namely, a parent is someone who is a parent of at least one individual. In DLs, this relationship can be captured by the concept equivalence

$$\mathsf{Parent} \equiv \exists \mathsf{parentOf}.\top \tag{3.15}$$

where the *existential restriction* $\exists \mathsf{parentOf}.\top$ is a complex concept that describes the set of individuals that are parents of at least one individual (instance of $\top$). Similarly, the concept $\exists \mathsf{parentOf}.\mathsf{Female}$ describes those individuals that are parents of at least one female individual, i.e., those that have a daughter.

To denote the set of individuals all of whose children are female, we use the *universal restriction*

$$\forall \mathsf{parentOf.Female} \qquad (3.16)$$

It is a common error to forget that (3.16) also includes those that have no children at all. More accurately (and less naturally), the axiom can be said to describe the set of all individuals that have "no children other than female ones," i.e., no "no children that are not female." Following this wording, the concept (3.16) could indeed be equivalently expressed as $\neg \exists \mathsf{parentOf.}\neg \mathsf{Female}$ (recall the equivalences on page 40). If this meaning is not intended, one can describe the individuals who have at least one child and with all their children being female by the concept $(\exists \mathsf{parentOf.}\top) \sqcap (\forall \mathsf{parentOf.Female})$. To state the difference between Eq. 3.16 and the latter in another way: Eq. 3.16 says "if has children, then all female" and latter "does have children, and all female".

Existential and universal restrictions are useful in combination with the top concept for expressing *domain* and *range restrictions* on roles; that is, restrictions on the kinds of individual that can be in the domain and range of a given role. To restrict the domain of sonOf to male individuals we can use the axiom

$$\exists \mathsf{sonOf.}\top \sqsubseteq \mathsf{Male} \qquad (3.17)$$

and to restrict its range to parents we can write

$$\top \sqsubseteq \forall \mathsf{sonOf.Parent} \qquad (3.18)$$

In combination with the assertion sonOf(john, julia), these axioms would then allow us to deduce that John is male and Julia is a parent.

Number restrictions allow us to restrict the number of individuals that can be reached via a given role. For example, we can form the *at-least restriction*

$$\geqslant 2\,\mathsf{childOf.Parent} \qquad (3.19)$$

to describe the set of individuals that are children of at least two parents, and the *at-most restriction*

$$\leqslant 2\,\mathsf{childOf.Parent} \qquad (3.20)$$

for those that are children of at most two parents. The axiom Person $\sqsubseteq$ $\geqslant 2\,$childOf.Parent $\sqcap\;\leqslant 2\,$childOf.Parent then states that every person is a child of exactly two parents. A shorthand notation is Person $\sqsubseteq$ $=2\,$childOf.Parent

Finally, *local reflexivity* can be used to describe the set of individuals that are related to themselves via a given role. For example, the set of individuals that are talking to themselves is described by the concept

$$\exists\mathsf{talksTo}.\mathit{Self} \qquad\qquad (3.21)$$

Nominals   As well as defining concepts in terms of other concepts (and roles), it may also be useful to define a concept by simply enumerating its instances. For example, we might define the concept Beatle by enumerating its instances: john, paul, george, and ringo. Enumerations are not supported natively in DLs, but they can be simulated in DLs using *nominals*. A nominal is a concept that has exactly one instance. For example, {john} is the concept whose only instance is (the individual denoted by) john. Combining nominals with union, the enumeration in our example could be expressed as

$$\mathsf{Beatle} \equiv \{\mathsf{john}\} \sqcup \{\mathsf{paul}\} \sqcup \{\mathsf{george}\} \sqcup \{\mathsf{ringo}\} \qquad (3.22)$$

It is interesting to note that, using nominals, a concept assertion Mother(julia) can be turned into a concept inclusion {julia} $\sqsubseteq$ Mother and a role assertion parentOf(julia, john) into a concept inclusion {julia} $\sqsubseteq$ $\exists$parentOf.{john}. This illustrates that the distinction between ABox and TBox does not have a deeper logical meaning[5].

Role Constructors   In contrast to the variety of concept constructors, DLs provide only few constructor for forming complex roles. In practice, *inverse roles* are the most important such constructor. Intuitively, the relationship between the roles parentOf and childOf is that, for example, if Julia is a parent of John, then John is a child of Julia and vice versa. More formally, parenfOf is the inverse of childOf, which in DLs can be expressed by the equivalence

$$\mathsf{parentOf} \equiv \mathsf{childOf}^- \qquad\qquad (3.23)$$

---

[5]It does so ontologically, to which we shall return in Block II.

where the complex role childOf⁻ denotes the inverse of childOf.

In analogy to the top concept, DLs also provide the *universal role*, denoted by U, which always relates all pairs of individuals. It typically plays a minor role in modelling,[6] but it establishes symmetry between roles and concepts w.r.t. a top element. Similarly, an *empty role* that corresponds to the bottom concept is also available in OWL but has rarely been introduced as a constructor in DLs; however, we can define any role R to be empty using the axiom $\top \sqsubseteq \neg \exists R.\top$ ("all things do not relate to anything through R"). Interestingly, the universal role cannot be defined by TBox axioms using the constructors introduced above, and in particular universal role restrictions cannot express that a role is universal.

More RBox Axioms: Role Characteristics In Section 3.1.1 we introduced three forms of RBox axioms: role inclusions, role equivalences and role disjointness. OWL provides a variety of others, namely role transitivity, symmetry, asymmetry, reflexivity and irreflexivity. These are sometimes considered as basic axiom types in DLs as well, using some suggestive notation such as *Trans*(ancestorOf) to express that the role ancestorOf is transitive. However, such axioms are just syntactic sugar; all role characteristics can be expressed using the features of DLs that we have already introduced.

Transitivity is a special form of complex role inclusion. For example, transitivity of ancestorOf can be captured by the axiom ancestorOf ∘ ancestorOf ⊑ ancestorOf. A role is *symmetric* if it is equivalent to its own inverse, e.g., marriedTo ≡ marriedTo⁻, and it is *asymmetric* if it is disjoint from its own inverse, as in *Disjoint*(parentOf, parentOf⁻). If desired, *global reflexivity* can be expressed by imposing local reflexivity on the top concept as in $\top \sqsubseteq$ ∃knows.*Self*. A role is *irreflexive* if it is never locally reflexive, as in the case of $\top \sqsubseteq \neg\exists$marriedTo.*Self*.

3.1.3 Description Logic semantics

The formal meaning of DL axioms is given by their semantics. In particular, the semantics specifies what the logical consequences of an ontology

---

[6]Although there are a few interesting things that could be expressed with U, such as *concept products* [RKH08a], tool support is rarely sufficient for using this feature in practice.

are. The formal semantics is therefore the main guideline for every tool that computes logical consequences of DL ontologies, and a basic understanding of its working is vital to make reasonable modelling choices and to comprehend the results given by software applications. Luckily, the semantics of description logics is not difficult to understand provided that some common misconceptions are avoided.

Intuitively speaking, an ontology describes a particular situation in a given domain of discourse. For example, the axioms in Sections 3.1.1 and 3.1.2 describe a particular situation in the "families and relationships" domain. However, ontologies usually cannot fully specify the situation that they describe. On the one hand, there is no formal relationship between the symbols we use and the objects that they represent: the individual name julia, for example, is just a syntactic identifier with no intrinsic meaning. Indeed, the intended meaning of the identifiers in our ontologies has no influence on their formal semantics: what we know about them stems only from the axioms. On the other hand, the axioms in an ontology typically do not provide complete information. For example, Eqs. (3.3) and (3.4) in Section 3.1.1 state that some individuals are equal and that others are unequal, but in many other cases this information might be left unspecified.

Description logics have been designed to deal with such incomplete information. Rather than making default assumptions in order to fully specify one particular interpretation for each ontology, the DL semantics generally considers all the possible situations (i.e., states of the world) where the axioms of an ontology would hold (we also say: where the axioms are *satisfied*). This characteristic is called the *Open World Assumption* since it keeps unspecified information open.[7] A logical consequence of an ontology is an axiom that holds in all interpretations that satisfy the ontology, i.e., something that is true in all conceivable states of the world that agree with what is said in the ontology. The more axioms an ontology contains, the more specific are the constraints that it imposes on possible interpretations, and the fewer interpretations exist that satisfy all of the axioms (recall Section 1.2.3 on good ontologies with high precision). Conversely, if fewer interpretations satisfy an

---

[7]A *Closed World Assumption* "closes" the interpretation by assuming that every fact not explicitly stated to be true is actually false. Both terms are not formally specified and rather outline the general flavour of a semantics than any particular definition.

Table 3.1: Syntax and semantics of $\mathcal{SROIQ}$ constructors.

	Syntax	Semantics
Individuals:		
individual name	a	$a^{\mathcal{I}}$
Roles:		
atomic role	R	$R^{\mathcal{I}}$
inverse role	R^-	$\{\langle x, y\rangle \mid \langle y, x\rangle \in R^{\mathcal{I}}\}$
universal role	U	$\Delta^{\mathcal{I}} \times \Delta^{\mathcal{I}}$
Concepts:		
atomic concept	A	$A^{\mathcal{I}}$
intersection	$C \sqcap D$	$C^{\mathcal{I}} \cap D^{\mathcal{I}}$
union	$C \sqcup D$	$C^{\mathcal{I}} \cup D^{\mathcal{I}}$
complement	$\neg C$	$\Delta^{\mathcal{I}} \setminus C^{\mathcal{I}}$
top concept	$\top$	$\Delta^{\mathcal{I}}$
bottom concept	$\bot$	$\emptyset$
existential restriction	$\exists R.C$	$\{x \mid \text{some } R^{\mathcal{I}}\text{-successor of } x \text{ is in } C^{\mathcal{I}}\}$
universal restriction	$\forall R.C$	$\{x \mid \text{all } R^{\mathcal{I}}\text{-successors of } x \text{ are in } C^{\mathcal{I}}\}$
at-least restriction	$\geqslant n\, R.C$	$\{x \mid \text{at least } n\ R^{\mathcal{I}}\text{-successors of } x \text{ are in } C^{\mathcal{I}}\}$
at-most restriction	$\leqslant n\, R.C$	$\{x \mid \text{at most } n\ R^{\mathcal{I}}\text{-successors of } x \text{ are in } C^{\mathcal{I}}\}$
local reflexivity	$\exists R.Self$	$\{x \mid \langle x, x\rangle \in R^{\mathcal{I}}\}$
nominal	$\{a\}$	$\{a^{\mathcal{I}}\}$

where $a, b \in \mathsf{N}_I$ are individual names, $A \in \mathsf{N}_C$ is a concept name, $C, D \in \mathbf{C}$ are concepts, and $R \in \mathbf{R}$ is a role

ontology, then more axioms hold in all of them, and more logical consequences follow from the ontology. The previous two sentences imply that the semantics of description logics is *monotonic*: additional axioms always lead to additional consequences, or, more informally, the more knowledge we feed into a DL system the more results it returns.

An extreme case is when an ontology is not satisfied in any interpretation. The ontology is then called *unsatisfiable* or *inconsistent*. In this case *every* axiom holds vacuously in all of the (zero) interpretations that satisfy the ontology. Such an ontology is clearly of no utility, and avoiding inconsistency (and checking for it in the first place) is therefore an important task during ontology development.

We have outlined above the most important ideas of DL semantics. What remains to be done is to define what we really mean by an "inter-

Table 3.2: Syntax and semantics of $\mathcal{SROIQ}$ axioms.

	Syntax	*Semantics*
ABox:		
concept assertion	$C(a)$	$a^{\mathcal{I}} \in C^{\mathcal{I}}$
role assertion	$R(a,b)$	$\langle a^{\mathcal{I}}, b^{\mathcal{I}} \rangle \in R^{\mathcal{I}}$
individual equality	$a \approx b$	$a^{\mathcal{I}} = b^{\mathcal{I}}$
individual inequality	$a \not\approx b$	$a^{\mathcal{I}} \neq b^{\mathcal{I}}$
TBox:		
concept inclusion	$C \sqsubseteq D$	$C^{\mathcal{I}} \subseteq D^{\mathcal{I}}$
concept equivalence	$C \equiv D$	$C^{\mathcal{I}} = D^{\mathcal{I}}$
RBox:		
role inclusion	$R \sqsubseteq S$	$R^{\mathcal{I}} \subseteq S^{\mathcal{I}}$
role equivalence	$R \equiv S$	$R^{\mathcal{I}} = S^{\mathcal{I}}$
complex role inclusion	$R_1 \circ R_2 \sqsubseteq S$	$R_1^{\mathcal{I}} \circ R_2^{\mathcal{I}} \subseteq S^{\mathcal{I}}$
role disjointness	$Disjoint(R,S)$	$R^{\mathcal{I}} \cap S^{\mathcal{I}} = \emptyset$

pretation" and which conditions must hold for particular axioms to be satisfied by an interpretation. For this, we closely follow the intuitive ideas established above: an interpretation $\mathcal{I}$ consists of a set $\Delta^{\mathcal{I}}$ called the *domain* of $\mathcal{I}$ and an interpretation function $\cdot^{\mathcal{I}}$ that maps each atomic concept A to a set $A^{\mathcal{I}} \subseteq \Delta^{\mathcal{I}}$, each atomic role R to a binary relation $R^{\mathcal{I}} \subseteq \Delta^{\mathcal{I}} \times \Delta^{\mathcal{I}}$, and each individual name a to an element $a^{\mathcal{I}} \in \Delta^{\mathcal{I}}$. The interpretation of complex concepts and roles follows from the interpretation of the basic entities. Table 3.1 shows how to obtain the semantics of each compound expression from the semantics of its parts. By "$R^{\mathcal{I}}$-successor of x" we mean any individual y such that $\langle x, y \rangle \in R^{\mathcal{I}}$. The definition should confirm the intuitive explanations given for each case in Section 3.1.2. For example, the semantics of Female ⊓ Parent is indeed the intersection of the semantics of Female and Parent.

Since an interpretation $\mathcal{I}$ fixes the meaning of all entities, we can unambiguously say for each axiom whether it holds in $\mathcal{I}$ or not. An axiom *holds* in $\mathcal{I}$ (we also say $\mathcal{I}$ *satisfies* α and write $\mathcal{I} \models \alpha$) if the corresponding condition in Table 3.2 is met. Again, these definitions fully agree with the intuitive explanations given in Section 3.1.1. If all axioms in an ontology $\mathcal{O}$ hold in $\mathcal{I}$ (i.e., if $\mathcal{I}$ satisfies $\mathcal{O}$, written $\mathcal{I} \models \mathcal{O}$), then $\mathcal{I}$ is a *model* of $\mathcal{O}$. Thus a model is an abstraction of a state of the world that satisfies all axioms in the ontology. An ontology is *consistent* if it has at least one model. An axiom α is a *consequence* of an ontology $\mathcal{O}$ (or $\mathcal{O}$ *entails* α written $\mathcal{O} \models \alpha$) if α holds in every model of $\mathcal{O}$. In particular, an inconsistent ontology entails every axiom.

A noteworthy consequence of this semantics is the meaning of individual names in DL ontologies. We already remarked that DLs do not usually make the Unique Name Assumption, and indeed our formal definition allows two individual names to be interpreted as the same individual (element of the domain). Possibly even more important is the fact that the domain of an interpretation is allowed to contain many individuals that are not denoted by any individual name. A common confusion in modelling arises from the implicit assumption that interpretations must only contain individuals that are denoted by individual names (such individuals are also called *named individuals*). For example, one could wrongly assume the ontology consisting of the axioms

$$\mathsf{parentOf(julia, john), manyChildren(julia), manyChildren} \sqsubseteq {\geqslant} 3 \, \mathsf{parentOf}.\top$$

to be inconsistent since it requires Julia to have at least 3 children when only one (John) is given. However, there are many conceivable models where Julia does have three children, even though only one of them is explicitly named. A significant number of modelling errors can be traced back to similar misconceptions that are easy to prevent if the general open world assumption of DLs is kept in mind.

Another point to note is that the above specification of the semantics does not provide any hint as to how to compute the relevant entailments in practical software tools. There are infinitely many possible interpretations, each of which may have an infinite domain (in fact there are some ontologies that are satisfied only by interpretations with infinite domains). Therefore it is impossible to test all interpretations to see if they model a given ontology, and impossible to test all models of an ontology to see if they entail a given axiom. Rather, one has to devise concrete deduction procedures and prove their correctness with respect to the above specification. The interplay of certain expressive features can make reasoning algorithms more complicated and in some cases it can even be shown that no correct and terminating algorithm exists at all (i.e., that reasoning is undecidable). For our purposes it suffices to know that entailment of axioms is decidable for $\mathcal{SROIQ}$ (with the structural restrictions explained in Section 3.2.2, below) and that a number of free and commercial tools are available. Such tools are typically optimised for more specific reasoning problems, such as consistency checking, the entailment of concept subsumptions (subsumption checking) or of concept assertions (instance checking). Many of these standard inferencing problems can be expressed in terms of each other, so they can be handled by very similar reasoning algorithms.

3.2   Important DLs

There are very many DLs, of which some are used more often than others. In this section, we will first look at $\mathcal{ALC}$, for it is typically one of the languages used in DL courses, a basis to add various language features to, and it is much easier for showing how the principles of tableau work for DLs. Subsequently, we list the more expressive $\mathcal{SROIQ}$, and finally comment on leaner fragments that are computationally better behaved.

3.2.1   A basic DL to start with: $\mathcal{ALC}$

The DL language $\mathcal{ALC}$—which stands for $\mathcal{A}$ttributive $\mathcal{L}$anguage with $\mathcal{C}$oncept negation—contains the following elements:

- *Concepts* denoting entity types/classes/unary predicates/universals, including top $\top$ and bottom $\bot$;
- *Roles* denoting relationships/associations/binary predicates/properties;
- *Constructors*: and $\sqcap$, or $\sqcup$, and not $\neg$; quantifiers $\forall$ and $\exists$;
- *Complex concepts* using constructors: Let C and D be concept names, R a role name, then
    - $\neg C$, $C \sqcap D$, and $C \sqcup D$ are concepts, and
    - $\forall R.C$ and $\exists R.C$ are concepts
- *Individuals*

Some examples that can be represented in $\mathcal{ALC}$ are, respectively:

- Concepts (primitive, atomic); e.g., Book, Course
- Roles; e.g., enrolled, reads
- Complex concepts; e.g.,
    - Student $\sqsubseteq \exists$enrolled.(Course $\sqcup$ DegreeProgramme)
      (this is a *primitive concept*)
    - Mother $\sqsubseteq$ Woman $\sqcap \exists$ParentOf.Person
    - Parent $\equiv$ (Male $\sqcup$ Female)$\sqcap$
          $\exists$ParentOf.Mammal $\sqcap \exists$caresFor.Mammal

(this is a *defined concept*)
- Individuals;   e.g.,   Student(Andile),   ¬Student(Katniss), Mother(Katniss), enrolled(Andile, COMP101)

As usual, the meaning is defined by the *semantics* of $\mathcal{ALC}$, and it follows the same approach as we have seen for the other languages that have passed the revue (recollect FOL and model-theoretic semantics from Section 2.1). First, there is a *domain of interpretation*, and an *interpretation*, where:

- Domain Δ is a non-empty set of objects
- Interpretation: $\cdot^{\mathcal{I}}$ is the *interpretation function*, domain $\Delta^{\mathcal{I}}$
  - $\cdot^{\mathcal{I}}$ maps every concept name A to a subset $A^{\mathcal{I}} \subseteq \Delta^{\mathcal{I}}$
  - $\cdot^{\mathcal{I}}$ maps every role name R to a subset $R^{\mathcal{I}} \subseteq \Delta^{\mathcal{I}} \times \Delta^{\mathcal{I}}$
  - $\cdot^{\mathcal{I}}$ maps every individual name a to elements of $\Delta^{\mathcal{I}}$: $a^{\mathcal{I}} \in \Delta^{\mathcal{I}}$

Note that $\top^{\mathcal{I}} = \Delta^{\mathcal{I}}$ and $\bot^{\mathcal{I}} = \emptyset$.

Using the typical notation where C and D are concepts, R a role, and a and b are individuals, then they have the following meaning, with on the left-hand side of the "=" the syntax of $\mathcal{ALC}$ under an interpretation and on the right-hand side its semantics:

- $(\neg C)^{\mathcal{I}} = \Delta^{\mathcal{I}} \backslash C^{\mathcal{I}}$
- $(C \sqcap D)^{\mathcal{I}} = C^{\mathcal{I}} \cap D^{\mathcal{I}}$
- $(C \sqcup D)^{\mathcal{I}} = C^{\mathcal{I}} \cup D^{\mathcal{I}}$
- $(\forall R.C)^{\mathcal{I}} = \{x \mid \forall y.R^{\mathcal{I}}(x,y) \rightarrow C^{\mathcal{I}}(y)\}$
- $(\exists R.C)^{\mathcal{I}} = \{x \mid \exists y.R^{\mathcal{I}}(x,y) \wedge C^{\mathcal{I}}(y)\}$

Observe that this list is a subset of those listed in Table 3.1, as there are fewer features in $\mathcal{ALC}$ cf. $\mathcal{SROIQ}$.

One also can specify the notion of *satisfaction*:

- An interpretation $\mathcal{I}$ satisfies the statement $C \sqsubseteq D$ if $C^{\mathcal{I}} \subseteq D^{\mathcal{I}}$
- An interpretation $\mathcal{I}$ satisfies the statement $C \equiv D$ if $C^{\mathcal{I}} = D^{\mathcal{I}}$
- $C(a)$ is satisfied by $\mathcal{I}$ if $a^{\mathcal{I}} \in C^{\mathcal{I}}$
- $R(a,b)$ is satisfied by $\mathcal{I}$ if $(a^{\mathcal{I}}, b^{\mathcal{I}}) \in R^{\mathcal{I}}$
- An interpretation $\mathcal{I} = (\Delta^{\mathcal{I}}, \cdot^{\mathcal{I}})$ is a *model* of a knowledge base $\mathcal{KB}$ if every axiom of $\mathcal{KB}$ is satisfied by $\mathcal{I}$
- A knowledge base $\mathcal{KB}$ is said to be *satisfiable* if it admits a model

Many DLs have be defined over the past 25 years and their complexity proved. For instance, one could add $\mathcal{I}$nverses to $\mathcal{ALC}$, giving $\mathcal{ALCI}$, or a $\mathcal{H}$ierarchy of roles, $\mathcal{ALCH}$, or $\mathcal{Q}$ualified cardinality restrictions; the appendix of the DL Handbook [BCM+08] has the full list of letters and the features they denote. You also may like to have a look at the DL Complexity Navigator[8]. In the next chapter about OWL 2, we shall introduce a few more expressive languages, whereas ontology-based data access in Chapter 8 introduces *DL-Lite* that is less expressive than $\mathcal{ALC}$.

3.2.2   The DL $\mathcal{SROIQ}$

In this section, we summarise the various features that have been introduced informally above to provide a comprehensive definition of DL syntax. Doing so yields the description logic called $\mathcal{SROIQ}$, which is one of the most expressive DLs commonly considered today. It also largely agrees in expressivity with the ontology language OWL 2 DL, though there are still some differences as will be discussed in Chapter 4.

Formally, every DL ontology is based on three finite sets of signature symbols: a set N_I of *individual names*, a set N_C of *concept names* and a set N_R of *role names*. Usually these sets are assumed to be fixed for some application and are therefore not mentioned explicitly. Now the set of $\mathcal{SROIQ}$ *role expressions* **R** (over this signature) is defined by the following grammar:

$$\mathbf{R} ::= U \mid N_R \mid N_R^-$$

where U is the universal role (Section 3.1.2). Based on this, the set of $\mathcal{SROIQ}$ *concept expressions* **C** is defined as:

$$\mathbf{C} ::= N_C \mid (\mathbf{C} \sqcap \mathbf{C}) \mid (\mathbf{C} \sqcup \mathbf{C}) \mid \neg\mathbf{C} \mid \top \mid \bot \mid$$
$$\exists\mathbf{R}.\mathbf{C} \mid \forall\mathbf{R}.\mathbf{C} \mid \geqslant n\,\mathbf{R}.\mathbf{C} \mid \leqslant n\,\mathbf{R}.\mathbf{C} \mid \exists\mathbf{R}.Self \mid \{N_I\} \qquad (3.24)$$

where n is a non-negative integer. As usual, expressions like $(\mathbf{C}\sqcap\mathbf{C})$ represent any expression of the form $(C \sqcap D)$ with $C, D \in \mathbf{C}$. It is common to omit parentheses if this cannot lead to confusion with expressions of different semantics. For example, parentheses do not matter for $A \sqcup B \sqcup C$ whereas the expressions $A \sqcap B \sqcup C$ and $\exists R.A \sqcap B$ are ambiguous.

Using the above sets of individual names, roles and concepts, the *axioms* of $\mathcal{SROIQ}$ can be defined to be of the following basic forms:

ABox:	$\mathbf{C}(N_I)$	$\mathbf{R}(N_I, N_I)$	$N_I \approx N_I$	$N_I \not\approx N_I$
TBox:	$\mathbf{C} \sqsubseteq \mathbf{C}$	$\mathbf{C} \equiv \mathbf{C}$		
RBox:	$\mathbf{R} \sqsubseteq \mathbf{R}$	$\mathbf{R} \equiv \mathbf{R}$	$\mathbf{R} \circ \mathbf{R} \sqsubseteq \mathbf{R}$	$Disjoint(\mathbf{R}, \mathbf{R})$

---

[8]http://www.cs.man.ac.uk/ezolin/logic/complexity.html

with the intuitive meanings as explained in Section 3.1.1 and 3.1.2.

Roughly speaking, a $\mathcal{SROIQ}$ ontology (or *knowledge base*) is simply a set of such axioms. To ensure the existence of reasoning algorithms that are correct and terminating, however, additional syntactic restrictions must be imposed on ontologies. These restrictions refer not to single axioms but to the structure of the ontology as a whole, hence they are called *structural restrictions*. The two such conditions relevant for $\mathcal{SROIQ}$ are based on the notions of *simplicity* and *regularity*. Notably, both are automatically satisfied for ontologies that do not contain complex role inclusion axioms.

A role R in an ontology $\mathcal{O}$ is called *non-simple* if some complex role inclusion axiom (i.e., one that uses role composition ∘) in $\mathcal{O}$ implies instances of R; otherwise it is called *simple*. A more precise definition of the non-simple role expressions of the ontology $\mathcal{O}$ is given by the following rules:

- if $\mathcal{O}$ contains an axiom $S \circ T \sqsubseteq R$, then R is non-simple,

- if R is non-simple, then its inverse R^- is also non-simple,[9]

- if R is non-simple and $\mathcal{O}$ contains any of the axioms $R \sqsubseteq S$, $S \equiv R$ or $R \equiv S$, then S is also non-simple.

All other roles are called simple[10]. For a $\mathcal{SROIQ}$ ontology it is required that the following axioms and concepts contain simple roles only:

Restricted axioms:	$Disjoint(\mathbf{R}, \mathbf{R})$
Restricted concept expressions:	$\exists \mathbf{R}.Self \qquad \geqslant n\,\mathbf{R}.\mathbf{C} \qquad \leqslant n\,\mathbf{R}.\mathbf{C}$

The other structural restriction that is relevant for $\mathcal{SROIQ}$ is called *regularity* and is concerned with RBox axioms only. Roughly speaking, the restriction ensures that cyclic dependencies between complex role inclusion axioms occur only in a limited form. For details, please see [HKS06]. For the introductory treatment in this paper, it suffices to note that regularity, just like simplicity, is a property of the ontology as a whole that cannot be checked for each axiom individually. An important

---

[9]If $R = S^-$ already is an inverse role, then R^- should be read as S. We do not allow expressions like S^{--}.

[10]Whether the universal role U is simple or not is a matter of preference that does not affect the computational properties of the logic [RKH08b]. However, the universal role in OWL 2 is considered non-simple.

practical consequence is that the union of two regular ontologies may
no longer be regular. This must be taken into account when merging
ontologies in practice.

The semantics of $\mathcal{SROIQ}$ is shown in Tables 3.1 and 3.2.

3.2.3   Important fragments of $\mathcal{SROIQ}$

Many different description logics have been introduced in the literature.
Typically, they can be characterised by the types of constructors and
axioms that they allow, which are often a subset of the constructors in
$\mathcal{SROIQ}$. For example, the description logic $\mathcal{ALC}$ is the fragment of
$\mathcal{SROIQ}$ that allows no RBox axioms and only $\sqcap$, $\sqcup$, $\neg$, $\exists$ and $\forall$ as its
concept constructors. It is often considered the most basic DL. The ex-
tension of $\mathcal{ALC}$ with transitive roles is traditionally denoted by the letter
$\mathcal{S}$. Some other letters used in DL names hint at a particular constructor, such as inverse roles $\mathcal{I}$, nominals $\mathcal{O}$, qualified number restrictions
$\mathcal{Q}$, and role hierarchies (role inclusion axioms without composition) $\mathcal{H}$.
So, for example, the DL named $\mathcal{ALCHIQ}$ extends $\mathcal{ALC}$ with role hierarchies, inverse roles and qualified number restrictions. The letter $\mathcal{R}$ most
commonly refers to the presence of role inclusions, local reflexivity $Self$,
and the universal role U, as well as the additional role characteristics
of transitivity, symmetry, asymmetry, role disjointness, reflexivity, and
irreflexivity. This naming scheme explains the name $\mathcal{SROIQ}$.

In recent years, fragments of DLs have been specifically developed in
order to obtain favourable computational properties. For this purpose,
$\mathcal{ALC}$ is already too large, since it only admits reasoning algorithms that
run in worst-case exponential time. More light-weight DLs can be obtained by further restricting expressivity, while at the same time a number of additional $\mathcal{SROIQ}$ features can be added without loosing the
good computational properties. The three main approaches for obtaining light-weight DLs are $\mathcal{EL}$, *DLP* and *DL-Lite*, which also correspond
to language fragments OWL EL, OWL RL and OWL QL of the Web
Ontology Language.

The $\mathcal{EL}$ family of description logics is characterised by allowing un-
limited use of existential quantifiers and concept intersection. The original description logic $\mathcal{EL}$ allows only those features and $\top$ but no unions,
complements or universal quantifiers, and no RBox axioms. Further
extensions of this language are known as $\mathcal{EL}^+$ and $\mathcal{EL}^{++}$. The largest
such extension allows the constructors $\sqcap$, $\top$, $\bot$, $\exists$, $Self$, nominals and

the universal role, and it supports all types of axioms other than role symmetry, asymmetry and irreflexivity. Interestingly, all standard reasoning tasks for this DL can still be solved in worst-case polynomial time. One can even drop the structural restriction of regularity that is important for $\mathcal{SROIQ}$. $\mathcal{EL}$-type ontologies have been used to model large but light-weight ontologies that consist mainly of terminological data, in particular in the life sciences. A number of reasoners are specifically optimised for handling $\mathcal{EL}$-type ontologies, the most recent of which is the ELK reasoner[11] for OWL 2 EL.

DLP is short for *Description Logic Programs* and comprises various DLs that are syntactically restricted in such a way that axioms could also be read as rules in first-order Horn logic without function symbols. Due to this, DLP-type logics can be considered as kinds of rule languages (hence the name OWL 2 RL) contained in DLs. To accomplish this, one has to allow different syntactic forms for subconcepts and superconcepts in concept inclusion axioms. We do not provide the details here. While DLs in general may require us to consider domain elements that are not denoted by individual names, for DLP one can always restrict attention to models in which all domain elements are denoted by individual names. This is why DLP is often used to augment databases (interpreted as sets of ABox axioms), e.g., in an implementation of OWL 2 RL in the Oracle 11g database management system.

DL-Lite is a family of DLs that is also used in combination with large data collections and existing databases, in particular to augment the expressivity of a query language that retrieves such data. This approach, known as Ontology Based Data Access, considers ontologies as a language for constructing *views* or *mapping rules* on top of existing data. The core feature of DL-Lite is that data access can be realised with standard query languages such as SQL that are not aware of the DL semantics. Ontological information is merely used in a query preprocessing step. Like DLP, DL-Lite requires different syntactic restrictions for subconcepts and superconcepts. It is the basis for the OWL 2 QL species of OWL ontology languages, and we will present its DL definition and its use in Chapter 8.

---

[11]http://elk-reasoner.googlecode.com/

3.3   Reasoning services

The reasoning services for DLs can be divided into so-called 'standard' reasoning services and 'non-standard' reasoning services. The former are more common and provided by all extant DL reasoners, whereas for the latter, new problems had been defined that needed specific algorithms, extensions, and interfaces to the standard ones. In this section, only the standard ones are considered; an example example of the latter is deferred to Section 7.5, because the 'non-standard' ones are typically focussed on assisting modellers in the ontology authoring process, rather than purely deriving knowledge only.

3.3.1   Standard reasoning services

Recalling the four essential components of (automated) reasoning listed in Section 2.2.2, the formal language in this case is a DL, and we take a closer look the choice of class of problems the software has to solve. The standard reasoning services are as follows, i.e., generally, all DL-focussed automated reasoners offer these services.

- Consistency of the knowledge base ($\mathcal{KB} \not\models \top \sqsubseteq \bot$)

    - Is the $\mathcal{KB} = (\mathcal{T}, \mathcal{A})$ consistent (non-selfcontradictory), i.e., is there at least one model for $\mathcal{KB}$, i.e.: "can *all* concepts and roles be instantiated without leading to a contradiction?"

- Concept (and role) satisfiability ($\mathcal{KB} \not\models C \sqsubseteq \bot$)

    - is there a model of $\mathcal{KB}$ in which C (resp. R) has a nonempty extension, i.e., "can that concept (role) have instances without leading to contradictions?"

- Concept (and role) subsumption ($\mathcal{KB} \models C \sqsubseteq D$)

    - i.e., is the extension of C (resp. R) contained in the extension of D (resp. S) in every model of $\mathcal{T}$ (the TBox), i.e., 'are all instances of C also instances of D?

- Instance checking ($\mathcal{KB} \models C(a)$ or $\mathcal{KB} \models R(a,b)$)

    - is a (resp. (a,b)) a member of concept C (resp. R) in $\mathcal{KB}$, i.e., is the fact $C(a)$ (resp. $R(a,b)$) satisfied by every interpretation of $\mathcal{KB}$?

- Instance retrieval ($\{a \mid KB \models C(a)\}$)

  - find all members of C in KB, i.e., compute all individuals a s.t. $C(a)$ is satisfied by every interpretation of KB

You have used the underlying idea of concept subsumption both with EER and UML class diagrams, but then you did it all manually, like declaring that all cars are vehicles. Now, instead of you having to model a hierarchy of entity types/classes, we let the automated reasoner compute it for us thanks to the properties that have been represented for the DL concepts.

The following two examples illustrate logical implication and concept subsumption.

Example 3.1. Logical implication *Consider logical implication—i.e.,* $KB \models \phi$ *if every model of* KB *is a model of* ϕ—*with the following example:*

- *TBox:* $\exists$teaches.Course $\sqsubseteq \neg$Undergrad $\sqcup$ Professor

  "*The objects that teaches a course are not undergrads or professors*"

- *ABox:* teaches(Thembi, cs101), Course(cs101), Undergrad(Thembi)

This is depicted graphically in Figure 3.2. What does it entail, if anything? The only possibility to keep this logical theory consistent and satisfiable is to infer that Thembi is a professor ($KB \models$ Professor(Thembi)), because anything that teaches a course must be either not an undergrad or a professor. Given that Thembi is an undergrad, she cannot be not an undergrad, hence, she has to be a professor. ◇

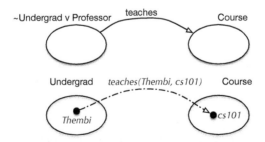

Figure 3.2: Top: Depiction of the TBox according to the given axiom; bottom: depiction of the ABox. See Example 3.1 for details.

What will happen if we have the following knowledge base?

- TBox: ∃teaches.Course ⊑ Undergrad ⊔ Professor
- ABox: teaches(Thembi, cs101), Course(cs101), Undergrad(Thembi)

That is, do we obtain $\mathcal{KB} \models$ Professor(Thembi) again? No.

Perhaps the opposite, that $\mathcal{KB} \models \neg$Professor(Thembi)? No. Can you explain why?

Example 3.2. Concept subsumption *As an example of concept subsumption, consider the knowledge base $\mathcal{KB}$ that contains the following axioms and is depicted graphically in Figure 3.3 (for intuitive purpose only):*

- HonsStudent ≡ Student ⊓ ∃enrolled.BScHonsDegree
- X ≡ Student ⊓ ∃enrolled.BScHonsDegree⊓
      ∃hasDuty.TeachingAssistantShip
- Y ≡ Student ⊓ ∃enrolled.BScHonsDegree⊓
      ∃hasDuty.ProgrammingTask
- X(John), BScHonsDegree(comp4), TeachingAssistantShip(cs101), enrolled(John, comp4), hasDuty(John, cs101), BScHonsDegree(maths4).

$\mathcal{KB} \models$ X ⊑ HonsStudent? *That is, is the extension of* X *contained in the extension of* HonsStudent *in every model of* $\mathcal{KB}$? *Yes. Why? We know that both* HonsStudent *and* X *are subclasses of* Student *and that both are enrolled in an* BScHonsDegree *programme. In addition, every instance of* X *also has a duty performing a* TeachingAssistantShip *for an undergrad module, whereas, possibly, not all honours students work as a teaching assistant. Thus, all* X*'s are always also an instance of* HonsStudent *in every possible model of* $\mathcal{KB}$, *hence* $\mathcal{KB} \models$ X ⊑ HonsStudent. *And likewise for* $\mathcal{KB} \models$ Y ⊑ HonsStudent. *This deduction is depicted in green in Figure 3.4.*

Let us modify this a bit by adding the following two axioms to $\mathcal{KB}$:

- Z ≡ Student ⊓ ∃enrolled.BScHonsDegree ⊓
      ∃hasDuty.(ProgrammingTask ⊓ TeachingAssistantShip)
- TeachingAssistantShip ⊑ ¬ProgrammingTask

What happens now? The first step is to look at Z: *it has the same properties as* HonsStudent, X, *and* Y, *but now we see that each instance of* Z *has as duty soothing that is both a* ProgrammingTask *and* TeachingAssistantShip; *hence, it must be a subconcept of both* X *and* Y, *because it refines them both. So far, so good. The second axiom tells us that the intersection of* ProgrammingTask *and* TeachingAssistantShip *is empty, or: they are disjoint, or: there is no object that is both a teaching assistantship and a programming task. But each instance of* Z *has as duty*

to carry out a duty that is both a teaching assistantship and a program-
ming task! This object cannot exist, hence, there cannot be a model
where Z is instantiated, hence, Z is an unsatisfiable concept. ◇

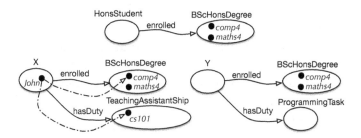

Figure 3.3: Graphical depiction of an approximation of $\mathcal{KB}$ before checking concept subsumption ($\equiv$ not shown, nor are the subsumptions to Student, so as to avoid too much clutter).

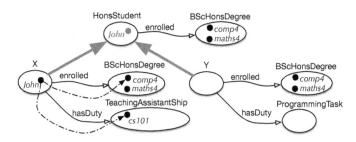

Figure 3.4: Graphical depiction of $\mathcal{K}$ after checking concept subsumption; content in green is deduced.

3.3.2   Techniques: a tableau for $\mathcal{ALC}$

The description of the deductions illustrated in the previous paragraph is an informal, high-level way of describing what the automated reasoner does when computing the concept hierarchy and checking for satisfiability. Clearly, such an informal way will not work as an algorithm to be implemented in a computer. There are several proof techniques both in theory and in practice to realise the reasoning service. The most widely used technique at the time of writing (within the scope of DLs and the Semantic Web) is *tableau reasoning*, and is quite alike what we have seen with tableau with full FOL. In short, it:

1. Unfold the TBox
2. Convert the result into negation normal form (NNF)
3. Apply the tableau rules to generate more ABoxes
4. Stop when none of the rules are applicable

Then:

- $\mathcal{T} \vdash C \sqsubseteq D$ if all ABoxes contain clashes
- $\mathcal{T} \nvdash C \sqsubseteq D$ if some ABox does not contain a clash

First, recall that one enters the tableau in Negation Normal Form (NNF), i.e., "$\neg$" only in front of concepts. For DLs and C and D are concepts, R a role, we use equivalences to obtain NNF, just like with FOL:

- $\neg\neg C$ gives C
- $\neg(C \sqcap D)$ gives $\neg C \sqcup \neg D$
- $\neg(C \sqcup D)$ gives $\neg C \sqcap \neg D$
- $\neg(\forall R.C)$ gives $\exists R.\neg C$
- $\neg(\exists R.C)$ gives $\forall R.\neg C$

Second, there are the tableau rules. If there are more features, there will be more rules. These are the ones for $\mathcal{ALC}$:

$\sqcap$-rule: If $(C_1 \sqcap C_2)(a) \in S$ but S does not contain both $C_1(a)$ and $C_2(a)$, then
$$S = S \cup \{C_1(a), C_2(a)\}$$

$\sqcup$-rule: If $(C_1 \sqcup C_2)(a) \in S$ but S contains neither $C_1(a)$ nor $C_2(a)$, then
$$S = S \cup \{C_1(a)\}$$
$$S = S \cup \{C_2(a)\}$$

$\forall$-rule: If $(\forall R.C)(a) \in S$ and S contains $R(a,b)$ but not $C(b)$, then
$$S = S \cup \{C(b)\}$$

$\exists$-rule: If $(\exists R.C)(a) \in S$ and there is no b such that $C(b)$ and $R(a,b)$, then
$$S = S \cup \{C(b), R(a,b)\}$$

With these ingredients, it is possible to construct a tableau to prove that the aforementioned deductions hold. There will be an exercise about it, and we will see more aspects of automated reasoning in the lectures and exercises about OWL.

3.4   Exercises

Review question 3.1. How are DLs typically different from full FOL?

Review question 3.2. What are the components of a DL knowledge base?

Review question 3.3. What are (in the context of DLs) the concept and role constructors? You may list them for either $\mathcal{ALC}$ or $\mathcal{SROIQ}$.

Review question 3.4. What distinguishes one DL from another? That is, e.g., $\mathcal{ALC}$ is different from $\mathcal{SROIQ}$ and from $\mathcal{EL}$; what is the commonality of those differences?

Review question 3.5. Explain in your own words what the following $\mathcal{ALC}$ reasoning tasks involve and why they are important for reasoning with ontologies:
a. Instance checking.
b. Subsumption checking.
c. Checking for concept satisfiability.

Exercise 3.1. Consider the following TBox $\mathcal{T}$:
$$Vegan \equiv Person \sqcap \forall eats.Plant$$
$$Vegetarian \equiv Person \sqcap \forall eats.(Plant \sqcup Dairy)$$
We want to know if $\mathcal{T} \vdash Vegan \sqsubseteq Vegetarian$.
This we convert to a constraint system $S = \{(Vegan \sqcap \neg Vegetarian)(a)\}$, which is unfolded (here: complex concepts on the left-hand side are replaced with their properties declared on the right-hand side) into:

$$S = \{Person \sqcap \forall eats.Plant \sqcap \neg(Person \sqcap \forall eats.(Plant \sqcup Dairy))(a)\}$$
$$(3.25)$$

Tasks:
a. Rewrite Eq. 3.25 into negation normal form
b. Enter the tableau by applying the rules until either you find a completion or only clashes.
c. $\mathcal{T} \vdash Vegan \sqsubseteq Vegetarian$?

3.5 Literature and reference material

This material is listed mainly for the curious who would like to delve deeper into Description Logics. At the time of writing, a DL textbook is in the making.

1. Ulrike Sattler. Reasoning in description logics: Basics, extensions, and relatives. In G. Antoniou et al., editors, *Reasoning Web 2007*, volume 4636 of LNCS, page 154-182. Springer, 2007. OR Anni-Yasmin Turhan. Reasoning and explanation in EL and in expressive Description Logics. In U. Assmann, A. Bartho, and C. Wende,

    editors, *Reasoning Web 2010*, volume 6325 of LNCS, pages 1-27.
    Springer, 2010.
 2. F. Baader, D. Calvanese, D. L. McGuinness, D. Nardi, and P. F.
    Patel-Schneider (Eds). *The Description Logics Handbook*. Cam-
    bridge University Press, 2008. Chapters 1 and 2 (and the rest if
    you can't get enough of it).

Chapter 4

The Web Ontology Language OWL 2

In the previous two chapters we have seen first FOL and then a version of it that was slightly changed with respect to notation and number of features in the language (easier, and less, respectively), being the DL family of languages. They haven't gotten us anywhere close to implementations, however. This is set to change in this chapter, where we will look at 'implementation versions' of DLs that have rich tooling support. We will take a look at the computational use of DLs with a so-called *serialization* to obtain computer-processable versions of an ontology and *automated reasoning* over it. The language that we will use to serialise the ontology is the most widely used ontology language for computational purposes, being the Web Ontology Language OWL. OWL was standardised first in 2004 and a newer version was standardised in 2009, which has fuelled tool development and deployment of ontologies in ontology-driven information systems. OWL looks like yet another a language and notation to learn, but the ones that we will consider (the DL-based ones) have the same underlying principles. It does have a few engineering extras, which also has as consequence that there are several ways to serialise the ontology so as to cater for software developers' preferences. Thus, theoretically, there is not really anything substantially new in this chapter, but there will be many more options and exercises to practically engage with the ontology languages, automated reasoning, and toy ontologies to play with on the computer. Depending on your interests, things start to get 'messy' (for a theoretician) or finally concrete (for an engineer).

OWL actually constitutes a family of languages consisting of OWL "species", and we will focus on those species that are based on DLs, which are all fragments of the most expressive one, OWL 2 DL. To understand how these species came about in the way they are, with these features and not others, we will touch upon OWL in Section 4.1 first, which will shed light on questions such as: What goes into standardising a language? Why precisely these ones came out of the efforts, and in this way? Why should an ontology engineer even consider the previous version and not only the latest?

Afterward, an overview of the DL-based OWL 2 languages is provided in Section 4.2. Yes, plural; that's not a typo. As we shall see, there are good reasons for it both from a computational viewpoint for scalable implementations and to please the user-base. The computational aspect is summarised in Section 4.2.4. If you have completed a course on theory of computation, this will be easy to follow. If not, you would want to consult Appendix C, which provides an explanation why one *cannot* have it all, i.e., both a gazillion of language features and good performance of an ontology-driven information system. Experience has seen that that sort of trade-off can annoy a domain expert become disappointed with ontologies; Section 4.2.4 (and the background in Appendix C) will help you explain to domain experts it's neither your fault nor the ontology's fault. Finally, OWL does not exist in isolation—if it were, then there would be no tools that can use OWL ontologies in information systems. Section 4.3 therefore sets it in context of the Semantic Web—heralded as a 'next generation' World Wide Web—and shows that, if one really wants the extra expressiveness, it can fit in another logic framework and system even up to second order logic with the Distributed Ontology, Model, and Specification Language (DOL) and its software infrastructure.

4.1 Standardizing an ontology language

This section and the next one are intentionally kept short, as listing language features isn't the most interesting of content, those lists exist also online in the standard[1], and are not meant to be memorised but to be consulted as the need arises. This section and the next one, instead, focus on the gist of it and provide some contextual information.

4.1.1 Historical notes

Before OWL, there were a plethora of ontology languages, such as the `obo` format (directed acyclic graphs) initiated by the Gene Ontology Consortium, KL-ONE, and F-logic (frames, and older versions of the Protégé ODE). Unsurprisingly, this caused ontology interoperation problems even at the syntactic level and hampered development and use of ontology tools, hence, its uptake. To solve those issues, researchers set out to standardise a logic language. At the time that people sat at the standardisation table (first around 2001) of the World Wide Web Consortium (W3C), there were several logics that had a considerable influence on the final product, most notably the SHOE, DAML-ONT, OIL, and DAML+OIL languages, and, more generally, the fruits of 20 years of research on languages and prototyping of automated reasoners by the DL community.

Following good engineering practices, a document of requirements and objectives was devised to specify what such an ontology language for the Semantic Web should meet. It is useful to list them here, so that you can decide yourself how well OWL meets them, as well as any contender languages, or if you would want to design one of your own. It specified the following *design goals*: Shareable; Change over time; Interoperability; Inconsistency detection; Balancing expressivity and complexity; Ease of use; Compatible with existing standards; and Internationalisation. There were also *requirements* on the features of the language. They were: Ontologies are objects on the Web; they have their own meta-data, versioning, etc.; Ontologies are extendable; They contain classes, properties, data-types, range/domain, individuals; they must be able to express equality for classes and for individuals; Classes as instances; Cardinality constraints; and XML syntax[2].

---

[1]start with a general non-technical overview in the OWL primer `http://www.w3.org/TR/owl2-primer/`.

[2]The "making of an ontology language" article [HPSvH03] gives a longer general historical view and it also summarises OWL with its three species (OWL lite, OWL-DL, and OWL full). The details of the standard are freely available at `http://www.w3.org/TR/owl-ref/`.

First, as standardisation is typically consensus-based, there was, on the one hand, a language called *OWL full* with RDF-based semantics (graphs) and two DL-based species, being *OWL lite* and *OWL DL*. But what makes OWL a Semantic Web language compared to the regular DL languages that were introduced in the previous chapter? This is the second step. There are the following main differences:

- OWL uses URI references as names; e.g., `http://www.mysite.co.za/UniOnto.owl#Student` is the URI of the class `Student` in the ontology with file name `UniOnto.owl` file that is online at `http://www.mysite.co.za`;

- It gathers information into ontologies stored as documents written in RDF/XML including things like `owl:imports` to import one ontology into another; e.g. another ontology, `HigherEd.owl` can import the `UniOnto.owl` so that the class `http://www.mysite.co.za/UniOnto.owl#Student` becomes part of `HigherEd.owl` in a way (though it still exists independently as well);

- It adds RDF data types and XML schema data types for the ranges of data properties (attributes), so one can use, e.g., `string` and `integer` in a similar way as you are familiar with in UML class diagrams and databases.

- A different terminology: a DL concept is now called a *class*, a DL role is called an *object property*, and *data property* is added for attributes (i.e., the relation that relates a class to a data type).

With this information, we can start going from a paper-based representation to its computational version. The first steps are illustrated in the next example, which will be extended in later chapters.

Example 4.1. *The African Wildlife Ontology (AWO) is a basic tutorial ontology based on the examples in the "A Semantic Web Primer" book [AvH03]. The fist step is to represent that in OWL, using your favourite ontology development environment (ODE). An OWL version of it,* `AfricanWildlifeOntology0.owl`*, has 10 classes and 3 object properties concerning animals such as* Lion*,* Giraffe*,* Plant*, and object properties* eats *and* is-part-of*, and has annotations that give an idea of what should be modelled (else: see 4.3.1 pages 119-133 in [AvH03]). Upon running* the reasoner, it will classify, among others, that Carnivore *is a subclass of* Animal *(i.e, $AWO \models$ Carnivore $\sqsubseteq$ Animal).*

This is not really exciting, and the tutorial ontology is not of a particularly good quality. First, we extend it by having loaded the ontology and adding knowledge to it: among others, proper parthood, a few more plant parts and animals, such as Impala, Warthog, and RockDassie. This version of the AWO is named `AfricanWildlifeOntology1.owl`. With this additional knowledge, warthogs are classified as omnivores, lions as carnivores, giraffes as herbivores, and so on.

Another aspect is purely engineering practice: if the intention is to put the ontology online, it should be named properly, i.e., the URI has to be set so that its contents can be identified appropriately on the Semantic Web; that is, do not simply use the default URI generated by the tool (e.g., `http://www.semanticweb.org/ontologies/2018/0/Ontology1357204526617.owl`), but specify an appropriate one where the ontology will be published, like `http://www.meteck.org/files/ontologies/myAWO.owl`. ◇

4.1.2 The OWL 1 family of languages

Purely for legacy purposes, I include here the first three 'species' of OWL (version 1). This because 1) there are still plenty of ontologies around that are represented in either of these languages and you may have to deal with them, and 2) OWL DL seems to be a fairly good 'sweet spot' in the expressivity/complexity trade-off, meaning: still being able to represent the domain fairly well, or at least sufficiently to the extent that the increased expressiveness of OWL 2 DL doesn't weigh up against the increased slowness of completing the reasoning tasks. The key points to remember are:

- OWL Lite and OWL DL are DL-based, with model-theoretic semantics.
- OWL DL is more expressive than OWL Lite, but there's not a lot of gain computationally, so OWL Lite was hardly used specifically.
- OWL full never really took off either.
- There are multiple syntaxes for the serialisation: functional-style syntax (optional) and RDF/XML (required for tool interoperability).

OWL Lite has a classification hierarchy and (relative to OWL DL) simple constraints. While OWL Lite has strong syntactic restrictions, it has only limited semantics restrictions compared to OWL DL[3]. OWL Lite corresponds to the DL $\mathcal{SHIF}(D)$. Putting the DL symbols to the names of the features, we have:

- Named classes (A)
- Named properties (P)
- Individuals $(C(o))$
- Property values $(P(o, a))$
- Intersection $(C \sqcap D)$
- Union $(C \sqcup D)$
- Negation $(\neg C)$
- Existential value restrictions $(\exists P.C)$
- Universal value restrictions $(\forall P.C)$
- Unqualified $(0/1)$ number restrictions $(\geq nP, \leq nP, = nP)$, $0 \leq n \leq 1$

OWL DL had, at the time, 'maximal' expressiveness while maintaining tractability, and has, as the name suggestion, an underlying DL. It has all the features of OWL-lite, and, in addition: Negation, Disjunction, (unqualified) Full cardinality, Enumerated classes, and hasValue. OWL DL corresponds to the DL $\mathcal{SHOIN}(D)$. It has the following features:

- All OWL Lite features
- Arbitrary number restrictions $(\geq nP, \leq nP, = nP)$, with $0 \leq n$
- Property value $(\exists P.\{o\})$
- Enumeration $(\{o_1, ..., o_n\})$

OWL Full, has a very high expressiveness (losing tractability) and all syntactic freedom of RDF (self-modifying). OWL full has meta-classes and on can modify the language. Note that OWL Full is *not* a Description Logic.

---

[3]More specifically regarding the latter, if you really want to know: negation can be encoded using disjointness and with negation an conjunction, you can encode disjunction. Take, for instance:
```
Class(C complete unionOf(B C))
```
This is equivalent to
```
DisjointClasses(notB B)
DisjointClasses(notC C)
Class(notBandnotC complete notB notC)
DisjointClasses(notBandnotC BorC)
Class(C complete notBandnotC)
```

As mentioned earlier, OWL and DLs are tightly related, in particular OWL Lite and OWL DL. They have, just like their base DLs, a model theoretic semantics. Table 4.1 shows a few examples of some OWL syntax and its DL counterpart notation. There is also the not-for-human-consumption RDF/XML serialisation.

Table 4.1: Some examples of OWL's construct, the same in DL notation, and an example.

OWL Construct	DL notation	Example
`intersectionOf`	$C_1 \sqcap ... \sqcap C_n$	Human $\sqcap$ Male
`unionOf`	$C_1 \sqcup ... \sqcup C_n$	Doctor $\sqcup$ Lawyer
`complementOf`	$\neg C$	$\neg$Male
`oneOf`	$\{o_1, ..., o_n\}$	{giselle, juan}
`allValuesFrom`	$\forall P.C$	$\forall$hasChild.Doctor
`someValuesFrom`	$\exists P.C$	$\exists$hasChild.Lawyer
`value`	$\exists P.\{o\}$	$\exists$citizenOf.{RSA}
`minCardinality`	$\geq nP$	$\geq$ 2 hasChild
`maxCardinality`	$\leq nP$	$\leq$ 6 enrolledIn

4.2 OWL 2

Over the past 16 years, OWL has been used across subject domains, but in the early years mostly by the health care and life sciences disciplines. Experimentation with the standard revealed expected as well as unexpected shortcomings in addition to the ideas mentioned in the "Future extensions" section of [HPSvH03], so that a successor to OWL was deemed to be of value. Work towards a standardisation of an OWL 2 took shape after the OWL Experiences and Directions workshop in 2007 and a final draft was ready by late 2008. On October 27 2009 it became the official OWL 2 W3C recommendation[4]. What does OWL 2 consists of—new and improved!—and what does it fix with respect to the OWL standard of 2004? Let's consider the answers to these questions in the remainder of this section.

---

[4]`http://www.w3.org/TR/2009/REC-owl2-overview-20091027/`

Table 4.2: Some examples of OWL's axioms, the same in DL notation, and an example.

OWL Axiom	DL	Example
SubClassOf	$C_1 \sqsubseteq C_2$	Dog $\sqsubseteq$ Animal $\sqcap$ Quadruped
EquivalentClasses	$C_1 \equiv ... \equiv C_n$	Man $\equiv$ Human $\sqcap$ Male
SubPropertyOf	$P_1 \sqsubseteq P_2$	hasSon $\sqsubseteq$ hasChild
EquivalentProperties	$P_1 \equiv ... \equiv P_n$	cost $\equiv$ price
SameIndividual	$o_1 = ... = o_n$	Mr_Zuma $=$ J_Zuma
DisjointClasses	$C_i \sqsubseteq \neg C_j$	Male $\sqsubseteq \neg$Female
DifferentIndividuals	$o_i \neq o_j$	Thabo $\neq$ Andile
inverseOf	$P_1 \equiv P_2^-$	hasChild $\equiv$ hasParent$^-$
transitiveProperty	$P^+ \sqsubseteq P$	ancestor$^+ \sqsubseteq$ ancestor, denoted also as Trans(ancestor)
symmetricProperty	$P \equiv P^-$	Sym(connectedTo)
functionalProperty	$\top \sqsubseteq\, \leq 1P$	$\top \sqsubseteq\, \leq$ 1hasPresident
inverseFunctionalProperty	$\top \sqsubseteq\, \leq 1P^-$	$\top \sqsubseteq\, \leq$ 1hasIDNo$^-$

Limitations of OWL—as experienced by the practitioners

OWL 2 aims to address the issues described in section 2 of [CGHM⁺08] to a greater or lesser extent, which is neither a superset nor subset of [HPSvH03]'s ideas for possible extensions. For instance, an OWL 1 possible future feature was catering for the Unique Name Assumption, but that did not make it into OWL 2, despite that it has quite an effect on the complexity of a language [ACKZ09]. We briefly summarise the interesting issues; refer to [CGHM⁺08] for details.

Expressivity limitations. First, it is not possible to express *qualified cardinality restrictions* in OWL. For instance, one can state Bicycle $\sqsubseteq\, \geq$ 2 hasComponent.$\top$ or Bicycle $\sqsubseteq\, \exists$ hasComponent.Wheel, but not Bicycle $\sqsubseteq\, \geq$ 2 hasComponent.Wheel. This was deemed an important shortcoming in OWL DL by its modellers. Second, some relational properties were perceived to be missing, notably reflexivity and irreflexivity, so one could not represent the class Narcissist (someone who loves him/herself), and not state that proper parthood is irreflexive, yet an irreflexive partOf relation is import in medicine and biology. Third, there were also limitations on data types; e.g., one cannot express restrictions to a subset of datatype values (ranges) and relationships between values of data properties on one object. Last, there were also some 'housekeeping' features missing, such as annotations, imports, versioning, and species validation (see p315 of [CGHM$^+$08] for details).

Syntax problems. OWL has both a frame-based legacy (Abstract syntax) and axioms (DL), which was deemed too confusing. For instance, take the following axiom:

`Class(A partial restriction(hasB someValuesFrom(C))`

What type of ontology elements do we have? Is `hasB` is data property and `C` a datatype, or is `hasB` an object property and `C` a class? OWL-DL has a strict separation of the vocabulary, but the specification does not precisely specify how to enforce this separation at the syntactic level. In addition, RDF's triple notation is difficult to read and process.

Problems with the semantics. We shall not cover this issue. (For the curious: this has to do with RDF's blank nodes, but unnamed individuals not directly available in $\mathcal{SHOIN}(D)$, and frames and axioms).

Overview of OWL 2

Complex systems have a tendency to become more, rather than less, complex, and so it is for OWL 2, mainly regarding new features and more new languages. First, have a look at the 'orchestration' of the various aspects of OWL 2 in Figure 4.1. The top section indicates several syntaxes that can be used to serialize the ontology, where RDF/XML is required and the other four are optional. There are mappings between an OWL ontology and RDF graph in the middle, and the lower half depicts that there is both a direct semantics, for OWL 2 DL-based species, and an RDF-based one, for OWL 2 full. Note that while that "mapping" between "ontology structure" and "RDF Graph" and that "correspondence theorem" between "Direct semantics" and "RDF-based semantics" exist, this does not mean they're all the same thing. The DL-based OWL 2 species have a mapping into RDF for the serialisation, but they do not have an RDF-based semantics.

Second, the OWL 2 DL species is based on the DL $\mathcal{SROIQ}(D)$ [HKS06]. It is more expressive than the underlying DL of OWL DL ($\mathcal{SHOIN}(D)$) and therewith meeting some of the modellers' requests, such as more properties of properties and qualified number restrictions (see below). There is cleaner support for annotations, debatable (from an ontological perspective, that is) punning for metamodelling, and a

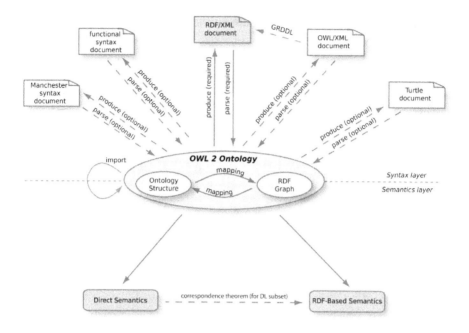

Figure 4.1: Orchestration of syntax and semantics of OWL 2. (Source: http://www.w3.org/TR/2009/REC-owl2-overview-20091027/).

'key' that is not a key in the common sense of keys in conceptual data models and databases. Also, it irons out some difficulties that tool implementers had with the syntaxes of OWL and makes importing ontologies more transparent.

Third, there are three OWL 2 profiles, which are sub-languages of (syntactic restrictions on) OWL 2 DL so as to cater for different purposes of ontology usage in applications. At the time of standardisation, they already enjoyed a considerable user base. This choice has its consequences that very well can, but may not necessarily, turn out to be a positive one in praxis; this will be explored further in the block on ontology engineering. The three profiles are:

- **OWL 2 EL**, which is based on the $\mathcal{EL}^{++}$ language [BBL05], intended for use with large relatively simple type-level ontologies;

- **OWL 2 QL**, which is is based on the $DL\text{-}Lite_R$ language [CGL+07], intended for handling and querying large amounts of instances through the ontology;

- **OWL 2 RL**, which is inspired by Description Logic Programs and pD, intended for ontologies with rules and data in the form of RDF triples.

Like with OWL 2 DL, each of these languages has automated reasoners tailored to the language so as to achieve the best performance for the application scenario. Indirectly, the notion of the profiles and automated reasoners says you cannot have both many modelling features together in one language and expect to have good performance with the ontology and ontology-driven information system. Such is life with the limitations of computers, but one can achieve quite impressive results with the languages and its tools that are practically not really doable with paper-based manual efforts.

4.2.1   New OWL 2 features

OWL 2 DL is based on $\mathcal{SROIQ}(D)$ [HKS06], which we have seen in Chapter 3, which is 2NExpTime-complete in taxonomic complexity [Kaz08]; hence, it is a more expressive language than OWL-DL ($\mathcal{SHOIN}$, which is NExpTime-complete [Tob01]). Compared to OWL DL, it has fancier metamodelling and annotations, improved ontology publishing, imports and versioning control. In addition to all the OWL-DL features (recall Section 4.1.2), one can use the following ones in OWL 2 DL as well, which are illustrated afterwards:

- Qualified cardinality restrictions, $\geq nR.C$ and $\leq nR.C$ (the $\mathcal{Q}$ in $\mathcal{SROIQ}$):
  - $(\geq nR.C)^{\mathcal{I}} = \{x \mid \sharp\{y \mid (x,y) \in R^{\mathcal{I}} \cap y \in C^{\mathcal{I}}\} \geq n\}$
    In OWL 2: ObjectMinCardinality(n OPE CE); an example in DL notation: ≥ 3 hasPart.Door
  - $(\leq nR.C)^{\mathcal{I}} = \{x \mid \sharp\{y \mid (x,y) \in R^{\mathcal{I}} \cap y \in C^{\mathcal{I}}\} \leq n\}$
    In OWL 2: ObjectMaxCardinality(n OPE CE), an example in DL notation: ≤ 2 enrolledIn.UGDegree
  - The difference between the *unqualified* cardinality constraint (the $\mathcal{N}$ in OWL DL's $\mathcal{SHOIN}$) and *qualified* cardinality constraint (the $\mathcal{Q}$ in OWL 2 DL's $\mathcal{SROIQ}$) is the difference between aforementioned Bicycle $\sqsubseteq \geq 2$ hasComponent.⊤ and Bicycle $\sqsubseteq \geq 2$ hasComponent.Wheel, respectively.

- Properties of roles (the $\mathcal{R}$ in $\mathcal{SROIQ}$):

- Reflexive (globally): $\mathsf{Ref}(R)$, with semantics:
  $\forall x : x \in \Delta^{\mathcal{I}}$ implies $(x, x) \in (R)^{\mathcal{I}}$
  Example: the connection relation (everything is connected to itself).
- Reflexive (locally): $\exists R.\mathsf{Self}$, with semantics:
  $\{x \mid (x, x) \in R\}$
  In OWL 2: `ObjectHasSelf` (OPE); e.g., $\exists \mathsf{knows}.\mathsf{Self}$ to state you know yourself.
- Irreflexive: $\mathsf{Irr}(R)$, with semantics:
  $\forall x : x \in \Delta^{\mathcal{I}}$ implies $(x, x) \notin (R)^{\mathcal{I}}$
  For instance, proper parthood is irreflexive: something cannot be proper part of itself.
- Asymmetric: $\mathsf{Asym}(R)$, with semantics:
  $\forall x, y : (x, y) \in (R)^{\mathcal{I}}$ implies $(y, x) \notin (R)^{\mathcal{I}}$
  For instance, $\mathsf{Asym}(\mathsf{parentOf})$: if John is the parent of Divesh, then Divesh cannot be the parent of John.

- *Limited* role chaining (also covered with the $\mathcal{R}$ in $\mathcal{SROIQ}$): e.g., $R \circ S \sqsubseteq R$, with semantics: $\forall y_1, \ldots, y_4 : (y_1, y_2) \in (R)^{\mathcal{I}}$ and $(y_3, y_4) \in (S)^{\mathcal{I}}$ imply $(y_1, y_4) \in (R)^{\mathcal{I}}$, and regularity restriction (strict linear order ("<") on the properties). For instance: $\mathsf{childOf} \circ \mathsf{childOf} \sqsubseteq \mathsf{grandchildOf}$ so that one can deduce that the child of a child is that person's grandchild, and the uncle example in Chapter 3.

The tricky part especially in practical ontology development is that some object property features and axioms work only on *simple* object properties, 'simple' meaning that it has no direct or indirect subproperties that are either transitive or are defined by means of property chains; see section 11.1 of the OWL Structural Specification and Functional-Style Syntax for the exact specification of this limitation. Practically, this means that the following features can be used only on simple object properties: `ObjectMinCardinality`, `ObjectMaxCardinality`, `ObjectExact-Cardinality`, `ObjectHasSelf`, `FunctionalObjectProperty`, `Inverse-FunctionalObjectProperty`, `IrreflexiveObjectProperty`, `Asym-metricObjectProperty`, and `DisjointObjectProperties`. Two examples of what this concretely means when you're trying to develop an ontology are illustrated next.

Example 4.2. *In the first example, the ontologist has to choose between transitivity or qualified number restrictions, but cannot have both. This gives a modeller options within OWL 2 DL, using cake with its ingredients as example:*

    1) Cake has ingredient *any number of* Edible substances *and one would be able to infer that if* Milk *is an* ingredient of Butter *that is an* ingredient of Cake, *then* Milk *is an* ingredient of Cake; *i.e.,* hasIngredient *and its inverse,* ingredientOf *is transitive; or*

    2) a *(standard)* Cake has ingredients *at least four* Edible substances, *but it cannot be inferred that the* Milk *is an* ingredient of *the* Cake; *i.e.,* hasIngredient *participates in a qualified number restriction.*

Another modelling trade-off is the following one. Alike the uncle *example in Chapter 3, one can specify a role chain for aunts, e.g.:* hasMother ∘ hasSister ⊑ hasAunt. *It certainly holds that* hasMother *is asymmetric (your mother cannot be your child), i.e.,* Asym(hasMother). *Each axiom can be represented in an OWL 2 DL ontology, yet, one cannot assert both the property chain and antisymmetry in the same OWL 2 DL ontology.*
◇

The ontology development environment probably will warn you about such syntax violations, and will prevent you from running the reasoner. It may say something cryptic like "internal reasoner error" and the log file will have an entry returned by the OWL API with the offending axioms, along the line of:

```
An error occurred during reasoning:  Non-simple property
'<ex#hasIngredient>' or its inverse appears in the
cardinality restriction 'ObjectMaxCardinality(4
<ex#hasIngredient> <ex#EdibleSubstance>)'.
```

where the **ex** is the ontology's URI. If it happens, you will have to decide which of the two axioms is the more important one to keep, or choose another, more expressive, logic beyond OWL 2 DL. One 'way out' to this problem will pass the revue in Section 4.3.2.

4.2.2 OWL 2 Profiles

The main rationale for the profiles are computational complexity considerations and robustness of implementations with respect to *scalable* applications. Their features are summarised here. Note that you are not expected to learn the following lists of features by heart (it can be used as a quick 'cheat sheet'), but you do need to know, at least, their intended purpose. The more you practice developing ontologies, the easier it becomes to remember them. To assist with grasping language features actually used in a particular ontology—be it the three OWL 1 species or the five OWL 2 species—the OWL Classifier can be used. It lists in which OWL species one's OWL ontology is and why it violates the other species (i.e., creates a justification of the reported expressivity)[5], and therewith provides features that are not available in currently popular ontology editors such as Protégé.

OWL 2 EL

OWL 2 EL is intended for large 'simple' ontologies and focuses on type-level knowledge (TBox). It has a better computational behaviour than OWL 2 DL . It is based on the DL language $\mathcal{EL}^{++}$ (PTime complete), and it is used for the large medical terminology SNOMED CT [SNO12], among others. The listing of OWL 2 EL features is included in Appendix B.

OWL 2 QL

OWL 2 QL aims at scenarios for query answering over a large amount of instances with the same kind of performance as relational databases (Ontology-Based Data Access; see Chapter 8). Its expressive features cover several used features of UML Class diagrams and ER models. It is based on *DL-Lite$_\mathcal{R}$* (though more is possible with the Unique Name Assumption and in some implementations).

The supported axioms in OWL 2 QL take into account what one can use on the left-hand side of the inclusion operator ($\sqsubseteq$, `SubClassOf`) and what can be asserted on the right-hand side, which turns it into a fairly long list due to the intricate exclusions. The listing of OWL 2 QL features is included in Appendix B.

OWL 2 RL

OWL 2 RL's development was motivated by what fraction of OWL 2 DL can be expressed by rules (with equality) and scalable reasoning in the

---

[5]Source code and tool: `https://github.com/muhummadPatel/OWL_Classifier`; for a brief explanation of its use, see `https://keet.wordpress.com/2016/06/19/an-exhaustive-owl-species-classifier/`.

context of RDF(S) application. It uses rule-based technologies (forward chaining rule system, over *instances*) and is inspired by Description Logic Programs and pD*. Reasoning in PTime.

The list of features supported in OWL 2 RL is easily specified:

- More restrictions on class expressions (see table 2 of [MGH⁺09]; e.g., no SomeValuesFrom on the right-hand side of a subclass axiom)
- All axioms in OWL 2 RL are constrained in a way that is compliant with the restrictions in Table 2.
- Thus, OWL 2 RL supports all axioms of OWL 2 apart from disjoint unions of classes and reflexive object property axioms.

A quick one-liner of the difference with OWL 2 DL is: No $\forall$ and $\neg$ on the left-hand side, and $\exists$ and $\sqcup$ on right-hand side of $\sqsubseteq$.

4.2.3 OWL 2 syntaxes

There are more syntaxes for OWL 2 than for OWL, as we have see in Figure 4.1. Consider the DL axiom

FirstYearCourse $\sqsubseteq$ $\forall$isTaughtBy.Professor

Rendering this in RDF/XML yields:

```
<!−− http://www.semanticweb.org/ontologies/
              2017/6/exOKB17.owl#FirstYearCourse −−>

<owl:Class rdf:about="&exOKB17;FirstYearCourse">
    <rdfs:subClassOf rdf:resource="&owl;Thing"/>
    <rdfs:subClassOf>
        <owl:Restriction>
            <owl:onProperty rdf:resource="&exOKB17;isTaughtBy"/>
            <owl:allValuesFrom rdf:resource="&exOKB17;Professor"/>
        </owl:Restriction>
    </rdfs:subClassOf>
</owl:Class>
```

This RDF/XML fragment tells us that the ontology is called `exOKB17` (abbreviated name for the full URI), `FirstYearCourse` is a `subClassOf` the root-class `Thing`, and a subclass of the restriction on `FirstYearCourse`, being that the restriction is `owl:onProperty` object property `isTaughtBy` and the 'filler', i.e., to which the restriction applies, is `allValuesFrom` (i.e., $\forall$) `Professor`.

In OWL/XML (also not intended for human consumption), we have the same as follows:

```
<SubClassOf>
    <Class IRI="#FirstYearCourse"/>
    <Class abbreviatedIRI="owl:Thing"/>
</SubClassOf>
<SubClassOf>
    <Class IRI="#FirstYearCourse"/>
    <ObjectAllValuesFrom>
        <ObjectProperty IRI="#isTaughtBy"/>
        <Class IRI="#Professor"/>
    </ObjectAllValuesFrom>
</SubClassOf>
```

The functional syntax equivalent is as follows:

```
Declaration(Class(:FirstYearCourse))
SubClassOf(:FirstYearCourse owl:Thing)
SubClassOf(:FirstYearCourse ObjectAllValuesFrom(:isTaughtBy :Professor))
```

The Manchester syntax rendering is intended exceedingly for human reading, for non-logicians, and for ease of communication in, say, emails that do not render mathematical symbols well. On the one hand, there is a Protégé-generated Manchester syntax rendering:

```
Class: <http://www.semanticweb.org/ontologies/
                2017/6/exOKB17.owl#FirstYearCourse>

    SubClassOf:
        owl:Thing,
        <http://www.semanticweb.org/ontologies/
                2017/6/exOKB17.owl#isTaughtBy> only
            <http://www.semanticweb.org/ontologies/
                2017/6/exOKB17.owl#Professor>
```

But this usually gets abbreviated as follows:

```
Class: FirstYearCourse
SubClassOf:
        owl:Thing,
        isTaughtBy only Professor
```

or, even shorter:

```
FirstYearCourse SubClassOf isTaughtBy only Professor
```

There are several really non-standard representations of OWL ontologies for various reasons, such as interface design and making it easier for non-logicians to contribute to ontology development. For instance, in pseudo-natural language (which is a topic of Chapter 9), and graphical renderings, like with Ontograf and depicted in Figure 4.2, where the axiom shows when hovering over the coloured line representing the object

property. These informal variants are all 'syntactic sugar' renderings of
the ontology.

Figure 4.2: Screenshot of the FirstYearCourse ⊑ ∀isTaughtBy.Professor in the
Ontograf plugin for the Protégé ontology development environment; the axiom
appears when hovering over the coloured dashed line representing the object
property.

4.2.4 Complexity considerations for OWL

We have seen different 'species' of OWL, which have more or less language features, and that this was motivated principally by scalability
issues of the very expressive languages. Different languages/problems
have different complexity (NP-complete, PSPACE, EXPTIME etc.).
Appendix C contains a very brief recap on computational complexity,
whereas here we jump straight to the specifics for OWL.

In this setting of ontologies, we are interested in the following reasoning problems: ontology consistency, class expression satisfiability, class
expression subsumption, instance checking, and (Boolean) conjunctive
query answering (recall Section 3.3). When evaluating complexity, the
following parameters are considered (copied from section 5 of the OWL
2 Profiles standard [MGH+09]):

- **Data Complexity**: the complexity measured with respect to the
  total size of the assertions in the ontology.
- **Taxonomic Complexity**: the complexity measured with respect
  to the total size of the axioms in the ontology.
- **Query Complexity**: the complexity measured with respect to
  the total size of the query.
- **Combined Complexity**: the complexity measured with respect
  to both the size of the axioms, the size of the assertions, and, in
  the case of conjunctive query answering, the size of the query as
  well.

Table 4.3 summarises the known complexity results for OWL 2 under

Table 4.3: Complexity of OWL species (Source: [MGH+09]).

Language	Reasoning Problems	Taxonomic Complexity	Data Complexity	Query Complexity	Combined Complexity
OWL2 RDF-Based Semantics	Ontology Consistency, Class Expression Satisfiability, Class Expression Subsumption, Instance Checking, Conjunctive Query Answering	Undecidable	Undecidable	Undecidable	Undecidable
OWL 2 Direct Semantics	Ontology Consistency, Class Expression Satisfiability, Class Expression Subsumption, Instance Checking	2NEXPTIME-complete (NEXPTIME if property hierarchies are bounded)	Decidable, but complexity open (NP-Hard)	Not Applicable	2NEXPTIME-complete (NEXPTIME if property hierarchies are bounded)
	Conjunctive Query Answering	Decidability open	Decidability open	Decidability open	Decidability open
OWL 2 EL	Ontology Consistency, Class Expression Satisfiability, Class Expression Subsumption, Instance Checking	PTIME-complete	PTIME-complete	Not Applicable	PTIME-complete
	Conjunctive Query Answering	PTIME-complete	PTIME-complete	NP-Complete	PSPACE-Complete
OWL 2 QL	Ontology Consistency, Class Expression Satisfiability, Class Expression Subsumption, Instance Checking,	NLogSpace-complete	in AC^0	Not Applicable	NLogSpace-complete
	Conjunctive Query Answering	NLogSpace-complete	in AC^0	NP-complete	NP-complete
OWL 2 RL	Ontology Consistency, Class Expression Satisfiability, Class Expression Subsumption, Instance Checking,	PTIME-complete	PTIME-complete	Not Applicable	PTIME-complete
	Conjunctive Query Answering	PTIME-complete	PTIME-complete	NP-complete	NP-complete
OWL DL	Ontology Consistency, Class Expression Satisfiability, Class Expression Subsumption, Instance Checking,	NEXPTIME-complete	Decidable, but complexity open (NP-Hard)	Not Applicable	NEXPTIME-complete
	Conjunctive Query Answering	Decidability open	Decidability open	Decidability open	Decidability open

both RDF and the direct semantics, OWL 2 EL, OWL 2 QL, OWL 2 RL, and OWL 1 DL. The results refer to the *worst-case complexity* of these reasoning problems and, as such, do not say that implemented algorithms necessarily run in this class on all input problems, or what space/time they use on some/typical/certain kind of problems.

For X-complete problems, these results only say that a reasoning algorithm cannot use less time/space than indicated by this class on all input problems, where "X" is one of the complexity classes listed in the previous section.

4.3 OWL in context

OWL was designed for the World Wide Web, and has a place there, which is outlined in the next subsection. A different notion of 'positioning' OWL is with respect to the language features, or: options to link OWL to more expressive languages, which is described afterward.

4.3.1 OWL and the Semantic Web

OWL does not exist in isolation, but is part of the Semantic Web stack—also called the (in)famous 'layer cake'—to make the Semantic Web work. This layer cake is shown in Figure 4.3. Stepwise working our way up from the bottom layer, there is XML, which is a surface syntax that has no semantics, and then XML Schema, which describes structure of XML documents.

RDF is intended for describing data and facilitating data exchange; it is a data model for "relations" between "things", which also has a RDF Schema and an RDF Vocabulary Definition Language. RDF data can be queried with the SPARQL query language (one can draw an analogue with SQL for relational databases, but then tailored to the Internet). At the time of writing, RDF with its Linked Data—be it open or not—is quite popular. One of the central nodes in the Linked Data cloud is DBpedia [BLK+09], an RDF-ised version of Wikipedia's info boxes. Such systems may be users of lightweight ontologies or structured controlled vocabularies. The reason for lightweight is because the RDF store tends to be large with a lot of data stored in triples.

On top of that, we have the ontology language for the Web, OWL, to handle the knowledge and reasoning, and rules (RIF). RIF does not seem to be used much.

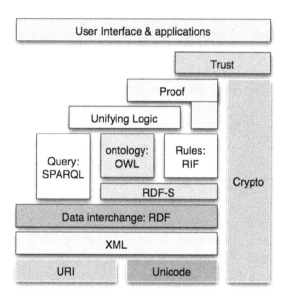

Figure 4.3: The Semantic Web layer cake.

There are many user interfaces for the whole range of Semantic Web applications. The details of the "trust" and "crypto", on the other hand, are still sketchy. Perhaps the "crypto" will receive more attention with the increasing popularity of BlockChain. There are, at the time of writing, some preliminary explorations on using RDF with BlockChain. Also, as there are several BlockChain systems, and they will need to interoperate at some point, so perhaps there is a job for ontologies there as well in the near future.

Finally, several directions for extensions to OWL proposed. These include the 'leftover' from OWL 1's "Future extensions", such as the unique name assumption, closed world assumption, making parthood a primitive object property alike subsumption is, syntactic sugar for, e.g., 'macros' and 'n-aries', a better integration with rules (RIF, DL-safe rules, SBVR), some orthogonal dimensions such as temporal, fuzzy, rough, and/or probabilistic, and better support for multilingual ontologies. Most of these desires were known during the standardisation of OWL 2. At the time of writing, it does not seem likely that a version 2.5 or even 3 will be started any time soon (but that does not mean there are no such extensions or solutions proposed for them; in fact, we will

see some of them pass the revue later in the book). Perhaps this is a sign
that realising the 'Semantic Web' may not happen after all. Regardless,
OWL itself has a life of its own, were OWL files are integrated into a
wide range of applications on and off the Web in standalone 'intelligent'
applications anyway.

4.3.2 The Distributed ontology, model, and specification language DOL

A few limitations of OWL 2 DL were illustrated in Example 4.2, showing that entirely reasonable combinations of features, like asymmetry of
hasMother and inferring who has whom as aunt, are not possible within
that framework. There are alternatives, but they do come at the cost
of scalability. If one needs scalability as well, one could choose to first
develop the more precise ontology that has a higher precision and coverage, check that all is consistent and satisfiable, and then simplify it to
the profile needed for the application.

One option is to use the Distributed ontology, model, and specification language (DOL), which has been approved as a standard of the
Object Management Group (OMG) in 2016[6]. DOL is not yet a new
language for representing the axioms, but provides a *unified metalan-
guage* where one can slot in one's logic of choice—including OWL—as
one pleases (roughly), and put the axioms that violate the OWL 2 DL
restrictions in another ontology module that is then linked to the OWL
file. The system can treat them both as one larger ontology and reason over it (that will take a bit more time to complete, if at all). It
comes with a tool for realising reasoning over the combination of ontologies (the Heterogeneous ToolSet[7]) and the OntoHub repository to store
heterogeneous ontologies [CKK+17].

How this is achieved behind the scenes is not trivial; the general theoretical background of DOL is described in [KML10], with a detailed
description in [MCNK15]. It uses the notion of *institutions* (in the
mathematical sense) to tie the logics together, which were first introduced in [GB92]. Institutions capture commonalities across logics—like
FOL and DLs both using a model-theoretic semantics, the overlap in
constructors—and therewith provide a means of interoperability across

---

[6]http://www.omg.org/spec/DOL/
[7]http://hets.dfki.de

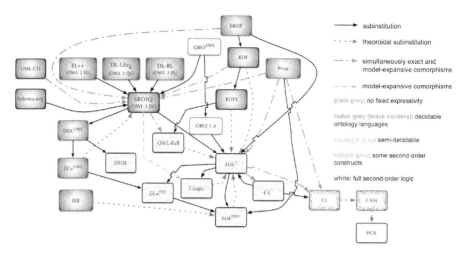

Figure 4.4: A sub-graph of logics supported by DOL/Ontohub (at the time of writing), linked with a variety of logic translations; the arrow shapes indicate some technical differences in translation from one logic to another and the different colours of the boxes give a ballpark figure of the expressivity/complexity of that language. (Source: [KK17b])

logics.

The orchestration of languages DOL supports currently is depicted in Figure 4.4, which is organised along two dimensions: the quality of logic translation (the different shapes of the arrows) and expressivity of the logic (coloured boxes). The expressivity ranges from the Semantic Web languages RDF and the OWL species all the way up to (variants of) first- and second-order logic, so as to cater for a wide range of requirements from the different communities that use models in one way or another.

DOL has many more features that, at this stage in the book, may not make a lot of sense or seem not really needed, but they probably will be perceived useful as one advances in ontology engineering and/or are facing a concrete ontology development and maintenance project in government or industry. This for the simple reason that ontologies 'out there' are definitely not as small and simple as the African Wildlife Ontology. For instance, one could create a network of ontologies rather than a monolithic one, which can be useful if several groups at different locations contribute to the ontology, or create mappings between elements in ontologies once one has imported one for reuse. We will see such scenarios in Block II. In addition, or, perhaps: moreover, besides being able to represent the aforementioned expressiveness example with the cake and the aunts (Example 4.2), one can also do other things that are still in the 'future extensions' list for OWL, such as playing with open vs. closed world semantics and declare n-ary relations fully.

4.3.3 Common Logic

Ontology development does not need to occur with OWL. The main other logic that has been serialised is Common Logic (CL) [CLs07], which has been standardised by the ISO. It is a family of first-order logics that share a common abstract syntax, have a model-theoretic semantics, and it uses XML as well. It has three "dialects" (syntaxes): 1) the Common Logic Interchange Format CLIF (one textual notation); 2) the Conceptual Graph Interchange Format (diagrams), CGIF; and 3) eXtended Common Logic Markup Language (XCL), based on XML (another textual notation).

It had its own design goals, which wasn't concerned with computability. More specifically[8], and in comparison with the there earlier listed design goals of OWL, they were: 1) Common interlingua for variety of KR notations; 2) Syntactically as unconstrained as possible; 3) Semantically as simple and conventional as possible; 4) Full first-order logic with equality, at least; 5) web-savvy, up-to-date; 6) Historical origins in Knowledge Interchange Format (KIF).

Because CL is more expressive, the Semantic Web languages (including the OWL species) all can map into CL. Further, since DOL, it need not be 'self standing', as the DOL framework as well as the tooling with Hets do provide support for CL; see also the "CL$^-$" and "CL" boxes in the right-bottom corner in Figure 4.4.

4.4 Exercises

Review question 4.1. How does OWL/OWL 2 differ from a DL language?

Review question 4.2. Describe what were the motivations to develop OWL 2.

---

[8]A clear brief overview can be found at https://www.w3.org/2004/12/rules-ws/slides/pathayes.pdf

Review question 4.3. What are the new features in OWL 2 DL compared to OWL-DL?

Review question 4.4. Which is the required format one has to serialise an OWL ontology in?

Review question 4.5. List all the species of OWL (both standards).

Review question 4.6. Which language features can be used on simple object properties only?

Review question 4.7. What are OWL 2 QL, OWL 2 RL, and OWL 2 EL tailed toward, respectively?

Review question 4.8. What is the major advantage of the OWL 2 Profiles over OWL 2 DL and OWL 2 full?

Review question 4.9. Which four 'parameters' are considered for complexity of an OWL species?

Review question 4.10. Describe in one sentence the purpose of DOL.

Exercise 4.1. Complete Table 4.4: Verify the question marks in the table (tentatively all "−"), fill in the dots, and any "±" should be qualified at to what the restriction is. You may prefer to distribute this exercise among your class mates.

Exercise 4.2. Consider some medical ontology. You know that an injury (a cut, a fracture) to a bone in your hand is also an injury to your hand. How can you model this, and similar, information in an OWL 2 DL ontology such that it infers this not only for injuries to hands, but for any injury to any anatomical body part to an injury to its (direct/indirect) whole? Which OWL 2 DL feature do you need for this? Try to formalise it.

Exercise 4.3. Install your ODE of choice, if not already done so, and acquaint yourself with the software. If you installed Protégé (5.x it is in 2018), you may want to have a look at the Pizza Ontology Tutorial (can be downloaded from the Web), but note that it was for a prior Protégé version, so there are slight differences in the screenshots there and the current interface. Also note that the Pizza tutorial was designed with the intention to acquaint the user the tool, not as a cookbook for best practices in ontology development (which it certainly is not).

Exercise 4.4. Several axioms were listed in the chapter. You will now add them to a new 'test ontology' and experiment a bit with it.

(a. Create a new ontology, give it a new URI, and save it in RD-F/XML.

(b. Add either Bicycle $\sqsubseteq \geq 2$ hasComponent.$\top$ or Bicycle $\sqsubseteq \exists$ hasComponent.Wheel.

(c. Take the OWL classifier (see footnote 5) and inspect the least expressive OWL species and violations.

(d. Update the previous axiom with the following one: Bicycle $\sqsubseteq \geq 2$ hasComponent.Wheel.

(e. Reload the ontology in the OWL classifier and inspect the OWL species and violations. What is the main difference?

(f. Experiment in a similar way with one or more of the other axioms listed in the chapter.

Exercise 4.5. Create a new ontology, add the vegan and vegetarian from Exercise 3.1, and check both $\mathcal{O} \vdash Vegan \sqsubseteq Vegetarian$ and $\mathcal{O} \vdash Vegetarian \sqsubseteq Vegan$. Describe the outcomes.

Exercise 4.6. Have a look at another ontology development environment, e.g., MoKi (at `https://moki.fbk.eu`), which uses a semantic wiki.

a. Repeat the previous exercise.

b. Compare the tools by considering, among others: do they both support OWL 2 DL? Which one is easier to navigate? Which one has the most features to help ontology development? Which one is easier for a collaborative ontology development project?

Exercise 4.7. Load `university.owl` (note the OWL species) in your ODE, inspect the contents, and try to represent:

a. A `Joint Honors Maths & Computer Science Student`, who is one who takes both Computer Science and Mathematics modules.

b. A `Single Honours Maths Student` (or [Computer Science, Economics]) is one who takes only Maths [Computer Science, Economics] modules.

Is it possible? If yes, how, if not, why not?

Exercise 4.8. Classify the ontology of the previous question, and describe what happened and changed.

Table 4.4: Partial comparison of some OWL features.

Language ⇒ Feature ⇓	OWL 1 Lite	DL	OWL 2 DL	OWL 2 Profiles EL	QL	RL
Role hierarchy	+	+	+	.	+	.
N-ary roles (where $n \geq 2$)	−	−	−	.	?	.
Role chaining	−	−	+	.	−	.
Role acyclicity	−	−	−	.	−	.
Symmetry	+	+	+	.	+	.
Role values	−	−	−	.	−	.
Qualified number restrictions	−	−	+	.	−	.
One-of, enumerated classes	?	+	+	.	−	.
Functional dependency	+	+	+	.	?	.
Covering constraint over concepts	?	+	+	.	−	.
Complement of concepts	?	+	+	.	+	.
Complement of roles	−	−	+	.	+	.
Concept identification	−	−	−	.	−	.
Range typing	−	+	+	.	+	.
Reflexivity	−	−	+	.	.	.
Antisymmetry	−	−	−	.	−	.
Transitivity	+	+	+	.	−	.
Asymmetry	?	?	+	−	+	+
Irreflexivity	−	−	+	.	−	.
.	.	.	.	.	.	.

Exercise 4.9. The university has a regulation that each undergraduate student must take exactly 2 modules. Add this restriction the the ontology of the previous question.

  a. `Student 9` takes `MT101`, `CS101`, and `CS102`. Do you think your ontology is consistent? Describe why. Check your answer by adding the student and his courses, run the reasoner and examine the inferences.

  b. `Student 10` takes `MT101`, `CS101`, and `EC101`. Do you think your ontology is consistent? Describe why. Check your answer by adding the data, running the reasoner, and examining the inferences.

Exercise 4.10. Open the `computerscience.owl` file, find the principal errors in the ontology, and distinguish them from the 'knock-on' errors that are merely a consequence of the principal errors. What would you propose to a modeller how to fix it, and why? Note that "fixing" is to be understood as obtaining a satisfiable ontology other than just deleting the unsatisfiable classes.

Exercise 4.11. From an educational perspective, you could do Practical Assignment 1 now (see Section A.1) or at the end of Block II. The advantage of doing it now is that you will appreciate the contents of Block II more and can revisit this assignment at the end of Block II, and it gives you a better understanding of both the language features and the automated reasoner. The disadvantage is that it might be harder to do now than at the end of Block II and the quality of the ontology of your first attempt to create one is likely going to be low (which, on the other hand, is a good learning opportunity).

4.5 Literature and reference material

1. Ian Horrocks, Peter F. Patel-Schneider, and Frank van Harmelen. From SHIQ and RDF to OWL: The making of a web ontology language. *Journal of Web Semantics*, 1(1):7, 2003.
2. OWL Guide: http://www.w3.org/TR/owl-guide/
3. OWL Reference: http://www.w3.org/TR/owl-ref/
4. OWL Abstract Syntax and Semantics: http://www.w3.org/TR/owl-semantics/
5. B. Cuenca Grau, I. Horrocks, B. Motik, B. Parsia, P. Patel-Schneider, and U. Sattler. OWL 2: The next step for OWL. *Journal of Web Semantics: Science, Services and Agents on the World Wide Web*, 6(4):309-322, 2008.
6. Pascal Hitzler, Markus Kroetzsch, Sebastian Rudolph. *Foundations of Semantic Web Technologies.* Chapman & Hall/CRC, 2009, 455p.
7. OWL 2 quick Reference: http://www.w3.org/TR/owl2-quick-reference/
8. OWL 2 Web Ontology Language Structural Specification and Functional-Style Syntax: http://www.w3.org/TR/owl2-syntax/

9. OWL 2 Profiles: `http://www.w3.org/TR/owl2-profiles/`

Part II

Developing good ontologies

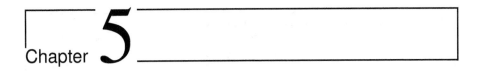

Chapter **5**

Methods and Methodologies

In Block I we looked at languages for representing ontologies, and you obtained experience in reading existing ontologies, adding and removing some axioms, and using the automated reasoner. But how exactly did someone come up with the whole ontology in the first place? What can, or should, you do when you have to develop your own ontology? When is an ontology a good one? Just like in software engineering, there are methods and methodologies to guide you through it so that you will be able to answer these questions, or they at least will help out with one or more of the steps in the development of an ontology.

There is not just one way of doing it or a single up-to-date comprehensive *methodology* for ontology development that covers everything you possibly probably need, but there some useful steps and combinations. There are several proposals along the line of generic 'waterfall' and 'agile' approaches that were inspired by software development methodologies. They are at the level of general guidelines and more and less detailed stages, which we shall cover in this chapter in Section 5.1. Diagrammatically, such (generalised!) methodologies have the tasks as shown in Figure 5.1: this one may look like a 'waterfall', but practically, it can be an iterative one not only within the ontology development, but within the "maintenance" that may involve substantial redesign or adding a new module that follows those development steps again, and a further refinement are methodologies for ontology authoring that permeate the whole development process. Particular aspects of such methodologies can be assisted by one or more *methods* and guidelines of the many ones available. A main reason for this state of affairs is that there is still much to be done, there are many different use-case scenarios, and it is—scientifically—hard to prove one methodology is better than another. This is easier to demonstrate for particular methods.

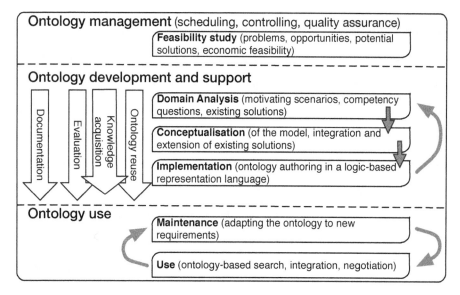

Figure 5.1: Main tasks in ontology engineering. (Source: based on [SMB10])

More specifically, in this chapter we start with high-level methodologies reminiscent of those in software development—dubbed (process-oriented) 'macro-level' methodologies—and more detailed ones that focus on ontology authoring—called 'micro-level' development—in Section 5.1. We then proceed to a sampling of methods that can be used as a component within those methodologies (Section 5.2), which are roughly divided into one of the four categories of methods: logic-based only, purely based on philosophy, a combination of the two, and heuristics.

5.1   Methodologies for ontology development

Several specific methodologies for ontology development exist following the general idea depicted in Figure 5.1, notably the older METHONTOLOGY and On-To-Knowledge, the more recent NeON and Melting Point methodologies, and the authoring-focused recent ones OntoSpec,

DiDOn, and TDDonto, and the older "Ontology Development 101" (OD101)[1]. They are not simply interchangeable in that one could pick any one of them and it will work out well. Besides that some are older or outdated by now, they can be distinguished in core approach, being between:

- micro-level ontology authoring vs. a macro-level systems-view of ontology development;

- isolated, single, stand-alone, ontology development vs. collaborative development of ontologies and ontology networks.

Micro-level methodologies focus on the viewpoint of the details emphasising formalisation aspects, which goes into *ontology authoring*, for it is about writing down the actual axioms and design choices that may even be driven by the language. Macro-level methodologies, on the other hand, emphasise the processes from an information systems and IT viewpoint, such as depicted in Figure 5.1. They may merge into comprehensive methodologies in the near future.

Regarding the second difference, this reflects a division between 'old' and 'new' methodologies in the sense that the older ones assume a setting that was typical of 20 years ago: the development of a single monolithic ontology by one or a few people residing in one location, who were typically the knowledge engineers doing the actual authoring after having extracted the domain knowledge from the domain expert. The more recent ones take into account the changing landscape in ontology development over the years, being towards collaboratively building ontology networks that cater for characteristics such as *dynamics, context, collaborative, and distributed development*. For instance, domain experts and knowledge engineers may author an ontology simultaneously, in collaboration, and residing in two different locations, or the ontology may have been split up into inter-related modules so that each sub-group of the development team can work on their section, and the automated reasoning may well be distributed over other locations or remotely with more powerful machines.

The remainder of this section provides an overview of these two types of guidelines.

---

[1]details can be found in [FGPPP99, SSSS01, SFdCB+08, GOG+10, Kas05, Kee12b, KL16, NM01], respectively.

5.1.1   Macro-level development methodologies

Waterfalls

The macro-level methodologies all will get you started with domain on-tology development in a structured fashion, albeit not all in the exact same way, and sometimes that is even intended like that. For instance, one may commence with a feasibility study and assessment of potential economic benefits of the ontology-driven approach to solving the prob-lem(s) at hand, or assume that is sorted out already or not necessary and commence with the actual development methodology by conducting a requirements analysis of the ontology itself and/or find and describe case studies. A well-known instantiation of the generic notions of the develop-ment process depicted in Figure 5.1, is the comparatively comprehensive METHONTOLOGY methodology [GPFLC04], which has been applied to various subject domains since its development in the late 1990s (e.g., the chemicals [FGPPP99] and legal domain [CMFL05]). This method-ology is for single ontology development and while several practicalities are superseded with more recent and even newer languages, tools, and methodologies, the core procedure still holds. Like Figure 5.1, it has a distinct flavour of a waterfall methodology. The five main steps are:

1) Specification: why, what are its intended uses, who are the prospec-tive users
2) Conceptualization: with intermediate representations such as in text or diagrams
3) Formalization: transforms the domain-expert understandable 'con-ceptual
   model' into a formal or semi-computable model
4) Implementation: represent it in an ontology language
5) Maintenance: corrections, updates, etc.

In addition, there are various management activities, such as planning activities, control, and quality assurance, and supporting tasks, such as documentation and version control. Ontology management may vary somewhat across the methodologies, such as helping with development of a Gantt chart for several ontology development scenarios. A refinement over the years is, among others, the better provision of 'intermediate rep-resentations'; e.g., the MOdelling wiKI MoKi [GKL+09] has a feature for automatic translation between formal and semi or informal specifi-cations by the different experts, which is also reflected in the interface

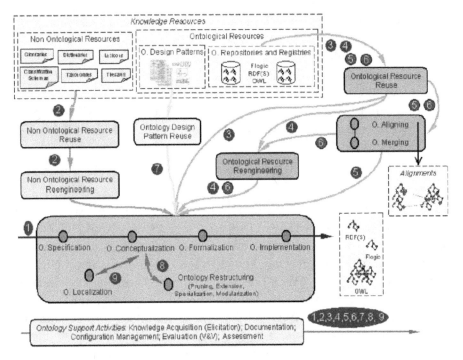

Figure 5.2: Graphical depiction of several different steps in ontology development, where each step has its methods and interactions with other steps (Source: [SFdCB+08])

so as to let domain experts, ontologists, and logicians work together on a single project, which is further facilitated by chat-like features where discussions take place during the modelling stage [DGR12].

METHONTOLOGY is, practically, superseded by the NeON methodology. Instead of the straight-forward five steps, there are many possible routes composed of multiple steps; see Figure 5.2. Various development scenarios are then specified by combining a subset of those steps and in some order, which results in a different planning of the ontology activities. Each number in Figure 5.2 denotes a scenario. For instance, Scenario 4 is that of "Building ontology networks by reusing and reengineering ontological resources." [SFdCB+08]. How to actually *do* this Scenario 4, is another matter. For instance, one may/will have to

a) be able to find ontologies in the domain of interest, evaluate them on the relevance and choose which would be the best fit—a research problem of its own (see, e.g., [KG17, KK12, McD17]);

b) extract only a module from an ontology, rather than reusing the whole ontology (see, e.g., [Daw17] for a recent overview, new methods, and tools);

c) convert the representation language of the ontology; e.g., from OWL 2 DL to OWL 2 QL, or from OBO to OWL; and

d) align ontologies, which is even a sub-field within ontology engineering that is large and active enough for a second edition of a handbook [ES07].

Each of these tasks has its own theoretical foundations, methods, and tools.

NeON also includes more details for the specification stage, especially with respect to so-called *Competency Questions* (CQs). CQs, first introduced in [GF95], specify the questions one's ontology should be able to answer and therewith what knowledge the ontology should contain. For instance, with the AWO, one may want the ontology to be able to answer "Which animal eats which other animal?" and "Which animals are endangered?". The AWO you have inspected does contain some information to answer the former (lions eat impalas), but not the latter, for it does not contain information about endangered species.

NeOn also has a "Glossary of Activities", identifying and defining 55 activities when ontology networks are collaboratively built, such as ontology localisation (for another natural language), alignment (linking to another ontology), and diagnosis (of errors), which are divided into a matrix with "required" and "if applicable" [SFdCB+08].

Not even the NeON methodology covers all options—i.e., all the steps and all possible permutations at each step—that should be in an ontologist's 'tool box', though. For instance, some mention "non-ontological resource reuse" for bottom-up ontology development (number 2 in Figure 5.2), and note NLP and reuse of thesauri, but lack detail on how this is to be done—for that, one has to search the literature and look up specific methods and tools and the other bottom-up routes (the topic of Chapter 7) that can, or have to be, 'plugged in' the methodology actually being applied. A glaring absence from the methodologies is that none of them incorporates a 'top-down' step on foundational ontology use to enforce precision and interoperability with other ontologies and reuse generic classes and object properties to facilitate domain ontology development. We will look at this in some detail in Chapter 6. For the older methodologies this may be understandable, given that at the time they were hardly available, but it is a missed opportunity for the more recent methodologies.

Lifecycles

A recent addition to the ontology development methodology landscape is the Ontology Summit 2013 Communiqué's[2] take on the matter with the *ontology lifecycle model*; see Figure 5.3. Each stage has its own set of questions that ought to be answered satisfactorily. To provide a flavour of those questions that need to be answered in an ontology development project, I include here random selection of such questions at several stages, which also address evaluation of the results of that stage (see the communiqué or [N+13] for more of such questions):

- Requirements development phase
  - Why is this ontology needed? (What is the rationale? What are the expected benefits)?
  - Are there existing ontologies or standards that need to be reused or adopted?
  - What are the competency questions? (what questions should the ontology itself be able to answer?)
- Ontological analysis phase
  - Are all relevant terms from the use cases documented?
  - Are all entities within the scope of the ontology captured?
- System design phase
  - What operations will be performed, using the ontology, by other system components? What components will perform those operations? How do the business requirements identified in the requirements development phase apply to those specific operations and components?
  - How will the ontology be built, evaluated, and maintained? What tools are needed to enable the development, evaluation, configuration management, and maintenance of the ontology?

At this point, you are not expected to be able to answer all questions already. Some possible answers will pass the revue in the remainder of the book, and others you may find when working on the practical assignment.

---

[2]http://ontolog.cim3.net/cgi-bin/wiki.pl?OntologySummit2013_Communique

Figure 5.3: Ontology Summit 2013's lifecycle model. (Source: http://ontolog.cim3.net/cgi-bin/wiki.pl?OntologySummit2013_Communique)

Agile

Agile approaches to ontology development are being investigated at the time of writing this book. That is, this is in flux, hence, perhaps, too early at this stage to give a full account of it. For some preliminary results, one may wish to have a look at, e.g., the Agile-inspired OntoMaven that has OntoMvnTest with 'test cases' for the usual syntax checking, consistency, and entailment [PS15], simplified agile [Per17], a sketch of a possible Test-Driven Development methodology is introduced in [KL16], and eXtreme Design was added to NeON [PD+09].

It is beyond the current scope to provide a comparison of the methodologies (see for an overview [GOG+10]). Either way, it is better to pick one of them to structure your activities for developing a domain ontology than using none at all. Using none at all amounts to re-inventing the wheel and stumbling upon the same difficulties and making the same mistakes developers have made before, but a good engineer has learned from previous mistakes. The methodologies aim to prevent common mistakes and omissions, and let you to carry out the tasks better than otherwise would have occurred without using one.

5.1.2 Micro-level development

OntoSpec, OD101, and DiDOn can be considered 'micro-level' methodologies: they focus on guidelines to formalise the subject domain, i.e.,
providing guidance *how* to go from an informal representation to a logic-
based one. While this could be perceived to be part of the macro-level
approach, as it happens, such a 'micro-level view' actually does affect
some macro-level choices and steps. It encompasses not only axiom
choice, but also other aspects that affect that, such as the following ones
(explained further below):

1) Requirements analysis, with an emphasis on purpose, use cases
   regarding expressiveness (temporal, fuzzy, n-aries etc.), types of
   queries, reasoning services needed;
2) Design of an ontology architecture (e.g., modular), distributed or
   not, which (logic-based) framework to use;
3) Choose principal representation language and consider encoding
   peculiarities (see below);
4) Consider and choose a foundational ontology and make modelling
   decisions (e.g., on attributes and n-aries as relations or classes;
   Chapter 6);
5) Consider domain ontology, top-domain level ontology, and ontology design pattern ontology reuse, if applicable, and any ontology
   matching technique required for their alignment;
6) Consider semi-automated bottom-up approaches, tools, and language transformations, and remodel if needed to match the decisions in steps 3 and 4 (Chapter 7);
7) Formalization (optionally with intermediate representations), including:
   a) examine and add the classes, object properties, constraints,
      rules taking into account the imported ontologies;
   b) use an automated reasoner for debugging and detecting anoma-
      lous deductions in the logical theory;
   c) use ontological reasoning services for ontological quality checks
      (e.g., OntoClean and RBox Compatibility);
   d) add annotations;
8) Generate versions in other ontology languages, 'lite' versions, etc.,
   if applicable;
9) Deployment, with maintenance, updates, etc.

Some of them are incorporated also in the macro-level methodologies, but do not yet clearly feature in the detail required for authoring ontologies. There is much to say about these steps, and even more yet to be investigated and developed (and they will be revised and refined in due time); some and its application to bio-ontologies can be found in [Kee12b].

For the remainder of this section, we shall consider briefly the language choice and some modelling choices on formalising it, in order to demonstrate that the 'micro' is not a 'single step' as it initially might seem from the macro-level methodologies, and that the 'micro' level does not simply consist of small trivial choices to make in the development process.

The representation language

Regarding formalisation, the first aspect is to choose a suitable logic-based language, which ought to be the optimal choice based on the required language features and automated reasoning requirements (if any), that, in turn, ought to follow from the overall purpose of the ontology (due to computational limitations), if there is a purpose at all [Kee10a]. Generalising slightly, they fall into two main group: lightweight ontologies—hence, languages—to be deployed in systems for, among others, annotation, natural language processing, and ontology-based data access, and there are 'scientific ontologies' for representing the knowledge of a subject domain in science, such as human anatomy, biological pathways, and data mining [D+10, HND+11, KLd+15, RMJ03]. More importantly for choosing the suitable language, is that the first main group of ontologies require support for navigation, simple queries to retrieve a class in the hierarchy, and scalability. Thus, a language with low expressiveness suffices, such as the Open Biological and biomedical Ontologies' obo-format, the W3C standardised Simple Knowledge Organisation System (SKOS) language [MB09], and the OWL 2 EL or OWL 2 QL profile [MGH+09]. For a scientific ontology, on the other hand, we need a very expressive language to capture fine-grained distinctions between the entities. This also means one needs (and can use fruitfully) more reasoning services, such as satisfiability checking, classification, and complex queries. One can choose any language, be it full first order predicate logic with or without an extension (e.g., temporal, fuzzy), or one of the very expressive OWL species to guarantee termina-

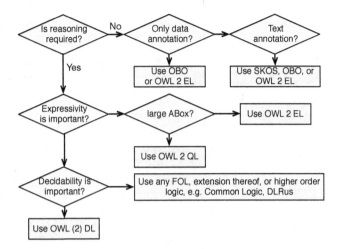

Figure 5.4: A preliminary decision diagram to choose a suitable ontology language for one's prospective ontology, with indications of current typical usage and suggestions for use. (Source: extended from [Kee12b])

tion of the reasoning services and foster interoperability and reuse with other ontologies. The basic idea is summarised in Figure 5.4, which is yet to be refined further with more ontology languages, such as the OWL 2 RL profile or SWRL for rules and the $\mathcal{DLR}$ and $\mathcal{CFD}$ families of DL languages that can handle n-ary relationships (with $n \geq 2$) properly.

The analysis of the language aspects can be pushed further, and one may wish to consider the language in a more fine-grained way and prefer one semantics over another and one ontological commitment over another. For instance, assessing whether one needs access to the components of a relationship alike UML's association ends, the need for n-aries, or whether asymmetry is essential, and, e.g., graph-based versus model-theoretic semantics. This is interesting from a logic and philosophical perspective at a more advanced level of ontology engineering and research, which we will not cover in this introductory course to a practically usable detail.

Encoding Peculiarities

This is tricky to grasp at the start: there may be a difference between what the domain expert sees in the tool—what it is 'understood to represent'—and what you, as the computer scientist, know how it works regarding the computational representation at the back-end that a domain expert need not know about. Ontologies need not be stored in an OWL file. For instance, it may be the case that a modeller sees an ontology in the interface of a software application, but those classes, relations, and constraints are actually stored in a database, or an n-ary relationship is depicted in the diagrammatic rendering of the ontology, but this is encoded as 3 binaries behind the scenes. The former plays a trick logically: in that case, mathematically, classes are stored as instances in the system (not classes-as-instances in the ontology!). For instance, `Chair` may be represented in the OWL ontology as the class `Chair`, but one equally well can store `Chair` in a database table, by which it mathematically has become an instance when it is a tuple or a value when it is stored in a cell, yet it is 'thought of' and pretended to be a universal, class, or concept in the graphical interface. This is primarily relevant for SKOS and OBO ontologies. Take the Gene Ontology, among others, which is downloadable in OBO or OWL format—i.e., its taxonomy consists of, mathematically, classes—and is available in database format—i.e., mathematically it is a taxonomy of instances. This does not have to be a concern of the subject domain experts, but it does affect how the ontology can be used in ontology-driven information systems. A motivation for storing the ontology in a database, is that databases are much better scalable, which is nice for querying large ontologies. The downside is that data in databases are much less usable for automated reasoning. As an ontology engineer, you will have to make a decision about such trade-offs.

There is no such choice for SKOS 'ontologies', because each SKOS concept is always serialised as an OWL individual, as we shall see in Chapter 7. One has to be aware of this distinction when converting between SKOS and OWL, and it can be handled easily in the application layer in a similar way to GO.

One also could avail of "punning" as a way to handle second-order logic rules in a first-order setting and use the standard reasoners instead of developing a new one (that is, not in the sense of confusing class as instance, but for engineering reasons), or 'push down' the layers. This can be done by converting the content of the TBox into the ABox, encode the second-order or meta rules in the TBox, and classify the classes-converted-into-individuals accordingly. We will come across one such example with OntoClean in Section 5.2.2.

In short: one has to be careful with the distinction between the 'intended meaning' and the actual encoding in an implemented system.

On formalising it

The *'how to formalise it?'* question is not new, neither in IT and Computing [Hal01, HP98] nor in logic [BE93], and perhaps more of those advances made elsewhere should be incorporated in ontology development methodologies. For ontologies, they seem to be emerging as so-called *modelling styles* that reflect formalisation choices. These formalisation choices can have a myriad of motivations, but also consequences for linking one's ontology to another or how easily it is to use the ontology in, say, an OBDA system. The typical choices one probably has come across in conceptual modelling for database systems or object-oriented software also appear here, as well as others. For instance:

- will you represent 'marriage' as a class Marriage or as an object property isMarriedTo?
- will you represent 'skill' as a class Skill, as an object property hasSkill, or as a data property (attribute) with values?

At this stage, it may look like an arbitrary choice of preference or convenience. This is not exactly the case, as we shall see in Chapter 6. Others have to do with a certain axiom type or carefulness:

- On can declare, say, hasPart and partOf and state they are inverses, i.e., adding two vocabulary elements to the ontology and the axiom hasPart $\equiv$ partOf$^-$. In OWL 2, one also could choose to add only one of the two and represent the other through an inverse directly; e.g., with only hasPart, one could state C $\sqsubseteq$ hasPart$^-$.D "Each C is part of at least one D", i.e., partOf would not be a named object property in the ontology.
- The Pizza Ontology Tutorial cautions against declaring domain and range axioms, mainly because the inferences can come as a surprise to novice ontology developers. Should one therefore avoid them? Ideally, no, for this results in a lower precision and actually may hide defects in the ontology.
- n-aries ($n \geq 3$) cannot be represented fully, only approximated, in OWL and there are different ways to manage that, be it through reification or choosing another logic.

Whichever way you choose to represent a particular recurring pattern, do try to do it consistently throughout. There are some methods and tools to assist with such matters, which will be introduced gradually, starting with the next section.

5.2   Methods to improve an ontology's quality

The methodologies we have seen in the previous section may include one or more methods at a particular step in the process. These methods aim to assist the ontologist in certain tasks of the ontology engineering process, such as to assist the modelling itself and to integrate ontologies, which may have supporting software tools. The methods can be divided roughly into: logic-based only, purely based on philosophy, a combination of the two, and practical rules or guidelines. Each of these categories has several methods with more or less tool support. In this section, we take an illustrative sampling of each of them, respectively:

1. The 'debugging' of deductions that caused, e.g., one or more classes to have become unsatisfiable, where we'll see some detail as to what creates such justifications;
2. OntoClean to 'clean up' a 'dirty' taxonomy;
3. The RBox compatibility service for coherent hierarchies and role chains of object properties;
4. OOPS! with TIPS to catch common pitfalls and how to avoid them.

5.2.1   Logic-based methods: explanation and justification

People make errors with respect to what they intend to represent in the ontology, or do it correctly, but are somewhat surprised by one or more deductions. The automated reasoners can help explain that, or: 'justify' the deduction. The more recent versions of ODEs may have this feature already implemented, and you may have come across it during the exercises (e.g., by having clicked on the "?" on the right of the yellow deduction in Protégé). Put differently: you have been using an automated reasoner to 'debug' the ontology. Where do they come from, and what is a good strategy to explain deductions to the modeller or domain expert?

As a first step to obtain the answers, researchers looked at what were the most common logical mistakes that modellers made. Typical mistakes that cause a class to be unsatisfiable, result in undesirable inferred subsumptions, or inconsistent ontologies, are the following ones:

- The basic set of clashes for concepts (w.r.t. tableaux algorithms) resulting in an *incoherent* ontology are:
  - Atomic: Any individual of a class would belong to a class and its complement;
  - Cardinality: A class has a max cardinality restriction declared, but its subclass has a higher min cardinality on that same object or data property;
  - Datatype: A literal value violates the (global or local) range restrictions on a data property (i.e., conflicting data types).

- The basic set of clashes for the ontology resulting in an *inconsistent* ontology are:
  - Inconsistency of assertions about individuals, e.g., an individual is asserted to belong to disjoint classes or has a cardinality restriction but related to more individuals;
  - Individuals related to unsatisfiable classes;
  - Defects in class axioms involving nominals (`owl:oneOf`, if present in the language).

The second step was to integrate this with what the reasoner computes along the way to the final deduction: which axioms are involved that lead to the unsatisfiable class or inconsistent ontology? Any such explanation feature thus uses at least the standard reasoning services. It adds further and new reasoning services tailored to pinpointing the errors and explaining the entailments to, e.g., try to find the least number of axioms among the alternative explanation. Such 'debugging' goes under terms like glass box reasoning, (root) justification, explanation, and pinpointing errors. This may sound easy: just get a log from the reasoner. It is not that simple, however. Consider the following example.

Example 5.1. *The ontology $\mathcal{O}$ under consideration contains, among many other axioms, the following two:*

$A \sqsubseteq B \sqcap C \sqcap \neg C$
$A \sqsubseteq \neg B$

One deduces $A \sqsubseteq \bot$. Why? There are two routes that explain this deduction purely based on the axioms, with the relevant classes indicated in italics:

1. $A \sqsubseteq B \sqcap C \sqcap \neg C$
2. $A \sqsubseteq B \sqcap C \sqcap \neg C$
   $A \sqsubseteq \neg B$

Which of the two 'explanations' should be shown to the user, or both? And the whole axiom, or only the relevant part(s) of it, or like the colour highlighting? Or, given a set of explanations, those axioms that appear in all explanations or, vv., that are unique (i.e., appear only once across all explanations)? Or maybe to not show a whole set of axioms, but instead only the essence in natural language, alike "A is a subclass of both a class and its complement, which causes it to be unsatisfiable" or perhaps a Venn diagram can be drawn? ◇

Both the theory and how to present it to the user have been investigated. If you use Protégé, it is based on the work presented in [HPS08]. They use the notions of *laconic* justifications, which are justifications— i.e., a set of relevant axioms—whose axioms do not contain any superfluous parts (and all of whose parts are as weak as possible[3]) and *precise* justifications, which are laconic justifications where each axiom is a minimal repair in the sense that changing something to any axiom may result in fixing the undesirable deduction. While they are useful topics, we will spend little time on it here, because it requires some more, and more in-depth, knowledge of Description Logics and its reasoning algorithms (suitable for a Description Logics course).

Proposing possible fixes automatically is yet a step further and research is still under way to address that. This is in no small part because it is hard to second-guess the user. Taking the axioms in Example 5.1 as example, there are already multiple options, such as removing $A \sqsubseteq \neg B$, or deleting $A \sqsubseteq B$, and likewise for C, yet showing all possible ways to fix the undesirable deduction results in too much clutter.

5.2.2   Philosophy-based methods: OntoClean to correct a taxonomy

OntoClean [GW09] helps the ontologist to find errors in a taxonomy, and explains why. One might ask oneself: who cares, after all we have the reasoner to classify our taxonomy anyway, right? Indeed, but that works only if you have declared many properties for the classes so that the reasoner can sort out the logical issues. However, it is not always the

---

[3]an axiom β is deemed weaker than another one, α if and only if $\alpha \models \beta$ and $\beta \not\models \alpha$

case that many property expressions have been declared for the classes in the ontology and those reasoners do not detect certain ontological issues.

OntoClean fills this gap for taxonomies. It uses several notions from philosophy, such as rigidity, identity criteria, and unity (based on [GW00a, GW00b]) to provide modelling guidelines. Let's take rigidity as example, for it can be used elsewhere as well. There are four different types of rigidity, but the useful ones are *rigid* and *anti-rigid*, which are defined as follows:

Definition 5.1. *(+R [GW09]) A* rigid *property ϕ is a property that is essential to all its instances, i.e., $\forall x\phi(x) \rightarrow \Box\phi(x)$.*

Definition 5.2. *($\sim$R [GW09]) An* anti-rigid *property ϕ is a property that is not essential to all its instances, i.e., $\forall x\phi(x) \rightarrow \neg\Box\phi(x)$.*

OntoClean takes these sort of metaproperties to annotate each class in the ontology. For instance, a modeller may want to assert that Apple is rigid (each instance remains an apple during its entire existence) and being a Professor is anti-rigid (all individuals that are professors now were at some time not a professor).

Subsequently, we apply meta-rules to reclassify the classes. For our rigid and anti-rigid meta-property, the applicable rule is as follows:

- *Given two properties (classes), p and q, when q subsumes p the following constraint hold:*

  1. *If q is anti-rigid, then p must be anti-rigid*

Or, in shorthand: $+R \not\sqsubset \sim R$, i.e., it cannot be the case that a class that is annotated as being rigid is subsumed by a class that is annotated as being anti-rigid. For instance, if we have, say, both Student and Person in our ontology, then the former is subsumed by the latter, not vice versa, because Person is rigid and Student anti-rigid. If Person $\sqsubseteq$ Student were asserted, it would say that each person is a student, which we know not to be the case: 1) it is not the case that all persons come into existence as students and die as students, and 2) it is not the case that if a student cease to be a student (e.g., graduates), then that object also ceases to be a person.

Besides manual analyses, currently, two approaches have been proposed for incorporating the ideas of OntoClean in OWL ontologies.

One is to develop a separate application to handle the annotations of the classes and the rules, another is to leverage the capabilities of the standard reasoning services of the OWL reasoners, which is done by [GRV10, Wel06]. They differ in the details, but they have in common the high-level approach:

1) develop the domain ontology (TBox);
2) push it into the ABox (i.e., convert everything from the TBox into ABox assertions);
3) encode the OntoClean 'meta rules' in the TBox;
4) run the standard OWL reasoner and classify the 'instances';
5) transfer the reclassifications in the taxonomy back into the domain-ontology-in-TBox.

Finally, observe that this machinery of OntoClean also provides one with the theory to solve the "green apple issue" we encountered in Section 1.2.3 on good and bad ontologies: Apple is rigid (and a sortal), but its greenness is not. It is the rigid entities that provide a backbone of an ontology, not the other ones (like Green, Student) that depend on the existence of rigid entities.

5.2.3   Combining logic and philosophy: role hierarchies

OntoClean does little to help solving so-called *undesirable deductions*, be they logically consistent or not, and the justifications computed may not always point to the root problem from a modelling viewpoint. The *RBox Compatibility* service [KA08] and its extension to *SubProS* and *ProChainS* [Kee12a] can assist with at least some of that. They check for *meaningful* object property hierarchies and property chains. This has as prerequisite to know when a property hierarchy is 'good' (e.g.: guaranteed not lead to an undesirable deduction). Only afterward can one test for violations of those principles, and finally have guidance on how a mistake can be revised.

The hierarchy of object properties must be well-formed, which entails the principles as to what it means for one property to be a sub-property of another. In analogy to a class hierarchy, where the instances of a subclass necessarily are a subset of the set of instances of the superclass, one can state that in every model, the tuples (individual relations) of the sub-property are a subset of the tuples of its parent property. This can be guaranteed in two distinct ways. The most-straightforward case is that the domain and/or range of the sub-property must be a subclass of the domain and/or range of its super-property. This is similar to UML's 'subsetting' for associations. The other has to do with implications of property characteristics; e.g., asymmetry can be derived from antisymmetry and irreflexivity, hence, it is a stronger constraint. This is presented informally in Figure 5.5.

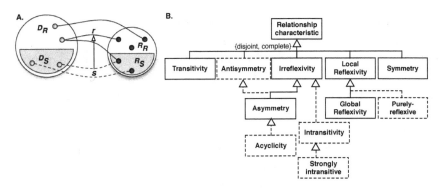

Figure 5.5: Constraining a property: A: an example, alike the so-called 'subsetting' idea in UML; B: hierarchy of property characteristics (structured based on information in [Hal01, HC11]), where the dashed ones are not available in OWL 2 DL. (Source: based on [Kee14])

To state the subsetting notion formally into the *RBox Compatibility service* (a subset of *SubProS*), let's introduce in the following definition the notation to denote the user-defined domain and range of an object property.

Definition 5.3. *(User-defined Domain and Range Concepts [KA08]). Let R be a role and $R \sqsubseteq C_1 \times C_2$ its associated Domain & Range axiom. Then, with the symbol D_R we indicate the* User-defined Domain *of R— i.e., $D_R = C_1$—while with the symbol R_R we indicate the* User-defined Range *of R—i.e., $R_R = C_2$.*

The RBox Compatibility can then be defined as follows, covering each permutation of domain and range of the sub- and super property in the hierarchy in the RBox $\mathcal{R}$, with the domains and ranges from the TBox $\mathcal{T}$:

Definition 5.4. *(RBox Compatibility [KA08]) For each pair of roles, R, S, such that $\langle \mathcal{T}, \mathcal{R} \rangle \models R \sqsubseteq S$, check whether:*

Test 1. $\langle \mathcal{T}, \mathcal{R} \rangle \models D_R \sqsubseteq D_S$ *and* $\langle \mathcal{T}, \mathcal{R} \rangle \models R_R \sqsubseteq R_S$;

Test 2. $\langle \mathcal{T}, \mathcal{R} \rangle \not\models D_S \sqsubseteq D_R$;

Test 3. $\langle \mathcal{T}, \mathcal{R} \rangle \not\models R_S \sqsubseteq R_R$.

An RBox is said to be compatible iff Test 1 *and (*2 *or* 3*) hold for all pairs of role-subrole in the RBox.*

An ontology that does not respect the RBox compatibility criterion can be considered as *ontologically flawed*, as it may not generate a logical inconsistency and the criterion—or: semantics of object property subsumption—is at least an extra-logical, if not ontological, criterion. This holds also for the extended version, *SubProS*, that has a longer list of tests to also cover the hierarchy of property characteristics.

Checking for RBox compatibility—hence, for ontological RBox correctness—can be implemented by availing of the standard DL/OWL automated subsumption reasoning service. It may serve to have further tooling assistance in correcting any flaws that may be detected.

On can extend this further to 'safe' property chains, as, essentially, they are also inclusions, just with a chain on the left rather than a single property. Basically, the domain and range class from left to right in the chain on the left-hand side of the inclusion has to be equal or a superclass, and likewise for the outer domain (resp. range) on the left-hand side and range of the object property on the right-hand side of the inclusion; the complete test to check for a safe chain is described in [Kee12a]. This is illustrated in the following example.

Example 5.2. *Take the property chain* hasMainTable ∘ hasFeature ⊑ hasFeature *in the Data Mining and OPtimisation (DMOP) ontology, which is depicted in Figure 5.6. The two properties have the domain and range axioms as follows:* hasMainTable ⊑ DataSet × DataTable *and* hasFeature ⊑ DataTable × Feature. *The range of* hasMainTable *and domain of* hasFeature *match neatly, i.e., both are* DataTable. *However, the domain of* hasMainTable *is* DataSet *and the domain of* hasFeature *is* DataTable, *and* DataSet *and* DataTable *are non-disjoint sibling classes. The reasoner infers* DataSet ⊑ DataTable *because of the property chain, which is undesirable, because a set is not a subclass of a table. The ProChainS tests helps detecting such issues, and proposals how to revise such a flaw are also described in [Kee12a]. Note that in this case, there was not a logical inconsistency according to the language and the automated reasoning services, but instead it was a modelling issue.* ◇

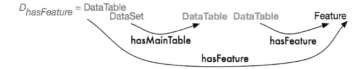

Figure 5.6: The property chain hasMainTable ∘ hasFeature ⊑ hasFeature with the domain and range axioms of the two object properties. (Source: [Kee12a])

There are further aspects to the semantics of relations (roles/object properties), such as material vs formal relations and the 'standard view' vs 'positionalist' commitment as to what relations are [Fin00, GW08, Leo08, Loe15] that may influence the formalisation as well as language design [FK15, Leo08, Loe15]. At present, within the scope of ontology development, there is only one preliminary model and corresponding Protégé plugin [KC16] that takes some of this into account and therefore it will not be elaborated on further here.

5.2.4   Heuristics: OntOlogy Pitfall Scanner OOPS!

Besides the theoretical guidance, there are other ways to address glitches in ontology authoring. Early works aimed at identifying typical modelling mistakes in OWL are described in [RDH+04], which moved onward to the notion of "anti-patterns" of the 'don't do this' variety [RCVB09], and a growing catalogue of pitfalls [PVSFGP12] of which 21 can be scanned automatically online with the OntOlogy Pitfall Scanner! (OOPS!)[4]. A selection of those pitfalls are: Creating synonyms as classes (P2); Creating the relationship "is" instead of using `rdfs:subClassOf`, `rdf:type` or `owl:sameAs` (P3); Defining wrong inverse relationships (P5); Including cycles in the hierarchy (P6); Merging different concepts in the same class (P7); Missing disjointness (P10); Missing domain or range in properties (P11); Swapping intersection and union (P19); Using a miscellaneous class (P21); Using different naming criteria in the ontology (P22); Defining a relationship inverse to itself (P25); Defining inverse relationships for a symmetric one (P26); and Defining wrong transitive relationships (P29). Pitfall P19 is illustrated in the following example.

---

[4]`http://www.oeg-upm.net/oops`

Example 5.3. *You have to represent "a pizza Hawaii has as topping ham and pineapple"⁵. A modeller may be inclined to take the natural language description of the toppings quite literally, and add*

$$\exists \mathsf{hasTopping}.(\mathsf{Ham} \sqcap \mathsf{Pineapple}) \tag{5.1}$$

However, this is not what the modeller really wants to say. The "⊓" means 'and', i.e., an intersection, and thus the "(Ham ⊓ Pineapple)" is the OWL class with those objects that are both ham and pineapple. However, nothing is both, for meat and fruit are disjoint, so the pizza Hawaii in our ontology has a topping that is Nothing. *What we want to represent, is that from* PizzaHawaii *there are at least two outgoing relations for the toppings, being one to* Ham *and one to* Pineapple, *i.e.,*

$$\exists \mathsf{hasTopping}.\mathsf{Ham} \sqcap \exists \mathsf{hasTopping}.\mathsf{Pineapple} \tag{5.2}$$

In addition, one may want to add a so-called 'closure axiom' to say that all pizzas Hawaii "have as topping only ham and pineapple",

$$\forall \mathsf{hasTopping}.(\mathsf{Ham} \sqcup \mathsf{Pineapple}) \tag{5.3}$$

Note also here that there is not a one-to-one mapping between the imprecise natural language and the constructors: ham and pineapple, but using an 'or' ⊔, which becomes clearer when we rephrase it as "all toppings are either ham or pineapple". ◇

An evaluation of the presence of those 21 pitfalls showed that it does not make much difference whether the ontology is one developed by novices, an arbitrary ontology, or is a well-known ontology [KSFPV13]. It may well be that the notion of a good quality ontology is not tightly related to absence of pitfalls, or maybe the modelling pitfalls are propagated from the well-known ones by novice modellers; whichever be the case, it is fertile ground for research. Notwithstanding this, the ontology can be scanned quickly with OOPS! and the results provides pointers where the ontology may be improved.

The error, anti-pattern, and pitfall efforts look at quality of an ontology from the negative side—what are the mistakes?—whereas, e.g.,

---

⁵and we ignore the fact that, according to Italians, pizzas are not supposed to have any fruit on a pizza—other than tomatoes—so the pizza Hawaii is not really an Italian pizza.

OntoClean and the RBox compatibility view it from the positive side, i.e., what does a good representation look like? To this end, one also can turn around the pitfalls, into authoring guidelines, which is dubbed the **T**ypical p**I**tfall **P**revention **S**cheme, TIPS [KSFPV15], which describe the tips in the imperative so as to indicate what a developer should be checking. The one that includes trying to avoid the problem illustrated in Example 5.3 is the following:

> **T7: Intended formalization** (includes P14, P15, P16, P19, C1, and C4): A property's domain (resp., range) may consist of more than one class, which is usually a union of the classes (an **or**), not the intersection of them. Considering the property's participation in axioms, the `AllValuesFrom`/`only`/ ∀ can be used to 'close' the relation, i.e., that no object can relate with that relation to the class other than the one specified. If you want to say there is at least one such relation (more common), then use `SomeValuesFrom`/`some`/∃ instead. To state there is *no* such relation in which the class on the left-hand side participates, put the negation before the quantifier (¬∀ or ¬∃), whereas stating that there is a relation but just not with some particular class, then the negation goes in front of the class on the right-hand side; e.g., a vegetarian pizza does not have meat as ingredient (¬∃hasIngredient.Meat), not that it can have all kinds of ingredients—cucumber, marsh mellow, etc.—as long as it is not meat (∃hasIngredient.¬Meat). To avoid the latter (the unintended pizza ingredients), one ought not to introduce a class with negation, like NotMeat, but use negation properly in the axiom. Finally, when convinced *all* relevant properties for a class are represented, consider making it a defined class, if not already done so. [KSFPV15]

One that has nothing to do with logic foundations, but enters the picture for ontology development is the aspect where it is still more of a craft and engineering, is the following.

> **T1: Class naming and identification** (includes P1, P2, P7, C2, and C5): When identifying and naming classes in ontologies, avoid synonymy and polysemy: distinguish the concept itself from the different names such a concept can

have (the synonyms) and create just one class for the concept and provide, if needed, different names for such a class
using `rdfs:label` annotations. Regarding polysemy, where
the same name has different meanings, try to disambiguate
the term, use extension mechanisms and/or axioms. Other
important cases regarding class naming and identification are
(a) creating a class whose name refers to two or more different concepts by including "and" or "or" in the name (e.g.,
StyleAndPeriod or ProductOrService) and (b) using modality
("can", "may", "should") in the ontology element's names.
In situation (a) consider dividing the class into different subclasses, and in case (b) consider a more appropriate name
avoiding the use of modality or change to a logic language
that can express it. Take care about about providing proper
names for both the ontology file and the URI. [KSFPV15]

The topic of pitfalls, anti-patterns, and modelling suggestions spills
over into a broader setting of ontology quality, which includes aspects
such as accuracy, adaptability, clarity, completeness, computational ef-
ficiency, conciseness, consistency/coherence and organisational fitness,
and domain and task-independent evaluation methods that cover, among
others, syntax, semantics, representation, and context aspects. (see, e.g.,
[Vra09] for an early overview.)

5.2.5 Tools

There are many tools around that help you with one method or with a
methodology. Finding the right tool to solve the problem at hand (if it
exists) is a skill of its own and it is a necessary one to find a feasible
solution to the problem at hand. From a technologies viewpoint, the
more you know about the goals, features, strengths, and weaknesses of
available tools (and have the creativity to develop new ones, if needed),
the higher the likelihood you bring a potential solution of a problem to
successful completion.

Honesty requires me to admit that not all Semantic Web tools are being maintained and there is typically little documentation. In particular,
plugins may falter when they have been developed for one ODE but not
another, or for a prior version but aren't compatible with a later version
of the ODE. This short section it merely intended to give you an idea

that there *are* tools for a range of activities, and if the one listed does not work anymore, then there is likely some open source code or at least a paper describing what it does and how, so that one could re-implement it, if needed[6]. The tools are grouped along five categories—to support methodologies, ODEs, implementing methods, portals, and exports—and where to start when you want to develop your own one.

Software-supported methodologies. They are few and far between. WebODE provided software support for METHONTOLOGY, the NeOn toolkit[7] aims to support the NeON methodology for distributed development of ontologies.

Ontology Development Environments (ODEs). Clearly, the tools listed under the 'Software-supported methodologies' are ODEs, but there are also ODEs that are not tailored to a particular methodology. They mainly lack project management features, and/or the possibility to switch back and forth between informal, intermediate, and formal representations, or do not have features for activities such as project documentation. It may well be the case that such functionality is available in part or in whole as a set of plug-ins to the ODE. Some of those ODEs are stand-alone tools, such as Protégé desktop and Racer, others have a web interface, such as WebProtégé and the Modeling Wiki MOKI. The HOZO ontology editor is the only editor that was specifically designed to explicitly accommodate for certain ontological commitments, in particular regarding roles [MSKK07].

Most ODEs are packaged with one or more automated reasoners, but one also can use another one, given that there is a plethora of ontology reasoners and editors[8]. This includes tools that have a pseudo-natural language interface or a graphical interface to adding axioms to an ontology, which serves as 'syntactic sugar' to the underlying logic.

Software-supported methods and other features. Additional features and implemented methods may exist as stand-alone tool or as plugin for an ODE, or, thanks to the widespread uptake, may have been in-

---

[6]Inclusion in this section does not mean I have tested all of them and give a quality judgement on it.

[7]`http://neon-toolkit.org/`

[8]`https://www.w3.org/wiki/Ontology_editors` and `http://owl.cs.manchester.ac.uk/tools/list-of-reasoners/`

tegrated in the ODEs already upon installation. For instance, Racer has extensive features for sophisticated querying and OWL ontology visualisation with Ontograf is already included in the standard installation of Protégé. For the axiom tests component of test-driven development, there is a TDDonto2 plugin for Protégé [KL16], and plugins for very specific tasks, such as the DroolsTab for visual authoring of complex spatial process simulation, and the CompGuide Editor for obtaining Computer-Interpretable Guidelines for Clinical Practice Guidelines. There are many more Protégé plug-ins[9], which are sorted by topic (e.g., NLP, biomedical) and type (e.g., API, viewing), but do verify the versioning of the plugins and the ODE before installation.

Some of the recent stand-alone tools focussed on improving the quality of the ontology are the Possible World Explorerthat helps with adding disjointness axioms [FR12, Fer16], the OntOlogy Pitfall Scanner (OOPS!) that implements an automated check of the ontology with 21 common modelling pitfalls [PVSFGP12], and OntoParts to represent part-whole relations better [KFRMG12].

There are many more tools, such as for ontology alignment, converting one language into another, tools for language extensions, and so on.

Portals. Other tools that can make an ontology developer's life easier, are portals to more easily find ontologies and search them, and easily obtain some additional information. For instance, BioPortal [WNS⁺11] also lists an ontology's use, OntoHub [CKK⁺17] analyses the characteristics of the ontology and which features have been used, and ROMULUS [KK16] and COLORE [GHH⁺12] zoom in on advanced aspects of foundational ontologies (the topic of the next chapter).

Exporting ontologies. There are tools for exporting the knowledge represented in the ontology and rendering it in another format for documentation purposes. These include, notably, a conversion from OWL to latex so as to obtain the—to some, more readable—DL notation of the ontology (see "save as" in Protégé, select latex), and to automatically generate documentation alike software documentation, like in LiveOWL, LODE, and its successor WIDOCO [Gar17].

Develop your own tool. There are many plugins and stand-alone

---

[9]https://protegewiki.stanford.edu/wiki/Protege_Plugin_Library

tools. Still, it may be that what you need doesn't exist yet. To develop your own tool, be it a standalone tool or as plugin, one does not have to start from scratch. For applications that have to read in or write to OWL files: rather than declaring your own regular expressions to find things in an OWL file and declaring methods to write into an OWL file, use the OWL API[10], OWLink [LLNW11], or Apache Jena[11] for Java-based applications and Owlready for Python-based applications [Lam17].

5.3 Exercises

Review question 5.1. List the main high-level tasks in a 'waterfall' ontology development methodology.

Review question 5.2. Explain the difference between macro and micro level development.

Review question 5.3. What is meant by 'encoding peculiarities' of an ontology?

Review question 5.4. Methods were grouped into four categories. Name them and describe their differences.

Review question 5.5. Give two examples of types of modelling flaws, i.e., that are possible causes of undesirable deductions.

Review question 5.6. Ontology development methodologies have evolved over the past 20 years. Compare the older METHONTOLOGY with the newer NeON methodology.

Exercise 5.1. Consider the following CQs and evaluate the `AfricanWildlifeOntology1.owl` against them. If these were the requirements for the content, is it a 'good' ontology?
  1. Which animal eats which other animal?
  2. Is a rockdassie a herbivore?
  3. Which plant parts does a giraffe eat?
  4. Does a lion eat plants or plant parts?
  5. Is there an animal that does not drink water?
  6. Which plants eat animals?

---

[10]https://github.com/owlcs/owlapi
[11]https://jena.apache.org/

7. Which animals eat impalas?
8. Which animal(s) is(are) the predators of rockdassies?
9. Are there monkeys in South Africa?
10. Which country do I have to visit to see elephants?
11. Do giraffes and zebras live in the same habitat?

Exercise 5.2. Carry out at least subquestion a) and if you have started with, or already completed, the practical assignment at the end of Block I, do also subquestion b).

    a. Take the Pizza ontology `pizza.owl`, and submit it to the OOPS! portal. Based on its output, what would you change in the ontology, if anything?

    b. Submit your ontology to OOPS! How does it fare? Do you agree with the critical/non-critical categorisation by OOPS!? Would you change anything based on the output, i.e.: does it assist you in the development of your ontology toward a better quality ontology?

Exercise 5.3. There is some ontology O that contains the following expressions:

$R \sqsubseteq PD \times PD,$	$PD \sqsubseteq PT,$	$A \sqsubseteq ED,$	$A \sqsubseteq \exists R.B,$
$S \sqsubseteq PT \times PT,$	$ED \sqsubseteq PT,$	$B \sqsubseteq ED,$	$D \sqsubseteq \exists S.C.$
$S \sqsubseteq R,$	$ED \sqsubseteq \neg PD,$	$C \sqsubseteq PD,$	
$\mathrm{Trans}(R),$		$D \sqsubseteq PD,$	

Answer the following questions:

    a. Is A consistent? Verify this with the reasoner and explain why.

    b. What would the output be when applying the *RBox Compatibility service*? Is the knowledge represented ontologically flawed?

Exercise 5.4. Apply the OntoClean rules to the flawed ontology depicted in Figure 5.7, i.e., try to arrive at a 'cleaned up' version of the taxonomy by using the rules. The other properties are, in short:

  - *Identity*: being able to recognise individual entities in the world as being the same (or different); Any property carrying an IC: +I (-I otherwise); Any property supplying an IC: +O (-O otherwise) ("O" is a mnemonic for "own identity"); +O implies +I and +R.

  - *Unity*: being able to recognise all the parts that form an individual entity; e.g., ocean carries unity (+U), legal agent carries no unity (-U), and amount of water carries anti-unity ("not necessarily wholes", ~U)

- *Identity criteria* are the criteria we use to answer questions like, "is that my dog?"
- Identity criteria are conditions used to determine equality (sufficient conditions) and that are entailed by equality (necessary conditions)

With the rules:

- Given two properties, p and q, when q subsumes p the following constraints hold:
  - If q is anti-rigid, then p must be anti-rigid
  - If q carries an IC, then p must carry the same IC
  - If q carries a UC, then p must carry the same UC
  - If q has anti-unity, then p must also have anti-unity
- Incompatible IC's are disjoint, and Incompatible UC's are disjoint
- And, in shorthand:
  - $+R \not\subset \sim R$
  - $-I \not\subset +I$
  - $-U \not\subset +U$
  - $+U \not\subset \sim U$
  - $-D \not\subset +D$

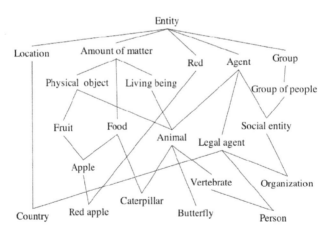

Figure 5.7: An 'unclean' taxonomy. (Source: OntoClean teaching material by Guarino)

Exercise 5.5. Pick a topic—such as pets, buildings, government—and step through one of the methodologies to create an ontology. The point here is to try to apply a methodology, not to develop an ontology, so even one or two CQs and one or two axioms in the ontology will do.

5.4 Literature and reference material

1. Mari Carmen Suarez-Figueroa, Guadalupe Aguado de Cea, Carlos Buil, Klaas Dellschaft, Mariano Fernandez-Lopez, Andres Garcia, Asuncion Gomez-Perez, German Herrero, Elena Montiel-Ponsoda, Marta Sabou, Boris Villazon-Terrazas, and Zheng Yufei. NeOn Methodology for Building Contextualized Ontology Networks. NeOn Deliverable D5.4.1. 2008.
2. Alexander Garcia, Kieran ONeill, Leyla Jael Garcia, Phillip Lord, Robert Stevens, Oscar Corcho, and Frank Gibson. Developing ontologies within decentralized settings. In H. Chen et al., editors, *Semantic e-Science. Annals of Information Systems 11*, pages 99-139. Springer, 2010.
3. Fabian Neuhaus, Amanda Vizedom, Ken Baclawski, Mike Bennett, Mike Dean, Michael Denny, Michael Grüninger, Ali Hashemi, Terry Longstreth, Leo Obrst, Steve Ray, Ram Sriram, Todd Schneider, Marcela Vegetti, Matthew West, and Peter Yim. Towards ontology evaluation across the life cycle. *Applied Ontology*, 8(3):179-194, 2013.
4. Guarino, N. and Welty, C. An Overview of OntoClean. in S. Staab, R. Studer (eds.), *Handbook on Ontologies*, Springer Verlag 2009, pp. 201-220.
5. C. Maria Keet. Preventing, detecting, and revising flaws in object property expressions. *J. on Data Semantics*, 3(3):189-206, 2014.

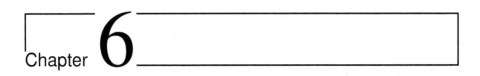

Chapter **6**

Top-down Ontology Development

Having an ontology language is one thing, but *what* to represent, and *how*, is quite another. In the previous chapter, we looked at answering "Where do you start?" and "How to proceed" with methodologies, but we are still left with answering: How can you avoid reinventing the wheel? What can guide you to make the process easier to carry it out successfully? How can you make the best of 'legacy' material? There are two principal approaches, being the so-called *top-down* and *bottom-up* ontology development approaches with their own set of methods, tools, and artefacts. In this chapter, we focus on the former and in the next chapter on the latter, where each can be seen as a refinement of some aspects of an overall methodology like introduced in Chapter 5.

We look at 'avoiding to reinvent the wheel' and 'what can guide you to make the process of adding those axioms easier' by reusing some generic principles. Those generic modelling aspects are typically represented in *foundational ontologies*, assisted by further details on specific sub-topics. We will cover each in sequence: foundational ontologies, also called top-level or upper ontologies, are introduced in Section 6.1 and subsequently parthood and part-whole relations, as one of the sub-topics, are introduced in Section 6.2. (The notion of *ontology design patterns* partially could fit here as well, but also partially as bottom up or practice-oriented; for the latter reason and chapter size considerations, it has been moved to the next chapter.)

6.1   Foundational ontologies

The basic starting point for top-down ontology development is to consider several core principles of Ontology for ontologies; or: some philosophical guidance for the prospective engineering artefact[1]. Although we will not delve into deep debates about philosophical theories in this course, it is useful to know it has something to offer to the development of ontologies, and we will see several examples where it has had influence. A few examples where results from philosophy can be useful when deciding what is going to be represented in one's ontology, and how, are the following ones.

- One can commit to a 3-Dimensional view of the world with objects persisting in time or take a(4-Dimensional (perdurantist) stance with space-time worms; e.g., are you convinced that you after reading this sentence is a different you than you before reading this sentence? If so, then you may well be a perdurantist, if you consider yourself to be the very same entity before and after, then you lean toward the 3D, endurantist, commitment (but before proclaiming to be one or the other based on this single example, do read up on the details and the implications).

- The distinction between (in OWL terminology) classes and individuals: the former can have instances, but the latter cannot be instantiated further; e.g., a class Chair can have instances, such as the one you are sitting on now, but that chair cannot be instantiated further (it is already an individual object). Generally, philosophers tend to agree on such a distinction, but one has to decide whether one's ontology is for individuals or for classes, or

---

[1]As philosophy enters, a note about terminology may be in order, because some ideas are borrowed and changed, and some terms that are the same do mean different things in different disciplines. In the literature, you will come across *material* ontology and *formal* ontology. The former (roughly) concerns making an 'inventory' of the things in the universe (we have the vase, the clay, the apple, etc.), whereas the latter concerns laying bare the formal structure of (and relation between) entities, which are assumed to have general features and obey some general laws that hold across subject domains, like identity, constitution, and parthood (the latter will be introduced in Section 6.2). So, in ontology engineering the 'formal' may refer to *logic-based* but also to the usage of 'formal' in philosophy, which concerns the topic of investigation and does not imply there is a formalisation of it in a logic language. In most computer science and IT literature, when 'formal' is written, it generally refers to logic-based.

both.

- In the previous chapters, we have used terms like class and concept as they are used in that specific field. Philosophically, however, terms like class, concept, universal, type, and category each have their very specific meaning and this brings us back to comments in Section 1.2.2: concepts live in the mind/one's thoughts, whereas universals are out there in the world (if one is convinced universals exist). OWL and its reasoners are entirely agnostic about this distinction, but the people who are reading, developing, and evaluating the ontologies typically are not.

- Descriptivist vs. prescriptivist: should the ontology try to *describe* as best as possible the subject domain, i.e., give an account of it, or should that what is represented in the ontology *prescribe* how the world is, i.e., that the entities in the ontology and constraints represented necessarily must hold, and shown to hold, in reality? Conversely, if something is not represented in the ontology, then a descriptivist may say it was unintentionally incomplete whereas a prescriptivist may say not only that, but also, pedantically, argue that if it's not in the ontology, then it does not exist in reality.

Then there more detailed decision to make, such as whether you are convinced that there are entities that are not in space/time (i.e., that are abstract), whether two entities can be co-located (the vase and the amount of clay it is made of), and what it means that one entity is [dependent on/constituted by/part of/...] another. There are more of such questions and decision to make. If you do not want to entertain yourself with these questions, you can take someone else's design decisions and use that in ontology development. Someone else's design decisions on Ontology for a set of such questions typically is available in a **foundational ontology**, and the different answers to such questions end up as different foundational ontologies. Even with the same answers they may be different[2]. The intricacies of, and philosophical debates about, the more subtle details and differences are left to another course, as here the focus is one *why to use one, where,* and *how*.

In the remainder of this section, we'll first have a look at typical content of a foundational ontology (Section 6.1.1) and that there are

---

[2]see, e.g. beyond concepts [Smi04], the WonderWeb deliverable [MBG+03], and a synopsis of the main design decisions for DOLCE [BM09]

multiple foundational ontologies (Section 6.1.2) to subsequently proceed
to the why, where, and how to use them (Section 6.1.3).

6.1.1   Typical content of a foundational ontology

Foundational ontologies provide a high-level categorisation about the
kinds of things that will be represented in the ontology, such as *process*
and *physical object*, relations that are useful across subject domains,
such as *participation* and *parthood*, and (what are and) how to represent
'attributes' in a particular subject domain, such as Colour and Height
(recall Section 1.3), which can be done, e.g., as *quality* or some kind of
dependent continuant or *trope*. To make sense of this, let us start with
the two main ingredients: the 'class' taxonomy and the relationships.

Universals, categories, class hierarchy

Just like with other ontologies we have seen, also a foundational ontology represented in OWL has a hierarchy in the TBox. However, there
are some differences with a domain ontology or tutorial ontology such
as the AWO and the Pizza ontology. The hierarchy in a foundational
ontology does not contain subject domain classes such as Boerewors and
PizzaHawaii, but *categories* (or, loosely, 'conceptual containers') of kinds
of things. For instance, all instances of PizzaHawaii can be considered to
be *physical objects*, as are those sausages that are an instance of Boerewors. If we assume there to be physical objects, then presumably, there
can also be entities that can be categorised as *non-physical objects*; e.g.,
the class (concept/universal/...) Organisation, with instances such as the
United Nations, fall in the category of *social object*, which are a type of
non-physical object. Non-physical objects typically 'inhere in' physical
objects, or physical objects are the 'bearer' of the non-physical ones;
e.g., being an instance of Student is a role you play[3] where the physical
object is you as an instance of Human.

Likewise, one can categorise kinds of processes. For instance, writing
an exam is something that unfolds in time and has various sub-activities,
such as thinking, writing, erasing pencil marks, and so on; taken together, writing an exam is an *accomplishment*. Contrast this with, say,
an instance of Sitting: for the whole duration you sit, each part of it is
still an instance of sitting, which thereby may be categorised as a *state*.

---

[3]not 'role' as in DLs or ORM, but role in the common sense meaning.

None of the things mentioned in *slanted font type* in this paragraph actually are specific entity types that one would encounter in an ontology about subject domain entities only, yet we would want to be able to categorise the kinds of things we represent in our domain ontology in a systematic way. It is these and other categories that are represented in a foundational ontology.

The categories introduced with the examples above actually are from the Descriptive Ontology for Linguistic and Cognitive Engineering (DOLCE) foundational ontology, and a screenshot of its hierarchy is shown in Figure 6.1-B. Behind this simple taxonomy in the picture, is a comprehensive formalisation in first order predicate logic that was introduced in [MBG+03]. The taxonomy of the Basic Formal Ontology (BFO) v1 is shown in Figure 6.1-A, to illustrate that the DOLCE categories and their hierarchical organisation are not the only way of structuring such core entities. (How to deal with such variety will be addressed further below).

Being a pedantic ontologist, one could go as far as saying that if a category is not in the foundational ontology, then its developers are of the opinion it does not exist in reality. It is more likely that the ontology is incomplete in some way. There are efforts ongoing to harmonise the foundational ontologies better, to create a 'core' foundational ontology, and to standardise such a core. At the time of writing, this is under construction.

Relations in foundational ontologies

In analogy to the 'subject domain classes' in domain ontologies versus categories in foundational ontologies, one can identify generic relations/relationships/object properties that are different from those in domain ontologies. For instance, a domain ontology about universities may have a relation enrolled to relate Student to Course, or in a sports ontology that a runner runs a marathon. These relations are specific to the subject domain, but there are several that re-appear across domains, or: they are subject domain-independent. Such subject domain-independent relations are represented in a foundational ontology. Notable core relations are *parthood* (which we shall look at in some detail in Section 6.2), *participation* of an object in an event, *constitution* of an object (e.g., a vase) from an amount of matter (such as clay), and *dependency* when the existence of one entity depends on the existence of another. The

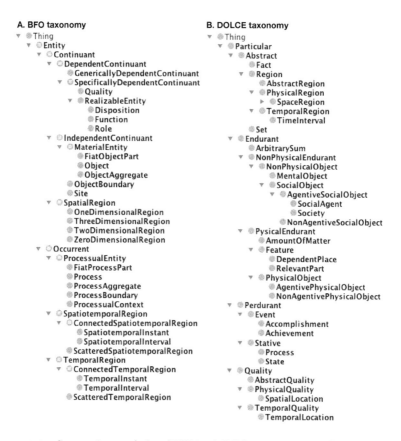

A. BFO taxonomy
- ▼ ● Thing
  - ▼ ○ Entity
    - ▼ ○ Continuant
      - ▼ ○ DependentContinuant
        - ● GenericallyDependentContinuant
        - ▼ ○ SpecificallyDependentContinuant
          - ● Quality
          - ▼ ● RealizableEntity
            - ● Disposition
            - ● Function
            - ● Role
      - ▼ ○ IndependentContinuant
        - ▼ ○ MaterialEntity
          - ● FiatObjectPart
          - ● Object
          - ● ObjectAggregate
        - ● ObjectBoundary
        - ● Site
      - ▼ ○ SpatialRegion
        - ● OneDimensionalRegion
        - ● ThreeDimensionalRegion
        - ● TwoDimensionalRegion
        - ● ZeroDimensionalRegion
    - ▼ ○ Occurrent
      - ▼ ○ ProcessualEntity
        - ● FiatProcessPart
        - ● Process
        - ● ProcessAggregate
        - ● ProcessBoundary
        - ● ProcessualContext
      - ▼ ○ SpatiotemporalRegion
        - ▼ ○ ConnectedSpatiotemporalRegion
          - ● SpatiotemporalInstant
          - ● SpatiotemporalInterval
        - ● ScatteredSpatiotemporalRegion
      - ▼ ○ TemporalRegion
        - ▼ ○ ConnectedTemporalRegion
          - ● TemporalInstant
          - ● TemporalInterval
        - ● ScatteredTemporalRegion

B. DOLCE taxonomy
- ▼ ● Thing
  - ▼ ● Particular
    - ▼ ● Abstract
      - ● Fact
      - ▼ ● Region
        - ● AbstractRegion
        - ▼ ● PhysicalRegion
          - ▶ ● SpaceRegion
        - ▼ ● TemporalRegion
          - ● TimeInterval
      - ● Set
    - ▼ ● Endurant
      - ● ArbitrarySum
      - ▼ ● NonPhysicalEndurant
        - ▼ ● NonPhysicalObject
          - ● MentalObject
          - ▼ ● SocialObject
            - ▼ ● AgentiveSocialObject
              - ● SocialAgent
              - ● Society
            - ● NonAgentiveSocialObject
      - ▼ ● PysicalEndurant
        - ● AmountOfMatter
        - ▼ ● Feature
          - ● DependentPlace
          - ● RelevantPart
        - ▼ ● PhysicalObject
          - ● AgentivePhysicalObject
          - ● NonAgentivePhysicalObject
    - ▼ ● Perdurant
      - ▼ ● Event
        - ● Accomplishment
        - ● Achievement
      - ▼ ● Stative
        - ● Process
        - ● State
    - ▼ ● Quality
      - ● AbstractQuality
      - ▼ ● PhysicalQuality
        - ● SpatialLocation
      - ▼ ● TemporalQuality
        - ● TemporalLocation

Figure 6.1: Screenshots of the OWLized BFO v1 and DOLCE taxonomies; for indicative purpose: Perdurant ≈ Occurrent, Endurant ≈ IndependentContinuant.

characterisation of such relations go hand in hand with the categories from a foundational ontology, so as to be precise rather than alluding to 'object' or 'event' and assuming your and my intuition about what those things really mean are the same. For instance, one thus could assert that, say, *participates in* holds only between exactly a *dolce:Endurant*, which is an entity that is wholly present at a time, and a *dolce:Perdurant* (an entity that unfold in time).

It is a typical characteristic of foundational ontologies to have a set of relations that are used heavily in axioms so as to constrain the possible models as much as one reasonably can.

Attributions

The third main component of representing knowledge the foundational ontology way is attributions, as, just like in conceptual data modelling, 'attributes' have to be represented somehow. There is a domain-specific component to it and there are general, recurring, principles of attributions, and it is the latter that are captured in a foundational ontology— to some extent at least. However, this is represented quite differently from attributes you have modelled in UML or EER.

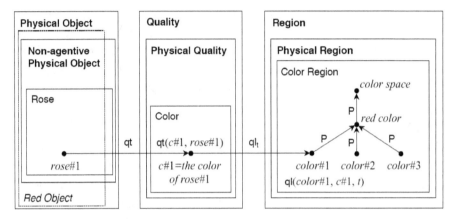

Figure 6.2: DOLCE's approach for qualities ('attributes') (Source: [MBG+03])

Let us first revisit the 'attribute' Colour that we have come across in Section 1.3.1 and Figure 1.5 when trying to integrate legacy systems. One could decide to make it a data property in OWL, declare its domain to be Rose and choose the data type String, i.e.,

hasColour $\mapsto$ Rose$\times$String

in ontology $\mathcal{O}_1$, or, in OWL functional syntax style notation:

```
DataPropertyDomain(ex:hasColour ex:Rose)
DataPropertyRange(ex:hasColour xsd:string)
```

That is, a binary relationship, which is the same approach as in UML class diagrams. Now, if another ontology developer decided to record the values in integers in $\mathcal{O}_2$, then the hasColour properties in $\mathcal{O}_1$ and $\mathcal{O}_2$ are incompatible in the representation. Or consider the scenario where $\mathcal{O}_1$ = AWO.owl that has a data property hasWeight for any object, including elephants, and its XML data type set to integer. One can declare, e.g., Elephant $\sqsubseteq$ =1 hasWeight.integer. Perhaps a hasWeightPrecise with as data type **real** may be needed elsewhere; e.g., in ontology $\mathcal{O}_2$ that will be used for monitoring all the animals in the zoo's in your country in, say, Europe. Implicitly, it was assumed by the developers that the weight would be measured in kg. Then someone from the USA wants to use the ontology, but wants to record the weight in lbs instead, which then amounts to adding, say, hasWeightImperial or the developer has to fork the ontology with such a data property, and so on, all about weights. Now the WWF wants to link both zoo management systems across the pond and compare it with African wildlife. What should the WWF IT specialists do? What is happening here is a replication of the very same issues encountered in database integration. But this was precisely what ontologies were supposed to solve! Copying the problem from information systems into the ontologies arena (perhaps because you're more familiar with that way of modelling things), is not going to solve the interoperability problem. It is still the case that there's a sameness of conceptualisation and/or reality—like Colour, and the *meaning* of Weight is all the same throughout as well. Thus, we need something else.

The first step toward resolving the issue is to realise that the choice of datatype is an *implementation decision*, just like it is in database development from the EER diagram to SQL schema. Even EER as conceptual data model already has the underlying principle to be implementation-independent, so surely should the ontology be, for it is typically expected to be even application-independent. In short: if one indeed aims for the purposes of interoperability and reusability across applications by means of an ontology, then don't use data properties and data types.

The next step then is: how to solve that problem? That other way of handing attributions is the one typical of foundational ontologies and their respective OWL-ized versions. The idea is to *generalise* (more precisely: reify) the attribute into a class so that we can reuse the core notion that is the same throughout (Colour and Weight in the examples), and this new entity is then related to the endurants and perdurants on the one side and instead of datatypes, we use value regions on the other side. Thus, an unfolding from one attribute/OWL data property into at least two properties: there is one OWL object property from the endurant/perdurant to the reified attribute—a *quality* property, represented as an OWL class—and a second object property from *quality* to the value region. In this way, the shared understanding can be shared, and any specifics on how one has to store the data is relegated to the implementation, therewith solving the problem of the limited reusability of attributes and preventing duplication of data properties. For instance, Colour would be a subclass of Quality in DOLCE [MBG$^+$03] and a Specifically dependent continuant in BFO. An example of the approach taken in DOLCE is depicted in Figure 6.2: rose1 is an instance of Rose, which is a subclass of Non-Agentive Physical Object, and it is related by the qt relation to its colour property, c1, which is an instance of the quality Colour that is a subclass of Physical Quality. The actual value—the [measured] redness—of the colour of the rose at a given time is a region red colour as instance of the Colour Region, which is a subclass of Physical Region, and they are related by means of the ql$_t$ relation[4].

The remaining step one may have to take is the case when one really has to represent some values in the ontology itself, which is something that the foundational ontologies are silent about. The least complicated and most reusable option is to create a data property, say, hasDataValue with the Region class as domain and XML data type anyType as range. This allows one to use the attributions across ontologies and tools, yet leaves the flexibility to the implementer to choose the actual data type.

This concludes the brief idea of what is in a foundation ontology. As you will have observed, there are several foundational ontologies, which may be confusing or look like overcomplicating things, so we spend a few words on that now.

6.1.2 Several foundational ontologies

In this section, a selection of the foundation ontologies are summarised with respect to their ontological commitments.

DOLCE

As the name suggests, the Descriptive Ontology for Linguistic and Cognitive Engineering (DOLCE) has a strong cognitive/linguistic bias. It takes a descriptive (as opposite to prescriptive) attitude and the categories mirror cognition, common sense, and the lexical structure of natural language. The emphasis is on cognitive invariants and the categories

---

[4]There are alternative theories in philosophy one can commit to whilst taking the unaries approach to attributes, but this would be more suitable for an intermediate level of ontology engineering.

are intended as 'conceptual containers' in the sense that there are no
deep metaphysical implications. Further, its documentation [MBG⁺03]
focuses on design rationale so as to facilitate a comparison with different ontological options. It is rigorous, systematic, and has a rich
axiomatisation. Concerning the size, it may look 'small' from an OWL
ontologies viewpoint, having 37 basic categories, 7 basic relations, 80
axioms, 100 definitions, and 20 theorems, but it is a rather dense ontology nonetheless. Besides the paper-based version in [MBG⁺03], there
are also several versions in OWL (Dolce-lite, Dolce-lite Plus, ultralight),
where some concessions have been made to force the formalisation into
a less expressive language. Some more information and downloads of
the various versions are available⁵.

BFO and the RO

The Basic Formal Ontology (BFO)⁶ sees Ontology as reality representation. It aims at reconciling the 3-dimensionalist and 4-dimensionalist
views with a 'Snap' ontology of endurants, which is reproduced at each
moment of time and is used to characterise static views of the world,
and a 'Span' ontology of happenings and occurrents and, more generally,
of entities which persist in time by perduring. It has a limited granularity and is heavily influenced by parthood relations, boundaries, and
dependence.

   Its version 1 is a bare taxonomy, i.e., there are no relations/ob-
ject properties. There is a separate Relation Ontology (RO) [SCK⁺05],
which was developed to assist ontology developers in avoiding errors in
modelling and assist users in using the ontology for annotations, and
such that several ontologies would use the same set of agreed-upon defined relations to foster interoperability among the ontologies. Philosophically, it is still a debate what then the 'essential' relations are to
represent reality, and if those included are good enough, are too many, or
too few. Several extensions to the RO are under consideration and refine-
ments have been proposed, such as for RO's *transformation_of* [Kee09]
that avails of theory underlying OntoClean and *derived_from* [Bro06].

   Meanwhile, BFO v2.0 is richly annotated, the forked ROcore⁷ does
use relevant BFO classes for the domain and range of the incorporated

---

⁵http://www.loa.istc.cnr.it/old/DOLCE.html
⁶http://basic-formal-ontology.org/
⁷https://github.com/oborel/obo-relations/wiki/ROCore

RO relations, whereas the forked draft release of BFO v2.1 (of 2014) takes yet another route where most names of the relations suggest temporality and thus indicate a different intended meaning, yet OWL is atemporal. There is also a BFO Core with mereological theories[8].

GFO

The General Formal Ontology (GFO)[9] [HH06] is a component of an integrated system of foundational ontologies that has a three-layered meta-ontological architecture. The three layers are the abstract core level (ACO), the entities of the world (ATO) that are exhaustively divided into *categories* and *individuals*, where individuals instantiate categories, and among individuals, there is a distinction between objects and attributives, and the basic level ontology that contains all relevant top-level distinctions and categories. It has (3D) objects and (4D) processes, admitting universals, concepts, and symbol structures and their interrelations. There are also modules for functions and for roles, and s slimmed version GFO-basic.

Other foundational ontologies

There are several other foundational ontologies that did not receive their separate paragraph in this version of the textbook as the aim is to have about 20 pages per chapter. They include, in alphabetical order:
- GIST minimalist upper ontology [McC10];
- GUM, the Generalized Upper Model, driven by natural language [BMF95];
- SUMO, the Standard Upper Merged Ontology [NP01], which was an early FO and has relatively very many classes and relations;
- UFO, the Unified Foundational Ontology [Gui05];
- YAMATO, the Yet Another More Advanced Top-level Ontology, which focuses on qualities and processes and events [Miz10].

To the best of my knowledge, only GIST, UFO, and YAMATO are being maintained or extended at the time of writing.

---

[8]http://www.acsu.buffalo.edu/~bittner3/Theories/BFO/
[9]http://www.onto-med.de/ontologies/gfo/

On multiple foundational ontologies

The documentation of the foundational ontologies contain further details about their formalisation and the rationale for having modelled it in the way they did; e.g., that DOLCE takes a multiplicative approach, GFO lets one represent both universals and individuals in the same ontology, BFO claims a realist approach, and so on. Their properties have be structured and are included in the ONSET tool that assists an ontologist with selecting a suitable foundational ontology for one's own domain ontology based on the selected requirements [KK12]. It saves the user reading the foundational ontology literature to large extent, and all of those new terms that have been introduced (like "multiplicative") have brief informal explanations. There will be an exercise about it at the end of the chapter.

One can wonder whether such foundational ontologies just use different names for the same kind of entities, but are essentially all the same anyway. Only very few detailed comparisons have been made. If we ignore some intricate philosophical aspects, such as whether universals and properties exist or not, then still only few entity-by-entity alignments can be made, and even less mappings. An alignment is a mapping only if asserting the alignment in the new ontology containing the (foundational) ontologies does not lead to an inconsistency. Table 6.1 lists the common alignments among DOLCE, BFO, and GFO. More alignments and mappings are described and discussed in [KK15] and a searchable version is online in the foundational ontology library ROMULUS [KK16].

In closing, observe that there are different versions of each foundational ontology, not only differentiating between a formalisation on paper versus what is representable in OWL, but also more and less detailed versions of an ontology. The other main aspect from an engineering perspective, is to choose the most suitable foundational ontology for the task at hand.

6.1.3   Using a foundational ontology

Having some idea of what a foundational ontology is, is one thing, but how to use them is a different story, and one that is not fully resolved yet. In this subsection, we start first with answering why one would want to use one at all, and some examples where it helps a modeller in

Table 6.1: Common alignments between DOLCE-Lite, BFO and GFO; the ones numbered in bold can also be mapped. (Source: [KK13a])

	DOLCE-Lite	BFORO	GFO
		Class	
1.	endurant	Independent Continuant	Presential
2.	physical-object	Object	Material_object
3.	perdurant	Occurrent	Occurrent
4.	process	Process	Process
5.	quality	Quality	Property
6.	space-region	SpatialRegion	Spatial_region
7.	temporal-region	Temporal-Region	Temporal_region
		Relational property	
1.	proper-part	has_proper_part	has_proper_part
2.	proper-part-of	proper_part_of	proper_part_of
3.	participant	has_participant	has_participant
4.	participant-in	participates_in	participates_in
5.	generic-location	located_in	occupies
6.	generic-location-of	location_of	occupied_by

making modelling decisions for the overall (domain) ontology. We then turn to some practical aspects, such as their files, language used, and how (where) to link one's domain entities to those generic categories in a foundational ontology.

Why use a foundational ontology?

Foundational ontologies exist, but does that means one necessarily must use one? Not everybody agrees on the answer. There are advantages and disadvantages to it. The principal reasons for why it is beneficial are:

- one does not have to 'reinvent the wheel' with respect to the basic categories and relations to represent the subject domain,

- it improves overall quality of the ontology by using principled design decisions, and

- it facilitates interoperability among ontologies that are aligned to the same foundational ontology.

From the viewpoint of Ontology, a foundational ontology serves to clarify philosophical details and be upfront about them, bring assumptions to the fore and justify them, and, with that, it may become clear where there are any philosophical agreements and disagreements and what their underlying causes are.

A subset of domain ontology developers do not see a benefit:
- they consider them too abstract, too expressive and comprehensive for the envisioned ontology-driven information system, and
- it takes excessive effort to understand them in sufficient detail such that it would not weigh up to the benefits.

A controlled experiment has been carried out with 52 novice ontology developers, which showed that, on average, using a foundational ontology resulted in an ontology with more new classes and class axioms, and significantly less new ad hoc object properties than those who did not, there were no part-of vs. is-a mistakes, and, overall, "the 'cost' incurred spending time getting acquainted with a foundational ontology compared to starting from scratch was more than made up for in size, understandability, and interoperability already within the limited time frame of the experiment" [Kee11b]. There is room for further experimentation, but results thus far point clearly to a benefit.

Modelling guidance: examples of some principal choices

An immediate practical benefit is that Ontology and foundational ontologies help preventing making novice ontology developer's mistakes, such as confusing parthood with subsumption and class vs instance mix-ups. The former will become clear in Section 6.2 (e.g., a province is part of a country, not a subclass). Regarding the latter, ontologically, instances/individuals/particulars are, roughly, those things that cannot be instantiated, whereas classes (or universals or concepts) can. For instance, the chair you are sitting on is an instance whereas the class Chair can be instantiated (the one you are sitting on is one such instance). Likewise, MacBookPro is a type of laptop, which in an OWL ontology would be added as a *subclass* of Laptop, not as an instance of Laptop—the MacBook I have with serial number ♯123456 is an instance, and, likewise, GoldenDelicious is a subclass of Apple, not an instance (the actual instances grow on the tree and are on the shelves in the supermarket).

An example on choosing how to represent relations is described next.

Example 6.1. *A relation, i.e., an n-ary with $n > 1$, can be represented as an unary entity (a class in OWL) or as a n-ary relation (object property in OWL if it is a binary). It is certainly more intuitive to keep the n-aries as such, because it indicates a close correspondence with natural language. For instance, in formalising "Person runs marathon", it is tempting to represent "runs" as an object property* runs *and assert, say,* Marathon $\sqsubseteq$ $\exists$runs⁻.Person.

The foundational ontologies take a different approach. Such perdurants, like running, and the verbs we use to label them, are included as an unary (OWL class) suitably positioned as a subclass of 'processes', being Perdurant in DOLCE and Occurrent in BFO, which are then related with a new relation to 'objects', which are suitably positioned subclasses of Endurant in DOLCE (Continuant in BFO), in such a way that an endurant is a participant in a perdurant. For instance, still with the TBox-level knowledge that "Person runs marathon", then Running *(being a subclass of* Process*) has_participant some* Person *(i.e.,* Running $\sqsubseteq$ $\exists$has_participant.Person*) and another binary to* Marathon *(e.g.,* Marathon $\sqsubseteq$ $\exists$involves.Running*), but there is no 1-to-1 formalisation with an object property* runs *that has as domain and range* Person *and* Marathon.

The option with runs *results in a more compact representation, is intuitively closer to the domain expert's understanding, and makes it easier to verbalise the ontology, and therefore is likely to be more useful in praxis. The* Running *option is more generic, and thereby likely to increase reusability of the ontology. No scientific experiments have been conducted to test which way would be better to represent such knowledge, and current mapping tools do not deal with such differences of representing roughly the same knowledge in syntactically very different ways. Theoretical foundations for mappings between such distinct modelling styles have been proposed [FK17], and this may be resolved soon.*

Whichever way one chooses to represent such information, adhering to that choice throughout the ontology makes the ontology easier to process and easier to understand by the human reader. ◇

A longer and practical example and exercises with the African Wildlife

Ontology is included in the next section.

Practical aspects on using a foundational ontology

It was already mentioned that there are OWL-ized versions of several foundational ontologies, but there is more to it. Once the most appropriate foundational ontology is selected, the right version needs to be imported either in full or a module thereof, and it has to be linked to the entities in your ontology. The latter means you will have to find out which category each of your entity is and which object properties to use.

Some 15 years ago researchers already realised it might not be feasible to have one singe foundational ontology that pleases everybody; hence, the idea emerged to create a library of foundational ontologies with appropriate mappings between them so that each modeller can choose her pet ontology and the system will sort out the rest regarding the interoperability of ontologies that use different foundational ontologies. The basis for this has been laid with the Wonderweb deliverable D18, but an implementation was yet to be done and new foundational ontology developments have taken place since 2003. A first step in the direction of such a foundational ontology library has been laid recently with the Repository of Ontology for MULtiple USes, ROMULUS [KK13b]. ROMULUS focuses on OWL ontologies in particular.

The leaner OWL versions of DOLCE and BFO have been made available and are intended to be used for development of ontologies in one's domain of interest. These files can be found on their respective websites (see earlier footnotes), which also lists domain ontologies that use them. Observe that DOLCE-Lite is encoded in the DL language that is characterised by $\mathcal{SHI}$, BFO is simpler (in $\mathcal{ALC}$); that is, neither one uses all OWL-DL capabilities of $\mathcal{SHOIN}(D)$, let alone all OWL 2 DL features. Recall that another difference is that BFO-in-owl is only a bare taxonomy (extensions with the RO do exist; see Section 6.1.2), whereas DOLCE-Lite makes heavy use of object properties.

To make reuse easier, 'clever modules' of foundational ontologies may be useful, such as light/basic and full versions according to the developers' taste, a separate major branch of the ontology (e.g., using only *Endurants*), and a computationally better behaved fragment with the best semantic approximation of the full version (i.e., not merely dropping the violating axioms), such as an OWL 2 EL compliant fragment of DOLCE. Some of those are also available from the aforementioned

ROMULUS and, by extension, the OntoHub ontology libraries.

Once the foundational ontology is *imported* (not leaded and extended), the task is to find the right classes to link one's domain classes to, and likewise for the object properties. The whole process is illustrated in the following example, starting with a very basic African Wildlife Ontology, and gradually extending it and improving its quality.

Example 6.2. *Continuing with the African Wildlife Ontology from Example 4.1, a first step to improve its quality may be to add knowledge to ensure a better coverage of the subject domain. Adding classes and object properties to an ontology does not necessarily make a better quality ontology. One aspect that does with respect to the subject domain, is to refine the represented knowledge further and with more constraints so as to limit the possible models; e.g.: 1) giraffes eat not only leaves but also twigs, 2) they are disjoint from impalas, and 3) more object property characteristics, e.g., that the* is-part-of *is not only transitive, but also reflexive, and* is-proper-part-of *is transitive and irreflexive or asymmetric (recall that the latter can be added thanks to the increased expressiveness of OWL 2 DL compared to OWL-DL, but not both irreflexivity and asymmetry).*

Third, we can improve the ontology's quality by using a foundational ontology, as mentioned in Section 6.1.3; e.g., one of DOLCE, BFO, GFO, SUMO, and YAMATO that were introduced in Section 6.1.1 and all happen to have OWLized version of them.

For the sake of example, let us take DOLCE to enrich the African Wildlife Ontology (AWO). To do this, we need to import into the AWO an OWLized version of DOLCE; in this case, this means importing DOLCE-lite.owl. *Then, consider first the taxonomic component of DOLCE in Figure 6.1-B (for details, see Wonderweb deliverable D18 Fig 2 p14 and Table 1 p15 or explore the imported ontology with its annotations).*

1. *Where does* Plant *fit in in the DOLCE categorisation?*
2. *Giraffes drink water: where should we put* Water*?*
3. *Impalas run (fast); where should we put* Running*?*
4. *Lions eat impalas, and in the process, the impalas die; where should we put* Death*?*

To answer such questions, we have to look at the principal distinctions made in DOLCE among its categories. Let us take Plant*: is* Plant *wholly presents during its existence (enduring), or is it happening in time (per-*

*during)? With a 3D versus 4D worldview, the former applies. Within
endurants, we look at its subclasses, which are Arbitrary Sum, Physical
Endurant, and Non-Physical Endurant: a plant is certainly not some
arbitrary collection of things, like the set of this lecture notes and your
pencil are, and a plant takes up physical space, so one chooses Physical Endurant. We repeat this for the subclasses of Physical Endurant,
which are Feature, Amount of Matter, and Physical Object. A feature (in DOLCE) is something like a bump in the road or the hole in
a swiss cheese, hence quite distinct from Plant (but a plant can have
such things). Amount of matter is in natural language normally denoted with a mass noun, such as gold and water, and it can be counted
only in quantities (a litre of water); however, plants can be counted, so
they are physical objects and, hence, we can add* AWO:Plant ⊑ dolce:
PhysicalObject *to the ontology. One can find the alignments for the other
ones in a similar step-wise way, which may be assisted by the decision
diagram in Figure 6.3. The answers can be found in* AfricanWildlife-
Ontology2a.owl.

   *DOLCE is more than a taxonomy, and we can also inspect in more
detail its object properties and reuse the properties already defined instead of re-inventing them. First, the African Wildlife Ontology's* is-
part-of *is the same as DOLCE's part-of, and likewise for their respective
inverses, so declare them equivalent. Concerning the subject domain,
here are a few modelling questions.*

   1. *The* Elephant*'s* Tusks *(ivory) are made of* Apatite *(calcium phos-
      phate, an amount of matter); which DOLCE relation can be reused?*
   2. *Giraffes eat leaves and twigs; how do* Plant *and* Twig *relate?*
   3. *How would you represent the* Size *(*Height, Weight, *etc.) of an
      average adult elephant; with DOLCE's* Quality *or an OWL data
      property?*

Answers to the first two questions are included in AfricanWildlife-
Ontology2a.owl. *Note first that* AWO:Tusk ⊑ dolce:PhysicalObject *and*
AWO:Apatite ⊑ dolce:Amount- OfMatter, *so we need to find an object
property that has as domain a physical object and as range an amount
of matter; at present, the easiest way to find out, is to run it through the*
ONTOPARTS *tool [KFRMG12], which returns the constitution relation
as the only one that fits these constraints.* ONTOPARTS*'s constitution
is more restrictive than DOLCE's, so one can either 1) use* dolce:generic-
constituent *that relates perdurants or endurants or 2) add*

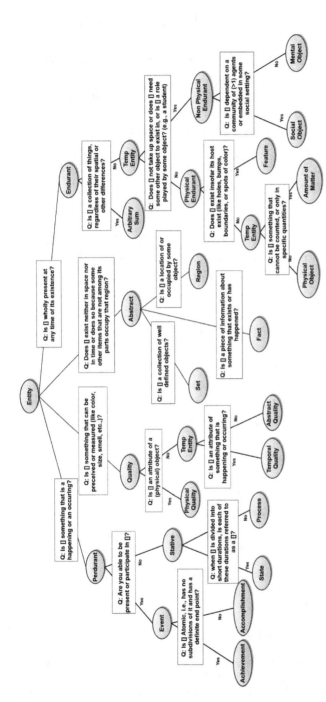

Figure 6.3: The Decision Tree of D3; a single branch can be selected at a time. (Source: [KKG13])

AWO:constituted-of *with domain and range* dolce:PhysicalObject *and range* dolce:AmountOfMatter *and add* AWO:constituted-of ⊑ dolce:generic- constituent, *and then assert* Tusk ⊑ ∃constituted-of.Apatite *in the ontology. Option 1 has the benefit of direct reuse of a relation from DOLCE instead of inventing one's own from scratch, whereas option 2 is more restrictive and precise, thereby also improving the ontology's quality.*

How does it work out when we import the OWL version of BFO v2.0 into AfricanWildlifeOntology1.owl? *Aside from minor differences— e.g.,* Death *is not a type of Achievement as in DOLCE, but a Process- Boundary instead, and animals and plants are subtypes of Object, see also Figure 6.1-A—there is a major difference with respect to the object properties (BFO has none). A possible outcome of linking the same entities of the wildlife ontology to BFO is included in* AfricanWildlife- Ontology3a.owl. *To do these last two exercises with DOLCE and BFO in a transparent and reusable way, a mapping between the two foundational ontologies is needed. Even more so: with a mapping, only one of the two exercises would have sufficed and software would have taken care of the mappings between the two. ROMULUS has both mapping and a solid method and tool to 'swap' a foundational ontology [KK14].*

One could take the development a step further by adding types of part-whole relations so as to be more precise than only a generic part-of relation: e.g., Root *is a* structural part of *some* Plant *and* NatureReserve *is* located-in *some* Country, *which will be discussed in some detail in the next section. Another option is to consider a Content Ontology Design Pattern*[10], *such as being more finicky about names for plants and animals with, perhaps, a Linnaean Taxonomy content pattern or adding some information on Climatic Zones where the plants and animals live, and so on*[11]. *Such patterns are the topic of Section 7.6.* ◇

You may like to inspect a real ontology that is linked to DOLCE as well. There are multiple examples, such as BioTop [BSSH08] that is linked to both DOLCE and BFO-RO, and the Data Mining Optimization Ontology we have come across in Section 1.3.2 [KLd+15]. A selection of the links is depicted in Figure 6.4.

---

[10]http://www.ontologydesignpatterns.org/

[11]But note that regarding content, one also can take a bottom-up approach to ontology development with resources such as the Environment Ontology (http://www.environmentontology.com/) or pick and choose from 'semantified' Biodiversity Information Standards (http://www.tdwg.org/) etc. Bottom-up approaches are the topic of the next chapter.

Methods and supporting tools are being developed that are informed by foundational ontologies or provide actual support using them, e.g., [HOD+10, KK12, KKG13, KK16, Hep11], but more can be done to assist the modeller in the ontology authoring process involving foundational ontologies.

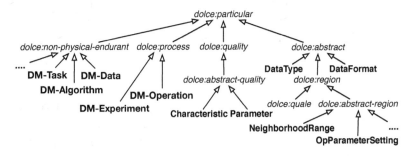

Figure 6.4: Selection of DMOP classes linked to DOLCE.

6.2 Part-whole relations

A, if not *the*, essential relation in Ontology and ontologies is the part-whole relation, which is deemed as essential as subsumption by the most active adopters of ontologies—i.e., bio- and medical scientists—while its full potential is yet to be discovered by, among others, manufacturing to manage components of devices. Let's start with a few modelling questions to get an idea of the direction we are heading at:

- Is City a subclass of or a part of Province?
- Is a tunnel part of the mountain? If so, is it a 'part' in the same way as the sand of your sandcastle on the beach?
- What is the difference, if any, between how Cell nucleus and Cell are related and how Cell Receptor and Cell wall are related? Or between the circuit on the ethernet card embedded on the motherboard and the motherboard in the computer?
- Assuming boxers must have their own hands and boxers are humans, is Hand part of Boxer in the same way as Brain is part of Human?
- Consider that "Hand is part of Musician" and "Musician part of Orchestra". Clearly, the musician's hands are not part of the orchestra. Is part-of then not transitive, or is there a problem with

the example?

To shed light on part-whole relations in its broadest sense and sort out such modelling problems, we will look first at mereology, which is the Ontology take on part-whole relations, and to a lesser extent meronymy, which is more popular in linguistics. Subsequently, the different terms that are perceived to have something to do with part-whole relations are structured into a taxonomy of part-whole relations, based on [KA08], which has been adopted elsewhere, such as in NLP.

6.2.1   Mereology

The most 'simple' mereological theory is commonly considered to be Ground Mereology. We take the one where parthood is primitive[12], i.e., part-of is not defined but only characterised with some properties. In particular, the three characterising properties are that parthood is re-flexive (everything is part of itself, Eq. 6.1), antisymmetric (two distinct things cannot be part of each other, or: if they are, then they are the same thing, Eq. 6.2), and transitive (if x is part of y and y is part of z, then x is part of z, Eq. 6.3):

$$\forall x(\mathsf{part\_of}(x,x)) \tag{6.1}$$

$$\forall x,y((\mathsf{part\_of}(x,y) \wedge \mathsf{part\_of}(y,x)) \rightarrow x = y) \tag{6.2}$$

$$\forall x,y,z((\mathsf{part\_of}(x,y) \wedge \mathsf{part\_of}(y,z)) \rightarrow \mathsf{part\_of}(x,z)) \tag{6.3}$$

With parthood, on can define *proper parthood*:

$$\forall x,y(\mathsf{proper\_part\_of}(x,y) \equiv \mathsf{part\_of}(x,y) \wedge \neg\mathsf{part\_of}(y,x)) \tag{6.4}$$

and its characteristics are that it is transitive (Eq. 6.5), asymmetric (if x is part of y then y is not part of x, Eq. 6.6) and irreflexive (x is not part of itself, Eq. 6.7). Irreflexivity follows from the definition of proper parthood and then, together with antisymmetry, one can prove asymmetry of proper parthood (proofs omitted).

$$\forall x,y,z((\mathsf{proper\_part\_of}(x,y) \wedge \mathsf{proper\_part\_of}(y,z)) \rightarrow \mathsf{proper\_part\_of}(x,z)) \tag{6.5}$$

---

[12]one also can take proper parthood as primitive and define parthood in terms of it [Var04], and one can argue about including other things (see below for some examples) or remove some (see, e.g., [Cot10])

$$\forall x, y(\text{proper\_part\_of}(x, y) \rightarrow \neg\text{proper\_part\_of}(y, x)) \qquad (6.6)$$

$$\forall x \neg(\text{proper\_part\_of}(x, x)) \qquad (6.7)$$

These basic axioms already enables us to define several other common relations. Notably, overlap (x and y share a piece z):

$$\forall x, y(\text{overlap}(x, y) \equiv \exists z(\text{part\_of}(z, x) \land \text{part\_of}(z, y))) \qquad (6.8)$$

and underlap (x and y are both part of some z):

$$\forall x, y(\text{underlap}(x, y) \equiv \exists z(\text{part\_of}(x, z) \land \text{part\_of}(y, z))) \qquad (6.9)$$

The respective definitions of proper overlap & proper underlap are similar.

But there are 'gaps' in Ground Mereology, some would say; put differently: there's more to parthood than this. For instance: what to do—if anything—with the 'remainder' that makes up the whole? There are two options:

- Weak supplementation: every proper part must be supplemented by another, disjoint, part, resulting in Minimal Mereology (MM).
- Strong supplementation: if an object fails to include another among its parts, then there must be a remainder, resulting in Extensional Mereology (EM).

There is a problem with EM, however: non-atomic objects with the same proper parts are identical (extensionality principle), but sameness of parts may not be sufficient for identity. For instance, two objects can be distinct purely based on arrangement of its parts, like there is a difference between statue and its marble and between several flowers bound together and a bouquet of flowers. This is addressed in General Extensional Mereology (GEM); see also Figure 6.5.

One can wonder about parts some more: does it go on infinitely down to even smaller than the smallest, or must it stop at some point? If one is convinced it stops with a smallest part, this means a 'basic element' exists, which is called Atom in mereology. The alternative—going on infinitely down into parts of parts—is that at the very basis there is so-called atomless 'gunk'. These different commitments generate additional mereological theories. If that is not enough for extensions: one could, e.g., *temporalise* each mereological theory, so that one can assert that something used to be part of something else; this solves the boxer, hand, and brain example mentioned in the introduction (we'll look at the solution in Section 10.2.2). Another option is to also consider space or topology, which should solve the tunnel/mountain question, above; see also, e.g., [Var07]. These extensions do not yet solve the cell and the musician questions. This will be addressed in the next section.

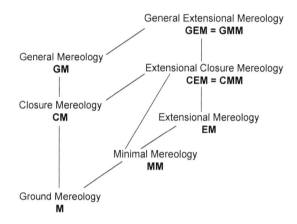

Fig. 1: Hasse diagram of mereological theories; from weaker to stronger, going uphill (after [44]).

Figure 6.5: Hasse diagram of mereological theories; from weaker to stronger, going uphill (after [Var04]). Atomicity can be added to each one.

6.2.2 Modelling and reasoning in the context of ontologies

Mereology is not enough for ontology engineering. This is partially due to the 'spill-over' from conceptual data modelling and cognitive science, where a whole range of relations are sometimes referred to as a parthood relation, but which are not upon closer inspection. In addition, if one has only **part-of** in one's ontology with no domain or range axiom, the reasoner will not complain when one adds, say, Hand⊑ ∃part-of.Musician and Musician⊑ ∃part-of.Performance, even though ontologically this is not quite right. A philosopher might say "yeah, well, then don't do this!", but it would be more useful for an ontology developer to have relations at one's disposal that are more precise, both for avoiding modelling mistakes and for increasing precision to obtain a better quality ontology.

This issue has been investigated by relatively many researchers. We shall take a closer look at a taxonomy of part-whole relations [KA08] that combines, extends, and formalises them. The basic version of the informal graphical rendering is depicted in Figure 6.6.

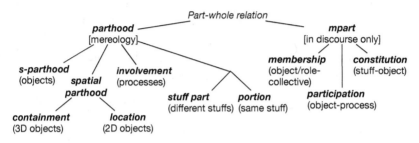

Figure 6.6: Taxonomy of basic mereological (left-hand branch) and meronymic (right-hand branch) part-whole relations, with an informal summary of how the relations are constrained by their domain and range; s-parthood = structural parthood. (Source: based on [KA08])

The relations have been formalised in [KA08]. It uses DOLCE in order to be precise in the domain and range axioms; one could have taken another foundational ontology, but at the time it was a reasonable choice (for an assessment of alternatives, see [Kee17a]). The more precise characterisations (cf. the figure) and some illustrative examples are as follows.

- *involvement* for processes and sub-processes; e.g. Chewing (a perdurant, PD) is involved in the grander process of Eating (also a perdurant), or vv.:

$$\forall x, y(\mathsf{involved\_in}(x, y) \equiv \mathsf{part\_of}(x, y) \wedge PD(x) \wedge PD(y)) \quad (6.10)$$

- *containment* and *location* for object and its 2D or 3D region; e.g., contained-in(John's address book, John's bag) and located_in(Joburg, South Africa). They are formalised as Eqs. 6.11 and 6.12, respectively, where *has_2D* and *has_3D* are shorthand relations standing for DOLCE's qualities and qualia:

$$\forall x, y(\mathsf{contained\_in}(x, y) \equiv \mathsf{part\_of}(x, y) \wedge R(x) \wedge R(y) \wedge$$
$$\exists z, w(\mathsf{has\_3D}(z, x) \wedge \mathsf{has\_3D}(w, y) \wedge ED(z) \wedge ED(w)))$$
$$(6.11)$$

$$\forall x, y(\text{located\_in}(x, y) \equiv \text{part\_of}(x, y) \land R(x) \land R(y) \land$$
$$\exists z, w(\text{has\_2D}(z, x) \land \text{has\_2D}(w, y) \land ED(z) \land ED(w)))$$
$$(6.12)$$

Observe that the domain and range is *Region* (R), which has an object occupying it, i.e., this does not imply that those objects are related also by structural parthood. Also, the 2D vs 3D distinction is not strictly necessary, but prior research showed that modellers like to make that difference explicit.

- *structural parthood* between endurants (ED) specifically:

$$\forall x, y(\text{s\_part\_of}(x, y) \equiv \text{part\_of}(x, y) \land ED(x) \land ED(y)) \qquad (6.13)$$

Practically, this is probably better constrained by PED, physical endurant, such as a wall being a structural part of a house.

- *stuff part* or "quantity-mass", e.g., Salt as a stuff part of SeaWater relating different types of amounts of matter (M) or stuffs, which are typically indicated with mass nouns and cannot be counted other than in quantities. A *partial formalisation* is as follows (there is a more elaborate one [Kee16]):

$$\forall x, y(\text{stuff\_part}(x, y) \equiv \text{part\_of}(x, y) \land M(x) \land M(y)) \qquad (6.14)$$

- *portion*, elsewhere also called "portion-object", relating a smaller (or sub) part of an amount of matter to the whole, where both are of the same type of stuff; e.g., the wine in the glass of wine & wine in the bottle of wine. A *partial formalisation* is as follows (there is a more elaborate one [Kee16]):

$$\forall x, y(\text{portion\_of}(x, y) \equiv \text{part\_of}(x, y) \land M(x) \land M(y)) \qquad (6.15)$$

- *membership* for so-called "member-bunch": collective nouns (e.g., Herd, Orchestra) with their members (Sheep, Musician, respectively), where the subscript "n" denotes non-transitive and POB physical object and SOB social object:

$$\forall x, y(\text{member\_of}_n(x, y) \equiv \text{mpart\_of}(x, y) \land (POB(x) \lor$$
$$SOB(x)) \land SOB(y)) \qquad (6.16)$$

That is, sometimes transitivity might hold in a chain of member-ships, but as soon as POB and SOB are mixed, that stops working, like with the hand in the example at the start of the section, for it is a POB.

- *participation* where an entity participates in a process (also called "noun-feature/ activity"), like Enzyme that participates in CatalyticReaction or a Musician participating in a Performance, where the subscript "it" denotes intransitive:

$$\forall x, y(\text{participates\_in}_{it}(x, y) \equiv \text{mpart\_of}(x, y) \wedge \\ ED(x) \wedge PD(y)) \tag{6.17}$$

From this definition, it becomes obvious why a 'musician is part of a performance' does not work: the domain and range are disjoint categories, so they never can line up in a transitivity chain.

- *constitution* or "material-object", to relate that what something is made of to the object, such as the Vase and the (amount of) Clay it is constituted of, where the subscript "it" denotes intransitive:

$$\forall x, y(\text{constitutes}_{it}(x, y) \equiv \text{constituted\_of}_{it}(y, x) \equiv \\ \text{mpart\_of}(x, y) \wedge POB(y) \wedge M(x)) \tag{6.18}$$

This can be put to use with manual or software-supported guide-lines, such as ONTOPARTS [KFRMG12], to choose the most appropriate part-whole relation for the modelling problem at hand. Several OWL files with taxonomies of part-whole relations, including aligned to other foundational ontologies are also available[13].

Note that the mereological theories from philosophy are, as of yet, not feasible to implement in OWL: there is no DL that actually allows one to represent all of even the most basic mereological theory (Ground Mereology), as shown in Table 6.2, let alone add definitions for relations. This is possible within the DOL framework (recall Section 4.3.2). More precisely with respect to the table's languages beyond OWL: $\mathcal{DLR}_\mu$ is a peculiar DL [CDGL99] and HOL stands for higher order logic (like, second order, beyond first order). Acyclicity means that an object x does not have a path to itself through one or more relations R on which

---

[13]http://www.meteck.org/swdsont.html

acyclicity is declared. The reason why acyclicity is included in the table is that one actually can prove acyclicity with the axioms of proper parthood. It needs second order logic, though; formally, acyclicity is $\forall x(\neg\varphi(x,x))$ where φ ranges over one or more relations (of proper parthood, in this case).

Table 6.2: Properties of parthood ($.^p$) and proper parthood ($.^{pp}$) in Ground Mereology and their inclusion in the OWL family, FOL, $\mathcal{DLR}_\mu$, and HOL; Trans.: transitive, Antisymm: antisymmetry, Asymm: asymmetry.

Language $\Rightarrow$ Feature $\Downarrow$	DL	Lite	2DL	2QL	2RL	2EL	$\mathcal{DLR}_\mu$	FOL	HOL
Reflexive^p	$-$	$-$	$+$	$+$	$-$	$+$	$+$	$+$	$+$
Antisymm.^{p}	$-$	$-$	$-$	$-$	$-$	$-$	$-$	$+$	$+$
Trans.^{p,pp}	$+$	$+$	$+$	$-$	$+$	$+$	$+$	$+$	$+$
Asymm.^{pp}	$-$	$-$	$+$	$+$	$+$	$-$	$+$	$+$	$+$
Irreflexive^{pp}	$-$	$-$	$+$	$+$	$+$	$-$	$+$	$+$	$+$
Acyclicity	$-$	$-$	$-$	$-$	$-$	$-$	$+$	$-$	$+$

Notwithstanding this, what sort of things can be derived with the part-whole relations, and what use may it have? The following example provides a few of the myriad of illustrations.

Example 6.3. *Informally, e.g., when it is possible to deduce which part of the device is broken, then only that part has to be replaced instead of the whole it is part of (saving a company money), and one may want to deduce that when a soccer player has injured her ankle, she has an injury in her limb, but not deduce that if she has an amputation of her toe, she also has an amputation of her foot that the toe is (well, was) part of. If a toddler swallowed a Lego brick, it is spatially contained in his stomach, but one does not deduce it is structurally part of his stomach (normally it will leave the body unchanged through the usual channel). A consequence of asserting reflexivity of parthood in the ontology is that then for a domain axiom like* Twig $\sqsubseteq$ $\exists$s-part-of.Plant, *one deduces that each* Twig *is a* part-of *some* Twig *as well, which is an uninteresting deduction, and, in fact, points to a defect: it should have been asserted to be a proper part—which is irreflexive—of* Plant. $\diamondsuit$

A separate issue that the solution proposed in [KA08] brought afore, is that it requires one to declare the taxonomy of relations correctly.

This can be done by availing of the *RBox Compatibility* service that we have seen in Section 5.2.3. While the part-whole taxonomy, the *RBox Compatibility* service, and the ONTOPARTS tool's functionalities do not solve all modelling problems of part-whole relations, at least they provide an ontologist with a sound basis and some guidelines.

As noted before, various extensions to mereology are being investigated, such as mereotopology and mereogeometry, the notion of essential parthood, and portions and stuffs. For mereotopology, the interested reader may want to consult, among others, ontological foundations [Var07] and its applicability and modelling aspects in the Semantic Web setting with OWL ontologies [KFRMG12] and DOL [KK17b], the introduction of the RCC8 spatial relations [RCC92], and exploration toward integrating RCC8 with OWL [GBM07, SS09]. Useful starting points for portions and stuff parts from the viewpoint of ontology and formalisations are [BD07, DB09, Kee16].

Other foundational ontology aspects, such as philosophy of language, modal logic, change in time, properties, the ontology of of relations, and dependence, will not be addressed in this course. The free online Stanford Encyclopedia of Philosophy[14] contains comprehensive, entry-level readable, overviews of such foundational issues.

6.3 Exercises

Review question 6.1. Why would one want to at least consider using a foundational ontology in ontology development?

Review question 6.2. Name at least three fundamental ontological design decisions that affect how a foundational ontology will look like with respect to its contents.

Review question 6.3. What are the major differences between DOLCE and BFO in terms of philosophical approach?

Review question 6.4. What is the major difference between DOLCE and BFO in type of contents of the ontologies?

---

[14]http://plato.stanford.edu/

Review question 6.5. Name at least 2 common relations—in terms of definition or description and intention—in the OWLized DOLCE, GFO and RO.

Review question 6.6. Why can one not represent Ground Mereology fully in OWL 2 DL?

Review question 6.7. Which part-whole relation is appropriate to relate the following entities?
  1. Plant and Twig;
  2. Tusk/Ivory and Apatite;
  3. Musician and Performance;
  4. Musician and Orchestra

Exercise 6.1. Content comparison:
  a. Try to match the DOLCE classes Endurant, Process, Quality, Amount of Matter, Accomplishment, Spatial Region, Agentive Physical Object, and Set to a class in BFO.
  b. If you cannot find a (near) equivalence, perhaps as a subclass-of some BFO class? And if not even that, why do you think that (those) class(es) is (are) not mappable?

Exercise 6.2. Assume you are asked to develop an ontology about
  a. Sociological and organizational aspects of public administration
  b. The physiology and chemistry of medicinal plants
  c. A topic of your choice
Which (if any) foundational ontology would you choose for each one? Why?

Exercise 6.3. Download ONSET from `http://www.meteck.org/files/onset/` and do Exercise 6.2 again, but now use the ONSET tool to obtain an answer. Does it make any difference? Were you reasons for choosing a foundational ontology the same as ONSET's?

Exercise 6.4. Consider the following scenario.

> Both before and since the 2008 recession hit, banks have been merging and buying up other banks, which have yet to integrate their IT systems within each of the consolidated banks, and meet new regulations on transparency of business operations. To achieve that, you are tasked with developing an ontology of banks that will facilitate the database

integration and transparency requirements. In such an ontology there will be concrete entities e.g., Bank manager and ATM, and abstract entities e.g., Loans. For this to be possible, the ontological assumptions that are made by the ontology must be based on human common-sense. Processes, such as withdrawals and deposits must also be modelled. It must be possible to capture dates and times for operations that occur between entities and processes. Past and present transactions must be allowed in the ontology. Entities of the ontology may have properties and values associated with them e.g., an individual has a credit rating. It may be useful to refer to or possibly use components of an ontology that implements a particular mereology theory such as classical extensional mereology (CEM) or any other. This ontology must be represented in OWL 2 DL.

Which (if any) foundational ontology would you choose? Why?

Exercise 6.5. Consider the D3 decision diagram and answer the first four questions of Example 6.2.

Exercise 6.6. Download either `AfricanWildlifeOntology2.owl` (with DOLCE) or `AfricanWildlifeOntology3.owl` (with BFO), open it in the ontology development environment of choice, and inspect its contents. Modify the African Wildlife Ontology such that it contains, in some way, the following:

a. Add enough knowledge so that RockDassie will be classified automatically as a subclass of Herbivore.
b. Add information that captures that lions, impalas, and monkeys reside in nature reserves that are located in a country (like Kenya, well-known for safaris), and that monkeys can also be found on some university campuses in residential areas.
c. Rangers of nature reserves are Humans (or: it's a role that a human can perform).

Was there anything of use from DOLCE/BFO to assist with that?

6.4 Literature and reference material

1. Masolo, C., Borgo, S., Gangemi, A., Guarino, N., Oltramari, A.: WonderWeb Deliverable D18–Ontology library. WonderWeb. http:

//wonderweb.man.ac.uk/deliverables/documents/D18.pdf (2003).

2. Keet, C.M. and Artale, A. Representing and Reasoning over a Taxonomy of Part-Whole Relations. *Applied Ontology*, 2008, 3(1-2): 91-110.

Chapter 7

Bottom-up Ontology Development

Besides a top-down approach, another option to developing an ontology without starting with a blank slate, is to reuse exiting data, information, or knowledge. A motivation to consider this are the results obtained by Simperl et al [SMB10]: they surveyed 148 ontology development projects, which showed that "domain analysis was shown to have the highest impact on the total effort" of ontology development, "tool support for this activity was very poor", and the "participants shared the view that process guidelines tailored for [specialised domains or in projects relying on end-user contributions] are essential for the success of ontology engineering projects". In other words: the *knowledge acquisition bottleneck* is still an issue. Methods and tools have been, and are being, developed to make it less hard to get the subject domain knowledge out of the experts and into the ontology, e.g., through natural language interfaces and diagrams, and to make it less taxing on the domain experts by reusing the 'legacy' material they already may have to manage their information and knowledge. It is the latter we are going to look at in this chapter: *bottom-up ontology development* to get the subject domain knowledge represented in the ontology. We approach it from the other end of the spectrum compared to what we have seen in Chapter 6, being starting from more or less reusable non-ontological sources and try to develop an ontology from that.

Techniques to carry out bottom-up ontology development range from manual to (almost) fully automated. They differ according to their focus:

- Ontology learning to populate the TBox, where the strategies can be subdivided into:
  - transforming information or knowledge represented in one logic language into an OWL species;
  - transforming somewhat structured information into an OWL species;
  - starting at the base.

- Ontology learning to populate the ABox.

The latter is carried out typically by either natural language processing (NLP) or one or more data mining or machine learning techniques. In the remainder of this chapter, however, we shall focus primarily on populating the TBox. Practically, this means taking some 'legacy' material (i.e., not-Semantic Web and, mostly, not-ontology) and convert it into an OWL file with some manual pre- and/or post-processing. Input artefacts may be, but are not limited to:

1. Databases
2. Conceptual data models (ER, UML)
3. Frame-based systems
4. OBO format ontologies
5. Thesauri
6. Biological models
7. Excel sheets
8. Tagging, folksonomies
9. Output of text mining, machine learning, clustering

It is not equally easy (or difficult) to transform them into a domain ontology. Figure 7.1 gives an idea as to how far one has to 'travel' from the legacy representation to a 'Semantic Web compliant' one. The further the starting point is to the left of the figure, the more effort one has to put into realising the *ontology learning* such that the result is actually usable without the need of a full redesign. Given that this is an introductory textbook, not all variants will pass the revue. We shall focus on using a database as source material to develop an ontology (Section 7.1), spreadsheets (Section 7.2) , thesauri (Section 7.3), and a little bit NLP (Section 7.4). Lastly, we will introduce ontology design patterns in Section 7.6, which are a bit in the middle of bottom-up and top-down.

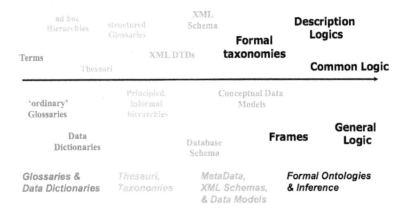

Figure 7.1: Various types of less and more comprehensively formalised 'legacy' resource.

7.1 Relational databases and related 'legacy' KR

The starting position for leveraging the knowledge encoded in a relational database to develop an ontology could be its conceptual data model. However, despite academics' best efforts to teach good design and maintenance methodologies in a degree programme, it is not uncommon in organisations that if there was a conceptual model for the database at all, it is outdated by the time you would want to use it for ontology development. New columns and tables may have been added in the database, constraints removed, tables joined (further denormalised) for better performance or vice versa for cleaner data, and so on, and no-one may have bothered to go back to the original conceptual, or even relational, model and update it with the changes made. Practically, there likely will be a database with multiple tables that have many (15-50) columns. This is represented at the bottom of Figure 7.2.

If one were to simply convert that SQL schema into an OWL ontology, the outcome would be a bunch of classes with many data properties and a unnamed object property between a subset of the classes based on the foreign key constraints. This won't do as an ontology. Let us have a look at the additional steps.

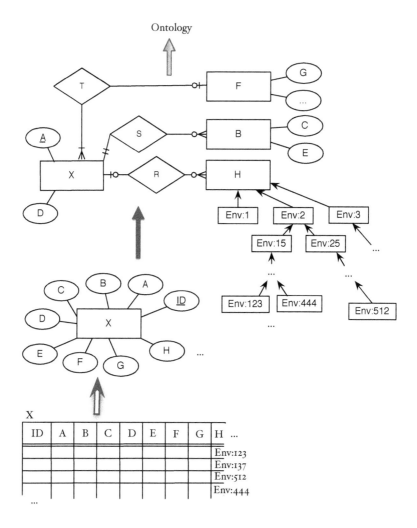

Figure 7.2: Denormalised relational database (bottom), where each table is reverse engineered into an entity in a 'flat' EER diagram (middle), and subsequently refined with respect to the hidden entity types and annotations, such as the Environment ontology (top), which then finally can be transformed/-translated into an ontology.

Reverse engineering the database

There are several reverse engineering tools for SQL schemas of relational databases, where a first pass results in one of the possible logical models (i.e., the relational model for an RDBMSs), and another iteration brings one up to the conceptual data model (such as ER, ORM) [HCTJ93]. Such a first draft version of the EER model is depicted in EER bubble notation in Figure 7.2, where each table (relation) has become an entity type and each column an attribute. The main problematic consequence for reverse engineering the conceptual data model to feed into an OWL ontology is that the database structure has been 'flattened out', which, if simply reverse engineered, ends up in the 'ontology' as a class with umpteen attributes with which one can do minimal (if at all) automated reasoning (see the first diagram above the table in Figure 7.2).

To avoid this, should one perform some normalization steps to try to get some structure back into the conceptual view of the data alike in the diagram at the top in Figure 7.2, and if so, how? Whether done manually or automatically, it can be cleaned up, and original entity types (re-)introduced, relationships added, and the attributes separated accordingly, thereby making some knowledge implicit in the database schema explicit, which is depicted in the top-half of Figure 7.2. A tried and tested strategy to do this semi-automatically is by discovering functional dependencies in the data stored in the database tables. Such reverse engineering opens up other opportunities, for one could use such a procedure to also establish some mechanism to keep a 'link' between the terms in the ontology and the source in the database so that the ontology can be used to enhance data analysis through conceptual model or ontology-based querying. A particular algorithm up to obtaining a DL-formalised conceptual data model based on a fully normalised database can be found in, e.g., [LT09]. Most of the reverse engineering achievements up to conceptual models were obtained in the 1990s.

Figure 7.2 may give the impression that it is easy to do, but it is not. Difficulties have to do with the formal apparatus of the representation languages[1], and the static linking between the layers and the procedures—conveniently depicted with the three arrows—hide the real complexity of the algorithms. Reverse engineering is not simply running the forward algorithm backwards, but has a heuristics component to

---

[1]For conceptual data modelling languages, among others, the Object Management Group's Ontology definition metamodel (http://www.omg.org/spec/ODM/1.0/) is exploring interactions between UML and OWL & RDF, and there are various results on mapping ER, EER, UML, ORM and/or ORM2 into a suitable or convenient DL language. This 'application of Ontology and ontologies' areas are deemed outside the book's current scope.

second-guess what the developers' design decisions may have been along the stages toward implementation and may have a machine learning algorithm to find constraints among instances. Most solutions to date set aside data duplication, violations of integrity constraints, hacks, outdated imports from other databases and assume to have a well-designed relational database in at least 3NF or BCNF, and, thus, the results are imperfect.

In addition to this procedure, one has to analyse the data stored in the database on its exact meaning. In particular, one may come across data in the database that are actually assumed to be concepts/universals/classes, whereas others represent real instances (typically, a tuple represents an instance). For instance, a Content Management System, such as Joomla, requires the content provider to store a document under a certain category that is considered a class by its user, which, however, is stored in a cell of a row in the back-end database, hence, mathematically an instance in the software. Somehow, we need to find that and extract it for use in the ontology in a way that they will become classes. Another typical case is where a structured controlled vocabulary, such as the Gene Ontology we have seen in Section 1.3, has been used in the database for annotation. This is depicted on the right-hand side with Env:444 and so on. Knowing this, one can reverse engineer that section of the database into a taxonomy in the conceptual data model (shown in Figure 7.2 in the top figure on the right-hand side). Finally, there is a so-called 'impedance mismatch' between database *values* and ABox *objects*, but this is relevant mainly for ontology-based data access (see Chapter 8). Thus, we end up having to process the case that some, or all, data where the values are actually concepts, should become OWL classes and values that should become OWL individuals.

Enhancing and converting the conceptual model

Having completed all the reverse engineering and data analysis to obtain the conceptual data model, one can commence with the ontological analysis. For instance, whilst improving the conceptual data model, one could add a section of another ontology for use or interoperability, alike the GO, improve on the naming and meaning of the relationships as perhaps some of them have the same meaning as those in a foundational ontology, add constraints (notably: disjointness), and so forth. Subsequently, it will have to be converted to a suitable logic.

There are several tools that convert a conceptual model, especially UML Class Diagrams, into OWL, but they have only partial coverage and its algorithms are unclear; for instance, on how one should transform ternaries and what to do with the attributes (recall Section 6.1.1). In addition, they work only with a subset of UML diagrams due to the differences in UML tool implementations (which is due to ambiguity emanating from the OMG standard and differences across versions); hence, a careful post-transformation analysis will have to be carried out.

One also could switch these steps by first converting a schema to OWL and then perform the ontological analysis.

Other languages and OWL

Imperfect transformations from other languages, such as the common OBO format [GH07, HOD⁺10] and a pure frames-based approach [ZBG06], are available, which also describe the challenges to create them.

OBO is a Directed Acyclic Graph mainly for classes and a few relationships (mainly **is a** and **part of**), which relatively easily can be mapped into OWL, and the extras (a.o., date, saved by, remark) could go in OWL's annotations. There are a few mismatches and 'workarounds', such as the **not-necessary** and **inverse-necessary**, and a non-mappable antisymmetry (cannot be represented in OWL). As a result, there are several OBO-in-OWL mappings, of which some are more comprehensive than others. The latest/official mapping available from http://oboformat.org (superseding the earlier mapping by [GH07]), which is also implemented in the OWL API. Most OBO ontologies now also have an OWL version (consult OBO Foundry, BioPortal), but keep both, for each has their advantages (at present). There is one salient difference between OWL and OBO ontologies—more precisely: the approach to modelling—which also affects multilingual ontologies (Section 9.1), and how an OBO ontology in Protégé is displayed. In OWL, you typically give a class a human readable *name*, whereas in OBO, a class is assigned an *identifier* and the name is associated to that with a label (OBO people who moved to OWL maintain that practice, so numbers as class names do not imply it was natively an OBO ontology). Newer versions of ontology editors let the user choose how to render the ontology in the interface, by name or by label. If you find an ontology online and the class names are something alike IAO12345, then it was likely an OBO ontology converted into OWL, and you'll have to change the view so that it will show the labels instead of those meaningless numbers.

While OBO and the older frames-based Protégé do serve a user base, their overall impact on widespread bottom-up ontology development for the Semantic Web is likely to be less than the potential that might possibly be unlocked with leveraging knowledge of existing (relational) databases to start developing ontologies.

7.2   From spreadsheets to OWL

Spreadsheets are normally intended to store data. There are two ways to leverage the structure of spreadsheet content in the process of developing an ontology. The first option is based on the 'standard' way of using a spreadsheet. Normally, the first row contains column headings that are essentially the 'attributes' or classes of something, and the rest of the columns or rows are the data. This can be likewise for the rows in the first column. This gives two opportunities for bottom-up development: extract those column/row headings and take that vocabulary to insert in the TBox. For instance, a row 1 that contains in columns A-D ⟨FlowerType, Colour, Height, FloweringSeason⟩ gives a clear indication what one could put in the ontology. It is a bit less structured than databases and their corresponding conceptual models, and there are no reverse engineering algorithms to discover the constraints, so still an analysis has to be carried out as to how one represents, say, Colour in the ontology. Subsequently, and having recorded how the column headings have been represented in the ontology, one could load the data into the ABox accordingly, if desired.

The second option of using a spreadsheet is that it can be seen as an easier interface to declare knowledge compared to adding axioms in an ODE such as Protégé, especially for domain experts. The idea works as follows. We have seen several axioms that adhere to a particular pattern, such as $C \sqsubseteq D$ and $C \sqsubseteq \exists R.D$, where the former could be called, say, "named class subsumption" and the latter "all-some". This can be converted into 'logical macros', i.e., a non-logician-friendly interface where *only* the vocabulary is entered into specific fields, and some script behind the scenes does the rest to insert it in the ontology. This is illustrated in the following example.

Example 7.1. *Consider Figure 7.3. On the left-hand side is a small spreadsheet, with in column A some data that one would want to have converted into classes in the TBox and to be asserted to be subclasses of those values-to-be-turned-into-classes in column B. That is, it is a table representation of the axiom type* C ⊑ D. *The script to do that may be, say, a JSON script to process the spreadsheet that, in turn, uses the OLW API to write into the OWL file. Such a script is shown on the right-hand side of the figure. Upon running it, it will add* Lion ⊑ Animal *etc. to the ontology, if not already present.*

The principle is similar for the data in columns D and E, but then for the "all-some" axiom type C ⊑ ∃R.D. *The values in column D will be the class that will have a property declared and in column E what the class in column D is doing (eating, in this case). Looking at it differently: the table consisting of columns D and E amounts to the* eats *relation and is intended to be converted into the two axioms* Lion ⊑ ∃eats.Impala *and* Giraffe ⊑ ∃eats.Twig. ◇

One such tool with which one can do this is cellfie[2] that uses the M^2 DSL for the transformation [OHWM10]. It still requires one to declare what the axiom pattern should be in the `rule` line, which could be seen as disadvantage but also as having the advantage to be more flexible. For instance, a table could have three columns, so that a domain expert can add arbitrary object properties in a row, like in row 2 ⟨`lion`, `eats`, `impala`⟩ and in row 3 ⟨`lion`, `drinks`, `water`⟩ and then declare in the rule that the second column has to become an object property in the ontology.

If there are many axioms to add, such an approach likely also will be faster when knowledge has to be added in batch compared to clicking around in the ODE.

7.3 Thesauri

A thesaurus is a simple concept hierarchy where the concepts are related through three core relations: **BT** broader term, **NT** narrower term, and **RT** related term (and auxiliary ones UF/USE, use for/use). For instance, a small section of the Educational Resources Information Center thesaurus looks like this:

---

[2]`https://github.com/protegeproject/cellfie-plugin`

Figure 7.3: Generating OWL axioms based on a 'macro' approach in spreadsheets. left: a spreadsheet with in column A the subclass and in column B its superclass, and in column D the subclass/class that will have a property declared and in column E what the class in column D is eating. Right: the JSON script to convert columns A and B into axioms of the type "A ⊑ B".

```
reading ability
   BT ability
   RT reading
   RT perception
```
and the AGROVOC thesaurus about agriculture of the Food and Agriculture Organisation (FAO) of the United Nations has the following asserted, among others:
```
milk
   NT cow milk
   NT milk fat
```
How to go from this to an ontology? Three approaches exists (thus far):

- Automatically translate the 'legacy' representation of the ontology into an OWL file and call it an ontology (by virtue of being represented in OWL, regardless the content);
- Find some conversion rules that are informed by the subject domain and foundational ontologies (e.g., introducing parthood, constitution, etc.);
- Give up on the idea of converting it into an ontology and settle for the W3C-standardised Simple Knowledge Organisation System[3] format to achieve compatibility with other Semantic Web Technologies.

---

[3]http://www.w3.org/2004/02/skos/

We will look at the problems with the first option, and achievements with the second and third option.

7.3.1 Converting a thesaurus into an ontology

Before looking at conversions, one first has to examine what a typical thesaurus really looks like, in analogy to examining databases before trying to port them into an ontology.

Problems

The main issues with thesauri, and for which thus a solution has to be found, are that:

- Thesauri are generally a lexicalisation of a conceptualisation, or: writing out and describing concepts in the name of the concept, rather than adding characterising properties;

- Thesauri have low ontological precision with respect to the categories and the relations: there are typically no formal details defined for the concept names, and BT/NT/RT are the *only* relations allowed in the concept hierarchy.

As thesauri were already in widespread use before ontologies came into the picture for ontology-driven information systems, they lack basic categories alike those in DOLCE and BFO. Hence, an alignment activity to such foundational ontology categories will be necessary. Harder to figure out, however, are the relations. RT can be *anything*, from parthood to transformation, to participation, or anything else, and BT/NT turns out not to be the same as class subsumption; hence, the relations are overloaded with (ambiguous) subject domain semantics. This has as result that those relationships are used inconsistently—or at least not precise enough for an ontology. For instance, in the aforementioned example, `milk` and `milk fat` relate in a different way to each other than `milk` and `cow milk`, for `milk fat` is a component of milk and `cow milk` indicates its origin (and, arguably, it is part of the cow), yet both were NT-ed to `milk`.

A sample solution: rules as you go

Because of the relatively low precision of a thesaurus, it will take a bit more work to convert it into an ontology cf. a database. Basically, the ontological analysis that hasn't been done when developing the thesaurus—in favour of low-hanging fruit for system development—will have to be done now. For instance, a nebulous term like "Communication (Thought Transfer)" in the ERIC thesaurus will have to be clarified and distinguished from other types of communication like in computer networks. They then could be aligned to a foundational ontology or a top-domain ontology after some addition analysis of the concepts in the hierarchy and aided by a decision diagram like D3. One also should settle on the relations that will replace BT/NT/RT. An approach to this particular aspect of refinement is presented in [KJLW12].

This is a lot of manual work, and there may be some ways to automate some aspects of the whole process. Soergel and co-authors [SLL+04] took a 'rules as you go' approach that can be applied after the aforementioned ontological analysis. This means that as soon some repetitiveness was encountered in the manual activity, a rule was devised, the rest of the thesaurus assessed on the occurrence of the pattern, and converted in one go. A few examples are included below.

Example 7.2. *For instance, Soergel and co-authors observed that, e.g.,* cow NT cow milk *should become* cow <hasComponent> cow milk. *There are more animals with milk; hence, a pattern could be* animal <hasComponent> milk, *or, more generally* animal <hasComponent> body part. *With that rule, one can find automatically, e.g.,* goat NT goat milk *and convert that automatically into* goat <hasComponent> goat milk. *Other pattern examples were, e.g.,* plant <growsIn> soil type *and* geographical entity <spatiallyIncludedIn> geographical entity. ◇

7.3.2 Avoiding ontologies with SKOS

Thesauri tend to be very large, and it may well be too much effort to convert them into a real ontology, yet one still would want to have some interoperation of thesauri with other systems so as to avail of the large amounts of information they contain. To this end, the W3C developed a standard called *Simple Knowledge Organisation System(s): SKOS*[4]

---

[4]http://www.w3.org/TR/swbp-skos-core-spec

[MB09]. More broadly, it is intended for converting thesauri, classification schemes, taxonomies, subject headings etc. into one interoperable syntax, thereby enabling concept-based search instead of text-based search, reuse of each other's concept definitions, facilitate the ability to search across institution boundaries, and to use standard software. This is a step forward compared to the isolated thesauri.

However, there are also some limitations to it: 'unusual' concept schemes do not fit into SKOS because sometimes the original structure too complex, skos:Concept is without clear properties like in OWL, there is still much subject domain semantics in the natural language text which makes it less amenable to advanced computer processing, and the SKOS 'semantic relations' have little semantics, as skos:narrower does not guarantee it is is a or part of, as it just is the standardised version of NT.

Then there is a peculiarity in the encoding. Let us take the example where Enzyme is a subtype of Protein, hence, we declare:

SKOSPaths:protein rdf:type skos:Concept

SKOSPaths:enzyme rdf:type skos:Concept

SKOSPaths:enzyme SKOSPaths:broaderGeneric SKOSPaths:protein

in the SKOSPaths SKOS file, which are, mathematically, statements about instances. This holds true also if we were to transform an OWL file to SKOS: each OWL class becomes a SKOS instance due to the mapping of skos:Concept to owl:Class [IS09]. This is a design decision of SKOS. From a purely technical point of view, that can be dealt with easily, but one has to be aware of it when developing applications.

As the scope of this book is ontology engineering, SKOS will not be elaborated on further.

7.4 Text processing to extract content for ontologies

If all else fails, and there happens to be a good amount of text available in the subject domain of the (prospective) ontology, one can try Natural Language Processing (NLP) to develop the ontology[5]. Which approaches and tools suit best depends on the goal (and background)

---

[5]of course, once the ontology is there, it can be used as a component in an ontology-driven information system, and an NLP application can be enhanced with an ontology, but that is a separate theme.

of its developers and prospective users, ontological commitment, and available resources.

There are two principal possibilities to use NLP for ontology development:

- Use NLP to populate the TBox of the ontology, i.e., obtaining candidate terms from the text, which is also called *ontology learning* (from text).

- Use NLP to populate the ABox of the ontology, i.e., obtaining named entities, which is also called *ontology population* (from text).

An review of NLP and (bio-)ontologies can be found in [LHC11] and some examples in [CSG+10, AWP+08].

But why the "if all else fails..." at the start of the section? The reason is that information in text is *unstructured* and natural language is *inherently ambiguous*. The first step researchers attempted was to find candidate terms for OWL classes. This requires a Part-of-Speech (POS) tagger so as to annotate each word in the text with its category; e.g., 'apple' is a noun and so forth. Then one selects the nouns only and counts how often it occurs, taking into account synonyms so as to group those together and assesses which ones are homonyms and used in different ways and therefore have to be split into different buckets. This process may be assisted by, e.g., WordNet[6]. Challenges arise with euphemisms, slang, and colloquialisms, as well as with datedness of texts as terms may have undergone concept drift (i.e., mean something else now) and new ones have been invented. The eventual resulting candidate list is then assessed by humans on relevance, and subsequently a selection will be added to the ontology.

The process for candidate relations is a bit more challenging. Although one easily can find the verbs with a POS tagger, it is not always easy to determine the scope of what denotes the subject and what denotes the object in the sentence, and authors are 'sloppy' or at least imprecise. For instance, one could say (each) 'human has a heart', where 'has' actually refers to structural parthood, 'human has a house' where 'has' probably means ownership, and 'human has a job' which again has a different meaning. The taxonomy of part-whole relations we have seen in Section 6.2 has been used to assist with this process (e.g., [THU+16]).

---

[6]https://wordnet.princeton.edu/

Consider that DOLCE and WordNet are linked and thus for a noun in the text that is also in WordNet, then one can find the DOLCE category. Knowing the DOLCE category, one can check which part-whole relation fits with that thanks to the formal definitions of the relations. For instance, 'human' and 'heart' are both physical endurants, which are endurants, which are particulars. One then can use ONTOPARTS's algorithm: return only those relations where the domain and range are either of those three, but not any others. In this case, it can be (proper) *structural parthood* or the more generic plain (proper) *parthood*, but not, say *involvement* because 'human' and 'heart' are not perdurants. A further strategy that could be used is, e.g., VerbNet[7] that uses compatible roles of the relations that the nouns play in the relation.

Intuitively, one may be led to think that simply taking the generic NLP tools will do also for specialised domains, such as (bio-)medicine. Any application does indeed use those techniques and tools, but, generally, they do not suffice to obtain 'acceptable' results. Domain specific peculiarities are many and wide-ranging. For instance, 1) to deal with the variations of terms (e.g., scientific name, variants, abbreviations, and common misspellings) and the grounding step (linking a term to an entity in a biological database) in the ontology-NLP preparation and instance classification [WKB07]; 2) to characterise the question in a question answering system correctly (e.g., [VF09]); and 3) to find ways to deal with the rather long strings and noun phrases that denote a biological entity or concept or universal [AWP+08]. Taking into account such peculiarities does generate better overall results than generic or other domain-specific usages of NLP tools, but it requires extra manual preparatory work and a basic understanding of the subject domain and its applications to include also such rules. For instance, enzyme names always end with '-ase', so one can devise a rule with a regular expression to detect these terms ending in '-ase' and add them in the taxonomy as a subclass of Enzyme.

Ontology population in the sense of actually adding a lot of objects in the ABox of the OWL file is not exciting, for it is not good in scalability of reasoning, partially due to the complexity of OWL 2 and partially because the default setting of the ODEs is that it will load the whole OWL file into main memory and by default settings at least, the ODE will run out of memory. There are alternatives to that, such as

---

[7]https://verbs.colorado.edu/verbnet/

putting the instances in a database or annotating the instances named in the text with the terms of the ontology and store those texts in a digital library, which then can be queried. The process to realise it requires, among others, a named entity tagger so that is can tag, say, the 'Kruger park' as a named entity. It then has to find a way to figure out that that is an instance of **Nature Reserve**. For geographic entities, a gazetteer can be used. As for nouns, also named entities can have different strings yet refer to the same entity; e.g., the strings 'Luis Fonsi' and 'L. Fonsi' refer to the same singer-songwriter of the smash-hit Despacito. It has further issues, such as referring expressions in the same as well as successive sentences; e.g., in the sentence "he wrote the song during a sizzling Sunday sunset", "he" refers to Fonsi and "the song" to Despacito, which has to be understood and represented formally as a triple, say, ⟨Fonsi, songwriter, Despacito⟩ and linked to the classes in the ontology.

NLP for ontology learning and population is its own subfield in ontology learning. The brief summary and illustration of some aspects of it does not cover the whole range, but may at least have given some idea of non-triviality of the task. If you are interested in this topic: a more comprehensive overview is described in [CMSV09] and there are several handbooks.

7.5 Other semi-automated approaches

Other (semi-)automated approaches to bottom-up ontology development include machine learning techniques, deploying so-called 'non-standard' DL reasoning services, and converting diagrams fro biology into (candidate) ontology terms and relations.

A short overview and relevant references of machine learning techniques for ontology development can be found in [dFE10], who also outline where such *inductive methods* can be used, being: classifying instances, learning new relationships among individuals, probabilistic ontologies, and probabilistic mapping for the ontology matching task, (semi)-automating the ontology population task, refining ontologies, and reasoning on inconsistent or noisy knowledge bases. Several 'hybrids' exists, such as the linking of Bayesian networks with probabilistic ontologies [dCL06] and improving data mining with an ontology [ZYS+05].

Other options are to resort to a hybrid of Formal Concept Analysis with OWL [BGSS07], least common subsumer [BST07, Tur08, PT11], and similar techniques. The notion of least common subsumer and most specific concept and motivations where and how it may be useful are described in [PT11]. The least common subsumer and most specific concept use non-standard reasoning services that helps with ontology development, and they are defined in terms of DL knowledge bases as follows.

Definition 7.1 (least common subsumer ([PT11])). *Let $\mathcal{L}$ be a Description Logic language, $\mathcal{K} = (\mathcal{T}, \mathcal{A})$ be a knowledge base represented in DL $\mathcal{L}$ (an $\mathcal{L}$-KB). The* least common subsumer *(lcs) with respect to $\mathcal{T}$ of a collection of concepts $C_1, \ldots, C_n$ is the $\mathcal{L}$-concept description C such that:*

1. *$C_i \sqsubseteq_{\mathcal{T}} C$ for all $1 \leq i \leq n$, and*
2. *for each $\mathcal{L}$-concept description D holds: if $C_i \sqsubseteq_{\mathcal{T}} D$ for all $1 \leq i \leq n$, then $C \sqsubseteq_{\mathcal{T}} D$.*

Definition 7.2 (most specific concept ([PT11])). *Let $\mathcal{L}$ be a Description Logic language, $\mathcal{K} = (\mathcal{T}, \mathcal{A})$ be a knowledge base represented in DL $\mathcal{L}$ (an $\mathcal{L}$-KB). The* most specific concept *(msc) with respect to $\mathcal{K}$ of an individual from $\mathcal{A}$ is the $\mathcal{L}$-concept description C such that:*

1. *$\mathcal{K} \models C(a)$, and*
2. *for each $\mathcal{L}$-concept description D holds: $\mathcal{K} \models D(a)$ implies $C \sqsubseteq_{\mathcal{T}} D$.*

The least common subsumer computes the common superclass of a concept and the most specific concept classifies an individual into a concept description.

One could exploit biological models to find candidate terms and relations when those models have been created with software. This allows for semi-automated approaches to formalise the graphical vocabulary in textbooks and drawing tools, and subsequently use an algorithm to populate the TBox with the knowledge taken from the drawings. This because such software has typical icons for categories of things, like a red oval meaning **Protein**, a yellow rectangle meaning **Cell Process**, and a pale green arrow with a grey hexagon in the middle meaning **Protein Modification**. Each individual diagram can thus be analysed, and the named shapes at least categorised as subclasses of such main classes and relations asserted for the arrows between the shapes. This has been attempted for STELLA and PathwayStudio models [Kee05, Kee12b].

Related are the efforts with converting models represented in the Systems Biology Markup Language (SMBL) into OWL [HDG+11].

7.6   Ontology Design Patterns

Ontology Design Patterns (ODPs) are a middle out way for developing ontologies. They can be viewed as an extremely lightweight version of design principles alike found in foundational ontologies, but then with less 'clutter'. That is, they can be cleverly modularised foundational ontology fragments that serve as design snippets for good modelling practices. They also can be viewed as a way of bottom-up pattern finding that is then reused across the ontology and offered to others as a 'best practices' design solution for some modelling aspect. ODPs have been proposed first a while ago [BS05, Gan05], and have gained some traction in research in recent years with various ideas and proposals. There is, therefore, no clear single, neat, core to extract from it and describe at present. A clear, informal overview is described in [GP09], but terms, descriptions, and categorisations are being reworked [FGGP13], and the sub-field better characterised with respect to the issues for using ODPs and possible research directions [BHJ+15].

Let us first introduce some definitions for a pattern for a specific ontology and their uses and then proceed to types of patterns. The definitions are geared to the OWL language, but one can substitute that for another language of choice.

Definition 7.3 (Language of pattern instantiation [FK17]). *OWL Ontology O with language specification adhering to the W3C standard [MPSP09], which has classes $C \in V_C$, object properties $OP \in V_{OP}$, data properties $D \in V_D$, data types $DT \in V_{DT}$ of the permitted XML schema types, axiom components ('language features') $X \in V_X$, and such that $Ax \in V_{Ax}$ are the axioms.*

The 'axiom components' include features such as, among others, subsumption, transitivity, existential quantification, and cardinality, which can be used according to the syntax of the language. A pattern itself is a *meta-level* specification, in a similar fashion as stereotyping in UML. Just in case a pattern also includes 'reserved' entities from, say, a foundational ontology, they get their own entry in the vocabulary to clearly distinguish them.

Definition 7.4 (Language for patterns: Vocabulary $\mathcal{V}$ [FK17]). *The meta-level (second order) elements (or* stereotypes*) for patterns are:*
- *class $C \in V_C$ as $\mathcal{C}$ in the pattern;*
- *object property $OP \in V_{OP}$ as $\mathcal{R}$ in the pattern;*
- *data property $D \in V_D$ as $\mathcal{D}$ in the pattern;*
- *data type $DT \in V_{DT}$ as $\mathcal{DT}$ in the pattern;*
- *reserved set of entities from a foundational ontology, as $\mathcal{F}$ in the pattern;*

where added subscripts i with $1 \leq i \leq n$ may be different elements. Two elements in the vocabulary are called homogeneous *iff they belong to the same type, i.e., they are both classes, or both object properties, and so on. Elements can be used in axioms $Ax \in V_{Ax}$ that consists of axiom components $x \in V_X$ in the pattern such that the type of axioms are those supported in the ontology language in which the instance of the pattern is represented.*

With these ingredients in place, one can then define an ontology pattern P as follows.

Definition 7.5 (Ontology Pattern P [FK17]). *An ontology pattern P consists of more than one element from vocabulary $\mathcal{V}$ which relate through at least one axiom component from V_X. Its specification contains the:*
- *pattern name;*
- *pattern elements from $\mathcal{V}$;*
- *pattern axiom component(s) from V_X;*
- *pattern's full formalisation.*

For instance, the *basic all-some* pattern that we have seen as 'macro' in Section 7.2 has as specification ([FK17]):
- *pattern name*: basic all-some
- *pattern elements*: $\mathcal{C}_1, \mathcal{C}_2, \mathcal{R}$
- *pattern axiom component(s)*: $\sqsubseteq, \exists$
- *pattern's full formalisation*: $\mathcal{C}_1 \sqsubseteq \exists \mathcal{R}.\mathcal{C}_2$

An instantiation of the *basic all-some* pattern in an ontology, say, the AWO, may be, e.g., Giraffe $\sqsubseteq \exists$drinks.Water.

As can be seen from the definition, they are referred to agnostically as *patterns*—it may be a pattern realised in the ontology and some algorithm has to search for (as was the scope in [FK17]) as well as one defined separately and applied during the design phase and is therewith thus also in line with some newly proposed terminology [FGGP13]. Ontology patterns tend to be more elaborate than the *basic all-some* pattern. For instance, one could specify a pattern for how to represent attributions with DOLCE's Quality rather than an OWL data property, as was discussed in Section 6.1.1, or how to systematically approximate representing an *n*-ary into *n* binaries in OWL. Furthermore, there are broader options for ontology patterns. A selection of them with a few examples is as follows.

- Architecture pattern. This specifies how the ontology is organised. For instance, one could choose to have a modular architecture in the sense of sub-domains. An example of a fairly elaborate architecture is illustrated in Figure 7.4 for BioTop [BSSH08].

- Logical pattern. This deals with the absence of some features of a representation language and how to work with that. The issue with *n*-aries in OWL is such an example.

- Content pattern. This pattern assists with representing similar knowledge in the same way for that particular ontology. Recalling the rules-as-you-go from thesauri bottom-up development, they can be specified as content patterns. A larger example is shown in Figure 7.5.

- 'Housekeeping' patterns, including so-called lexico-syntactic patterns. They refer to ensuring clean and consistent representations in the ontology. For instance, to write names in CamelCase or with dashes, and using IDs with labels throughout versus naming the classes throughout the ontology.

There are also practical engineering tasks in the process of using ODPs, such as a workflow for using ODPs and the usual requirements of documentation and metadata; recent first proposals include [FBR$^+$16, KHH16].

7.7   Exercises

Review question 7.1. Why can one not simply convert each database table into an OWL class and assume the bottom-up process is completed?

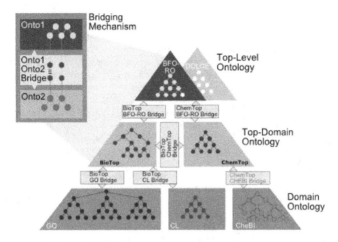

Figure 7.4: BioTop's Architecture, which links to both DOLCE and BFO-RO and small 'bridge' ontologies to link the modules. (Source: http://www.imbi.uni-freiburg.de/ontology/biotop).

Review question 7.2. Name two modelling considerations going from conceptual data model to ontology.

Review question 7.3. Name the type of relations in a thesaurus.

Review question 7.4. What are some of the issues one has to deal with when developing an ontology bottom-up using a thesaurus?

Review question 7.5. What are the two ways one can use NLP for ontology development?

Review question 7.6. Machine learning was said to use inductive methods. Recall what that means and how it differs from deductive methods.

Review question 7.7. The least common subsumer and most specific concept use non-standard reasoning services that helps with ontology development. Describe in your own words what they do.

Exercise 7.1. Examine Figure 7.6 and answer the following questions.
   a. Represent the depicted knowledge in an OWL ontology.
   b. Can you represent all knowledge? If not: what not?
   c. Are there any problems with the original conceptual data model? If so, which one(s)?

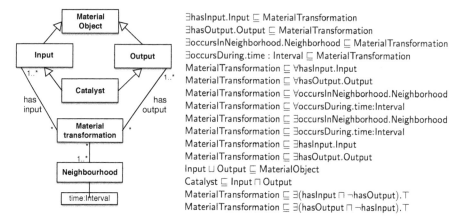

∃hasInput.Input ⊑ MaterialTransformation
∃hasOutput.Output ⊑ MaterialTransformation
∃occursInNeighborhood.Neighborhood ⊑ MaterialTransformation
∃occursDuring.time : Interval ⊑ MaterialTransformation
MaterialTransformation ⊑ ∀hasInput.Input
MaterialTransformation ⊑ ∀hasOutput.Output
MaterialTransformation ⊑ ∀occursInNeighborhood.Neighborhood
MaterialTransformation ⊑ ∀occursDuring.time:Interval
MaterialTransformation ⊑ ∃occursInNeighborhood.Neighborhood
MaterialTransformation ⊑ ∃occursDuring.time:Interval
MaterialTransformation ⊑ ∃hasInput.Input
MaterialTransformation ⊑ ∃hasOutput.Output
Input ⊔ Output ⊑ MaterialObject
Catalyst ⊑ Input ⊓ Output
MaterialTransformation ⊑ ∃(hasInput ⊓ ¬hasOutput).⊤
MaterialTransformation ⊑ ∃(hasOutput ⊓ ¬hasInput).⊤

Figure 7.5: Example of a content OP represented informally on the left in UML class diagram style notion and formally on the right. There is a further extension to this OPD described in [VKC+16] as well as several instantiations.

Exercise 7.2. Figure 7.7 shows a very simple conceptual data model in roughly UML class diagram notation: a partition [read: disjoint, complete] of employees between clerks and managers, plus two more subclasses of employee, namely rich employee and poor employee, that are disjoint from the clerk and the manager classes, respectively (box with cross). All the subclasses have the salary attribute restricted to a string of length 8, except for the clerk entity that has the salary attribute restricted to be a string of length 5. Another conceptual data model, in ORM2 notation (which is a so-called attribute-free language), is depicted in Figure 7.8, which is roughly similar.

    a. When you reason over the conceptual data model in Figure 7.7, you will find it has an inconsistent class and one new subsumption relation. Which class is inconsistent and what subsumes what (that is not already explicitly declared)? Try to find out manually, and check your answer by representing the diagram in an OWL ontology and run the reasoner to find out.

    b. Develop a proper ontology that can handle both conceptual data models. Consider the issue of how deal with attributes and add the information that clerks work for at most 3 projects and managers manage at least one project.

Exercise 7.3. Consider the small section of the Educational Resources

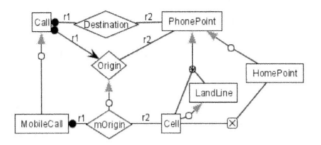

Figure 7.6: A small conceptual model in ICom (from its website http://www.inf.unibz.it/~franconi/~icom; see [FFT12] for further details about the tool); blob: mandatory, open arrow: functional; square with star: disjoint complete, square with cross: disjoint, closed arrow (grey triangle): subsumption.

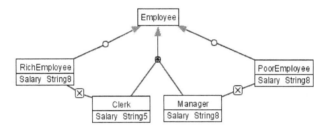

Figure 7.7: A small conceptual model in ICom (Source: http://www.inf.unibz.it/~franconi/~icom).

Information Center thesaurus, below.

    a. In which W3C-standardised (Semantic Web) language would you represent it, and why?

    b. Are all BT/NT assertions subsumption relations?

    c. There is an online tool that provides a semi-automatic approach to developing a domain ontology in OWL starting from SKOS. Find it. Why is it *semi*-automatic and can that be made fully automatic (and if so, how)?

```
Popular Culture
    BT Culture
        NT n/a
            RT Globalization
            RT Literature
            RT Mass Media
```

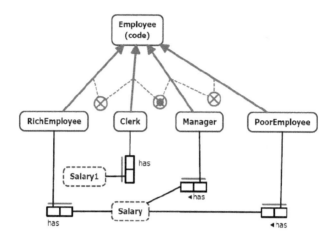

Figure 7.8: A small conceptual model in ORM2, similar to that in Figure 7.7.

```
                    RT Media Literacy
                    RT Films
                          UF Mass Culture (2004)
Mass Media
      BT n/a
            NT Films
            NT News Media
            NT Radio
                  RT Advertising
                  RT Propaganda
                  RT Publications;
                        UF Multichannel Programing (1966 1980) (2004)
Propaganda
      BT Communication (Thought Transfer)
      BT Information Dissemination
            NT n/a
                  RT Advertising
                  RT Deception
                  RT Mass Media
                        UF n/a
```

Exercise 7.4. In what way(s) may data mining be useful in bottom-up ontology development? Your answer should include something about the following three aspects:

a. populating the TBox (learning classes and hierarchies, relationships, constraints),

b. populating the ABox (assertions about instances), and

c. possible substitutes or additions to the standard automated reasoning service (consistency checking, instance classification, etc.).

Exercise 7.5. Define a pattern for how to represent attributions with DOLCE's Quality rather than an OWL data property.

Exercise 7.6. OWL permits only binary object properties, though n-aries can be approximated. Describe how they can be approximated, and how your OP would look like such that, when given to a fellow student, s/he can repeat the modelling of that n-ary exactly the way you did it and add other n-aries in the same way.

Exercise 7.7. Inspect the Novel Abilities and Disabilities OntoLogy for ENhancing Accessibility: ADOLENA; Figure 7.9 provides a basic informal overview. Can (any of) this be engineered into an ODP? If so, which type(s), how, what information is needed to document an OP?

Exercise 7.8. Figure 7.5 shows a content OP. How would you *evaluate* whether this is a good ODP? In doing so, describe your reasoning why it is, or is not, a good ODP.

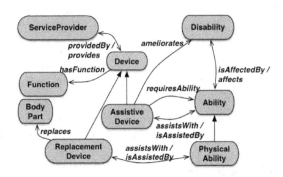

Figure 7.9: Informal view of the ADOLENA ontology.

Exercise 7.9. Discuss the feasibility of the following combinations of requirements for an ontology-driven information system (and make an informed guess about the unknowns):

a. Purpose: science; Language: OWL 2 DL, or an extension thereof; Reuse: foundational; Bottom up: form textbook models; Reasoning services: standard and non-standard.

b. Purpose: querying data through an ontology; Language: some OWL 2; Reuse: reference; Bottom up: physical database schemas and tagging; Reasoning services: ontological and querying.

c. Purpose: ontology-driven NLP; Language: OWL 2 EL; Reuse: unknown; Bottom up: a thesaurus and tagging experiments; Reasoning services: mainly just querying.

You may wish to consult [Kee10a] for a table about dependencies, or argue upfront first.

Exercise 7.10. You are an ontology consultant and have to advise the clients on ontology development for the following scenario. What would your advice be, assuming there are sufficient resources to realize it? Consider topics such as language, reasoning services, bottom-up, top-down, methods/methodologies.

> A pharmaceutical company is in the process of developing a drug to treat blood infections. There are about 100 candidate-chemicals in stock, categorised according to the BigPharma-ChemicalsThesaurus, and they need to find out whether it meets their specification of the 'ideal' drug, codename DruTopiate, that has the required features to treat that disease (they already know that DruTopiate must have as part a benzene ring, must be water-soluble, smaller than 1 μm, etc). Instead of finding out by trial-and-error and test all 100 chemicals in the lab in costly experiments, they want to filter out candidate chemicals by automatic classification according to those DruTopiate features, and then experiment only with the few that match the desired properties. This *in silico* (on-the-computer) biomedical research is intended as a pilot study, and it is hoped that the successes obtained in related works, such as that of the protein phosphatases and ideal rubber molecules, can be achieved also in this case.

7.8 Literature and reference material

A small selection of sample articles are the following ones, noting that there are, at the time of writing no 'common reference papers' on the topic:

1. L. Lubyte, S. Tessaris. Automatic Extraction of Ontologies Wrapping Relational Data Sources. In *Proc. of the 20th International Conference on Database and Expert Systems Applications (DEXA 2009)*.

2. Witte, R. Kappler, T. And Baker, C.J.O. Ontology design for biomedical text mining. In: *Semantic Web: revolutionizing knowledge discovery in the life sciences*, Baker, C.J.O., Cheung, H. (eds), Springer: New York, 2007, pp 281-313.

3. Dagobert Soergel, Boris Lauser, Anita Liang, Frehiwot Fisseha, Johannes Keizer and Stephen Katz. Reengineering thesauri for new applications: the AGROVOC example. *Journal of Digital Information* 4(4) (2004).

4. SKOS Core[8], SKOS Core guide[9], and the SKOS Core Vocabulary Specification[10].

---

[8]http://www.w3.org/2004/02/skos/core
[9]http://www.w3.org/TR/swbp-skos-core-guide
[10]http://www.w3.org/TR/swbp-skos-core-spec

Part III

Advanced topics in ontology engineering

Introduction

There are a myriad of advanced topics in ontology engineering, of which most require an understanding of both the logic foundations and of the modelling and engineering, albeit that each subtopic may put more emphasis on one aspect than another. A textbook at an introductory level cannot possibly cover all the specialised subtopics. Those included in this Block III aim to give an impression of the many possible directions with very distinct flavours and interests. They could have been other topics as well, and it was not easy to make a selection. For instance, machine learning is currently popular, and it is being used in ontology engineering, yet has not been included. Likewise, ontology mapping and alignment has a set of theories, methods, and tools drawing from various disciplines and topics that is of interest (graph matching, similarity measures, language technologies). Perhaps readers are interested in learning more about the various applications of ontologies in ontology-driven information systems to be motivated more thanks to demonstrations of some more concrete benefits of ontologies in IT and computing. I do have reasons for including the ones that have been included, though.

Ontology-Based Data Access could be seen as an application scenario of ontologies, yet it is also intricately linked with ontology engineering due to the representation limitations to achieve scalability, the sort of automated reasoning one does with it, handling the ABox, and querying ontologies, which can be done but hasn't been mentioned at all so far. That is, it adds new theory, methods, and tools into an ontology engineer's 'knapsack'. It principally provides an answer to the question:

- How can I have a very large ABox in my knowledge base and still have good performance?

The second topic (in Chapter 9) is of an entirely different nature compared to OBDA and brings afore two ontology development issues that have so far been ignored as well:

- What to do if one would want, say, the AWO not in English, or have it in several languages, like name the class Isilwane or Dier rather than Animal, and manage it all with several natural languages?

- How can one interact with domain experts in natural language, so that they can provide knowledge and verify that what has been represented in the ontology is what they want to have in there, without them having to learn logic?

That is, there is an interaction between ontologies and natural language, which oftentimes cannot be ignored.

A different topic is the tension between the expressivity of the logic and what one would like to—or need to—represent. Indeed, we have come across the DOL framework (Section 4.3.2), but that does neither cover all possibilities (yet), nor doe sit make immediately clear how to represent advanced features. For instance, what if the knowledge is not 'crisp', i.e. either true or false, but may be true *to a degree*? Or if one has used machine learning and induced some x, then that will be *probabilistically* true and it may be nicer to represent that uncertainty aspect in the ontology as well. Also, one of the BFO 2.x versions squeezed notions of time in the labels of the object properties (recall Section 6.1.2), but OWL is not temporal, so, logically, those labels have no effect whatsoever. Language extensions to some fragment of OWL and to DLs have been proposed, as there are requests for features to represent such knowledge and reason over it. The main question this strand of research tries to answer is:

- In what way(s) can ontology languages deal with, or be extended with, language features, such a time and vagueness, so that one also can use those extensions in automated reasoning (cf. workarounds with labels)?

That is, this topic has a tight interaction between modelling something even more precisely—obtaining a better quality ontology—and not just availability of language features and tinkering with workarounds, but actually getting them.

As mentioned in the introduction of the book, one can read either chapter in any order, as they do not depend on each other. They are short chapters and could perhaps have been combined into one large chapter with several sections, but that did not look nice aesthetically. Also, it is easier for lectures to cover a whole chapter at once and cover one topic at a time (though noting that each topic easily can cover more than one lecture).

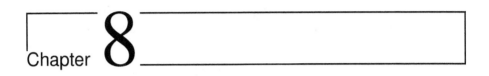

Chapter 8

Ontology-Based Data Access

Blocks I and II were rather theoretical in the sense that we have not seen many practical application infrastructures with ontologies. This is set to change in this chapter. We shall look at both theoretical foundations of *ontology-based data access* (OBDA) and one of its realisations, and you will set up an OBDA system yourself as an exercise. Also, this chapter will provide some technical details of the EPNet example of food in the Mediterranean [CLM+16] that was briefly described in Section 1.3.2 as an example of ontologies for data integration in the humanities.

From an education perspective, there are several 'starting points' for introducing OBDA, for it depends on one's background how one looks at it. The short description is that it links an OWL file (the 'ontology' in the TBox) to lots of data in a relational database (the 'Abox') by means of a newly introduced mapping layer, which subsequently can be used for automated reasoner-enhanced 'intelligent' queries. The sneer quotes on 'ontology' have to do with the fact that, practically, the 'ontology' is a logic-based simple conceptual data model formalised in ±OWL 2 QL. The sneer quotes on 'intelligent' refer to the fact that with the knowledge represented in the ontology/conceptual data model and an OBDA-enabled reasoner, one can pose more advanced queries to the database in an easier way in some cases than with just a plain relational database and SQL (although at the same time, one cannot use all of SQL).

In any case, in this chapter we divert from the "we don't really care about expressivity and scalability" of Block II to a setting that is driven

207

by the need for scalability of ontology-driven information systems. We start with some motivations why one should care (Section 8.1). There are many way to address the issues of query formulation and management, and several design choices are available even within the OBDA approach alone; they are described in Section 8.2. Sections 8.3 and 8.4 describe one of the architectures and its principal components.

8.1 Introduction: Motivations

To motivate the need for some version of an OBDA system, we start with two perspectives: the (end-)user and the database administrator.

A database administrator's perspective

Organisations normally have multiple database to store and manage their data; e.g., a PeopleSoft applications for student, course, degree, and grade management at a university, a database with employee data, a course management system like Moodle or Sakai for the university's course content management, and so on. Or take a city's public administration that wants to develop integrated services delivery and the separate databases of the individual services have to be integrated from separate electricity, sewerage, water, refuse collection, and cadastre databases. Health information systems sometimes need to be kept separate for privacy reasons, yet at the same time, some cross-database queries have to be executed. Hence, the databases have to be connected in some way, and doing all that manually is a tedious, time-consuming task in any case. Moreover, as database administrator, you will have to know *how* the data is stored in the database, write (very) large queries that can span pages, and there is no management for recurring queries.

Instead of knowing the structure of the database(s) by heart to construct such large queries, one can reduce the cognitive (over-)load by focusing only on *what* is in the database, without having to care about if, say, the class Student has a separate table or not, whether it uses the full name student or perhaps an abbreviation, like stud or stdnt, or whether the data about students is split into more than one table in more than one database. Provided the database was developed properly, there is a conceptual data model that has exactly the representation of what kind of data is stored in the database. Traditionally it is offline and shelved after the first implementation. However, this need not be the case, and OBDA can fill this gap.

The case from the viewpoint of the user

Did you ever not want to bother knowing how the data is stored in a database, but simply want to know what kind of things are stored in the database at, say, the conceptual layer? And did you ever not want to bother having to learn SQL in order to write queries in SQL (or, in the context of the Semantic Web, SPARQL), but have a graphical point-and-click interface with which you can compose a query using that 'what layer' of knowledge or some natural language interface such that the system will generate automatically the SQL query for you, in the correct syntax? (And all that not with a downloaded desktop application but in a Web browser?) Frustrated with rigid canned queries and pre-computed queries that limit your freedom to analyse the data? You don't want to keep on bothering the sysadmin for application layer updates to meet your whims and be dependent on whether she has time for your repeated requests?

Several domain experts in genetics, healthcare informatics, and oil processing, at least, wanted that and felt constrained in what they could do with their data, including at least pondering about, if not full desperation with, the so-called "write-only" databases. Especially in the biology and biomedical fields, there has been much ontology development as well as generation of much data, in parallel, which somehow has to be linked up again.

The notions of *query by diagram* or *conceptual queries* might fill this gap. These ideas are not new [CS94, BH96, BH97, SGJR+17], but now the technologies exist to realise it, even through a web interface and with reasoner-enabled querying. So, now one can do a sophisticated analysis of one's data and unlock new information from the database by using the OBDA approach. In one experiment, this resulted in the users—scientists conducting *in silico* experiments—coming up with new queries not thought of asking before [CKN+10].

8.2   OBDA design choices

Regardless whether you needed the motivation, the commonality of both cases described in the previous section is that it tries to 'cut out' several processes that were hitherto done manually by automating them, which is one of the core aims of computing. In essence, the aim is to link the knowledge layer to the data layer that contains gigabytes or even terabytes of data, and in some way still obtain inferences. From a knowledge engineering viewpoint, this is "logic-based knowledge representation + lots of data" where the latter is relegated to secondary storage rather than kept in the OWL file. From a database perspective, this is seen as "databases + background knowledge" where the latter happens to have been represented an OWL file. The following example illustrates how the knowledge can make a difference.

Example 8.1. *Consider we have the following:*
Prof(Mkhize)   *//explicit data represented and stored in a database*
Prof ⊑ Employee   *// knowledge represented in the ontology*
Then what is the answer to the query "list all employees"? In a database-only setting, it will tell you that there are no employees, i.e., return {}. *In the ontology-only setting, it wouldn't know if there are none. With the ontology + database, it will infer* Employee(Mkhize) *and return* {Mkhize} *as answer, which is what one may have expected intuitively by reading the example.* ◇

The question then becomes: how to combine the two? Data complexity for OWL 2 DL is decidable but open, and for query complexity the decidability is open (recall Table 4.2.4). Put differently: this is bad news. There are two ways we can restrict things to get the eventual algorithms 'well-behaved' for scalability:

1. Restrict the TBox somehow, i.e., decrease the expressivity of the language (at the cost of what one can model); within this option, there are two variants:

   v1: Incorporate the relevant parts of the TBox into the query and evaluate the query over a completed ABox;

   v2: Rewrite the query as needed, incorporate the TBox into the ABox, and then evaluate the query.

2. Restrict the queries one can ask in such a way that they are only those whose answer do *not* depend on the choice of model of the combination of the TBox + ABox.

First of all, when we're considering limiting the TBox, we end up with some minimalist language like OWL 2 QL or one of the DL-Lite flavours underpinning OWL 2 QL. Then, what does v1 and v2 mean for our example above? This is illustrated in the following example.

Example 8.2. *Consider again the query "list all employees" with the following:*
Prof(Mkhize)   *//explicit data represented and stored in a database*
Prof ⊑ Employee   *// knowledge represented in the ontology*
Option v1 will first notice Employee*'s subclass,* Prof*. It will then rewrite the query so as to ask for all instances of both* Employee *and* Prof*. It then returns* {Mkhize} *as answer.*

Option v2 first will notice Prof(Mkhize)*, and it sees* Prof*'s superclass* Employee*. It will extend the database with a new assertion,* Employee(Mkhize)*. Then it will try to answer the original query. It now sees* Employee(Mkhize) *and will return* {Mkhize} *as answer.* ◇

Does this difference in process matter? Of course, it does. There are advantages and disadvantages, as shown in Table 8.1: having to re-compute the whole extended database can be time-consuming, as is using the knowledge of the TBox to rewrite the query. Option 1 v1 is used more often, and we'll see the technicalities of it in the remainder of the chapter[1].

Option 2 tends to be more used in the database world for database's physical design, data structures, query optimisation, and materialised views [TW11].

8.3   An OBDA Architecture

Among the options described in the previous section, the architecture with its components that we will look at here are an example of Option 1 v1 [CGL+07]. The intuitive idea for solving the sysadmin issues is depicted in Figure 8.1, top-half (in blue): we add a "semantic layer" to a traditional database, or: we have a semantic layer and store information

---

[1]More details about the options can be found in[CGL+07, KLT+10, LTW09]

Table 8.1: Comparing v1 and v2 of the 'restrict your ontology language' option.

	v1 (query rewriting)	v2 (data completion)
Queries	rewriting is exponential in $|Query|$	data only grows polynomially in $|ABox|$
Updates	applies to original data	needs to rematerialise the data completion

about all individuals in the knowledge base not in the OWL ABox but in external storage (a relational database) and create a new link between the OWL TBox and the data store.

There are different tools for each component that make up a realised OBDA system. For instance, one can choose less or no reasoning, such as the Virtuoso system[2], and an RDF triple store versus relational database technology to store the data. We shall take a look at the OBDA system (and theory behind it) that was developed at "La Sapienza" University in Rome and Free University of Bozen-Bolzano, Italy, which is described in [CGL+09][3].

Its principal ingredients are:

- Formal language: a language in the *DL-Lite* family, (roughly OWL 2 QL);
- OBDA-enabled reasoner: e.g., QuOnto [ACDG+05], Quest [RMC12];
- Data storage: an RDBMS, e.g., Oracle, PostgreSQL, DB2;
- Developer interface: OWL ontology development environment, such as Protégé and an OBDA plugin [RMLC08], to manage the mappings and data access, and a developer API facing toward the application to be developed;
- End-user interface: OBDA plugin for Protégé for SPARQL queries[4] and results [RMLC08], and, optionally, a system for graphical

---

[2] http://virtuoso.openlinksw.com/, used for, among others DBPedia

[3] The latest version is *Ontop* [CCKE+17], which has more features, but introducing those here as well would distract for the core principles. It also compares Ontop to other OBDA and SPARQL query answering systems and lists where the system has been used in academia and industry.

[4] SPARQL is a query language, alike SQL but then for querying OWL and RDF. The W3C specification of SPARQL can be found at http://www.w3.org/TR/rdf-sparql-query/.

querying (e.g., [CKN$^+$10, SKZ$^+$ss]).
This is shown schematically in Figure 8.1, bottom-half.

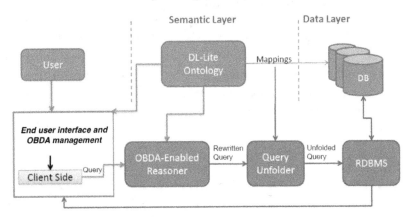

Figure 8.1: OBDA approach and some practical components (bottom-half): the relational database, mappings, an ontology, a reasoner, and a user interface both to hide the technicalities from the end-user and a way for the OBDA administrator to manage the ontology and mapping layer.

8.4 Principal components

The theoretical details are quite involved, and relevant papers span hundreds of pages. In essence, there are two principal aspects to it:

1. Ontology-Based Data Access systems (static components):
   - An ontology language, for representing the ontology
   - A mapping language, for declaring the mappings between vocabulary in the ontology and the data
   - The data

2. Query answering in Ontology-Based Data Access systems:
   - Reasoning over the TBox
   - Query rewriting
   - Query unfolding
   - Relational database technology

The mapping language and the items under 2 are new notions compared Blocks I and II and a regular database course, which will be described in the following subsections.

The ontology language

For the language, we remain, roughly, within the Semantic Web setting, and take a closer look at the OWL 2 QL profile and similar languages in the "DL-lite" family that is at the basis of OWL 2 QL, and *DL-Lite$_A$* in particular [CGL$^+$07]. Most significantly, the trade-off between expressive power and computational complexity of the reasoning services leans strongly towards the scalability of reasoning (including query answering) over large amounts of data; or: one can't say a lot with either OWL 2 QL or *DL-Lite$_A$*.

Syntax of *DL-Lite$_A$*.   As is common in DLs and OWL, we distinguish between (abstract) objects and (data) values. A *class expression* denotes a set of objects, a *datatype* denotes a set of values, an *object property* denotes a binary relationship between objects, and a *data property* denotes a binary relation between objects and values. We assume to have a set $\{T_1, \ldots, T_n\}$ of pairwise disjoint and unbounded datatypes, each denoting a set $val(T_i)$ of values (integers, strings, etc.), and $\top_d$ denotes the set of all values. Class expressions, C, and object property expressions, R, are formed according to the following syntax, where A denotes a class, P an object property, and U a data property:

$$C \longrightarrow A \mid \exists R \mid \delta(U), \qquad R \longrightarrow P \mid P^-.$$

Observe that $\exists R$ denotes an unqualified existential class expression, $\delta(U)$ denotes the domain of U, and P^- denotes the inverse of P.

A *DL-Lite$_A$* ontology $\mathcal{O} = \langle \mathcal{T}, \mathcal{A} \rangle$, consists of a TBox $\mathcal{T}$ and an ABox $\mathcal{A}$, where the TBox is constituted by a set of *axioms* of the form

$$C_1 \sqsubseteq C_2, \quad \rho(U) \sqsubseteq T_i, \quad R_1 \sqsubseteq R_2, \quad U_1 \sqsubseteq U_2,$$
$$(\mathsf{disj}\ C_1\ C_2), \qquad\qquad (\mathsf{disj}\ R_1\ R_2), \quad (\mathsf{disj}\ U_1\ U_2),$$
$$(\mathsf{funct}\ R), \qquad (\mathsf{funct}\ U).$$

The axioms in the first row denote *inclusions*, with $\rho(U)$ the range of U. The axioms in the second row denote *disjointness*; note that distinct datatypes are assumed to be disjoint. The axioms in the third row denote *functionality* (at most one) of an object property expression and of a data property expression, respectively. The ABox is constituted by a set of *assertions* of the form $A(a)$, $P(a, a')$, and $U(a, \ell)$, where a, a' are individuals denoting objects and ℓ is a literal (denoting a value).

To ensure that *DL-Lite*$_A$ maintains the computationally well-behaved computational properties of the *DL-Lite* family [CGL$^+$07], the form of the TBox has to be restricted (as we have seen for OWL 2 QL in Chapter 3). In particular, object and data properties occurring in functionality assertions cannot be specialized, i.e., the cannot appear in the right hand side of an inclusion axiom.

Semantics of *DL-Lite*$_A$. The semantics of *DL-Lite*$_A$ is based on first-order *interpretations* $\mathcal{I} = (\Delta^{\mathcal{I}}, \cdot^{\mathcal{I}})$, where $\Delta^{\mathcal{I}}$ is a nonempty interpretation domain, which is partitioned into a $\Delta^{\mathcal{I}}_O$ of objects, and a $\Delta^{\mathcal{I}}_V$ of values. The interpretation function $\cdot^{\mathcal{I}}$ maps each individual a to $a^{\mathcal{I}} \in \Delta^{\mathcal{I}}_O$, each class A to $A^{\mathcal{I}} \subseteq \Delta^{\mathcal{I}}_O$, each object property P to $P^{\mathcal{I}} \subseteq \Delta^{\mathcal{I}}_O \times \Delta^{\mathcal{I}}_O$, and each data property U to $U^{\mathcal{I}} \subseteq \Delta^{\mathcal{I}}_O \times \Delta^{\mathcal{I}}_V$, whereas each literal ℓ is interpreted as the value $\ell^{\mathcal{I}} = val(\ell)$, each datatype T_i as the set of values $T_i^{\mathcal{I}} = val(T_i)$, and $\mathsf{T}^{\mathcal{I}}_d = \Delta^{\mathcal{I}}_V$. The semantics of expressions:

$$(\exists R)^{\mathcal{I}} = \{o \mid \exists o'. (o, o') \in R^{\mathcal{I}}\}, \qquad (P^-)^{\mathcal{I}} = \{(o, o') \mid (o', o) \in P^{\mathcal{I}}\},$$

$$(\delta(U))^{\mathcal{I}} = \{o \mid \exists v. (o, v) \in U^{\mathcal{I}}\}, \qquad (\rho(U))^{\mathcal{I}} = \{v \mid \exists o. (o, v) \in U^{\mathcal{I}}\}.$$

Contrary to OWL, *DL-Lite*$_A$ (and its implementation) adopts the *unique name assumption*, meaning that for every interpretation $\mathcal{I}$ and distinct individuals or values c_1, c_2, we have that $c_1^{\mathcal{I}} \neq c_2^{\mathcal{I}}$ (which is the norm in the database setting).

As for other DLs and OWL species, $\mathcal{I}$ *satisfies* $\alpha_1 \sqsubseteq \alpha_2$ if $\alpha_1^{\mathcal{I}} \subseteq \alpha_2^{\mathcal{I}}$, it satisfies (disj α_1 α_2) if $\alpha_1^{\mathcal{I}} \cap \alpha_2^{\mathcal{I}} = \emptyset$, and it satisfies (funct S) if $S^{\mathcal{I}}$ is a function (that is, if $(o, z_1) \in S^{\mathcal{I}}$ and $(o, z_2) \in S^{\mathcal{I}}$, then $z_1 = z_2$)). $\mathcal{I}$ satisfies $A(a)$ if $a^{\mathcal{I}} \in A^{\mathcal{I}}$, it satisfies $P(a, a')$ if $(a^{\mathcal{I}}, a'^{\mathcal{I}}) \in P^{\mathcal{I}}$, and it satisfies $U(a, \ell)$ if $(a^{\mathcal{I}}, val(\ell)) \in U^{\mathcal{I}}$.

Mappings

Here, a few definitions and an example is included; the chapter literature contains further technical details and more examples of mappings.

Definition 8.1 (Mapping assertion between a database and a TBox). *A mapping assertion between a database $\mathcal{D}$ and a TBox $\mathcal{T}$ has the form $\Phi \rightsquigarrow \Psi$ where*

- Φ *is an arbitrary SQL query of arity $n > 0$ over $\mathcal{D}$;*

- Ψ is a conjunctive query over $\mathcal{T}$ of arity $n' > 0$ without non-distinguished variables, possibly involving variable terms.

Definition 8.2 (Mapping assertion in $\mathcal{M}$ in an OBDA system). *A mapping assertion between a database $\mathcal{D}$ and a TBox $\mathcal{T}$ in $\mathcal{M}$ has the form $\Phi(\vec{x}) \leadsto \Psi(\vec{t}, \vec{y})$ where*

- Φ is an arbitrary SQL query of arity $n > 0$ over $\mathcal{D}$;
- Ψ is a conjunctive query over $\mathcal{T}$ of arity $n' > 0$ without non-distinguished variables;
- $\vec{x}, \vec{y}$ are variables with $\vec{y} \subseteq \vec{x}$;
- $\vec{t}$ are variable terms of the form $f(\vec{z})$, with $f \in \Lambda$ and $\vec{z} \subseteq \vec{x}$.

Concerning the the semantics of mappings, intuitively: $\mathcal{I}$ satisfies $\Phi \leadsto \Psi$ with respect to $\mathcal{D}$ if all facts obtained by evaluating Φ over $\mathcal{D}$ and then propagating answers to Ψ, hold in $\mathcal{I}$.

Definition 8.3 (Satisfaction of a mapping assertion with respect to a database). *An interpretation $\mathcal{I}$ satisfies a mapping assertion $\Phi(\vec{x}) \leadsto \Psi(\vec{t}, \vec{y})$ in $\mathcal{M}$ with respect to a database $\mathcal{D}$, if for each tuple of values $\vec{v} \in Eval(\Phi, \mathcal{D})$, and for each ground atom in $\Psi[\vec{x}/\vec{v}]$, we have that:*

- *If the ground atom is $A(s)$, then $s^{\mathcal{I}} \in A^{\mathcal{I}}$;*
- *If the ground atom is $P(s_1, s_2)$, then $(s_1^{\mathcal{I}}, s_2^{\mathcal{I}}) \in P^{\mathcal{I}}$.*

(Note: $Eval(\Phi, \mathcal{D})$ denotes the result of evaluating Φ over $\mathcal{D}$, $\Psi[\vec{x}/\vec{v}]$ denotes Ψ where each x_i is substituted with v_i)

An example is shown in Figure 8.2 with the OBDA plugin for Protégé. There is an ontology that happens to have a class PromiscuousBacterium, among other things, and a relational database (HGT) with several tables, such as organisme and flexcount. Now we have to link the two with a mapping, which means (i) constructing a database query such that it retrieves only the promiscuous bacteria, and (ii) solving the 'impedance mismatch' (recollect Chapter 7) with a functor so that the values returned by the database query become objects in the ontology, which is what getPromBact does. Informally, the functor can be considered as a URI building mechanism for individuals in the ontology taken from the database (theoretically, they are skolem functions).

Query answering

Recall the outline of the ADOLENA ontology from the exercise and Figure 7.9. A query could be "retrieve the devices that ameliorate paraplegia"

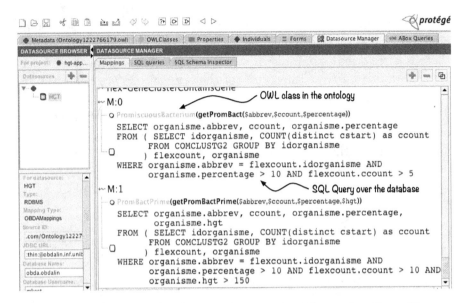

Figure 8.2: An example of a mapping; see text for explanation. (Source: based on [Kee10c])

```
q(x) :- Device(x), ameliorates(x,y), Paraplegia(y)
```
For this to work, we have to introduce three aspects. First, we need a computer-processable serialization of the query, a notion of what kind of queries we can pose, and a way how it will do the answering. The query language is SPARQL (see footnote 4). The kind of queries are (unions of) conjunctive queries. A conjunctive query (CQ) q over an ontology $\mathcal{O}$ is an expression of the form $q(\vec{x}) \leftarrow \exists \vec{y}.conj(\vec{x}, \vec{y})$, where $q(\vec{x})$ the head, $conj(\vec{x}, \vec{y})$ the body, the variables in $\vec{x}$ are distinguished variables and $\vec{y}$ the non-distinguished variables, and where $conj(\vec{x}, \vec{y})$ is a conjunction of atoms of the form $D(z)$, $S(z, z')$, $z = z'$, where D denotes a class or a datatype, S an object property or data property in $\mathcal{O}$, and z, z' are individuals or literals in $\mathcal{O}$ or variables in $\vec{x}$ or $\vec{y}$. Given an interpretation $\mathcal{I} = (\Delta^{\mathcal{I}}, \cdot^{\mathcal{I}})$, then $q^{\mathcal{I}}$ is the set of tuples of $\Delta^{\mathcal{I}}$ that, when assigned to the variables $\vec{x}$, make the formula $\exists \vec{y}.conj(\vec{x}, \vec{y})$ true in $\mathcal{I}$. The set $cert(q, \mathcal{O})$—certain answers to q over $\mathcal{O}$—is the set of tuples $\vec{a}$ of individuals or literals appearing in $\mathcal{O}$ such that $\vec{a}^{\mathcal{I}} \in q^{\mathcal{I}}$, for every model $\mathcal{I}$ of $\mathcal{O}$.

Regarding query answering, consider Figure 8.3, where q is our query, $\mathcal{T}$ the TBox (ontology or formal conceptual data model), and $\mathcal{A}$ the

ABox (our instances, practically stored in the relational database). Somehow, this combines to produce the answers, using all components. First, there is a "reformulation" (or: rewriting) step, which computes the perfect reformulation (rewriting), q_{pr}, of the original query q using the inclusion assertions of $\mathcal{T}$ so that we have a union of conjunctive queries. That is, it uses the knowledge of the ontology to come up with the 'real' query. For instance, recollect Figure 7.9 about the ontology of abilities and disabilities, then a query "retrieve all Devices that assistWith UpperLimbMobility", i.e.,

    q(x) :- Device(x), assistsWith(x,y), UpperLimbMobility(y)
or, in SPARQL notation:
    SELECT $device
       WHERE {$device rdf:type :Device.
              $device :assistsWith $y.
              $y rdf:type :UpperLimbMobility}
will traverse the hierarchy of devices until it finds those devices that have an object property declared with as range UpperLimbMobility. In this case, this is MotorisedWheelchair, hence, the 'real' query concerns only the retrieval of the motorised wheelchairs, not first retrieving all devices and then making the selection.

Second, the "unfolding" step computes a new query, q_{unf}, by using the (split version of) the mappings that link the terms of the ontology to queries over the database.

Third, the "evaluation" step delegates the evaluation of q_{unf} to the relational DBMS managing the data, which subsequently returns the answer.

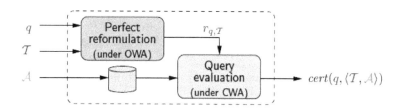

Figure 8.3: Intuition of the top-down approach to query answering.

Examples

Early trials and tribulations of trying to set up an OBDA system (and of which I know the details) are described in [KAGC08] and [CKN⁺10], which provided useful learning moments [CCKE⁺17]. The ontology in [KAGC08] practically was developed separately from the existing database, which caused some mismatches; or: the content in the ontology and database really should be compatible (as an aside: the query answering examples in the previous section were based on that system). This was much better aligned in the experiment described in [CKN⁺10]: the ontology was a reverse engineered physical (SQL) schema and dressed up with neater modelling, having following the steps described in Section 7.1. A downside with the knowledge of this particular scenario was that there was a considerable hierarchy, so the system ended up creating very big conjunctive queries, which slowed down the database side in actually answering the SQL query (albeit still faster than the original database). This has been optimised in the meantime, among other things [CCKE⁺17].

More recent examples from industry and with the 'next generation' OBDA, i.e., the extended *Ontop* setting, can be found in, e.g., [KHS⁺17], describing industry's motivations, mappings, a rather large SQL query, and streaming (i.e., temporal) data, and there are several references in [CCKE⁺17] that describe applications and usage of *Ontop*. It is, perhaps, also worth mentioning that OBDA has seen many people involved since the early days in 2005, and by now has been shown to be robust, albeit not a trivial matter to understand and set up from a system's development viewpoint. You can practice with this in the Chapter's exercises, as all the code and software is freely available online.

8.5 Exercises

Review question 8.1. Describe in your own words what an OBDA system is. Try to keep it short, such that you can explain it in less than 30 seconds.

Review question 8.2. What are the principal components of the OBDA system described in some detail in this chapter?

Review question 8.3. How is querying in the OBDA setting different compared to plain relational database?

Exercise 8.1. Inspect an ontology used for OBDA; e.g.,: the one of the EPnet[5] or one from the Ontop examples[6]. Consider again Section 1.2.1 regarding the differences between ontologies and conceptual models and Chapter 6 on foundational ontologies. Why does the 'ontology' in an OBDA system look more like an OWLized conceptual data model?

Exercise 8.2. You will set up an OBDA system. Consult the wiki at `https://github.com/ontop/ontop/wiki` for tutorials and sample data, and the software at `https://github.com/ontop/ontop`.

8.6   Literature and reference material

1. Diego Calvanese, Giuseppe De Giacomo, Domenico Lembo, Maurizio Lenzerini, Antonella Poggi, Mariano Rodriguez-Muro, and Riccardo Rosati. Ontologies and databases: The DL-Lite approach. In Sergio Tessaris and Enrico Franconi, editors, *Semantic Technologies for Information Systems - 5th Int. Reasoning Web Summer School (RW 2009)*, volume 5689 of Lecture Notes in Computer Science, pages 255-356. Springer, 2009.
2. Calvanese, D., Keet, C.M., Nutt, W., Rodríguez-Muro, M., Stefanoni, G. Web-based Graphical Querying of Databases through an Ontology: the WONDER System. *ACM Symposium on Applied Computing (ACM SAC'10)*, March 22-26 2010, Sierre, Switzerland.
3. D. Calvanese, P. Liuzzo, A. Mosca, J. Remesal, M. Rezk, and G. Rull. Ontology-based data integration in EPnet: Production and distribution of food during the roman empire. *Engineering Applications of Artificial Intelligence*, 51:212-229, 2016.

---

[5] `http://romanopendata.eu/sparql/doc/index.html`
[6] e.g., movies: `https://github.com/ontop/ontop/wiki/Example_MovieOntology`

Chapter 9

Ontologies and natural languages

The interaction of ontologies and natural language processing and even more so at the fundamental level—Ontology and linguistics—can be good for many conversations and debates about long-standing controversies. In this chapter, we shall focus on the former and take an engineering perspective to it[1]. In this case we can do that, because the points of disagreement are 'outside' the ontology as artefact, in a similar way as an OWL file is indifferent as to whether a human who reads the file assumes a particular OWL class to be a concept or a universal. Regardless whether you are convinced the reality is shaped, or even created, by language, or not, there are concrete issues that have to be resolved nonetheless. For instance, the OWL standard had as one of the design goals "internationalisation" (recall Section 4.1.1), which presumably means ontologies being able to handle multiple languages. How is that supposed to work? Anyone who speaks more than one language will know there are many words that do not have a simple 1:1 translation of the vocabulary. What can, or should, one do with those non-1:1 cases when translating an ontology in one's own language or from one's own language into, say, English? Where exactly is a good place to record natural language information pertaining to the vocabulary elements? Does translating an ontology into another language even make sense? The area of *multilingual ontologies* aims to find answers to such questions, which will be introduced in Section 9.1.

---

[1]Debates include the topic whether language shapes reality and therewith ontology or is used to approximate describing the world.

A quite different type of interaction between ontologies and languages is that of ontologies and Controlled Natural Language (CNL), which may avail of multilingual ontologies to a greater or lesser extent. One can *verbalise*—or: put into (pseudo-)natural language sentences— the knowledge represented in the ontology. This can be useful for, among others: interaction with domain expert during the knowledge acquisition and verification phases, automatically generating documentation about the ontology, and anywhere where the ontology is being used in an ontology-driven information system (e.g., SNOMED CT with an electronic health records system). The general idea will be described in Section 9.2.

Besides these two interactions between ontology and natural language, and the use of NLP for ontology learning that we have seen in Section 7.4. There are also areas of research and working technologies where ontologies enhance NLP applications[2]. This version of the textbook does not include a separate section on such ontology-driven information systems, however, for the scope is ontology engineering. It is duly acknowledged that some of the solutions that came out of the application areas can be useful for the aforementioned tasks, and the Semantic Web as application area in particular. This because the Web is global, so it makes sense to create a *Multilingual* Semantic Web (see also the recently published handbook [BC14]). It turned out there are some inherent problems of the original vision [BLHL01] to overcome [Hir14], and insights gained there assist with solutions for ontologies in the general case, regardless whether that is within the Semantic Web with OWL or another logic.

9.1   Toward multilingual ontologies

Let us first have a look at just one natural language and an ontology (Section 9.1.1) before complicating matters with multiple languages in Section 9.1.2.

---

[2]E.g., it has been shown to enhance precision and recall of queries (including enhancing dialogue systems [VF09]), to sort results of an information retrieval query to the digital library [DAA+08], (biomedical) text mining, and annotating textbooks for ease of navigation and automated question generation [CCO+13] as an example of adaptive e-learning.

9.1.1 Linking a lexicon to an ontology

Most, if not all, ontologies you will have inspected and all examples given in the preceding chapters simply gave a human-readable name to the DL concept or OWL class. Perhaps you have loaded an ontology in the ODE, and the class hierarchy showed numbers, alike GO:00012345, and you had to check the class's annotation what was actually meant with that cryptic identifier. This is an example of a practical difference between OBO and OWL (recall Section 7.1), which is, however, based on different underlying modelling principles. DLs assume that a concept is *identified* by the *name* given to it; that is, there is a 1:1 correspondence between what a concept, say, being a vegetarian, means and the name we give to it. Natural language and the knowledge, reality etc. are thus tightly connected and, perhaps, even conflated. Not everybody agrees with that underlying assumption. An alternative viewpoint is to assume that there are language-*independent* entities—i.e., they exist regardless whether humans name them or not—that somehow have to be identified and then one sticks one or more labels or names to it. Put differently: knowledge is one thing and natural language another, and they should be kept as distinct kinds of things.

My impression is that the second view is prevailing at least within the ontology engineering arena. To date, two engineering solutions have been proposed how to handle this in an ontology. The first one is the OBO solution, which was used since its inception in 1998 by the Gene Ontology Consortium [Gen00]: each language-independent entity gets an identifier and it must have at least one label that is human-readable. This solution clearly allows also for easy recording of synonyms, variants, and abbreviations, which were commonplace in genetics especially at the inception of the GO.

The second option emerged within the Semantic Web field [BCHM09]. It also acknowledges that distinction between the knowledge layer and the language layer, yet it places the latter explicitly *on top of* the knowledge layer. This has as effect that the solution does not 'overload' OWL's annotation fields, but proposes to store all the language and linguistic information in a *separate file* that interacts with the OWL file. How that separate file should look like, what information should be stored in it, and how it should interact with the OWL file is open to manifold possible solutions. One such proposal will be described here to illustrate how something like that may work, which is the *Lemon* model

[MdCB$^+$12, MAdCB$^+$12], of which a fragment has been accepted as a community standard by the W3C[3]. It also aims to cater for multilingual ontologies.

Consider the *Lemon* model as depicted in Figure 9.1, which depicts the kind of things one can make annotations of, and how those elements relate to each other. At the bottom-center of the figure, there is the ontology to which the language information is linked. Each vocabulary element of the ontology will have an entry in the *Lemon* file, with more or less lexical information, among others: in which sense that word is meant, what the surface string is, the POS tag (noun, noun

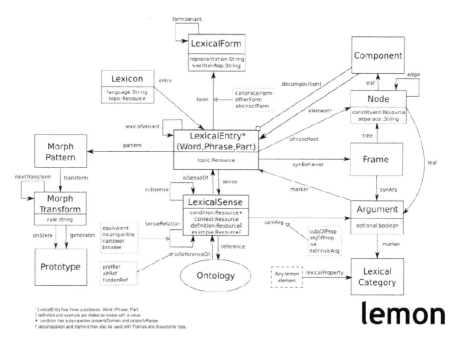

Figure 9.1: The *Lemon* model for multilingual ontologies (Source: [MdCB$^+$12])

phrase, verb etc.), gender, case and related properties (if applicable).

A simple entry in the *Lemon* file could look like this, which lists, in sequence: the location of the lexicon, the location of the ontology, the location of the *Lemon* specification, the lexical entry (including stating in which language the entry is), and then the link to the class in the OWL ontology:

---

[3]https://www.w3.org/community/ontolex/wiki/Final_Model_Specification

```
@base <http://www.example.org/lexicon>
@prefix ontology:  <http://www.example.org/AWO1#>
@prefix lemon: <http://www.monnetproject.eu/lemon#>

:myLexicon a lemon:Lexicon ;
  lemon:language "en" ;
  lemon:entry :animal .

:animal a lemon:LexicalEntry ;
  lemon:form [ lemon:writtenRep "animal"@en ] ;
  lemon:sense [ lemon:reference AWO1:animal ] .
```

One can also specify rules in the *Lemon* file, such as how to generate
the plural from a singular. However, because the approach is principally a declarative specification, it is not as well equipped at handling
rules compared to the well-established grammar systems for NLP. Also,
while *Lemon* covers a fairly wide range of language features, it may not
cover all that is needed; e.g., the noun class system emblematic for the
indigenous language spoken in a large part of sub-Saharan Africa does
not quite fit [CK14]. Nonetheless, *Lemon*, and other proposals with a
similar idea of separation of concerns, are a distinct step forward for
ontology engineering where interaction with languages is a requirement.
Such a separation of concerns is even more important when the scope
is broadened to a multilingual setting, which is the topic of the next
section.

9.1.2 Multiple natural languages

Although this textbook is written in one language, English, for it is
currently the dominant language in science, the vast majority of people
in the world speak another language and they both have information
systems in their own language as well as that they may develop an ontology in their own language, or else localise an ontology into their own
language. One could just develop the ontology in one's own language
in the same way as the examples were given in English in the previous
chapters and be done with it. But what if, say, SNOMED CT [SNO12]
should be translated in one's own language for electronic health records,
like with OpenMRS [Ope], or the ontology has to import an existing
ontology that happens to be not represented in the target language and
compatibility with the original ontology has to be maintained? What if

some named class is not translatable into one single term? For instance, in French, there are two words for the English 'river': one for a river that ends in the sea and another word for a river that doesn't (*fleuve* and *rivière*), and isiZulu has two words and corresponding meanings for the *participation* relation: one as we have see in Section 6.2 and another for participation of collectives in a process (*-hlanganyela*). The following example illustrates some actual (unsuccessful) 'struggling' trying to handle this when there is not even a name for the entity in the other language (example from [AFK12]); a more extensive list of the type of issues can be found in [LAF14].

Example 9.1. *South Africa has a project on indigenous knowledge management systems, but the example equally well can be generalised to cultural historic museum curation in any country (AI for cultural heritage). Take ingcula, which is a 'small bladed hunting spear' (in isiZulu), that has no equivalent term in English. Trying to represent it in the 'English understanding', i.e., adding it not as a single class but as a set of axioms, then one could introduce a class* Spear *that has two properties, e.g.,* Spear $\sqsubseteq$ $\exists$hasShape.Bladed $\sqcap$ $\exists$participatesIn.Hunting. *To represent the 'small', one could resort to fuzzy concepts; e.g., following* [BS11]*'s fuzzy OWL notation, then, e.g.,*

  MesoscopicSmall : Natural $\rightarrow$ [0, 1] *is a fuzzy datatype,*
  MesoscopicSmall(x) = trz$(x, 1, 5, 13, 20)$, *with* trz *the trapezoidal function,*
so that a small spear can be defined as
  SmallSpear $\equiv$ Spear $\sqcap$ $\exists$size.MesoscopicSmall
Then one can create a class in English and declare something alike
  SmallBladedHuntingSpear $\equiv$ SmallSpear $\sqcap$ $\exists$hasShape.Bladed $\sqcap$
      $\exists$participatesIn.Hunting
This is just one of the possibilities of a formalised transliteration of an English natural language description[4], not a definition of ingcula as it may appear in an ontology about indigenous knowledge of hunting.

  Let's assume for now the developer does want to go in this direction, then it requires more advanced capabilities than even lexicalised ontologies to keep the two ontologies in sync: lexicalised ontologies only link dictionaries and grammars to the ontologies, but here one now would need to map sets of axioms between ontologies. $\diamondsuit$

---

[4]Plain OWL cannot deal with this, though, for it deals with crisp knowledge only. Refer to Section 10.1.1 for some notes on fuzzy ontologies

That is, what was intended as a translation exercise ended up as a *different ontology* file at least[5]. It gets even more interesting in multilingual organisations and societies, like the European Union with over 20 languages and, e.g., South Africa that has 11 official languages, for then it would require some way of managing all those versions.

Several approaches have been proposed for the multilingual setting, for both localisation and internationalisation of the ontology with links to the original ontology and multiple languages at the same time in the same system. The simplest approach is called *semantic tagging*. This means that the ontology is developed 'in English', i.e., *naming* the vocabulary elements in one language and for other languages, labels are added, such as **Fakultät** and **Fakulteit** for the US-English **School**. This may be politically undesirable and anyhow it does not solve the issue of non-1:1 mappings of vocabulary elements. It might be a quick 'smart' solution if you're lucky (i.e., there happen to be only 1:1 mappings for the vocabulary elements in your ontology), but a solid reusable solution it certainly is not. OBO's approach of IDs and labels avoids the language politics: one ID with multiple labels for each language, so that it at least treats all the natural languages as equals.

However, both falter as soon as there is no neat 1:1 translation of a term into another single term in a different language—which is quite often the case except for very similar languages—though within the scientific realm, this is much less of an issue, where handling synonyms may be more relevant.

One step forward is a mildly "lexicalised ontology" [BCHM09], of which an example is depicted in Figure 9.2. Although it still conflates the entity and its name and promotes one language as the primary, at least the handling of other languages is much more extensive and, at least in theory, will be able to cope with multilingual ontologies to a greater extent. This is thanks to its relatively comprehensive information about the lexical aspects in its own linguistic ontology, with the **WordForm** etc., which is positioned orthogonally to the domain ontology. In Figure 9.2, the English **OralMucosa** has its equivalent in German as **Mundschleimhaut**, which is composed here of two sub-words that are nouns themselves, **Mund** 'mouth' and **Schleimhaut** 'mucosa'. It is this idea that has been made more precise and comprehensive in its successor, the *Lemon* model, that is tailored to the Semantic Web setting

---

[5]whether it is also a different conceptualisation is a separate discussion.

[MdCB$^+$12]. Indeed, the same *Lemon* from the previous section. The *Lemon* entries can become quite large for multiple languages and, as it uses RDF for the serialisation, it is not easily readable. An example for the class Cat in English, French, and German is shown diagrammatically in Figure 9.3, and two annotated short entries of the Friend Of A Friend (FOAF)[6] structured vocabulary in Chichewa (a language spoken in Malawi) are shown in Figure 9.4.

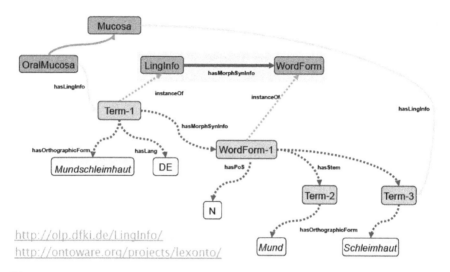

Figure 9.2: Ontologies in practice: Semantic Tagging—Lexicalized Ontologies. (Source: http://www.deri.ie/fileadmin/documents/teaching/tutorials/DERI-Tutorial-NLP.final.pdf)

There are only few tools that can cope with ontologies and multiple languages. A web-based tool for creating *Lemon* files is under development at the time of writing. It would be better if at least some version of language management were to be integrated in ODEs. At present, to the best of my knowledge, only MoKI provides such a service partially for a few languages, inclusive of a localised interface [BDFG14].

As a final note: those non-1:1 mappings of the form of having one class in ontology O_1 and one or more axioms in O_2, sets of axioms in both, like in Example 9.1 with the hunting spear, as well as non-1:1 property alignments, are feasible by now with the (mostly) theoretical

---

[6]http://xmlns.com/foaf/spec/

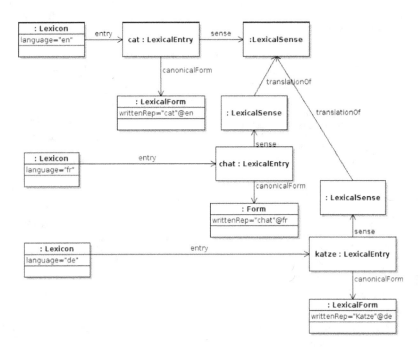

Figure 9.3: The *Lemon* model for multilingual ontologies to represent the class Cat (Source: [MdCB+12])

results presented in [FK17, Kee17b], so this *ingcula* example could be solved in theory at least. Its details are not pursued here, because it intersects with the topic of ontology alignment. Further, one may counter that an alternative might be to SKOSify it, for it would avoid the complex mapping between a named class to a set of axioms. However, then the differences would be hidden in the label of the concepts rather than solving the modelling problem.

9.2 Ontology verbalisation

The second topic of ontologies & natural language, ontology verbalisation, can build upon the previous, but need not if you happen to be interested in a grammatically 'simple' language, such as English. The core notion is to generate (pseudo-) natural language sentences from the axioms in the ontology. The introduction to Block III already noted that ontology verbalisation may be useful for, mainly:

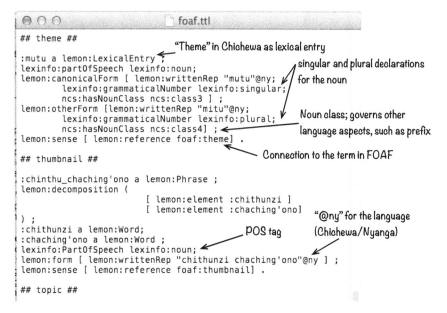

Figure 9.4: Annotated small section of part of the FOAF in Chichewa. (Source: `http://www.meteck.org/files/ontologies/foaf.ttl`, discussed in [CK14].

- Ameliorating the knowledge acquisition bottleneck; it:
  - helps the domain experts understand what exactly has been represented in the ontology, and thereby provides a means to validate that what has been represented is what was intended;
  - can be used to write axioms in pseudo-natural language, rather than the logic itself, to develop the ontology.

- Some ontology-driven information system purposes; e.g., e-learning (question generation, textbook search), readable medical information from medical terminologies in electronic health record systems.

The term 'ontology verbalisation' is rather specific and restricted, and it falls within the scope of Controlled Natural Language (CNL) and Natural Language Generation fields of research (NLG). While most papers on ontology verbalisation will not elaborate on the methodological approach specifically, there are clear parallels with the activities of the traditional NLG pipeline alike proposed in [RD97]. The pipeline is summarised in Figure 9.5, top section, and the corresponding answers for ontology verbalisation are described in the bottom section of the figure.

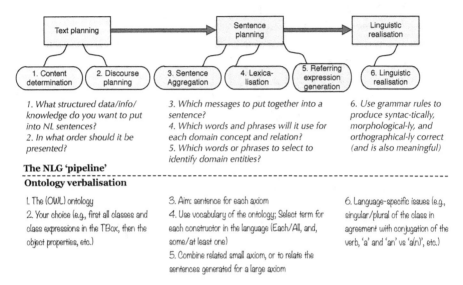

1. What structured data/info/ knowledge do you want to put into NL sentences?
2. In what order should it be presented?

The NLG 'pipeline'

3. Which messages to put together into a sentence?
4. Which words and phrases will it use for each domain concept and relation?
5. Which words or phrases to select to identify domain entities?

6. Use grammar rules to produce syntac-tically, morphological-ly, and orthographical-ly correct (and is also meaningful)

- -

Ontology verbalisation

1. The (OWL) ontology
2. Your choice (e.g., first all classes and class expressions in the TBox, then the object properties, etc.)

3. Aim: sentence for each axiom
4. Use vocabulary of the ontology; Select term for each constructor in the language (Each/All, and, some/at least one)
5. Combine related small axiom, or to relate the sentences generated for a large axiom

6. Language-specific issues (e.g., singular/plural of the class in agreement with conjugation of the verb, 'a' and 'an' vs 'a(n)', etc.)

Figure 9.5: The common NLG 'pipeline' and how that links to ontology verbalisation

9.2.1 Template-based approach

There are three principal approaches to generate the sentences: canned text, templates, and a grammar engine. The most commonly used approach for ontology verbalisation is templates, as it generally takes less effort to start with and therewith one may reap the low-hanging fruit. Let's look at two examples (analysed afterward):

(S1) **Giraffe ⊑ Animal**

<u>Each</u> Giraffe ___ Animal

(S2) **Herb ⊑ Plant**

<u>Each</u> Herb ___ Plant

The underlined text 'Each' is the natural language rendering of the silent "∀" at the start of the axioms, and 'is a(n)' for "⊑", which remain the same, and the vocabulary from the axiom is inserted on-the-fly by reading it in from the ontology file. One can construct a *template* for an axiom type with those pieces of text that remain the same for each construct, interspersed with variables that will take the appropriate entity

from the ontology. For instance, for this named class subsumption axiom type $C \sqsubseteq D$, one could declare the following template:

    Each *class*$_1$ is a(n) *class*$_2$

and for the *basic all-some* axiom type $C \sqsubseteq \exists R.D$ that we have come
across in Chapter 7, either one of the following ones may be selected:

    Each *class*$_1$ *op* at least one *class*$_2$
    Each *class*$_1$ *op* some *class*$_2$
    All *class*$_{1pl}$ *op*$_{inf}$ at least one *class*$_2$
    All *class*$_{1pl}$ *op*$_{inf}$ some *class*$_2$

The subscript "$_{pl}$" indicates that the first noun has to be pluralised
and "$_{inf}$" denotes that the object property has to be rendered in the
infinitive. The algorithms tend to be based on the assumption that
the ontology adheres to conventions of naming classes with nouns in
the singular and object properties in 3rd person singular. It is an implementation detail whether a plural or the infinitive is generated on-the-fly
from grammar rules or fetched from a *Lemon* file or another annotation
or precomputed lexicon.

One could declare templates of each axiom type, but because it is
'arbitrary' within the syntax constraints of the logic, a modular approach
makes sense. Essentially, each symbol in the language has one or more
ways of putting it in natural language, and based on that, one can create
a *controlled natural language* that can generate only those sentences
following the specified template. For instance, a template for $C \sqcap D$,
i.e., "*class*$_1$ and *class*$_2$" can be fetched as needed when it appears in
a class expression such as $E \sqsubseteq \exists R.(C \sqcap D)$. In this way, then a whole
ontology can be *verbalised* and presented as (pseudo-)natural language
sentences that hide the logic. Of course, it takes for granted one already
has an ontology in one's preferred language.

Two recent review papers describe the current state of the art with
respect to NLG and the Semantic Web [BACW14] and CNLs [SD17].
Both focus principally on English, largely because there are only few
efforts for other languages. Some 13 years ago we tried to create a ver-
baliser for multiple languages, which worked to some extent [JKD06];
that is, the technology did, but not all sentences were fluent. The main
lessons learned then, and which hold just as much now, were: 1) it is
easier to generate a new set of templates in a language based on an existing set of templates for a similar language, and 2) the template-based
approach is *infeasible* for grammatically richer languages. Regarding

the second aspect, it may be that a few additional rules suffice, which could be added to the same template file, even, or one could perhaps repurpose SimpleNLG [GR09], which has been adapted from English to French, Spanish, and Portuguese. For a language such as isiZulu, however, there are, thus far, no known templates, but only 'patterns'; that is, for the patterns designed for verbalising ontologies (roughly within $\mathcal{ALC}$), there is no single canned word in the 'template' as each word in the sentence requires some processing with language tags and grammar rules [KK17a].

9.2.2 Reusing the results for related activities

Having the route from axiom to (pseudo-)natural language sentence, one could wonder about the process in the reverse, i.e., using the CNL to generate the axioms. The most successful results for ontologies have been obtained with Attempto Controlled English (ACE) [FKK10] for OWL DL. A related line of work within the scope of from-text-to-axiom, is natural language-based query formulation (e.g., [FGT10]), which also uses a CNL. In this scenario, however, partial completions of an iteratively constructed sentence to query the ontology are based on the step-wise selected vocabulary and the (partial) axioms in which it appears.

One might take another step further: use machine translation in the verbalisation process. Such a system has been developed by [GB11]: it uses ACE for ontology verbalisation in English and Grammatical Framework for translations between English and Latvian. Which option is the 'better' one is not fully clear: a) make templates in one's language and translate the ontology, or b) skip the template specification by reusing an existing English one, develop a resource grammar for Grammatical Framework, and translate the generated English into the target language. This depends on one's aims and availability of resources. In theory, the Grammatical Framework should work better as a reusable solid solution but with (very) high start-up costs, whereas templates are easier to specify but the knowledge that goes into it is not easily reused elsewhere. Of course, the latter may not be useful if the ontology has its vocabulary elements already in the target language.

Ontology verbalisation can also be used for, e.g., automatically generating documentation of one's ontology, in a similar fashion as automated code documentation generation. A step toward interesting applications is, e.g., the ontology-enhanced museum guide (in Greek)

[ALG13], question generation for textbooks in biology that were annotated with an ontology [CCO+13], and language learning exercises [GK18].

9.3   Exercises

Review question 9.1. Name some of the problems with naming the classes in an OWL file, when considering multiple languages.

Review question 9.2. Describe in your own words the theoretical solution that *Lemon* exhibits, both in the content of a single natural language and in the multilingual setting.

Review question 9.3. What can ontology verbalisation be used for?

Review question 9.4. Describe how the template-based approach works for ontology verbalisation.

Exercise 9.1. Create a *Lemon* file for the ontology of your choice, in the language of your choice.

Exercise 9.2. Devise templates in English for the following axiom types:
1. $C \sqcap D \sqsubseteq \bot$
2. $\exists R.C \sqsubseteq D$
3. $C \sqsubseteq \forall R.D$

You may want to do this for a language of choice, but this may turn out a hard exercise then, depending on the chosen language.

Exercise 9.3. Devise a software architecture that combines both a solution to multilingualism and can verbalise an ontology.

9.4   Literature and reference material

1. John McCrae, Guadalupe Aguado de Cea, Paul Buitelaar, Philipp Cimiano, Thierry Declerck, Asunción Gómez-Pérez, Jorge Gracia, Laura Hollink, Elena Montiel-Ponsoda, Dennis Spohr, and Tobias Wunner. *The lemon cookbook*. Technical report, Monnet Project, June 2012. www.lemon-model.net.

2. Paul Buitelaar and Philipp Cimiano (Eds.). *Towards the Multilingual Semantic Web: Principles, Methods and Applications.* Springer, 2014.

3. N. Bouayad-Agha, G. Casamayor, and L. Wanner. Natural language generation in the context of the Semantic Web. *Semantic Web Journal*, 5(6):493-513, 2014.

4. Hazem Safwat and Brian Davis. CNLs for the semantic web: a state of the art. *Language Resources & Evaluation*, 51(1):191-220, 2017.

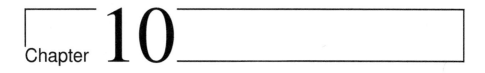

Chapter **10**

Advanced Modelling with Additional Language Features

When the representation of the subject domain in an ontology requires features not available in OWL, the default response is typically 'tough luck'. This is not exactly true. Common Logic (CL) and the Distributed Ontology, model and specification Language (DOL) were mentioned as an alternative way out in Section 4.3.2. It is not immediately clear, however, how exactly CL and DOL can assist with, say, probabilistic or temporal information. Also, for some 'minor' addition, one perhaps may not want to immediately leave behind all the Semantic Web tooling infrastructure. To some extent, such requirements have been met for especially uncertainty and vagueness, and extensions to OWL do exist, as we shall see. Temporal extensions have shown to be somewhat difficult, or: if one wants to remain within a decidable fragment of FOL, then there is not much temporal knowledge one would be able to represent. We will look at each in turn.

The main aim of this chapter is to provide several pointers to more advanced language features that allow the modeller to represent more than can be done with the DL-based OWL species only. We shall see some solutions to earlier-mentioned modelling question, among others: with which extension that "small" of the 'small bladed hunting spear' can be represented and how the essential and immutable behaviour of the parthood relation with the boxer and his hands vs. brain and human is resolved.

237

10.1 Uncertainty and vagueness

This advanced ontology engineering topic concerns how to cope with uncertainty and vagueness in ontology languages and their reasoners and what we can gain from all the extra effort. At the time of writing, this elective topic is mainly focused on theory and research, and a few proof-of-concept tools exist. Let's first clarify these two terms upfront:

- **Uncertainty**: statements are true or false, but *due to lack of knowledge* we can only estimate to which probability / possibility / necessity degree they are true or false;

- **Vagueness**: statements involve concepts for which *there is no exact definition* (such as tall, small, close, far, cheap, expensive), which are then true to some degree, taken from a truth space.

Consider, e.g., information retrieval: to which *degree* is a web site, a page, a paragraph, an image, or a video segment relevant to the information need and an acceptable answer to what the user was searching for? In the context of ontology alignment, one would want to know (automatically) to which *degree* the focal concepts of two or more ontologies represent the same thing, or are 'sufficiently' overlapping. In an electronic health record system, one may want to classify patients based on their symptoms, such as throwing up *often*, having a *high* blood pressure, and *yellow-ish* eye colour. Or compute the probability that a person is HIV positive is 23% and has been exposed to TB is 85%, or the probability that birds fly. How can ontology-driven software agents do the negotiation for your holiday travel plans that are specified imprecisely, alike "I am looking for a package holiday of *preferably less than* R15000, but really no more than R20000 , for *about* 12 days in a *cold* country that has snow"? One may want to classify, say, *ripe* apples, find the set of all individuals that *mostly* buy low calorie food, and patients that are possibly septic when having the properties of "infection and [temperature > 39C OR temperature < 36C, respiratory rate > 20 breaths/minute OR PaCO2 < 32 mmHg]". Of course, one can combine the two notions as well, e.g.: "It is *probable* to degree 0.915 that it will be *hot* in June in the Northern hemisphere".

The main problem to solve, then, is what and how to incorporate such *vague* or *uncertain* knowledge in OWL and its reasoners (or another logic, as one desires). The two principal approaches regarding uncertainty probabilistic and possibilistic languages, ontologies, and reasoning services, where the former way of dealing with uncertainty receives a lot more attention than the latter[1]. The two principal approaches regarding vagueness and the semantic web are fuzzy and rough extensions, where fuzzy used to receive more attention compared to the rough approach, but theories for the latter are catching up.

10.1.1 Fuzzy ontologies

In fuzzy logic[2], statements are true to some degree which is taken from a *truth space*, which is usually $[0, 1]$. This sounds easier than it is, especially the deductions that follow from them. Consider first the following example.

Example 10.1. *Take the statement that Hotel EnjoyYourStay is close to the train station to degree 0.83. A query on a hotel booking site may be "Find me the top-k cheapest hotels close to the train station", more formally:*

q(h) ← hasLocation(h, hl) ∧ hasLocation(train, cl)∧
        close(hl, cl) ∧ cheap(h)

Then what is the meaning—and logically: interpretation—of the query when filled in with values alike close(EnjoyYourStay, train) ∧ cheap(200)*? That is, how does that work out in the model (in the context of model-theoretic semantics)? We have to change the interpretation function a little to accommodate for the fuzzy concepts. The interpretation is a function I that maps atoms into a value between 0 and 1 inclusive, i.e., $I(A) \in [0, 1]$. Given that, then if the knowledge base states* I(close(EnjoyYourStay, train)) = 0.83 *and* I(cheap(200)) = 0.2, *then what is the result of* $0.83 \wedge 0.2$*? More generally, what is the result of* $n \wedge m$, *for* $n, m \in [0, 1]$*?* ◇

Many-valued formulae in fuzzy logic have the form $\phi \geq l$ or $\phi \leq u$ where $l, u \in [0, 1]$, meaning that the degree of truth is *at least l* and *at*

---

[1]We will not cover probabilistic ontologies in this chapter; a recent introductory overview is described in [Luk17]. Some pointers to reasoners are: Pronto, which is an extension to the Pellet reasoner (`http://pellet.owldl.com/pronto/`), PR-OWL (`http://www.pr-owl.org/` and others, such as a Probabilistic Ontology Mapping Tool (OMEN), and combinations with Bayesian networks (BayesOWL, OntoBayes).

[2]In this section, I assume the reader recalls something of fuzzy logic or fuzzy sets, and that the occasional examples suffice as refresher.

most u, respectively. Figure 10.1 visualises the intuition of the graded degrees of truth. The top-left chart shows the membership function of expensive: a value of 25 is definitely not expensive, i.e., it would evaluate to 0, then it slowly starts climbing toward expensive, where at 187.5, expensive(someObject) $= 0.5$, and climbing further up to 400, when, whatever it is, it is definitely expensive (evaluating to 1); this function has a so-called *right shoulder*. One can do the same with two opposite concepts, like hot and cold. There are no values, as what is perceived to be hot (cold) weather in Iceland is different from Ireland, that's again different from Italy and yet again from the Ivory Coast. An example of a fuzzy function passed the revue in Example 9.1 for 'mesoscopic small' for the hunting spear. More fuzzy functions exist, such as the trapezoidal function with both a left and a right shoulder, also depicted in Figure 10.1, which, perhaps, could refer to the optimal temperature of a cup of coffee—not too cold and not too hot.

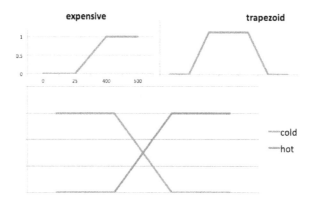

Figure 10.1: Some examples of fuzzy functions; see text for explanation.

Returning to Example 10.1, it noted that the interpretation has to be modified cf. the 'standard' way we have seen in Block I in order to take care of a truth value between 0 and 1 inclusive, rather than either 0 or 1. It is a mapping $I : Atoms \rightarrow [0, 1]$, which are extended to formulae as follows (the principal list is shown):

$$\mathcal{I}(\neg\phi) = \mathcal{I}(\phi) \rightarrow 0 \tag{10.1}$$

$$\mathcal{I}(\exists x\phi) = \sup_{c\in\Delta^{\mathcal{I}}}\mathcal{I}_x^c(\phi) \tag{10.2}$$

$$\mathcal{I}(\forall x\phi) = \inf_{c\in\Delta^{\mathcal{I}}}\mathcal{I}_x^c(\phi) \tag{10.3}$$

$$\mathcal{I}(\phi \wedge \psi) = \mathcal{I}(\phi) \otimes \mathcal{I}(\psi) \tag{10.4}$$

$$\mathcal{I}(\phi \vee \psi) = \mathcal{I}(\phi) \oplus \mathcal{I}(\psi) \tag{10.5}$$

$$\mathcal{I}(\phi \rightarrow \psi) = \mathcal{I}(\phi) \Rightarrow \mathcal{I}(\psi) \tag{10.6}$$

$$\mathcal{I}(\neg \phi) = \ominus \mathcal{I}(\phi) \tag{10.7}$$

where $\mathcal{I}_x^c$ is as $\mathcal{I}$ except that var x is mapped to individual c, the $\otimes$, $\oplus$, $\Rightarrow$, and $\ominus$ are *combination functions*: triangular norms (or t-norms), triangular co-norms (or s-norms), implication functions, and negation functions, respectively. Also, they extend the classical Boolean conjunction, disjunction, implication, and negation, respectively, to the many-valued case. In addition, it poses the notion of *degree of subsumption* between two fuzzy sets A and B, which is defined as $\inf_{x \in X} A(x) \Rightarrow B(x)$ and such that if $A(x) \leq B(x)$ for all $x \in [0,1]$ then $A \sqsubseteq B$ evaluates to 1. Finally, $\mathcal{I} \models \phi \geq l$ (resp. $\mathcal{I} \models \phi \leq u$) iff $\mathcal{I}(\phi) \geq l$ (respectively, $\mathcal{I}(\phi) \leq u$).

For notations of specific fuzzy DLs and fuzzy OWL extension, basically, the language specifications are the usual DL/OWL notation, with the above-mentioned modifications and additions. For details and examples, you are suggested to start with [Str08], which provides a good introductory overview and has a very long list of references to start delving into the topics, and a more technical take on it is provided in [LS08]. An alternative approach is taken in [BS11] (that also describes many examples), where all the fuzzy knowledge is put in the annotations of an OWL 2 file through a Protégé plugin[3] and then it is either ignored by a standard reasoner or parsed and handled by the fuzzyDL[4] or DeLorean[5] reasoner.

Fuzzy DLs can be classified according to the DL or OWL language that they extend, the allowed fuzzy constructs and the underlying fuzzy logics (notably, Gödel, Lukasiewicz, Zadeh), and their reasoning services. Regarding the latter, because we have those special new fuzzy features in the language, we get new reasoning services with it. They are:

- Consistency, Subsumption, Equivalence

- Graded instantiation: Check if individual a is an instance of class C to degree at least n, i.e., $KB \models \langle a : C, n \rangle$

---

[3]available at `http://www.umbertostraccia.it/cs/software/FuzzyOWL/` in July 2018, not the URL listed in the paper.

[4]`http://www.umbertostraccia.it/cs/software/fuzzyDL/fuzzyDL.html`

[5]`http://webdiis.unizar.es/~fbobillo/delorean.php`

- Best Truth Value Bound problem: determine tightest bound $n \in [0, 1]$ of an axiom α, i.e. $glb(KB, \alpha) = sup\{n, | KB \models \langle \alpha \geq n \rangle\}$ (likewise for *lub*, lowest upper bound)

- Best Satisfiability Bound problem: $glb(KB, C)$ determined by the max value of x s.t. $(\mathcal{R}, \mathcal{T}, \mathcal{A} \cup \{a : C \geq x\})$ (among all models, determine the max degree of truth that concept C may have over all individuals $x \in \Delta^{\mathcal{I}}$)

- $glb(KB, C \sqsubseteq D)$ is the minimal value of x such that $KB = (\mathcal{R}, \mathcal{T}, \mathcal{A} \cup \{a : C \sqcap \neg D \geq 1 - x\})$ is satisfiable, where a is a new individual; Therefore, the greatest lower bound problem can be reduced to the minimal satisfiability problem of a fuzzy knowledge base

There are several fuzzy reasoners, such as the aforementioned FuzzyDL for fuzzy $\mathcal{SHIF}(D)$ the DELOREAN reasoners.

How does this work out practically? Given some fuzzy $\mathcal{SHIF}(D)$, $\mathcal{SHOIN}(D)$, $\mathcal{SROIQ}(D)$ that is serialised in OWL syntax, then one can declare the fuzzy concepts with either modifiers (e.g., very) or 'concrete' fuzzy concepts (e.g., Young) using data properties, where both additions have explicit membership functions. Jumping over the technicalities here, it enables one to specify fuzzy concepts as follows, using 'minor' and 'young' as examples. Just by numbers, $\leq_{18}(x)$ over $\mathbb{N}$, evaluates to true if $x \leq 18$, false otherwise (i.e., $cr(0, 18)$). Let's define 'minor' as Minor $\equiv$ Person $\sqcap \exists$Age.$\leq_{18}$. Being a minor and being young is not exactly the same thing, so let's add something new for the latter: Young : Natural $\rightarrow [0, 1]$ is declared as a fuzzy datatype predicate denoting the degree of youngness, which then allows one to define 'young' as, say, Young(x) = ls(x, 10, 30), where *ls* is the left shoulder function (like the cold line in Figure 10.1). Then a young person may be defined as YoungPerson $\equiv$ Person $\sqcap \exists$Age.Young. What does the ontology entail with these axioms asserted? It entails, e.g.:

O $\models$ Minor $\sqsubseteq$ YoungPerson ≥ 0.6,
O $\models$ YoungPerson $\sqsubseteq$ Minor ≥ 0.4

The values of 0.6 and 0.4 follow from the fuzzy functions, were 'minor' covered the age range of 0 to 18 and the young covered 0-30 age range that was going downhill with being 'young' from the age of 10.

Example 9.1 describes the specification of a 'small bladed hunting spear' in a fuzzy way.

10.1.2 Rough ontologies

Rough ontologies are not an endpoint of themselves, but a means to an end—if one is lucky. If a concept turns out to be a rough concept, i.e., there are some individuals of which we don't know whether they are instances of that concept, it means that the concept is *underspecified* at least with respect to the properties one has represented in the ontology. More precision is good, from an ontological viewpoint at least, and rough ontologies can assist the modeller by providing an iterative way to add more properties so as to reduce the amount of uncertainty in an observable way. That is, adding more properties to the concept should lead to fewer individuals of which we don't know whether they are instances of that concept. If adding or removing a property does not make a difference, then that property is less important than others for that specific concept. Thus is, it can assist in making one's ontology more precise, be this regarding the representation only, or to press the domain expert for more subject domain details.

Rough DLs were first introduced in [Kee10b]. As 'roughness' is not commonly included in undergraduate education, a brief summary (based on [Kee10b]) is provided first, before porting it to DLs and demonstrating where it solves some representation and reasoning problems.

Rough sets

We consider here the typical rough set model of Pawlak, which is illustrated diagrammatically in Figure 10.2. Formally, $I = (U, A)$ is an *information system*, where U is a non-empty finite set of objects and A a finite non-empty set of attributes such that for every $a \in A$, we have the function $a : U \mapsto V_a$ where v_a is the set of values that attribute a can have. For any subset of attributes $P \subseteq A$, the equivalence relation $\text{IND}(P)$ is then defined as follows:

$$\text{IND}(P) = \{(x, y) \in U \times U \mid \forall a \in P, a(x) = a(y)\} \qquad (10.8)$$

which generates a partition of U, denoted with $U/\text{IND}(P)$, or U/P for short. If $(x, y) \in \text{IND}(P)$, then x and y are *indistinguishable* with respect to the attributes in P, which is referred to as *p-indistinguishable*.

From those objects in U, the aim is to represent set X such that $X \subseteq U$, using P (with $P \subseteq A$). That set X may not be crisp, i.e., it may include or exclude objects which are indistinguishable on the basis

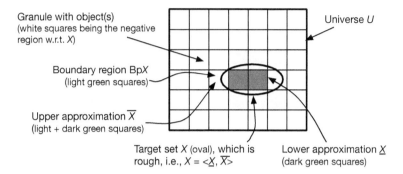

Figure 10.2: A rough set and associated notions (Source: based on [PS07]).

of the attributes in P, i.e., we do not know given the attributes under consideration. This can be approximated by using a *lower* and an *upper* approximation, which are defined as:

$$\underline{P}X = \{x \mid [x]_P \subseteq X\} \tag{10.9}$$
$$\overline{P}X = \{x \mid [x]_P \cap X \neq \emptyset\} \tag{10.10}$$

where $[x]_P$ denotes the equivalence classes of the p-indistinguishability relation. The *lower approximation* (10.9) is the set of objects that are *positively* members of set X (more precisely: it is the union of all equivalence classes in $[x]_P$). The *upper approximation* is the set of objects that are *possibly* in X and its complement, $U - \overline{P}X$, is the *negative region* that is the union of all equivalence classes of sets of objects that are definitely *not* in X (i.e., $\neg X$). Then, "with every rough set we associate two *crisp* sets, called *lower* and *upper approximation*" [PS07], which is denoted as a tuple $X = \langle \underline{X}, \overline{X} \rangle$. Finally, the difference between the lower and upper approximation, $B_P X = \overline{P}X - \underline{P}X$, is called the *boundary region*: this region contains the objects that neither can be classified as member of X nor that they are not in X. It follows that if $B_P X = \emptyset$ then X is a crisp set with respect to P and when $B_P X \neq \emptyset$ then X is rough w.r.t. P, i.e., then there are indistinguishable objects.

Given the boundary region, one can compute the *accuracy of approximation*, $\alpha_P X$, which indicates how well a rough set approximates the target set. There are several ways to compute it, e.g., $\alpha_P X = \frac{|\underline{P}X|}{|\overline{P}X|}$ or $\alpha_P X = 1 - \frac{|B_P X|}{|U|}$ (this is a separate topic not further discussed here). Note that $\underline{P}X \subseteq X \subseteq \overline{P}X$. There are further notions that we do not need in this summary, but are ontologically interesting: the *reduct* and *core*, which are the set of *sufficient* conditions (attributes) and the set of *necessary* conditions, respectively (still with respect to P).

Transferring rough sets into ontologies

In most ontology languages, there are more constructors than just attributes and 'attributes' may be, at least, represented with a role (object property) $R \in \mathcal{R}$ or value attributions (data property) $D \in \mathcal{D}$, which has to be accounted for: rough set's P is thus to be taken from $\mathcal{R} \cup \mathcal{D}$ where those attributes have the rough concept declared as domain. In addition, it requires an appropriate model-theoretic semantics for $\underline{C}$ and $\overline{C}$ as well as a 'rough concept', denoted here with "$\wr C$" to simplify notation. The semantics of the approximations can be transferred in a straightforward manner, where E denotes indistinguishability (equivalence) relation (which is reflexive, symmetric, and transitive):

$$\underline{C} = \{x \mid \forall y : (x, y) \in E \to y \in C\} \tag{10.11}$$
$$\overline{C} = \{x \mid \exists y : (x, y) \in E \land y \in C\} \tag{10.12}$$

Then there is rough sets' tuple notation, $X = \langle \underline{X}, \overline{X} \rangle$ to transfer into DL, but a $\wr C = \langle \underline{C}, \overline{C} \rangle$ is a rather unusual notation. Instead, one can use also two new binary relationships, dubbed *lapr* and *uapr*, to relate *any* rough concept and its associated approximations, which are typed as follows:

$$\forall \phi, \psi . lapr(\phi, \psi) \to \wr C(\phi) \land \underline{C}(\psi) \tag{10.13}$$
$$\forall \phi, \psi . uapr(\phi, \psi) \to \wr C(\phi) \land \overline{C}(\psi) \tag{10.14}$$

Note that they quantify over *sets*, not objects that are member of the respective sets, therewith making explicit the knowledge about the three sets and how they relate. Finally, we make explicit that $\wr C$ is identified by the combination of its lower and upper approximation, which the following axioms ensure:

$$\forall \phi. \wr C(\phi) \rightarrow \exists \psi. lapr(\phi, \psi),$$
$$\forall \phi. \wr C(\phi) \rightarrow \exists \psi. uapr(\phi, \psi),$$
$$\forall \phi, \psi, \varphi. lapr(\phi, \psi) \wedge lapr(\phi, \varphi) \rightarrow \psi = \varphi, \qquad (10.15)$$
$$\forall \phi, \psi, \varphi. uapr(\phi, \psi) \wedge uapr(\phi, \varphi) \rightarrow \psi = \varphi,$$
$$\forall \phi_1, \phi_2, \psi_1, \psi_2. lapr(\phi_1, \psi_1) \wedge uapr(\phi_1, \psi_2) \wedge$$
$$lapr(\phi_2, \psi_1) \wedge uapr(\phi_2, \psi_2) \rightarrow \phi_1 = \phi_2.$$

They say that: 1) there must be exactly one lower and one upper approximation for each rough concept, and 2) there is one rough concept for each combination of lower and upper approximation (i.e., if an approximation differs, it is a different rough concept).

Practically within an OWL-only setting, the $\overline{C}$ and $\underline{C}$ is reduced to, in OWL 2 DL functional syntax:

```
EquivalentClasses(C̄ ObjectSomeValuesFrom(a:Ind a:C))
EquivalentClasses(C ObjectAllValuesFrom(a:Ind a:C))
```

where **Ind** denotes the indistinguishability relation. Then Eq. 10.15 is approximated by adding object properties uapr, lapr that have $\wr$C as domain, and an exactly 1 cardinality constraint:

```
ObjectPropertyDomain(a:upar a:?C)
ObjectPropertyDomain(a:lapr a:?C)
ObjectExactCardinality(1 a:uapr a:C̄)
ObjectExactCardinality(1 a:lapr a:C)
```

One has to add this for each rough concept and its approximations. For instance, the promiscuous bacteria of [Kee10c]:

$$\text{PromiscuousBacterium} \equiv \text{Organism} \sqcap \exists \text{ Percentage.real}_{>10} \sqcap$$
$$\geq 6 \ \text{hasHGTCluster.FlexibleHGTGeneCluster}$$
$$\text{PromiscuousBacterium} \sqsubseteq = 1 \ \text{lapr.PromBactLapr}$$
$$\text{PromiscuousBacterium} \sqsubseteq = 1 \ \text{uapr.PromBactUapr}$$
$$\text{PromBactLapr} \equiv \forall \ \text{Ind.PromBact}$$
$$\text{PromBactUapr} \equiv \exists \ \text{Ind.PromBact}$$

$$(10.16)$$

Each such concept will have to be tested against the instances in the ABox: is the PromiscuousBacterium indeed a rough concept? This was experimented with in two ways: 'natively' in OWL files as well as in the OBDA setting (Figure 8.2 was taken from that experiment). Practically, at the time at least, putting the instances in the OWL file was a 'bad' idea, mainly because the reasoners are not optimised to deal efficiently with data properties, value restrictions, and instances (or: computing the rough concepts took quite some time even with just 17 individuals). The OBDA setting did work, but was at the time cumbersome to set up; this has improved in the meantime (see also Chapter 8).

One can add *rough subsumption* to rough concepts [Kee11a] as well, which is beyond the current introductory scope.

10.2   Time and Temporal Ontologies

There are multiple requests for including a temporal dimension in OWL. Some of those requirements are described in the ontology's annotation fields (see the OWL files of BFO and DOLCE), or the labels of the object properties in the BFO v2.1 draft, where they mention temporality that cannot be represented formally in OWL: e.g., DOLCE has a temporally indexed parthood in the paper-based version but this could not be transferred into the OWL file. This is, perhaps, even more an issue for domain ontologies. For instance, SNOMED CT [SNO12] has concepts like "Biopsy, *planned*", i.e., an event is expected to happen in the future, and "Concussion with loss of consciousness for *less than one hour*", i.e., a specific interval and where the loss of consciousness can be before or after the concussion, the symptom HairLoss *during* the treatment Chemotherapy, and Butterfly is a *transformation of* Caterpillar. Other examples are a business rule alike 'RentalCar must be returned *before* Deposit is reimbursed'. Adding an object property before in one's OWL ontology is not going to ensure that in all possible models, some return event happened before a reimbursement event, however, because it does not know when what happened.

There is no single computational solution to solve these examples all at once in another way beyond OWL. Thus far, it is a bit of a patchwork of various theories and some technologies, with, among many aspects, the Allen's interval algebra [All83] with the core qualitative temporal relations (such as *before* and *during*), Linear Temporal Logics (LTL) and Computational Tree Logics (CTL, with branching time). There is also a Time Ontology[6] that was recently standardised by the W3C (more explanation in [HP04]), but it is an ontology for annotations only—i.e., no temporal reasoning intended—and suffers from the class-as-instance modelling confusion[7].

In the remainder of this section, we will look at some motivations for temporal ontologies first, proceed to a very expressive temporal DL, $\mathcal{DLR}_{\mathcal{US}}$, and finally look at several modelling issues it helps solving. Although computationally, things do not look rosy at all, it is possible to squeeze out a bit here and there, which we shall touch upon at the end.

10.2.1   Why temporal ontologies?

There are two principal parts to answering this question: because of *what* we want to represent and *what* inferencing we want to do with it.

The things to represent

Quite common time aspects in conceptual data modelling for information systems are the requirements to record actual dates and intervals and calendar calculations. This is not particularly relevant for a domain ontology, but it would be useful to have an ontology about such things so that the applications use the same notions and, hence, will be interoperable in that regard.

In Chapter 6 we have seen BFO and the RO, where it was the intention by its developers to add a *precedes* and an *immediately precedes* relation to the OBO Foundry ontologies, which could not be done other than for annotation purposes. There are more such established qualitative temporal relations, also known as the 'Allen relations' or 'Allen's interval algebra', after the author who gave a first systematic and formal account of them [All83], which comprise relations such as *before, after, during, while,* and *meet*. Some might say they are all the temporal relations one will ever need, but one may wish to be more specific in specialised subject domains, such as a *transformation_of* a caterpillar

---

[6]http://www.w3.org/TR/owl-time/

[7]e.g., DayOfWeek(Friday) and, in the one for the Gregorian calendar, MonthOfYear(January): Friday does have instances, such as `Friday 6 July 2018` and `Friday 13 July 2018`, etc., and likewise for the other days and for the month instances.

into a butterfly, not just that a butterfly was a caterpillar 'before', and one thing *developed_from* another thing in developmental biology. Also, the latter two are *persistent* changes cf. permitting to go back to what it was before.

Modellers want to do even more than that: temporalising classes and relations. The former is well-known in databases as 'object migration'; e.g., an active project evolves to a completed project, and each divorcee in the census database must have been married before. Relation migration follows the idea of temporal classes, but applies to n-ary tuples (with $n \geq 2$); e.g. 'during x's lifetime, it always has y as part' and 'every passenger that boards the plane must have checked in before departure of that flight'.

More comprehensive and real examples, can be found in, among others, [AGK08, Kee09, KA10, SSBS09]. This is not to say that all ontologies have, or ought have, a temporal component to represent the subject domain as accurately as possible. It depends on the use case scenarios and CQs devised for the ontology.

Temporal reasoning services

As with a-temporal ontologies, one would want to have the same ones for temporal ontologies, such as satisfiability checking, subsumption reasoning, and classification. Logical implications are a bit more involved; e.g., given $B \sqsubseteq A$, then it must be the case that objects 'active' (alive) in B must be active in A and, e.g., to come up for promotion to become a company's manager (B), one must first exist as an employee (A) of that company. Also, an ontology should permit either a statement that 'X must happen before Y' or that 'Y must happen before X', but not both. That is, there are temporal constraints that are not permitted to be contradicted, and algorithms are needed to check for that.

One also would want to be able to query temporal information. For instance, to retrieve the answer to "Who was the South African president after Nelson Mandela?" and "Which library books have not been borrowed in the past five years?". This also suggests that the 'plain' OBDA may be extended to a temporal OBDA system; see [AKK+17] for a recent survey. There is a range of other examples that involve time in some way in information systems, and which have been solved and implemented already, such as querying with a calendar hierarchy and across calendars and finding a solution satisfying a set of constraints for scheduling the lecture hours of a study programme; there uses are outside the scope.

Open issues

There are many problems that are being investigated in temporal information and knowledge processing. On the one hand, there are the modelling issues in ontology development and figuring out what temporal features modellers actually require in a temporal logic cf. the logicians deciding which temporal features a modeller gets (typically only the computational well-behaved ones), the interaction between temporal logic and temporal databases (temporal OBDA), and further investigation into the interaction between temporal DLs with temporal conceptual data modelling. This, in turn, requires one to look into the computational properties of various fragments of expressive temporal logics. More fundamental issues have to do with making choices regarding linear time vs. branching time (LTL vs CTL), endurantism vs. perdurantism ('4D-fluents') as was noted in Chapter 6 as a choice for foundational ontologies, and dense time vs points in time.

10.2.2 Temporal DLs

If one assumes that recent advances in temporal DLs may have the highest chance of making it into a temporal OWL, then the following is 'on offer'.

- A very expressive (undecidable) DL language is $\mathcal{DLR}_{\mathcal{US}}$ (with the $\mathcal{U}$ntil and $\mathcal{S}$ince operators), which already has been used for temporal conceptual data modelling [APS07] and for representing essential and immutable parts and wholes [AGK08], which also solves the Boxer example of Section 6.2. It uses linear time and mostly qualitative temporal constraints.

- An inexpressive language is TDL-Lite [AKL+07], which is a member of the DL-Lite family of DL languages (of which one is the basis for OWL 2 QL). It also uses linear time and mostly qualitative temporal constraints, but fewer of them (e.g., one can't have temporal relations).

- Metric temporal logic, which zooms in on quantitative temporal constraints; e.g. [BBK+17].

- 4-D fluents/n-ary approach in OWL with SWRL rules [BPTA17], rather than a new language.

It is already known that $\mathcal{EL}^{++}$ (the basis for OWL 2 EL) does not keep the nice computational properties when extended with LTL, and results with $\mathcal{EL}^{++}$ with CTL are not out yet. If you are really interested in the topic, you may want to have a look at a survey [LWZ08] or take a broader scope with any of the four chapters from the KR handbook [vHLP08] that cover temporal knowledge representation and reasoning, situation calculus, event calculus, and temporal action logics, or the Handbook of temporal reasoning in artificial intelligence [EM05]. To give a flavour of how temporal logics may look like and what one can do with it, we shall focus on $\mathcal{DLR}_{\mathcal{US}}$, which has been extended with temporal relations and attributes and is also used for temporal conceptual modelling (including a graphical notation in the new TREND notation [KB17]).

The $\mathcal{DLR}_{\mathcal{US}}$ temporal DL

$\mathcal{DLR}_{\mathcal{US}}$ [AFWZ02] combines the propositional temporal logic with $\mathcal{S}ince$ and $\mathcal{U}ntil$ operators with the a-temporal DL $\mathcal{DLR}$ [CDG03] and can be regarded as an expressive fragment of the first-order temporal logic $L^{\{since, until\}}$ [CT98, HWZ99, GKWZ03].

As with other $\mathcal{DLR}$s, the basic syntactical types of $\mathcal{DLR}_{\mathcal{US}}$ are *classes* and *n*-ary *relations* ($n \geq 2$). Starting from a set of *atomic classes* (denoted by *CN*), a set of *atomic relations* (denoted by *RN*), and a set of *role symbols* (denoted by *U*), we can define complex class and relationship expressions (see upper part of Figure 10.3), where the restriction that binary constructors ($\sqcap, \sqcup, \mathcal{U}, \mathcal{S}$) are applied to relations of the same arity, i, j, k, n are natural numbers, $i \leq n$, j does not exceed the arity of R. All the Boolean constructors are available for both class and relation expressions. The selection expression $U_i/n : C$ denotes an *n*-ary relation whose *i*-th argument ($i \leq n$), named U_i, is of type C. (If it is clear from the context, we omit n and write $(U_i : C)$.) The projection expression $\exists^{\leq k}[U_j]R$ is a generalisation with cardinalities of the projection operator over argument U_j of relation R; the classical projection is $\exists^{\geq 1}[U_j]R$.

The model-theoretic semantics of $\mathcal{DLR}_{\mathcal{US}}$ assumes a flow of time $\mathcal{T} = \langle \mathcal{T}_p, < \rangle$, where $\mathcal{T}_p$ is a set of time points and $<$ a binary precedence relation on $\mathcal{T}_p$, assumed to be isomorphic to $\langle \mathbb{Z}, < \rangle$. The language of

$\mathcal{DLR}_{\mathcal{US}}$ is interpreted in *temporal models* over $\mathcal{T}$, which are triples of the form $\mathcal{I} \doteq \langle \mathcal{T}, \Delta^{\mathcal{I}}, \cdot^{\mathcal{I}(t)} \rangle$, where $\Delta^{\mathcal{I}}$ is non-empty set of objects (the *domain* of $\mathcal{I}$) and $\cdot^{\mathcal{I}(t)}$ an *interpretation function*. Since the domain, $\Delta^{\mathcal{I}}$, is time independent, we assume here the so called *constant domain assumption* with *rigid designator*—i.e., an instance is *always* present in the interpretation domain and it identifies the same instance at different points in time. The interpretation function is such that, for every $t \in \mathcal{T}$ (a shortcut for $t \in \mathcal{T}_p$), every class C, and every n-ary relation R, we have $C^{\mathcal{I}(t)} \subseteq \Delta^{\mathcal{I}}$ and $R^{\mathcal{I}(t)} \subseteq (\Delta^{\mathcal{I}})^n$. The semantics of class and relation expressions is defined in the lower part of Fig. 10.3, where $(u, v) = \{w \in \mathcal{T} \mid u < w < v\}$. For classes, the temporal operators $\Diamond^+$ (some time in the future), $\oplus$ (at the next moment), and their past counterparts can be defined via $\mathcal{U}$ and $\mathcal{S}$: $\Diamond^+ C \equiv \top \mathcal{U} C$, $\oplus C \equiv \bot \mathcal{U} C$, etc. The operators $\Box^+$ (always in the future) and $\Box^-$ (always in the past) are the duals of $\Diamond^+$ (some time in the future) and $\Diamond^-$ (some time in the past), respectively, i.e., $\Box^+ C \equiv \neg \Diamond^+ \neg C$ and $\Box^- C \equiv \neg \Diamond^- \neg C$, for both classes and relations. The operators $\Diamond^*$ (at some moment) and its dual $\Box^*$ (at all moments) can be defined for both classes and relations as $\Diamond^* C \equiv C \sqcup \Diamond^+ C \sqcup \Diamond^- C$ and $\Box^* C \equiv C \sqcap \Box^+ C \sqcap \Box^- C$, respectively.

A $\mathcal{DLR}_{\mathcal{US}}$ *knowledge base* is a finite set Σ of $\mathcal{DLR}_{\mathcal{US}}$ axioms of the form $C_1 \sqsubseteq C_2$ and $R_1 \sqsubseteq R_2$, with R_1 and R_2 being relations of the same arity. An interpretation $\mathcal{I}$ satisfies $C_1 \sqsubseteq C_2$ ($R_1 \sqsubseteq R_2$) if and only if the interpretation of C_1 (R_1) is included in the interpretation of C_2 (R_2) at *all time*, i.e., $C_1^{\mathcal{I}(t)} \subseteq C_2^{\mathcal{I}(t)}$ ($R_1^{\mathcal{I}(t)} \subseteq R_2^{\mathcal{I}(t)}$), for all $t \in \mathcal{T}$. Thus, $\mathcal{DLR}_{\mathcal{US}}$ axioms have a global reading. To see examples on how a $\mathcal{DLR}_{\mathcal{US}}$ knowledge base looks like we refer to the following sections where examples are provided.

Modelling

Let us look at some examples, both in shorthand $\mathcal{DLR}_{\mathcal{US}}$ notation and in their semantics. The second line provides a verbalisation of the axiom, using the CNL approach described in Section 9.2, but then tailored to verbalising the temporal features.

$$C \rightarrow \top \mid \bot \mid CN \mid \neg C \mid C_1 \sqcap C_2 \mid C_1 \sqcup C_2 \mid \exists^{\leq k}[U_j]R \mid$$
$$\diamond^+C \mid \diamond^-C \mid \square^+C \mid \square^-C \mid \oplus C \mid \ominus C \mid C_1 \, \mathcal{U} \, C_2 \mid C_1 \, \mathcal{S} \, C_2$$

$$R \rightarrow \top_n \mid RN \mid \neg R \mid R_1 \sqcap R_2 \mid R_1 \sqcup R_2 \mid U_i/n : C \mid$$
$$\diamond^+R \mid \diamond^-R \mid \square^+R \mid \square^-R \mid \oplus R \mid \ominus R \mid R_1 \, \mathcal{U} \, R_2 \mid R_1 \, \mathcal{S} \, R_2$$

$$\top^{\mathcal{I}(t)} = \Delta^{\mathcal{I}};$$
$$\bot^{\mathcal{I}(t)} = \emptyset;$$
$$CN^{\mathcal{I}(t)} \subseteq \top^{\mathcal{I}(t)};$$
$$(\neg C)^{\mathcal{I}(t)} = \top^{\mathcal{I}(t)} \setminus C^{\mathcal{I}(t)};$$
$$(C_1 \sqcap C_2)^{\mathcal{I}(t)} = C_1^{\mathcal{I}(t)} \cap C_2^{\mathcal{I}(t)};$$
$$(C_1 \sqcup C_2)^{\mathcal{I}(t)} = C_1^{\mathcal{I}(t)} \cup C_2^{\mathcal{I}(t)};$$
$$(\exists^{\leq k}[U_j]R)^{\mathcal{I}(t)} = \{ d \in \top^{\mathcal{I}(t)} \mid \sharp\{\langle d_1,\ldots,d_n \rangle \in R^{\mathcal{I}(t)} \mid d_j = d\} \lessgtr k\};$$
$$(C_1 \, \mathcal{U} \, C_2)^{\mathcal{I}(t)} = \{ d \in \top^{\mathcal{I}(t)} \mid \exists v > t.(d \in C_2^{\mathcal{I}(v)} \wedge \forall w \in (t,v).d \in C_1^{\mathcal{I}(w)})\};$$
$$(C_1 \, \mathcal{S} \, C_2)^{\mathcal{I}(t)} = \{ d \in \top^{\mathcal{I}(t)} \mid \exists v < t.(d \in C_2^{\mathcal{I}(v)} \wedge \forall w \in (v,t).d \in C_1^{\mathcal{I}(w)})\};$$

$$(\top_n)^{\mathcal{I}(t)} \subseteq (\Delta^{\mathcal{I}})^n;$$
$$RN^{\mathcal{I}(t)} \subseteq (\top_n)^{\mathcal{I}(t)};$$
$$(\neg R)^{\mathcal{I}(t)} = (\top_n)^{\mathcal{I}(t)} \setminus R^{\mathcal{I}(t)};$$
$$(R_1 \sqcap R_2)^{\mathcal{I}(t)} = R_1^{\mathcal{I}(t)} \cap R_2^{\mathcal{I}(t)};$$
$$(R_1 \sqcup R_2)^{\mathcal{I}(t)} = R_1^{\mathcal{I}(t)} \cup R_2^{\mathcal{I}(t)};$$
$$(U_i/n : C)^{\mathcal{I}(t)} = \{\langle d_1,\ldots,d_n \rangle \in (\top_n)^{\mathcal{I}(t)} \mid d_i \in C^{\mathcal{I}(t)}\};$$
$$(R_1 \, \mathcal{U} \, R_2)^{\mathcal{I}(t)} = \{\langle d_1,\ldots,d_n \rangle \in (\top_n)^{\mathcal{I}(t)} \mid \exists v > t.(\langle d_1,\ldots,d_n \rangle \in R_2^{\mathcal{I}(v)} \wedge$$
$$\forall w \in (t,v). \langle d_1,\ldots,d_n \rangle \in R_1^{\mathcal{I}(w)})\};$$
$$(R_1 \, \mathcal{S} \, R_2)^{\mathcal{I}(t)} = \{ \langle d_1,\ldots,d_n \rangle \in (\top_n)^{\mathcal{I}(t)} \mid \exists v < t.(\langle d_1,\ldots,d_n \rangle \in R_2^{\mathcal{I}(v)} \wedge$$
$$\forall w \in (v,t). \langle d_1,\ldots,d_n \rangle \in R_1^{\mathcal{I}(w)})\};$$
$$(\diamond^+R)^{\mathcal{I}(t)} = \{\langle d_1,\ldots,d_n \rangle \in (\top_n)^{\mathcal{I}(t)} \mid \exists v > t. \langle d_1,\ldots,d_n \rangle \in R^{\mathcal{I}(v)}\};$$
$$(\oplus R)^{\mathcal{I}(t)} = \{\langle d_1,\ldots,d_n \rangle \in (\top_n)^{\mathcal{I}(t)} \mid \langle d_1,\ldots,d_n \rangle \in R^{\mathcal{I}(t+1)}\};$$
$$(\diamond^-R)^{\mathcal{I}(t)} = \{\langle d_1,\ldots,d_n \rangle \in (\top_n)^{\mathcal{I}(t)} \mid \exists v < t. \langle d_1,\ldots,d_n \rangle \in R^{\mathcal{I}(v)}\};$$
$$(\ominus R)^{\mathcal{I}(t)} = \{\langle d_1,\ldots,d_n \rangle \in (\top_n)^{\mathcal{I}(t)} \mid \langle d_1,\ldots,d_n \rangle \in R^{\mathcal{I}(t-1)}\}.$$

Figure 10.3: Syntax and semantics of $\mathcal{DLR}_{\mathcal{US}}$.

- MScStudent $\sqsubseteq$ $\lozenge^*\neg$MScStudent
  Each MSc Student is not a(n) MSc Student for some time.

- marriedTo $\sqsubseteq$ $\lozenge^*\neg$marriedTo
  The objects participating in a fact in Person married to Person *do not relate through* married-to *at some time; or: people who are married now aren't married at another time.*

- $o \in Academic^{\mathcal{I}(t)} \land o \notin PhDStudent^{\mathcal{I}(t)} \land o \in PhDStudent^{\mathcal{I}(t-1)} \land$
  $o \notin Academic^{\mathcal{I}(t-1)}$
  A(n) Academic may have been a(n) PhD Student before, but is not a(n) PhD Student now.

- $o \in Frog^{\mathcal{I}(t)} \rightarrow \exists t' < t.o \in \mathrm{DEV}_{Tadpole,Frog}^{\mathcal{I}(t')}$
  Each Frog was a(n) Tadpole before, but is not a(n) Tadpole now.

The aforementioned 'planned' biopsy can now also be represented as something that will hold in the future $\lozenge^+$Biopsy and returning (the car) before reimbursement (of the deposit) as reimbursement $\sqsubseteq$ $\lozenge^-$return, i.e., "if reimbursement, then sometime in the past there was a return".

With this machinery, one can also solve the "Assuming boxers must have their own hands and boxers are humans, is Hand part of Boxer in the same way as Brain is part of Human?" that we have encountered in Section 6.2. Recasting this problem into the temporal dimension, we can encode it in $\mathcal{DLR}_{\mathcal{US}}$ and prove the correctness of the intended behaviour [AGK08]. The hand being part of the boxer is an *immutable* parthood, whereas the brain being part of the human is an *essential* parthood. That is: the 'essential' parthood relation means, informally, that 'that specific object must be part of the whole for entire lifetime of the whole object', whereas 'immutable' means, informally, 'for the time the objects are instance of that specific class (which is typically a role they play for some duration that is less that the lifetime of the object), it is essential'. The formal apparatus is quite lengthy, including recasting OntoClean's rigidity (recall Section 5.2.2) into the temporal modality, and is described in detail in [AGK08]. The short version showing the main axioms that represent that difference is as follows. First, for illustrative purpose, let's introduce a part-whole relation to relate brain to human:

HumanBrainPW $\sqsubseteq$ PartWhole

HumanBrainPW $\sqsubseteq$ part : Brain $\sqcap$ whole : Human

Subsequently, we add the 'essential' to it, which means it holds *at all times*, i.e., □*, for both human (once a human always a human for the whole lifetime of the object—it is a *rigid* property) and the essential parthood (once a part, always a part):

Human ⊑ □*Human

Human ⊑ ∃[whole]□*HumanBrainPW

Then, the boxer's hands. Also here, for illustrative purpose, we introduce the part-whole relation HumanHandPW to relate the hand to human:

HumanHandPW ⊑ PartWhole

HumanHandPW ⊑ part : Hand ⊓ whole : Human

To state that a boxer is at some time not (◊*¬) a boxer (an *anti-rigid* property), and is a human, the following axioms suffice:

Boxer ⊑ ◊*¬Boxer

Boxer ⊑ Human

The next step is the cardinality constraint that a boxer must have exactly two hands, if temporarily something is wrong with the boxer (e.g., the boxer has an injured hand for some time) he isn't a boxer either ('suspended'), and finally, that if that part-whole relation does not hold anymore ('disabled'), then the boxer ceases to be a boxer:

Boxer ⊑ ∃$^{=2}$[whole]HumanHandPW

Suspended-HumanHandPW ⊑ whole : Suspended-Boxer

Disabled-HumanHandPW ⊑ whole : Disabled-Boxer

Note that 'suspended' and 'disabled' are names for so-called *status relations* that are defined formally in [AGK08] and do not exactly have their colloquial meaning. If the boxer has to be continuously active by some rule from, say, the boxing association, then the 'suspended' axiom has to replaced by the following one, i.e., the relation is not allowed to be 'suspended':

Suspended-HumanHandPW ⊑ ⊥

Obviously, this can be defined for any essential or immutable relation, regardless whether it is a part-whole relation or not. The upside is that now we know how to represent it; the downside is that it uses both DL role hierarchies and temporal relations, which are computationally costly. What to do with this insight is something that a modeller has to decide.

10.3   Exercises

Review question 10.1. What is the difference between uncertainty and vagueness?

Review question 10.2. Name some examples of fuzzy concepts.

Review question 10.3. Rough ontologies contain rough concepts. Describe how they are approximated in an OWL ontology.

Review question 10.4. Name two conceptually distinct ways how time can be dealt with in/with ontologies.

Review question 10.5. The introductory paragraph of Section 10.1 lists a series of examples. State for each whether it refers to uncertainty or vagueness.

Exercise 10.1. Devise an example similar to the 'minor' and 'young', but then for 'senior citizen', 'old' and 'old person'. Compare this with another student. How well do you think fuzzy ontologies will fare with respect to 1) ontologies *in* information systems and 2) the original aim of ontologies *for* information systems?

Exercise 10.2. There are a few temporal reasoners for DLs and OWL. Find them (online) and assess what technology they use. As to the temporal things one can model, you may want to try to find out as follows: define a small example and see whether it can be represented and the deductions obtained in each of the tools.

Exercise 10.3. The Time Ontology was standardised recently. Inspect it. Can this be a viable alternative to $\mathcal{DLR}_{\mathcal{US}}$?

Exercise 10.4. BFO draft v2.1 has all those indications of time in the names of the object properties. Compare this to the Time Ontology and something like $\mathcal{DLR}_{\mathcal{US}}$ or TDL-Lite. What would your advice to its developers be, if any?

10.4 Literature and reference material

Suggested readings for fuzzy and rough ontologies:

1. Thomas Lukasiewicz and Umberto Straccia. 2008. Managing Uncertainty and Vagueness in Description Logics for the Semantic Web. *Journal of Web Semantics*, 6:291-308. NOTE: only the section on fuzzy ontologies

2. Umberto Straccia and Giulio Visco. DLMedia: an Ontology Mediated Multimedia Information Retrieval System. In: *Proceedings of the International Workshop on Uncertainty Reasoning for the Semantic Web (URSW-08)*, 2008. this is an example of an application that uses fuzzy DL

3. Keet, C.M. On the feasibility of Description Logic knowledge bases with rough concepts and vague instances. *23rd International Workshop on Description Logics (DL'10)*, 4-7 May 2010, Waterloo, Canada.

Suggested readings for temporal ontologies:

1. Alessandro Artale, Christine Parent, and Stefano Spaccapietra. Evolving objects in temporal information systems. *Annals of Mathematics and Artificial Intelligence (AMAI)*, 50:5-38, 2007. NOTE: only the $\mathcal{DLR}_{\mathcal{US}}$ part, the rest is optional.

2. J. R. Hobbs and F. Pan. An ontology of time for the semantic web. *ACM Transactions on Asian Language Processing (TALIP): Special issue on Temporal Information Processing*, 3(1):6685, 2004.

Optional readings with more technical details (in descending order of being optional):

1. Artale, A., Guarino, N., and Keet, C.M. Formalising temporal constraints on part-whole relations. *11th International Conference on Principles of Knowledge Representation and Reasoning (KR'08)*. Gerhard Brewka, Jerome Lang (Eds.) AAAI Press, pp 673-683. Sydney, Australia, September 16-19, 2008.

2. Alessandro Artale, Enrico Franconi, Frank Wolter and Michael Zakharyaschev. A Temporal Description Logic for Reasoning over Conceptual Schemas and Queries. In: *Proceedings of the 8th European Conference on Logics in Artificial Intelligence (JELIA'02)*, Cosenza, Italy, September 2002. LNAI, Springer-Verlag.

3. Alessandro Artale, Roman Kontchakov, Carsten Lutz, Frank Wolter

and Michael Zakharyaschev. Temporalising Tractable Description Logics. In: *Proc. of the 14th International Symposium on Temporal Representation and Reasoning (TIME'07)*, Alicante, June 2007.

Bibliography

[ACDG+05]   Andrea Acciarri, Diego Calvanese, Giuseppe De Giacomo, Domenico Lembo, Maurizio Lenzerini, Mattia Palmieri, and Riccardo Rosati. QuOnto: Querying Ontologies. In *Proc. of the 20th Nat. Conf. on Artificial Intelligence (AAAI 2005)*, pages 1670–1671, 2005.

[ACK+07]   Alessandro Artale, Diego Calvanese, Roman Kontchakov, Vladislav Ryzhikov, and Michael Zakharyaschev. Reasoning over extended ER models. In Christine Parent, Klaus-Dieter Schewe, Veda C. Storey, and Bernhard Thalheim, editors, *Proceedings of the 26th International Conference on Conceptual Modeling (ER'07)*, volume 4801 of *LNCS*, pages 277–292. Springer, 2007. Auckland, New Zealand, November 5-9, 2007.

[ACKZ09]   Alessandro Artale, Diego Calvanese, Roman Kontchakov, and Michael Zakharyaschev. DL-Lite without the unique name assumption. In *Proc. of the 22nd Int. Workshop on Description Logic (DL 2009)*, volume 477 of *CEUR-WS*, 2009. http://ceur-ws.org/.

[AFK12]   Ronell Alberts, Thomas Fogwill, and C. Maria Keet. Several required OWL features for indigenous knowledge management systems. In P. Klinov and M. Horridge, editors, *7th Workshop on OWL: Experiences and Directions (OWLED 2012)*, volume 849 of *CEUR-WS*, page 12p, 2012. 27-28 May, Heraklion, Crete, Greece.

[AFWZ02]   A. Artale, E. Franconi, F. Wolter, and M. Zakharyaschev. A temporal description logic for reasoning about conceptual schemas and queries. In S. Flesca, S. Greco, N. Leone, and G. Ianni, editors, *Proceedings of the 8th Joint European Conference on Logics in Artificial Intelligence (JELIA-02)*, volume 2424 of *LNAI*, pages 98–110. Springer Verlag, 2002.

[AGK08]   Alessandro Artale, Nicola Guarino, and C. Maria Keet. Formalising temporal constraints on part-whole relations. In Gerhard Brewka and Jerome Lang, editors, *11th International Conference on Principles of Knowledge Representation and Reasoning (KR'08)*, pages 673–683. AAAI Press, 2008. Sydney, Australia, September 16-19, 2008.

[AKK+17]   Alessandro Artale, Roman Kontchakov, Alisa Kovtunova, Vladislav Ryzhikov, Frank Wolter, and Michael Zakharyaschev. Ontology-mediated query answering over temporal data: A survey. In Sven Schewe, Thomas Schneider, and Jef Wijsen, editors, *Proceedings of the 24th International Symposium on Temporal Representation and Reasoning (TIME'17)*, pages 1:1–1:36. Leibniz International Proceedings in Informatics, 2017.

[AKL+07]   A. Artale, R. Kontchakov, C. Lutz, F. Wolter, and M. Zakharyaschev. Temporalising tractable description logics. In *Inter. Symposium on Temporal Representation and Reasoning (TIME07)*. IEEE Computer Society, 2007.

[ALG13]   I. Androutsopoulos, G. Lampouras, and D. Galanis. Generating natural language descriptions from owl ontologies: the naturalowl system. *Journal of Artificial Intelligence Research*, 48:671–715, 2013.

[Ali04]   A. Aliseda. Logics in scientific discovery. *Foundation of Science*, 9:339–363, 2004.

[All83]   James F. Allen. Maintaining knowledge about temporal intervals. *Communications of the ACM*, 26(11):832–843, 1983.

[APS07]   A. Artale, C. Parent, and S. Spaccapietra. Evolving objects in temporal information systems. *Annals of Mathematics and Artificial Intelligence*, 50(1-2):5–38, 2007.

[AvH03]   G. Antoniou and F. van Harmelen. *A Semantic Web Primer*. MIT Press, 2003.

[AWP+08]   Dimitra Alexopoulou, Thomas Wächter, Laura Pickersgill, Cecilia Eyre, and Michael Schroeder. Terminologies for text-mining; an experiment in the lipoprotein metabolism domain. *BMC Bioinformatics*, 9(Suppl 4):S2, 2008.

[BACW14]   N. Bouayad-Agha, G. Casamayor, and L. Wanner. Natural language generation in the context of the semantic web. *Semantic Web Journal*, 5(6):493–513, 2014.

[BBK+17]   Franz Baader, Stefan Borgwardt, Patrick Koopmann, Ana Ozaki, and Veronika Thost. Metric temporal description logics with interval-rigid names. In C. Dixon and M. Finger, editors, *Proceedings of the International Symposium on Frontiers of Combining Systems (FroCoS'17)*, volume 10483 of *LNCS*, pages 60–76. Springer, 2017.

[BBL05]   F. Baader, S. Brandt, and C. Lutz. Pushing the EL envelope. In *Proc. of the 19th Joint Int. Conf. on Artificial Intelligence (IJCAI 2005)*, volume 5, pages 364–369, 2005.

[BC14]   Paul Buitelaar and Philipp Cimiano, editors. *Towards the Multilingual Semantic Web: Principles, Methods and Applications*. Springer, 2014.

[BCDG05]   D. Berardi, D. Calvanese, and G. De Giacomo. Reasoning on UML class diagrams. *Artificial Intelligence*, 168(1-2):70–118, 2005.

[BCHM09]   P. Buitelaar, P. Cimiano, P. Haase, and Sintek M. Towards linguistically grounded ontologies. In L. Aroyo et al., editors, *Proceedings of
the Extended Semantic Web Conference (ESWC'09)*, volume 5554 of
LNCS, pages 111–125. Springer, 2009.

[BCM+08]   F. Baader, D. Calvanese, D. L. McGuinness, D. Nardi, and P. F. Patel-
Schneider, editors. *The Description Logics Handbook – Theory and
Applications*. Cambridge University Press, 2 edition, 2008.

[BD07]   T. Bittner and M. Donnelly. A temporal mereology for distinguish-
ing between integral objects and portions of stuff. In *Proceedings of
AAAI'07*, pages 287–292, 2007. Vancouver, Canada.

[BDFG14]   Alessio Bosca, Mauro Dragoni, Chiara Di Francescomarino, and
Chiara Ghidini. Collaborative management of multilingual ontologies.
In Paul Buitelaar and Philip Cimiano, editors, *Towards the Multilin-
gual Semantic Web*, pages 175–192. Springer, 2014.

[BE93]   Jon Barwise and John Etchemendy. *The language of first-order logic*.
Stanford, USA: CSLI Lecture Notes, 3rd edition, 1993.

[BGSS07]   F. Baader, B. Ganter, B. Sertkaya, and U. Sattler. Completing description logic knowledge bases using formal concept analysis. In *Proc. of
IJCAI 2007*, volume 7, pages 230–235, 2007. Hyderabad, India, 2007.

[BH96]   A. C. Bloesch and T. A. Halpin. ConQuer: a conceptual query language. In *Proceedings of ER'96: 15th International Conference on
conceptual modeling*, volume 1157 of *LNCS*, pages 121–133. Springer,
1996.

[BH97]   A. C. Bloesch and T. A. Halpin. Conceptual Queries using ConQuer-II.
In *Proceedings of ER'97: 16th International Conference on Conceptual
Modeling*, volume 1331 of *LNCS*, pages 113–126. Springer, 1997.

[BHJ+15]   E. Blomqvist, P. Hitzler, K. Janowicz, A. Krisnadhi, T. Narock, and
M. Solanki. Considerations regarding ontology design patterns. *Semantic Web*, 7(1):1–7, 2015.

[BLHL01]   Tim Berners-Lee, James Hendler, and Ora Lassila. The semantic web.
Scientific American Magazine, May 17, 2001, 2001.

[BLK+09]   Christian Bizer, Jens Lehmann, Georgi Kobilarov, Sören Auer, Christian Becker, Richard Cyganiak, and Sebastian Hellmann. Dbpedia – a
crystallization point for the web of data. *Journal of Web Semantics:
Science, Services and Agents on the World Wide Web*, 7:154165, 2009.

[BM09]   Stefano Borgo and Claudio Masolo. Foundational choices in DOLCE.
In Steffen Staab and Rudi Studer, editors, *Handbook on Ontologies*,
pages 361–381. Springer, 2 edition, 2009.

[BMF95]   John A. Bateman, Bernardo Magnini, and Giovanni Fabris. The Generalized Upper Model Knowledge Base: Organization and Use. In
N. J. I. Mars, editor, *Towards very large knowledge bases: knowledge
building and knowledge sharing*, pages 60–72, Amsterdam, 1995. IOS
Press.

[BPTA17] Sotiris Batsakis, Euripides Petrakis, Ilias Tachmazidis, and Grigoris Antoniou. Temporal representation and reasoning in OWL 2. *Semantic Web Journal*, 8(6):981–1000, 2017.

[Bro06] Matthias Brochhausen. The *Derives_from* relation in biomedical ontologies. *Studies in Health Technology and Informatics*, 124:769–774, 2006.

[BS05] E. Blomqvist and K. Sandkuhl. Patterns in ontology engineering - classification of ontology patterns. In *Proc. of the 7th International Conference on Enterprise Information Systems*, 2005. Miami, USA, May 2005.

[BS11] Fernando Bobillo and Umberto Straccia. Fuzzy ontology representation using OWL 2. *International Journal of Approximate Reasoning*, 52:1073–1094, 2011.

[BSSH08] Elena Beisswanger, Stefan Schulz, Holger Stenzhorn, and Udo Hahn. BioTop: An upper domain ontology for the life sciences - a description of its current structure, contents, and interfaces to OBO ontologies. *Applied Ontology*, 3(4):205–212, 2008.

[BST07] Franz Baader, Baris Sertkaya, and Anni-Yasmin Turhan. Computing the least common subsumer w.r.t. a background terminology. *Journal of Applied Logic*, 5(3):392–420, 2007.

[CCKE+17] Diego Calvanese, Benjamin Cogrel, Sarah Komla-Ebri, Roman Kontchakov, Davide Lanti, Martin Rezk, Mariano Rodriguez-Muro, and Guohui Xiao. Ontop: Answering SPARQL queries over relational databases. *Semantic Web Journal*, 8(3):471–487, 2017.

[CCO+13] V.K. Chaudhri, B. Cheng, A. Overholtzer, J. Roschelle, A. Spaulding, P. Clark, M. Greaves, and D Gunning. Inquire biology: A textbook that answers questions. *AI Magazine*, 34(3):55–72, 2013.

[CDG03] D. Calvanese and G. De Giacomo. *The DL Handbook: Theory, Implementation and Applications*, chapter Expressive description logics, pages 178–218. Cambridge University Press, 2003.

[CDGL99] Diego Calvanese, Giuseppe De Giacomo, and Maurizio Lenzerini. Reasoning in expressive description logics with fixpoints based on automata on infinite trees. In *Proc. of the 16th Int. Joint Conf. on Artificial Intelligence (IJCAI'99)*, pages 84–89, 1999.

[CGHM+08] B. Cuenca Grau, I. Horrocks, B. Motik, B. Parsia, P. Patel-Schneider, and U. Sattler. OWL 2: The next step for OWL. *Journal of Web Semantics: Science, Services and Agents on the World Wide Web*, 6(4):309–322, 2008.

[CGL+07] Diego Calvanese, Giuseppe De Giacomo, Domenico Lembo, Maurizio Lenzerini, and Riccardo Rosati. Tractable reasoning and efficient query answering in description logics: The DL-Lite family. *Journal of Automated Reasoning*, 39(3):385–429, 2007.

[CGL+09] Diego Calvanese, Giuseppe De Giacomo, Domenico Lembo, Maurizio Lenzerini, Antonella Poggi, Mariano Rodríguez-Muro, and Riccardo

Rosati. Ontologies and databases: The DL-Lite approach. In Sergio Tessaris and Enrico Franconi, editors, *Semantic Technologies for Informations Systems - 5th Int. Reasoning Web Summer School (RW 2009)*, volume 5689 of *LNCS*, pages 255–356. Springer, 2009. Brixen-Bressanone, Italy, 30 August - 4 September 2009.

[CK14] Catherine Chavula and C. Maria Keet. Is lemon sufficient for building multilingual ontologies for Bantu languages? In C. Maria Keet and Valentina Tamma, editors, *Proceedings of the 11th OWL: Experiences and Directions Workshop (OWLED'14)*, volume 1265 of *CEUR-WS*, pages 61–72, 2014. Riva del Garda, Italy, Oct 17-18, 2014.

[CKK⁺17] M. Codescu, E. Kuksa, O. Kutz, T. Mossakowski, and F. Neuhaus. Ontohub: A semantic repository for heterogeneous ontologies. *Applied Ontology*, 2017. Forthcoming.

[CKN⁺10] Diego Calvanese, C. Maria Keet, Werner Nutt, Mariano Rodríguez-Muro, and Giorgio Stefanoni. Web-based graphical querying of databases through an ontology: the WONDER system. In Sung Y. Shin, Sascha Ossowski, Michael Schumacher, Mathew J. Palakal, and Chih-Cheng Hung, editors, *Proceedings of ACM Symposium on Applied Computing (ACM SAC'10)*, pages 1389–1396. ACM, 2010. March 22-26 2010, Sierre, Switzerland.

[CLM⁺16] D. Calvanese, P. Liuzzo, A. Mosca, J. Remesal, M. Rezk, and G. Rull. Ontology-based data integration in epnet: Production and distribution of food during the roman empire. *Engineering Applications of Artificial Intelligence*, 51:212–229, 2016.

[CLs07] Common Logic (CL): a framework for a family of logic-based languages, 2007. https://www.iso.org/standard/39175.html.

[CMFL05] Oscar Corcho and Angel López-Cima Mariano Fernández-López, Asunción Gómez-Pérez. Building legal ontologies with methontology and webode. In *Law and the Semantic Web 2005*, volume 3369 of *LNAI*, pages 142–157. Springer LNAI, 2005.

[CMSV09] Philipp Cimiano, Alexander Mädche, Steffen Staab, and Johanna Völker. Ontology learning. In S. Staab and R. Studer, editors, *Handbook on Ontologies*, pages 245–267. Springer Verlag, 2009.

[Cot10] A. J. Cotnoir. Anti-symmetry and non-extensional mereology. *The Philosophical Quarterly*, 60(239):396–405, 2010.

[CS94] Tiziana Catarci and Giuseppe Santucci. Query by diagram: a graphical environment for querying databases. *ACM SIGMOD Record*, 23(2):515, 1994.

[CSG⁺10] Adrien Coulet, Nigam H. Shah, Yael Garten, Mark Musen, and Russ B. Altman. Using text to build semantic networks for pharmacogenomics. *Journal of Biomedical Informatics*, 43(6):1009–1019, 2010.

[CT98] J. Chomicki and D. Toman. *Logics for databases and information systems*, chapter Temporal logic in information systems. Kluwer, 1998.

[D⁺10]   Emek Demir et al. The BioPAX community standard for pathway data sharing. *Nature Biotechnology*, 28(9):935–942, 2010.

[DAA⁺08]   Heiko Dietze, Dimitra Alexopoulou, Michael R. Alvers, Liliana Barrio-Alvers, Bill Andreopoulos, Andreas Doms, Joerg Hakenberg, Jan Moennich, Conrad Plake, Andreas Reischuck, Loic Royer, Thomas Waechter, Matthias Zschunke, and Michael Schroeder. Gopubmed: Exploring pubmed with ontological background knowledge. In Stephen A. Krawetz, editor, *Bioinformatics for Systems Biology*. Humana Press, 2008.

[Daw17]   Zubeida C. Dawood. *A foundation for ontology modularisation*. Phd thesis, Department Computer Science, University of Cape Town, November 2017 2017.

[DB09]   Maureen Donnelly and Thomas Bittner. Summation relations and portions of stuff. *Philosophical Studies*, 143:167–185, 2009.

[dCL06]   P. C. G. da Costa and K. B. Laskey. PR-OWL: A framework for probabilistic ontologies. In *Proceedings FOIS'06*, pages 237–249. IOS Press, 2006.

[dFE10]   Claudia d'Amato, Nicola Fanizzi, and Floriana Esposito. Inductive learning for the Semantic Web: What does it buy? *Semantic Web Journal*, 1(1,2):53–59, 2010.

[DGR12]   Chiara Di Franscescomarino, Chiara Ghidini, and Marco Rospocher. Evaluating wiki-enhanced ontology authoring. In A ten Teije et al., editors, *18th International Conference on Knowledge Engineering and Knowledge Management (EKAW'12)*, volume 7603 of *LNAI*, pages 292–301. Springer, 2012. Oct 8-12, Galway, Ireland.

[DHI12]   A. Doan, A. Y. Halevy, and Z. G. Ives. *Principles of Data Integration*. Morgan Kaufmann, 2012.

[EGOMA06] H. El-Ghalayini, M. Odeh, R. McClatchey, and D. Arnold. Deriving conceptual data models from domain ontologies for bioinformatics. In *2nd Conference on Information and Communication Technologies (ICTTA'06)*, pages 3562 – 3567. IEEE Computer Society, 2006. 24-28 April 2006, Damascus, Syria.

[EM05]   J. Euzenat and A. Montanari. *Handbook of temporal reasoning in artificial intelligence*, chapter Time granularity, pages 59–118. Amsterdam: Elsevier, 2005.

[ES07]   Jerome Euzenat and Pavel Shvaiko. *Ontology Matching*. Springer, 2007.

[FBR⁺16]   R. A. Falbo, M. P. Barcelos, F. B. Ruy, G. Guizzardi, and R. S. S. Guizzardi. Ontology pattern languages. In A. Gangemi, P. Hizler, K. Janowicz, A. Krisnadhi, and V. Presutti, editors, *Ontology Engineering with Ontology Design Patterns: Foundations and Applications*. IOS Press, 2016.

[Fer16]   S. Ferré. Semantic authoring of ontologies by exploration and elimination of possible worlds. In E. Blomqvist, P. Ciancarini, F. Poggi, and

F. Vitali, editors, *Proceedings of the 20th International Conference on Knowledge Engineering and Knowledge Management (EKAW'16)*, volume 10024 of *LNAI*, pages 180–195. Springer, 2016. 19-23 November 2016, Bologna, Italy.

[FFT12]   Pablo R. Fillottrani, Enrico Franconi, and Sergio Tessaris. The ICOM 3.0 intelligent conceptual modelling tool and methodology. *Semantic Web Journal*, 3(3):293–306, 2012.

[FGGP13]   Ricardo A Falbo, Giancarlo Guizzardi, Aldo Gangemi, and Valentina Presutti. Ontology patterns: clarifying concepts and terminology. In *Proc. of OSWP'13*, 2013.

[FGPPP99] M. Fernández, A. Gómez-Pérez, A. Pazos, and J. Pazos. Building a chemical ontology using METHONTOLOGY and the ontology design environment. *IEEE Expert: Special Issue on Uses of Ontologies*, January/February:37–46, 1999.

[FGT10]   Enrico Franconi, Paolo Guagliardo, and Marco Trevisan. An intelligent query interface based on ontology navigation. In *Workshop on Visual Interfaces to the Social and Semantic Web (VISSW'10)*, 2010. Hong Kong, February 2010.

[Fin00]   Kit Fine. Neutral relations. *The Philosophical Review*, 109(1):1–33, 2000.

[FK15]   Pablo Rubén Fillottrani and C. Maria Keet. Evidence-based languages for conceptual data modelling profiles. In T. Morzy et al., editors, *19th Conference on Advances in Databases and Information Systems (ADBIS'15)*, volume 9282 of *LNCS*, pages 215–229. Springer, 2015. 8-11 Sept, 2015, Poitiers, France.

[FK17]   Pablo R. Fillottrani and C. Maria Keet. Patterns for heterogeneous tbox mappings to bridge different modelling decisions. In E. Blomqvist et al., editors, *Proceeding of the 14th Extended Semantic Web Conference (ESWC'17)*, volume 10249 of *LNCS*, pages 371–386. Springer, 2017. 30 May - 1 June 2017, Portoroz, Slovenia.

[FKK10]   Norbert E. Fuchs, Kaarel Kaljurand, and Tobias Kuhn. Discourse Representation Structures for ACE 6.6. Technical Report ifi-2010.0010, Department of Informatics, University of Zurich, Zurich, Switzerland, 2010.

[FR12]   Sebastien Ferré and Sebastian Rudolph. Advocatus diaboli — exploratory enrichment of ontologies with negative constraints. In A ten Teije et al., editors, *18th International Conference on Knowledge Engineering and Knowledge Management (EKAW'12)*, volume 7603 of *LNAI*, pages 42–56. Springer, 2012. Oct 8-12, Galway, Ireland.

[Gan05]   Aldo Gangemi. Ontology design patterns for semantic web content. In Yolanda Gil, Enrico Motta, V. Richard Benjamins, and Mark A. Musen, editors, *Proceedings of the 4th International Semantic Web Conference (ISWC'05)*, pages 262–276, Berlin, Heidelberg, 2005. Springer. Galway, Ireland, November 6-10, 2005.

[Gar17]   Daniel Garijo. WIDOCO: a wizard for documenting ontologies. In C. d'Amato et al., editors, *The Semantic Web ISWC 2017*, volume 10588 of *LNCS*, pages 94–102. Springer, 2017.

[GB92]   J. A. Goguen and R. M. Burstall. Institutions: Abstract Model Theory for Specification and Programming. *Journal of the Association for Computing Machinery*, 39(1):95–146, 1992. Predecessor in: LNCS 164, 221–256, 1984.

[GB11]   Normunds Gruzitis and Guntis Barzdins. Towards a more natural multilingual controlled language interface to OWL. In *Proceedings of the Ninth International Conference on Computational Semantics*, IWCS '11, pages 335–339, Stroudsburg, PA, USA, 2011. Association for Computational Linguistics.

[GBM07]   Rolf Grütter and Bettina Bauer-Messmer. Combining OWL with RCC for spatioterminological reasoning on environmental data. In *Third international Workshop OWL: Experiences and Directions (OWLED 2007)*, 2007. 6-7 June 2007, Innsbruck, Austria.

[Gen00]   Gene Ontology Consortium. Gene Ontology: tool for the unification of biology. *Nature Genetics*, 25:25–29, 2000.

[GF95]   M. Grüninger and M. S. Fox. Methodology for the design and evaluation of ontologies. In *IJCAI Workshop on Basic Ontological Issues in Knowledge Sharing*, 1995.

[GH07]   Christine Golbreich and Ian Horrocks. The OBO to OWL mapping, GO to OWL 1.1! In *Proc. of the Third OWL Experiences and Directions Workshop*, volume 258 of *CEUR-WS*, 2007. http://ceur-ws.org/.

[GHH+12]   Michael Grüninger, Torsten Hahmann, Ali Hashemi, Darren Ong, and Atalay Ozgovde. Modular first-order ontologies via repositories. *Applied Ontology*, 7(2):169–209, 2012.

[GK18]   Nikhil Gilbert and C. Maria Keet. Automating question generation and marking of language learning exercises for isiZulu. In *6th International Workshop on Controlled Natural language (CNL'18)*, page (in press). IOS Press, 2018. Co. Kildare, Ireland, 27-28 August 2018.

[GKL+09]   Chiara Ghidini, Barbara Kump, Stefanie Lindstaedt, Nahid Mabhub, Viktoria Pammer, Marco Rospocher, and Luciano Serafini. Moki: The enterprise modelling wiki. In *Proceedings of the 6th Annual European Semantic Web Conference (ESWC2009)*, 2009. Heraklion, Greece, 2009 (demo).

[GKWZ03]   D. Gabbay, A. Kurucz, F. Wolter, and M. Zakharyaschev. *Many-dimensional modal logics: theory and applications*. Studies in Logic. Elsevier, 2003.

[GOG+10]   Alexander Garcia, Kieran O'Neill, Leyla Jael Garcia, Phillip Lord, Robert Stevens, Óscar Corcho, and Frank Gibson. Developing ontologies within decentralized settings. In H. Chen et al., editors, *Semantic e-Science. Annals of Information Systems 11*, pages 99–139. Springer, 2010.

[GOS09]   Nicola Guarino, Daniel Oberle, and Steffen Staab. What is an ontology? In S. Staab and R. Studer, editors, *Handbook on Ontologies*, chapter 1, pages 1–17. Springer, 2009.

[GP09]   A. Gangemi and V. Presutti. Ontology design patterns. In S. Staab and R. Studer, editors, *Handbook on Ontologies*, pages 221–243. Springer Verlag, 2009.

[GPFLC04]   A. Gómez-Pérez, M. Fernández-Lopez, and O. Corcho. *Ontological Engineering*. Springer Verlag, 2004.

[GR09]   A. Gatt and E. Reiter. Simplenlg: A realisation engine for practical applications. In E. Krahmer and M. Theune, editors, *Proceedings of the 12th European Workshop on Natural Language Generation (ENLG'09)*, page 9093. ACL, 2009. March 30-31, 2009, Athens, Greece.

[Gru93]   T. R. Gruber. A translation approach to portable ontologies. *Knowledge Acquisition*, 5(2):199–220, 1993.

[GRV10]   Birte Glimm, Sebastian Rudolph, and Johanna Völker. Integrated metamodeling and diagnosis in OWL 2. In Peter F. Patel-Schneider, Yue Pan, Pascal Hitzler, Peter Mika, Lei Zhang, Jeff Z. Pan, Ian Horrocks, and Birte Glimm, editors, *Proceedings of the 9th International Semantic Web Conference*, volume 6496 of *LNCS*, pages 257–272. Springer, November 2010.

[Gua98]   Nicola Guarino. Formal ontology and information systems. In N. Guarino, editor, *Proceedings of Formal Ontology in Information Systems (FOIS'98)*, Frontiers in Artificial intelligence and Applications, pages 3–15. Amsterdam: IOS Press, 1998.

[Gua09]   Nicola Guarino. The ontological level: Revisiting 30 years of knowledge representation. In A.T. Borgida et al., editors, *Mylopoulos Festschrift*, volume 5600 of *LNCS*, pages 52–67. Springer, 2009.

[Gui05]   Giancarlo Guizzardi. *Ontological Foundations for Structural Conceptual Models*. Phd thesis, University of Twente, The Netherlands. Telematica Instituut Fundamental Research Series No. 15, 2005.

[GW00a]   Nicola Guarino and Chris Welty. A formal ontology of properties. In R. Dieng and O. Corby, editors, *Proceedings of 12th International Conference on Knowledge Engineering and Knowledge Management (EKAW'00)*, volume 1937 of *LNCS*, pages 97–112. Springer Verlag, 2000.

[GW00b]   Nicola Guarino and Chris Welty. Identity, unity, and individuality: towards a formal toolkit for ontological analysis. In W. Horn, editor, *Proceedings of ECAI'00*, pages 219–223. IOS Press, Amsterdam, 2000.

[GW08]   Giancarlo Guizzardi and Gerd Wagner. What's in a relationship: An ontological analysis. In Qing Li, Stefano Spaccapietra, Eric Yu, and Antoni Olivé, editors, *ER*, volume 5231 of *Lecture Notes in Computer Science*, pages 83–97. Springer, 2008.

[GW09]   N. Guarino and C. Welty. An overview of ontoclean. In S. Staab and
            R. Studer, editors, *Handbook on Ontologies*, pages 201–220. Springer
            Verlag, 2009.

[GWG+07]   Carole Goble, Katy Wolstencroft, Antoon Goderis, Duncan Hull, Jun
            Zhao, Pinar Alper, Phillip Lord, Chris Wroe, Khalid Belhajjame,
            Daniele Turi, Robert Stevens, Tom Oinn, and David De Roure. Knowl-
            edge discovery for biology with taverna. In C.J.O. Baker and H. Che-
            ung, editors, *Semantic Web: Revolutionizing knowledge discovery in
            the life sciences*, pages 355–395. Springer: New York, 2007.

[Hal01]   T.A. Halpin. *Information Modeling and Relational Databases*. San
            Francisco: Morgan Kaufmann Publishers, 2001.

[HC11]   Terry A. Halpin and Matthew Curland. Enriched support for ring
            constraints. In Robert Meersman, Tharam S. Dillon, and Pilar Herrero,
            editors, *OTM Workshops 2011*, volume 7046 of *LNCS*, pages 309–318.
            Springer, 2011. Hersonissos, Crete, Greece, October 17-21, 2011.

[HCTJ93]   J.-L. Hainaut, M. Chandelon, C. Tonneau, and M. Joris. Contribution
            to a theory of database reverse engineering. In *Reverse Engineering,
            1993., Proceedings of Working Conference on*, pages 161–170, May
            1993.

[HDG+11]   Robert Hoehndorf, Michel Dumontier, J H Gennari, Sarah
            Wimalaratne, Bernard de Bono, Daniel Cook, and George Gkoutos.
            Integrating systems biology models and biomedical ontologies. *BMC
            Systems Biology*, 5:124, 2011.

[HDN04]   N. Henze, P. Dolog, and W. Nejdl. Reasoning and ontologies for per-
            sonalized e-learning in the semantic web. *Educational Technology &
            Society*, 7(4):82–97, 2004.

[Hed04]   Shawn Hedman. *A first course in logic—an introduction to model
            theory, proof theory, computability, and complexity*. Oxford University
            Press, Oxford, 2004.

[Hep11]   Martin Hepp. SKOS to OWL. Online: `http://www.heppnetz.de/
            projects/skos2owl/`, Last accessed: Aug 30, 2011.

[HH06]   H. Herre and B. Heller. Semantic foundations of medical informa-
            tion systems based on top-level ontologies. *Knowledge-Based Systems*,
            19:107–115, 2006.

[Hir14]   Graeme Hirst. Overcoming linguistic barriers to the multilingual se-
            manticweb. In Buitelaar and Cimiano [BC14], chapter 1, pages 3–14.

[HKS06]   I. Horrocks, O. Kutz, and U. Sattler. The even more irresistible
            $\mathcal{SROIQ}$. *Proceedings of KR-2006*, pages 452–457, 2006.

[HND+11]   Melanie Hilario, Phong Nguyen, Huyen Do, Adam Woznica, and
            Alexandros Kalous. Ontology-based meta-mining of knowledge dis-
            covery workflows. In N. Jankowski, W. Duch, and K. Grabczewski,
            editors, *Meta-learning in Computational Intelligence*, pages 273–315.
            Springer, 2011.

[HOD+10]   Robert Hoehndorf, Anika Oellrich, Michel Dumontier, Janet Kelso, Dietrich Rebholz-Schuhmann, and Heinrich Herre. Relations as patterns: bridging the gap between OBO and OWL. *BMC Bioinformatics*, 11(1):441, 2010.

[HP98]   A. H. M. ter Hofstede and H. A. Proper. How to formalize it? formalization principles for information systems development methods. *Information and Software Technology*, 40(10):519–540, 1998.

[HP04]   J. R. Hobbs and F. Pan. An ontology of time for the semantic web. *ACM Transactions on Asian Language Processing (TALIP): Special issue on Temporal Information Processing*, 3(1):66–85, 2004.

[HPS08]   M. Horridge, B. Parsia, and U. Sattler. Laconic and precise justifications in OWL. In *Proc. of the 7th International Semantic Web Conference (ISWC 2008)*, volume 5318 of *LNCS*. Springer, 2008.

[HPSvH03] Ian Horrocks, Peter F. Patel-Schneider, and Frank van Harmelen. From SHIQ and RDF to OWL: The making of a web ontology language. *Journal of Web Semantics*, 1(1):7, 2003.

[HWZ99]   I. M. Hodgkinson, F. Wolter, and M. Zakharyaschev. Decidable fragments of first-order temporal logics. *Annals of pure and applied logic*, 106:85–134, 1999.

[IS09]   Antoine Isaac and Ed Summers. SKOS Simple Knowledge Organization System Primer. W3c standard, World Wide Web Consortium, August 2009 2009. http://www.w3.org/TR/skos-primer.

[JDM03]   M. Jarrar, J. Demy, and R. Meersman. On using conceptual data modeling for ontology engineering. *Journal on Data Semantics: Special issue on Best papers from the ER/ODBASE/COOPIS 2002 Conferences*, 1(1):185–207, 2003.

[JKD06]   Mustafa Jarrar, C. Maria Keet, and Paolo Dongilli. Multilingual verbalization of ORM conceptual models and axiomatized ontologies. Starlab technical report, Vrije Universiteit Brussel, Belgium, February 2006.

[KA08]   C. Maria Keet and Alessandro Artale. Representing and reasoning over a taxonomy of part-whole relations. *Applied Ontology – Special issue on Ontological Foundations for Conceptual Modeling*, 3(1-2):91–110, 2008.

[KA10]   C. Maria Keet and Alessandro Artale. A basic characterization of relation migration. In R. Meersman et al., editors, *OTM Workshops, 6th International Workshop on Fact-Oriented Modeling (ORM'10)*, volume 6428 of *LNCS*, pages 484–493. Springer, 2010. October 27-29, 2010, Hersonissou, Crete, Greece.

[KAGC08]   C. Maria Keet, Ronell Alberts, Aurona Gerber, and Gibson Chimamiwa. Enhancing web portals with Ontology-Based Data Access: the case study of South Africa's Accessibility Portal for people with disabilities. In Catherine Dolbear, Alan Ruttenberg, and Uli Sattler, editors, *Proceedings of the Fifth OWL: Experiences and Directions*

(OWLED 2008), volume 432 of *CEUR-WS*, 2008. Karlsruhe, Germany, 26-27 October 2008.

[Kas05]   Gilles Kassel.   Integration of the DOLCE top-level ontology into the OntoSpec methodology.   Technical Report HAL : hal-00012203/arXiv : cs.AI/0510050, Laboratoire de Recherche en Informatique d'Amiens (LaRIA), October 2005.   http://hal.archives-ouvertes.fr/ccsd-00012203.

[Kaz08]   Yevgeny Kazakov. RIQ and SROIQ are harder than SHOIQ. In *11th International Conference on Principles of Knowledge Representation and Reasoning (KR'08)*, pages 274–284, 2008. 16-19 August 2008, Sydney, Australia.

[KB17]   C. Maria Keet and Sonia Berman. Determining the preferred representation of temporal constraints in conceptual models. In H.C. Mayr et al., editors, *36th International Conference on Conceptual Modeling (ER'17)*, volume 10650 of *LNCS*, pages 437–450. Springer, 2017. 6-9 Nov 2017, Valencia, Spain.

[KC16]   C. M. Keet and T. Chirema. A model for verbalising relations with roles in multiple languages. In E. Blomqvist, P. Ciancarini, F. Poggi, and F. Vitali, editors, *Proceedings of the 20th International Conference on Knowledge Engineering and Knowledge Management (EKAW'16)*, volume 10024 of *LNAI*, pages 384–399. Springer, 2016. 19-23 November 2016, Bologna, Italy.

[Kee05]   C. Maria Keet. Factors affecting ontology development in ecology. In B Ludäscher and L. Raschid, editors, *Data Integration in the Life Sciences 2005 (DILS2005)*, volume 3615 of *LNBI*, pages 46–62. Springer Verlag, 2005. San Diego, USA, 20-22 July 2005.

[Kee09]   C. Maria Keet. Constraints for representing transforming entities in bio-ontologies. In R. Serra and R. Cucchiara, editors, *11th Congress of the Italian Association for Artificial Intelligence (AI*IA 2009)*, volume 5883 of *LNAI*, pages 11–20. Springer Verlag, 2009. Reggio Emilia, Italy, Dec. 9-12, 2009.

[Kee10a]   C. Maria Keet. Dependencies between ontology design parameters. *International Journal of Metadata, Semantics and Ontologies*, 5(4):265–284, 2010.

[Kee10b]   C. Maria Keet. On the feasibility of description logic knowledge bases with rough concepts and vague instances. In *Proceedings of the 23rd International Workshop on Description Logics (DL'10)*, CEUR-WS, pages 314–324, 2010. 4-7 May 2010, Waterloo, Canada.

[Kee10c]   C. Maria Keet. Ontology engineering with rough concepts and instances. In P. Cimiano and H.S. Pinto, editors, *17th International Conference on Knowledge Engineering and Knowledge Management (EKAW'10)*, volume 6317 of *LNCS*, pages 507–517. Springer, 2010. 11-15 October 2010, Lisbon, Portugal.

[Kee11a]   C. Maria Keet. Rough subsumption reasoning with rOWL. In *Proceeding of the SAICSIT Annual Research Conference 2011 (SAICSIT'11)*, pages 133–140. ACM Conference Proceedings, 2011. Cape Town, South Africa, October 3-5, 2011.

[Kee11b]   C. Maria Keet. The use of foundational ontologies in ontology development: an empirical assessment. In G. Antoniou et al., editors, *8th Extended Semantic Web Conference (ESWC'11)*, volume 6643 of *LNCS*, pages 321–335. Springer, 2011. Heraklion, Crete, Greece, 29 May-2 June, 2011.

[Kee12a]   C. Maria Keet. Detecting and revising flaws in OWL object property expressions. In A. ten Teije et al., editors, *18th International Conference on Knowledge Engineering and Knowledge Management (EKAW'12)*, volume 7603 of *LNAI*, pages 252–266. Springer, 2012. Oct 8-12, Galway, Ireland.

[Kee12b]   C. Maria Keet. Transforming semi-structured life science diagrams into meaningful domain ontologies with DiDOn. *Journal of Biomedical Informatics*, 45:482–494, 2012.

[Kee13]   C. Maria Keet. Ontology-driven formal conceptual data modeling for biological data analysis. In Mourad Elloumi and Albert Y. Zomaya, editors, *Biological Knowledge Discovery Handbook: Preprocessing, Mining and Postprocessing of Biological Data*, chapter 6, pages 129–154. Wiley, 2013.

[Kee14]   C. Maria Keet. Preventing, detecting, and revising flaws in object property expressions. *Journal on Data Semantics*, 3(3):189–206, 2014.

[Kee16]   C. M. Keet. Relating some stuff to other stuff. In E. Blomqvist, P. Ciancarini, F. Poggi, and F. Vitali, editors, *Proceedings of the 20th International Conference on Knowledge Engineering and Knowledge Management (EKAW'16)*, volume 10024 of *LNAI*, pages 368–383. Springer, 2016. 19-23 November 2016, Bologna, Italy.

[Kee17a]   C. M. Keet. A note on the compatibility of part-whole relations with foundational ontologies. In *FOUST-II: 2nd Workshop on Foundational Ontology, Joint Ontology Workshops 2017*, volume 2050 of *CEUR-WS*, page 10p, 2017. 21-23 September 2017, Bolzano, Italy.

[Kee17b]   C. M. Keet. Representing and aligning similar relations: parts and wholes in isizulu vs english. In J. Gracia, F. Bond, J. McCrae, P. Buitelaar, C. Chiarcos, and S. Hellmann, editors, *Language, Data, and Knowledge 2017 (LDK'17)*, volume 10318 of *LNAI*, pages 58–73. Springer, 2017. 19-20 June, 2017, Galway, Ireland.

[KFRMG12]   C. Maria Keet, Francis C. Fernández-Reyes, and Annette Morales-González. Representing mereotopological relations in OWL ontologies with ONTOPARTS. In E. Simperl et al., editors, *Proceedings of the 9th Extended Semantic Web Conference (ESWC'12)*, volume 7295 of *LNCS*, pages 240–254. Springer, 2012. 29-31 May 2012, Heraklion, Crete, Greece.

[KG17]   Megan Katsumi and Michael Grüninger. Choosing ontologies for reuse. *Applied Ontology*, 12(3-4):195–221, 2017.

[KHH16]   Nazifa Karima, Karl Hammar, and Pascal Hitzler. How to document ontology design patterns. In *Proceedings of the 7th Workshop on Ontology Patterns (WOP'16)*, 2016. Kobe, Japan, on 18th October 2016.

[KHS⁺17]   Evgeny Kharlamov, Dag Hovland, Martin G. Skaeveland, Dimitris Bilidas, Ernesto Jiménez-Ruiz, Guohui Xiao, Ahmet Soylu, Davide Lanti, Martin Rezk, Dmitriy Zheleznyakov, Martin Giese, Hallstein Lie, Yannis Ioannidis, Yannis Kotidis, Manolis Koubarakis, and Arild Waaler. Ontology based data access in statoil. *Web Semantics: Science, Services and Agents on the World Wide Web*, 44:3–36, 2017.

[KJLW12]   Daniel Kless, Ludger Jansen, Jutta Lindenthal, and Jens Wiebensohn. A method for re-engineering a thesaurus into an ontology. In M. Donnelly and G. Guizzardi, editors, *Proceedings of the Seventh International Conference on Formal Ontology in Information Systems*, pages 133–146. IOS Press, 2012.

[KK12]   Zubeida Khan and C. Maria Keet. ONSET: Automated foundational ontology selection and explanation. In A. ten Teije et al., editors, *18th International Conference on Knowledge Engineering and Knowledge Management (EKAW'12)*, volume 7603 of *LNAI*, pages 237–251. Springer, 2012. Oct 8-12, Galway, Ireland.

[KK13a]   Z. Khan and C. Maria Keet. Addressing issues in foundational ontology mediation. In Joaquim Filipe and Jan Dietz, editors, *5th International Conference on Knowledge Engineering and Ontology Development (KEOD'13)*, pages 5–16. INSTICC, SCITEPRESS – Science and Technology Publications, 2013. Vilamoura, Portugal, 19-22 September 2013.

[KK13b]   Zubeida Khan and C. Maria Keet. The foundational ontology library ROMULUS. In Alfredo Cuzzocrea and Sofian Maabout, editors, *Proceedings of the 3rd International Conference on Model & Data Engineering (MEDI'13)*, volume 8216 of *LNCS*, pages 200–211. Springer, 2013. September 25-27, 2013, Amantea, Calabria, Italy.

[KK14]   Zubeida C. Khan and C. Maria Keet. Feasibility of automated foundational ontology interchangeability. In K. Janowicz and S. Schlobach, editors, *19th International Conference on Knowledge Engineering and Knowledge Management (EKAW'14)*, volume 8876 of *LNAI*, pages 225–237. Springer, 2014. 24-28 Nov, 2014, Linkoping, Sweden.

[KK15]   Z. C. Khan and C. M. Keet. Foundational ontology mediation in ROMULUS. In A. Fred et al., editors, *Knowledge Discovery, Knowledge Engineering and Knowledge Management: IC3K 2013 Selected Papers*, volume 454 of *CCIS*, pages 132–152. Springer, 2015.

[KK16]   Zubeida C. Khan and C. Maria Keet. ROMULUS: a Repository of Ontologies for MULtiple USes populated with foundational ontologies. *Journal on Data Semantics*, 5(1):19–36, 2016.

[KK17a]   C. M. Keet and L. Khumalo. Toward a knowledge-to-text controlled natural language of isiZulu. *Language Resources and Evaluation*, 51(1):131–157, 2017.

[KK17b]   C. Maria Keet and Oliver Kutz. Orchestrating a network of mereo(topo)logical theories. In *Proceedings of the Knowledge Capture Conference*, K-CAP 2017, pages 11:1–11:8, New York, NY, USA, 2017. ACM.

[KKG13]   C. Maria Keet, M. Tahir Khan, and Chiara Ghidini. Ontology authoring with FORZA. In *Proceedings of the 22nd ACM international conference on Conference on Information & Knowledge Management (CIKM'13)*, pages 569–578. ACM proceedings, 2013. Oct. 27 - Nov. 1, 2013, San Francisco, USA.

[KL16]   C. M. Keet and A. Lawrynowicz. Test-driven development of ontologies. In H. Sack et al., editors, *Proceedings of the 13th Extended Semantic Web Conference (ESWC'16)*, volume 9678 of *LNCS*, pages 642–657. Springer, 2016. 29 May - 2 June, 2016, Crete, Greece.

[KLd+15]   C. Maria Keet, Agnieszka Lawrynowicz, Claudia d'Amato, Alexandros Kalousis, P. Nguyen, Raul Palma, Robert Stevens, and Melani Hilario. The data mining optimization ontology. *Web Semantics: Science, Services and Agents on the World Wide Web*, 32:43–53, 2015.

[KLT+10]   R. Kontchakov, C. Lutz, D. Toman, F. Wolter, and M. Zakharyaschev. The combined approach to query answering in DL-Lite. In Fangzhen Lin, Ulrike Sattler, and Miroslaw Truszczynski, editors, *Principles of Knowledge Representation and Reasoning: Proceedings of the Twelfth International Conference (KR 2010)*. AAAI Press, 2010. Toronto, Ontario, Canada, May 9-13, 2010.

[KML10]   O. Kutz, T. Mossakowski, and D. Lücke. Carnap, Goguen, and the Hyperontologies: Logical Pluralism and Heterogeneous Structuring in Ontology Design. *Logica Universalis*, 4(2), 2010. Special issue on 'Is Logic Universal?'.

[KSFPV13]   C. Maria Keet, Mari Carmen Suárez-Figueroa, and Maria Poveda-Villalón. The current landscape of pitfalls in ontologies. In Joaquim Filipe and Jan Dietz, editors, *5th International Conference on Knowledge Engineering and Ontology Development (KEOD'13)*, pages 132–139. INSTICC, SCITEPRESS – Science and Technology Publications, 2013. Vilamoura, Portugal, 19-22 September 2013.

[KSFPV15]   C. M. Keet, M. C. Suárez-Figueroa, and M. Poveda-Villalón. Pitfalls in ontologies and tips to prevent them. In A. Fred, J. L. G. Dietz, K. Liu, and J. Filipe, editors, *Knowledge Discovery, Knowledge Engineering and Knowledge Management: IC3K 2013 Selected papers*, volume 454 of *CCIS*, pages 115–131. Springer, 2015.

[KSH12]   Markus Krötzsch, František Simančík, and Ian Horrocks. A description logic primer. Technical Report 1201.4089v1, Department of Computer Science, University of Oxford, UK, 2012. arXiv:cs.LO/12014089v1.

[LAF14]   Pilar León-Araúz and Pamela Faber. Context and terminology in the multilingual semantic web. In Paul Buitelaar and Philip Cimiano, editors, *Towards the Multilingual Semantic Web: Principles, Methods and Applications*, chapter 3, pages 31–47. Springer, 2014.

[Lam17]   Jean-Baptiste Lamy. Owlready: Ontology-oriented programming in python with automaticclassification and high level constructs for biomedical ontologies. *Artificial Intelligence in Medicine*, 2017.

[Leo08]   Joop Leo. Modeling relations. *Journal of Philosophical Logic*, 37:353–385, 2008.

[LHC11]   Kaihong Liu, William R. Hogan, and Rebecca S. Crowley. Natural language processing methods and systems for biomedical ontology learning. *Journal of Biomedical Informatics*, 44(1):163–179, 2011.

[LLNW11]   Thorsten Liebig, Marko Luther, Olaf Noppens, and Michael Wessel. OWLlink. *Semantic Web Journal*, 2(1):23–32, 2011.

[Loe15]   Frank Loebe. *Ontological Semantics: An Attempt at Foundations of Ontology Representation*. Phd thesis, Fakultät für Mathematik und Informatik, Universität Leipzig, 2015.

[LS08]   Thomas Lukasiewicz and Umberto Straccia. Managing uncertainty and vagueness in description logics for the semantic web. *Journal of Web Semantics*, 6(4):291–308, 2008.

[LT09]   Lina Lubyte and Sergio Tessaris. Automated extraction of ontologies wrapping relational data sources. In *Proceedings of International Conference on Database and Expert Systems Applications (DEXA'09)*, pages 128–142. Springer, 2009.

[LTW09]   C. Lutz, D. Toman, and F. Wolter. Conjunctive query answering in the description logic EL using a relational database system. In *Proceedings of the 21st International Joint Conference on Artificial Intelligence IJCAI'09*. AAAI Press, 2009.

[Luk17]   Thomas Lukasiewicz. Uncertainty reasoning for the semantic web. In G. Ianni et al., editors, *Reasoning Web 2017*, volume 10370 of *LNCS*, pages 276–291. Springer, 2017.

[LWZ08]   Carsten Lutz, Frank Wolter, and Michael Zakharyaschev. Temporal description logics: A survey. In *Proc. of the Fifteenth International Symposium on Temporal Representation and Reasoning (TIME'08)*. IEEE Computer Society Press, 2008.

[MAdCB+12]   John McCrae, Guadalupe Aguado-de Cea, Paul Buitelaar, Philipp Cimiano, Thierry Declerck, Asunción Gómez-Pérez, Jorge Gracia, Laura Hollink, Elena Montiel-Ponsoda, Dennis Spohr, and Tobias Wunner. Interchanging lexical resources on the semantic web. *Language Resources and Evaluation*, 46(4):701–719, 2012.

[MB09]   Alistar Miles and Sean Bechhofer. SKOS Simple Knowledge Organization System Reference. W3c recommendation, World Wide Web Consortium (W3C), 18 August 2009.

[MBG+03]   C. Masolo, S. Borgo, A. Gangemi, N. Guarino, and A. Oltramari. Ontology library. WonderWeb Deliverable D18 (ver. 1.0, 31-12-2003)., 2003. http://wonderweb.semanticweb.org.

[MBSJ08]   Joshua S. Madin, Shawn Bowers, Mark P. Schildhauer, and
             Matthew B. Jones. Advancing ecological research with ontologies.
             Trends in Ecology & Evolution, 23(3):159–168, 2008.

[McC10]   Dave McComb. Gist: The minimalist upper ontology (abstract). Se-
             mantic Technology Conference, 2010. 21-25 June 2010, San Francisco,
             USA.

[McD17]   M. H. McDaniel. *An Automated System for the Assessment and Rank-
             ing of Domain Ontologies*. PhD thesis, Department of Computer Sci-
             ence, 2017.

[MCNK15]   T. Mossakowski, M. Codescu, F. Neuhaus, and O. Kutz. *The Road
             to Universal Logic–Festschrift for 50th birthday of Jean-Yves Beziau,
             Volume II*, chapter The distributed ontology, modelling and specifica-
             tion language - DOL. Studies in Universal Logic. Birkhäuser, 2015.

[MdCB+12]   John McCrae, Guadalupe Aguado de Cea, Paul Buitelaar, Philipp
             Cimiano, Thierry Declerck, Asunción Gómez-Pérez, Jorge Gracia,
             Laura Hollink, Elena Montiel-Ponsoda, Dennis Spohr, and Tobias
             Wunner. The lemon cookbook. Technical report, Monnet Project,
             June 2012. www.lemon-model.net.

[Mer10a]   G. H. Merrill. Ontological realism: Methodology or misdirection? *Ap-
             plied Ontology*, 5(2):79108, 2010.

[Mer10b]   Gary H. Merrill. Realism and reference ontologies: Considerations,
             reflections and problems. *Applied Ontology*, 5(3):189–221, 2010.

[MGH+09]   Boris Motik, Bernardo Cuenca Grau, Ian Horrocks, Zhe Wu, Achille
             Fokoue, and Carsten Lutz. OWL 2 Web Ontology Language Profiles.
             W3C recommendation, W3C, 27 Oct. 2009. `http://www.w3.org/TR/owl2-profiles/`.

[Miz10]   R. Mizoguchi. YAMATO: Yet Another More Advanced Top-level On-
             tology. In *Proceedings of the Sixth Australasian Ontology Workshop*,
             Conferences in Research and Practice in Information, pages 1–16. CR-
             PIT, 2010. Sydney : ACS.

[MPSP09]   Boris Motik, Peter F. Patel-Schneider, and Bijan Parsia. OWL 2 web
             ontology language structural specification and functional-style syntax.
             W3c recommendation, W3C, 27 Oct. 2009. `http://www.w3.org/TR/owl2-syntax/`.

[MR05]   M. C. MacLeod and E. M. Rubenstein. Universals. In *The Inter-
             net Encyclopedia of Philosophy*. 2005. `http://www.iep.utm.edu/u/universa.htm`.

[MSKK07]   R. Mizoguchi, E. Sunagawa, K. Kozaki, and Y. Kitamura. A model of
             roles within an ontology development tool: Hozo. *Applied Ontology*,
             2(2):159–179, 2007.

[N+13]   Fabian Neuhaus et al. Towards ontology evaluation across the life
             cycle. *Applied Ontology*, 8(3):179–194, 2013.

[Neu17]   Fabian Neuhaus. On the definition of ontology. In *FOUST-II: 2nd Workshop on Foundational Ontology, Joint Ontology Workshops 2017*, volume 2050 of *CEUR-WS*, page 10p, 2017. 21-23 September 2017, Bolzano, Italy.

[NM01]   N.F. Noy and D.L. McGuinness. Ontology development 101: A guide to creating your first ontology. Technical Report KSL-01-05, and Stanford Medical Informatics Technical Report SMI-2001-0880, Stanford Knowledge Systems Laboratory, March 2001.

[NP01]   I. Niles and A. Pease. Towards a standard upper ontology. In Chris Welty and Barry Smith, editors, *Proceedings of the 2nd International Conference on Formal Ontology in Information Systems (FOIS-2001)*, 2001. Ogunquit, Maine, October 17-19, 2001.

[OHWM10]   Martin J. O'Connor, Christian Halaschek-Wiener, and Mark A. Musen. Mapping master: A flexible approach for mapping spreadsheets to owl. In Patel-Schneider P. F. et al., editors, *Proceedings of the International Semantic Web Conference 2010 (ISWC'10)*, volume 6497 of *LNCS*, pages 194–208. Springer, 2010.

[Ope]   OpenMRS. https://www.transifex.com/openmrs/OpenMRS/.

[PD⁺09]   V. Presutti, E Daga, et al. extreme design with content ontology design patterns. In *Proc. of WS on OP'09*, volume 516 of *CEUR-WS*, pages 83–97, 2009.

[Per17]   Silvio Peroni. A simplified agile methodology for ontology development. In Dragoni M., Poveda-Villalón M., and Jimenez-Ruiz E., editors, *OWLED 2016, ORE 2016: OWL: Experiences and Directions Reasoner Evaluation*, volume 10161 of *LNCS*, pages 55–69. Springer, 2017.

[Por10]   F. Portoraro. Automated reasoning. In E. Zalta, editor, *Stanford Encyclopedia of Philosophy*. 2010. http://plato.stanford.edu/entries/reasoning-automated/.

[PS07]   Zdzislaw Pawlak and Andrzej Skowron. Rudiments of rough sets. *Information Sciences*, 177(1):3–27, 2007.

[PS15]   Adrian Paschke and Ralph Schaefermeier. Aspect OntoMaven - aspect-oriented ontology development and configuration with OntoMaven. Technical Report 1507.00212v1, Institute of Computer Science, Free University of Berlin, July 2015.

[PT11]   Rafael Peñaloza and Anni-Yasmin Turhan. A practical approach for computing generalization inferences in EL. In G. Antoniou et al., editors, *8th Extended Semantic Web Conference (ESWC'11)*, volume 6643 of *LNCS*, pages 410–423. Springer, 2011. Heraklion, Crete, Greece, 29 May-2 June, 2011.

[PVSFGP12]   María Poveda-Villalón, Mari Carmen Suárez-Figueroa, and Asunción Gómez-Pérez. Validating ontologies with OOPS! In A. ten Teije et al., editors, *18th International Conference on Knowledge Engineering and Knowledge Management (EKAW'12)*, volume 7603 of *LNAI*, pages 267–281. Springer, 2012. Oct 8-12, Galway, Ireland.

[RCB+07] Alan Ruttenberg, Tim Clark, William Bug, Matthias Samwald, Olivier Bodenreider, Helen Chen, Donald Doherty, Kerstin Forsberg, Yong Gao, Vipul Kashyap, June Kinoshita, Joanne Luciano, M Scott Marshall, Chimezie Ogbuji, Jonathan Rees, Susie Stephens, Gwendolyn T Wong, Elizabeth Wu, Davide Zaccagnini, Tonya Hongsermeier, Eric Neumann, Ivan Herman, and Kei-Hoi Cheung. Advancing translational research with the semantic web. *BMC Bioinformatics*, 8(Suppl 3):S2, 2007.

[RCC92] D. A. Randell, Z. Cui, and A. G. Cohn. A spatial logic based on regions and connection. In *Proc. 3rd Int. Conf. on Knowledge Representation and Reasoning*, pages 165–176. Morgan Kaufmann, 1992.

[RCVB09] C. Roussey, O. Corcho, and L. Vilches-Blázquez. A catalogue of OWL ontology antipatterns. In *Proc. of K-CAP'09*, pages 205–206, 2009.

[RD97] E. Reiter and R. Dale. Building applied natural language generation systems. *Natural Language Engineering*, 3:57–87, 1997.

[RDH+04] AL Rector, N Drummond, M Horridge, L Rogers, H Knublauch, R Stevens, H Wang, and C. Wroe, Csallner. OWL pizzas: Practical experience of teaching OWL-DL: Common errors & common patterns. In *Proceedings of the 14th International Conference Knowledge Acquisition, Modeling and Management (EKAW'04)*, volume 3257 of *LNCS*, pages 63–81. Springer, 2004. Whittlebury Hall, UK.

[RKH08a] Sebastian Rudolph, Markus Krötzsch, and Pascal Hitzler. All elephants are bigger than all mice. In Franz Baader, Carsten Lutz, and Boris Motik, editors, *Proc. 21st Int. Workshop on Description Logics (DL08)*, volume 353 of *CEUR-WS*, 2008. Dresden, Germany, May 1316, 2008.

[RKH08b] Sebastian Rudolph, Markus Krötzsch, and Pascal Hitzler. Cheap boolean role constructors for description logics. In Steffen Hölldobler, Carsten Lutz, and Heinrich Wansing, editors, *Proc. 11th European Conf. on Logics in Artificial Intelligence (JELIA08)*, volume 5293 of *LNAI*, page 362374. Springer, 2008.

[RMC12] Mariano Rodríguez-Muro and Diego Calvanese. Quest, an OWL 2 QL reasoner for ontology-based data access. In P. Klinov and M. Horridge, editors, *7th Workshop on OWL: Experiences and Directions (OWLED'12)*, volume 849 of *CEUR-WS*, 2012. 27-28 May, Heraklion, Crete, Greece.

[RMJ03] C. Rosse and J. L. V. Mejino Jr. A reference ontology for biomedical informatics: the foundational model of anatomy. *J. of Biomedical Informatics*, 36(6):478–500, 2003.

[RMLC08] Mariano Rodriguez-Muro, Lina Lubyte, and Diego Calvanese. Realizing Ontology Based Data Access: A plug-in for Protégé. In *Proc. of the Workshop on Information Integration Methods, Architectures, and Systems (IIMAS 2008)*. IEEE Computer Society, 2008.

[SAR⁺07]   B. Smith, M. Ashburner, C. Rosse, J. Bard, W. Bug, W. Ceusters, L.J. Goldberg, K. Eilbeck, A. Ireland, C.J. Mungall, The OBI Consortium, N. Leontis, A.B. Rocca-Serra, A. Ruttenberg, S-A. Sansone, M. Shah, P.L. Whetzel, and S. Lewis. The OBO Foundry: Coordinated evolution of ontologies to support biomedical data integration. *Nature Biotechnology*, 25(11):1251–1255, 2007.

[Sat07]   Ulrike Sattler. Reasoning in description logics: Basics, extensions, and relatives. In G. Antoniou et al., editors, *Reasoning Web 2007*, volume 4636 of *LNCS*, page 154182. Springer, 2007.

[SBF98]   R. Studer, R. Benjamins, and D. Fensel. Knowledge engineering: Principles and methods. *Data & Knowledge Engineering*, 25(1-2):161198, 1998.

[SC10]   Barry Smith and Werner Ceusters. Ontological realism: A methodology for coordinated evolution of scientific ontologies. *Applied Ontology*, 5(3):139–188, 2010.

[SCK⁺05]   B. Smith, W. Ceusters, B. Klagges, J. Köhler, A. Kumar, J. Lomax, C. Mungall, F. Neuhaus, A. L. Rector, and C. Rosse. Relations in biomedical ontologies. *Genome Biology*, 6:R46, 2005.

[SD17]   Hazem Safwat and Brian Davis. CNLs for the semantic web: a state of the art. *Language Resources & Evaluation*, 51(1):191–220, 2017.

[SFdCB⁺08] Mari Carmen Suarez-Figueroa, Guadalupe Aguado de Cea, Carlos Buil, Klaas Dellschaft, Mariano Fernandez-Lopez, Andres Garcia, Asuncion Gómez-Pérez, German Herrero, Elena Montiel-Ponsoda, Marta Sabou, Boris Villazon-Terrazas, and Zheng Yufei. NeOn methodology for building contextualized ontology networks. NeOn Deliverable D5.4.1, NeOn Project, 2008.

[SGJR⁺17] Ahmet Soylu, Martin Giese, Ernesto Jimenez-Ruiz, Evgeny Kharlamov, Dmitriy Zheleznyakov, and Ian Horrocks. Ontology-based enduser visual query formulation: Why, what, who, how, and which? *Universal Access in the Information Society*, 16(2):435–467, Jun 2017.

[SKC⁺08]   R. Schwitter, K. Kaljurand, A. Cregan, C. Dolbear, and G. Hart. A comparison of three controlled natural languages for OWL 1.1. In *Proc. of OWLED 2008 DC*, 2008. Washington, DC, USA metropolitan area, on 1-2 April 2008.

[SKZ⁺ss]   A. Soylu, E. Kharlamov, D. Zheleznyakov, E. Jimenez Ruiz, M. Giese, M.G. Skjaeveland, D. Hovland, R. Schlatte, S. Brandt, H. Lie, and I. Horrocks. Optiquevqs: a visual query system over ontologies for industry. *Semantic Web*, in press.

[SLL⁺04]   Dagobert Soergel, Boris Lauser, Anita Liang, Frehiwot Fisseha, Johannes Keizer, and Stephen Katz. Reengineering thesauri for new applications: the AGROVOC example. *Journal of Digital Information*, 4(4), 2004.

[SMB10]   Elena Simperl, Malgorzata Mochol, and Tobias Bürger. Achieving maturity: the state of practice in ontology engineering in 2009. *International Journal of Computer Science and Applications*, 7(1):45–65, 2010.

[Smi04]   B. Smith. Beyond concepts, or: Ontology as reality representation. In A. Varzi and L. Vieu, editors, *Formal Ontology and Information Systems. Proceedings of the Third International Conference (FOIS'04)*, pages 73–84. Amsterdam: IOS Press, 2004.

[SNO12]   SNOMED CT, last accessed: 27-1-2012. `http://www.ihtsdo.org/snomed-ct/`.

[Sol05]   D. Solow. *How to read and do proofs: An introduction to mathematical thought processes*. John Wiley & Sons, Hoboken NJ, USA., 4th edition, 2005.

[SS06]   Vijayan Sugumaran and Veda C. Storey. The role of domain ontologies in database design: An ontology management and conceptual modeling environment. *ACM Transactions on Database Systems*, 31(3):1064–1094, 2006.

[SS09]   Markus Stocker and Evren Sirin. Pelletspatial: A hybrid RCC-8 and RDF/OWL reasoning and query engine. In Rinke Hoekstra and Pieter Patel-Schneider, editors, *Proceedings of the 6th International Workshop OWL: Experiences and Directions (OWLED'09)*, volume 529 of *CEUR-WS*, 2009. Chantilly, Virginia, USA, 23-24 October 2009.

[SSBS09]   Stefan Schulz, Holger Stenzhorn, Martin Boekers, and Barry Smith. Strengths and limitations of formal ontologies in the biomedical domain. *Electronic Journal of Communication, Information and Innovation in Health (Special Issue on Ontologies, Semantic Web and Health)*, 3(1):31–45, 2009.

[SSSS01]   S. Staab, H.P. Schnurr, R. Studer, and Y. Sure. Knowledge processes and ontologies. *IEEE Intelligent Systems*, 16(1):26–34, 2001.

[STK16]   L. Sanby, I. Todd, and C. M. Keet. Comparing the template-based approach to gf: the case of afrikaans. In *2nd International Workshop on Natural Language Generation and the Semantic Web (WebNLG'16)*, page (in print). ACL, 2016. September 6, 2016, Edinburgh, Scotland.

[Str08]   Umberto Straccia. Managing uncertainty and vagueness in description logics, logic programs and description logic programs. In *Reasoning Web, 4th International Summer School*, 2008.

[THU+16]   Niket Tandon, Charles Hariman, Jacopo Urbani, Anna Rohrbach, Marcus Rohrbach, and Gerhard Weikum. Commonsense in parts: Mining part-whole relations from the web and image tags. In *Proceedings of the Thirtieth AAAI Conference on Artificial Intelligence (AAAI'16)*, pages 243–250. AAAI Press, 2016.

[Tob01]   S. Tobies. *Complexity Results and Practical Algorithms for Logics in Knowledge Representation*. PhD thesis, RWTH Aachen, 2001.

[Tur08]   Anni-Yasmin Turhan. *On the Computation of Common Subsumers in Description Logics*. PhD thesis, TU Dresden, Institute for Theoretical Computer Science, 2008, 2008.

[Tur10]   Anni-Yasmin Turhan. Reasoning and explanation in EL and in expressive Description Logics. In U. Assmann, A. Bartho, and C. Wende, editors, *Reasoning Web 2010*, volume 6325 of *LNCS*, pages 1–27. Springer, 2010.

[TW11]   David Toman and Grant E. Weddell. *Fundamentals of Physical Design and Query Compilation*. Synthesis Lectures on Data Management. Morgan & Claypool Publishers, 2011.

[Var04]   A. C. Varzi. Mereology. In E. N. Zalta, editor, *Stanford Encyclopedia of Philosophy*. Stanford, fall 2004 edition, 2004. http://plato.stanford.edu/archives/fall2004/entries/mereology/.

[Var07]   A.C. Varzi. *Handbook of Spatial Logics*, chapter Spatial reasoning and ontology: parts, wholes, and locations, pages 945–1038. Berlin Heidelberg: Springer Verlag, 2007.

[Var12]   Achille C. Varzi. On doing ontology without metaphysics. *Philosophical Perspectives*, 25(1):407–423, 2012.

[VF09]   K. Vila and A. Ferrández. Developing an ontology for improving question answering in the agricultural domain. In F. Sartori, M.Á. Sicilia, and N. Manouselis, editors, *3rd International Conference on Metadata and Semantics (MTSR'09)*, volume 46 of *CCIS*, pages 245–256. Springer, 2009. Oct 1-2 2009 Milan, Italy.

[vHLP08]   Frank van Harmelen, Vladimir Lifschitz, and Bruce Porter, editors. *Handbook of Knowledge Representation*. Elsevier, 2008.

[VKC+16]   Charles F. Vardeman, Adila A. Krisnadhi, Michelle Cheatham, Krzysztof Janowicz, Holly Ferguson, Pascal Hitzler, and Aimee P. C. Buccellato. An ontology design pattern and its use case for modeling material transformation. *Semantic Web Journal*, 8(5):719–731, 2016.

[Vra09]   Danny Vrandečić. Ontology evaluation. In S. Staab and R. Studer, editors, *Handbook on Ontologies*, pages 293–313. Springer, 2nd edition, 2009.

[Wel06]   Chris Welty. Ontowlclean: cleaning OWL ontologies with OWL. In B. Bennet and C. Fellbaum, editors, *Proceedings of Formal Ontologies in Information Systems (FOIS'06)*, pages 347–359. IOS Press, 2006.

[WHF+13]   Katherine Wolstencroft, Robert Haines, Donal Fellows, Alan Williams, David Withers, Stuart Owen, Stian Soiland-Reyes, Ian Dunlop, Aleksandra Nenadic, Paul Fisher, Jiten Bhagat, Khalid Belhajjame, Finn Bacall, Alex Hardisty, Abraham Nieva de la Hidalga, Maria P. Balcazar Vargas, Shoaib Sufi, , and Carole Goble. The taverna workflow suite: designing and executing workflows of web services on the desktop, web or in the cloud. *Nucleic Acids Research*, 41(W1):W557–W561, 2013.

[WKB07]   R. Witte, T. Kappler, and C.J.O. Baker. Ontology design for biomedical text mining. In C.J.O. Baker and H. Cheung, editors, *Semantic*

Web: revolutionizing knowledge discovery in the life sciences, pages 281–313. Springer, 2007.

[WNS⁺11]   Patricia L. Whetzel, Natalya Fridman Noy, Nigam H. Shah, Paul R. Alexander, Csongor Nyulas, Tania Tudorache, and Mark A. Musen. BioPortal: enhanced functionality via new web services from the national center for biomedical ontology to access and use ontologies in software applications. *Nucleic Acids Research*, 39(Web-Server-Issue), 2011.

[WSH07]   K. Wolstencroft, R. Stevens, and V. Haarslev. Applying OWL reasoning to genomic data. In C.J.O. Baker and H. Cheung, editors, *Semantic Web: revolutionizing knowledge discovery in the life sciences*, pages 225–248. Springer: New York, 2007.

[ZBG06]   S. Zhang, O. Bodenreider, and C. Golbreich. Experience in reasoning with the Foundational Model of Anatomy in OWL DL. In R. B. Altman, A. K. Dunker, L. Hunter, T. A. Murray, and T. E. Klein, editors, *Pacific Symposium on Biocomputing (PSB'06)*, pages 200–211. World Scientific, 2006.

[ZYS⁺05]   Y. Zhou, Jx A. Young, A. Santrosyan, K. Chen, Sx F. Yan, and Ex A. Winzeler. In silico gene function prediction using ontology-based pattern identification. *Bioinformatics*, 21(7):1237–1245, 2005.

Books about ontologies

Here used to be a section on different textbooks and handbooks. Meanwhile, this has been updated and moved to an online resource. It currently resides at the wikis of the Technical Committee on Education of the International Association for Ontology and its Applications, at `http://iaoaedu.cs.uct.ac.za/`, menu option "books" (this may have moved to some place on `http://www.iaoa.org/` by the time you read this).

Selection of journals that publish papers about ontologies

Research in ontologies

- Applied Ontology
- Journal of Web Semantics
- Semantic Web Journal
- Journal on Data Semantics
- International Journal of Metadata, Semantics and Ontologies
- Artificial Intelligence Journal
- Journal of Automated Reasoning

Ontologies and applications

- Journal of Biomedical Semantics
- Journal of Biomedical Informatics
- BMC Bioinformatics
- Data & Knowledge Engineering

Selection of conferences that publish papers about ontologies

Research in Ontology, ontologies, ontology engineering, ontology languages, and automated reasoning

- Formal Ontology in Information Systems (FOIS)
- International Conference on Knowledge Engineering and Knowledge Management (EKAW)
- International Conference on Knowledge Capture (K-CAP)
- Extended Semantic Web Conference (ESWC)
- International Conference on Knowledge Representation and Reasoning (KR)

Ontologies and applications

- International Conference on Biomedical Ontology (ICBO)
- Semantic Web Applications and Tools for the Life Sciences (SWAT4LS)
- International Semantic Web Conference (ISWC)

Appendix **A**

Assignments

Besides the exercises to engage with the material, there are two assignments. They have a strong integrative flavour to it and will take up more time than an exercise. You are expected to applying as much as you have learned, and look up more information online, be they tools, methods, other ontologies, or scientific papers.

The assignments in this appendix are described in such as way that they may serve as a draft description of the actual assignment. For instance, I include hard deadlines for hand-in, notwithstanding that I know the material will be better with more work put into it (ontologies are never really 'finished'). I consider both assignments to be group assignments, even though they could be done individually, and I assign people to groups and topics if they didn't make groups themselves by a give date. If the practical assignment is scheduled for the end of Block I rather than for hand in at the end of Block II, then remove the requirements on Block II topics form the description below.

Regarding the project assignment: most topics can be reused across years, and some of them can be done by more than one group as it invariable ends up in different results. Some of the previously listed projects that were carried out in earlier instalments have some material available online, which gives an indication of success (i.e., examples of projects that received top marks). One such mini-project from the OE course at the University of Havana (2010) resulted in ONTOPARTS—a tool and creative extension to the part-whole taxonomy of [KA08]—that was subsequently formalised, written up, and published [KFRMG12]. Another one is the OWL Classifier[1], which was developed as part of one of the mini-projects of the 2016 OE course at the University of Cape Town, and subsequently used toward conflict resolution in [KK17b]. These topics are not listed below anymore, for the obvious reasons.

A.1   Practical Assignment: Develop a Domain Ontology

The aim of this practical assignment is for you to demonstrate what you have learned about the ontology languages, top-down and bottom-up ontology development, and methods and methodologies, and experiment with how these pieces fit together.

You can do this assignment in groups of two or three students. It should be mentioned in the material you will hand in who did what.

Tasks

1. Choose a subject domain of interest for which you will develop a domain ontology. For instance, computers, tourism, furniture, some hobby you may be familiar with (e.g., diving, dancing), or some other subject domain you happen to be knowledgable about (or know someone who is).

2. Develop the domain ontology in the best possible way. You are allowed to use any resource you think is useful, be it other ontologies, non-ontological resources, tools, domain experts, etc.. If you do so (and you are encouraged to do so), then make sure to reference them in the write-up.

3. Write about 2-3 pages (excluding figures or screenshots) summarising your work. This can include—but is not limited to—topics such as an outline of the ontology, why (or why not) you have used a foundational ontology (if so, which, why), if you could reuse a top-domain or other subject domain ontology, which non-ontological resources you have used (if any, and if so, how), if you encountered subject domain knowledge that should have been in the ontology but could not be represented due to the limitations

---

[1]https://github.com/muhummadPatel/OWL_Classifier

of OWL, or perhaps a (real or imagined) purpose of the ontology and therefore a motivation for some OWL fragment, any particular reasoning services that was useful (and how and why, which deductions did you have or experimented with), any additional tools used.

Material to hand in

Send in/upload to the course's CMS the following items:

1. The OWL file of your ontology;

2. Imported OWL ontologies, if any;

3. The write up in pdf.

Assessment

1. Concerning the ontology: quality is more important that quantity. An ontology with more advanced constraints and appropriate reuse of foundational or general ontologies is a better illustration what you have learned than a large bare taxonomy.

2. Concerning the ontology: it will be checked on modelling errors in the general sense (errors such as is-a vs. part-of, class vs. instance, unsatisfiable classes). Regarding the subject domain itself, it will be checked only insofar as it indicates (mis)understanding of the ontology language or reasoning services.

3. Concerning the write up: a *synthesis* is expected, not a diary. For instance, "We explored a, b, and c, and b was deemed to be most effective because blabla" would be fine, but not "We tried a, but that didn't work out, then we had a go at b, which went well, then we came across c, tried it out of curiosity, but that was a dead end, so we went back to b.". In short: try to go beyond the 'knowledge telling' and work towards the so-called *knowledge transformation*.

4. Concerning the write up: while a brief description of the contents is useful, it is more important to include something about the *process* and *motivations* how you got there, covering topics such as, but not limited to, those mentioned under Tasks, item 3 (and

recollect the aim of the assignment—the more you demonstrate it, the better).

Notes

In random order:

1. The assignment looks easy. It isn't. If you start with the development of the ontology only the day or so before the deadline, there is an extremely high probability that you will fail this assignment. Your assignment will be of a higher quality if you start thinking about it some 2 weeks before the deadline, and the actual development at most one week before the deadline, and spread out the time you are working on it.

2. If you use non-English terms for the classes and properties, you should either add the English in the annotations (preferred), else lend me a dictionary if it is in a language I do not speak.

3. Use proper referencing when you use something from someone else, be it an ontology, other reused online resources (including uncommon software), textbooks, articles etc. Not doing so amounts to plagiarism.

4. Spell checkers tend to be rather useful tools.

5. Some of the mini-project topics can benefit from an experimental ontology that you know in detail, which you may want to take into consideration when choosing a subject domain or purpose so that your ontology might be reused later on.

A.2 Project Assignment

The project assignment aims to let you explore in more detail a specific subtopic within ontology engineering. There is enough variation in the list of topics below to choose either a software development project, literature review, experimentation, and occasionally a bit of research. The two subsections below could be used as is or function as a template for one's own specification of constraints and more or less project topics.

A.2.1 Suggested set-up of the assignment

The aim of this assignment is to work in a small group (2-4 students) and to investigate a specific theme of ontology engineering. The topics are such that either you can demonstrate the *integration of various aspects* of ontologies and knowledge bases or *going into quite some detail on a single topic*, and it can be either theory-based, implementation-focussed, or a bit of both.

Possible topics to choose from will be communicated in week x, and has to be chosen and communicated to me (topic + group members) no later than in week x+1, else you will be assigned a topic and a group.

Tasks

1. Form a group of 2-4 people and choose a topic, or vv.: choose a topic and find other people to work with. It should be mentioned in the material you will hand in who did what.

2. Carry out the project.

3. Write about 4-6 pages (excluding figures or screenshots) summarising your work. The page limit is flexible, but it surely has to be < 15 pages in total.

4. Give a presentation of your work during the last lecture (10 minutes presentation, ±5 minutes discussion). *Everyone must attend this lecture.*

Material to hand in

You have to upload/email the following items:

1. The write up.

2. Additional material: this depends on the chosen topic. If it is not purely paper-based, then the additional files have to be uploaded on the system (e.g., software, test data).

3. Slides of the presentation, if any.

Note that the deadline is after the last lecture so that you have the option to update your material for the mini-project with any feedback received during the presentation and discussion in class.

Assessment

1. Concerning the write up: a *synthesis* is expected, not a diary. For instance, "We explored a, b, and c, and b was deemed to be most effective because blabla" would be fine, but not "We tried a, but that didn't work out, then we had a go at b, which went well, then we came across c, tried it out of curiosity, but that was a dead end, so we went back to b.". In short: try to go beyond the 'knowledge telling' and work towards the so-called *knowledge transformation*.

2. Concerning the write up: use proper referencing when you use something from someone else, be it an ontology, other reused online resources (including uncommon software), textbooks, articles etc. Not doing so amounts to plagiarism, which has a minimum penalty of obtaining a grade of 0 (zero) for the assignment (for all group members, or, if thanks to the declaration of contribution the individual can be identified, then only that individual), and you will be recorded on the departmental plagiarism list, if you are not already on it, and further steps may be taken.

3. The presentation: respect the time limit, coherence of the presentation, capability to answer questions.

4. Concerning any additional material (if applicable): if the software works as intended with the given input, presentability of the code.

5. Marks will be deducted if the presentation or the write-up is too long.

Notes

Things you may want to take into consideration (listed in random order):

1. LaTeX is a useful typesetting system (including beamer for presentation slides), has a range of standard layouts as well as bibliography style files to save you the trouble of wasting time on making the write up presentable, and generates a pdf file that is portable[2]. This is much less so with MS Word; if you use MS Word nevertheless, please also include a pdf version of the document.

---

[2]in case you are not convinced: check http://openwetware.org/wiki/Word_vs. _LaTeX or http://ricardo.ecn.wfu.edu/~cottrell/wp.html

2. Regarding the bibliography: have complete entries. Examples of referencing material (for conference proceedings, books and book chapters, and journal articles) can be found in the scientific papers included in the lecture notes' bibliography, scientific literature you consult, or LaTeX documentation.

3. Spell checkers tend to be rather useful tools.

4. One or more of the domain ontologies developed in the previous assignment may be suitable for reuse in your chosen topic.

5. Some of the mini-projects lend themselves well for extension into an Honours/Masters project, hence, could give you a head-start.

A.2.2 Topics

You can select one of the following topics, or propose one of your own. If the latter, you first will have to obtain approval from you lecturer (if you are doing this assignment as part of a course).

The topics are listed in random order, have different flavours or emphases; e.g., more of a literature review project, or programming, or theory, or experimentation. The notes contain pointers to some more information, as does the corresponding section in the book.

Some descriptions may seem vague in that it still offers several possibilities with more or less work and/or more or less challenging activities; this is done on purpose. You should narrow it down as you see fit—bearing in mind the aims of the mini-project and the number of people in your group—and be able to justify why if asked to do so. If you choose a topic that involves processing OWL files, then try to use either the OWL API (for Java-based applications) or Owlready (Python), the Jena Toolkit (or similar), or OWLink, rather than spending time reinventing the wheel.

You probably will find out it's not as easy as it looked like initially, which may make it tempting wishing to change, but that also holds for the other topics, and by changing topic you very likely have lost too much time to bring the other one to passable completion.

Some topics can be done by more than one group simultaneously, after which it can be interesting to compare what came out of it. Based on my experience of previous years, these include topic numbers 5, 7, 14, 16, and 19.

1. Consider the *Lemon* model for monolingual and multilingual ontologies
   [MdCB$^+$12, MAdCB$^+$12]. Apply it to an ontology you developed for the practical assignment. You can choose any natural language, as long as it is a different one from the one the ontology is developed in or requires some redesign to bring it in line with best practices on the ontology-language interface.

2. There are some 15 working automated reasoners for various Description Logics (e.g., HermiT, FaCT++, TrOWL, Pellet, Racer, ELK, MoRE, Quonto, Quest). Conduct a comparison with a sensible subset, including their performance on a set of ontologies you select or create artificially, and possibly also along the direction of examining the effect of the use of different features in the ontology. Some ideas may be gleaned from the "short report" in the proceedings of the Ontology Reasoner Evaluation workshop[3].

3. Write a literature review about ontology-driven NLP or ontology-enhanced digital libraries (minimum amount of references to consider depends on group size and whether this is an undergraduate or postgraduate course).

4. Set up an OBDA system (that is not one of the samples of the Ontop website). You are advised to either reuse your ontology from the practical assignment or take an existing one. Regarding data, you may want to have a look at the GitHub list of publicly available data sets[4], or you can create a mock database.

5. There are various ways to verbalize an ontology (e.g., $\forall$ as 'each...' or 'for all ...', using the opposite, etc.). Write a web-based or stand-alone application that verbalises an ontology in a natural language of choice, where users will be able to choose their verbalization. Some of the examples you may want to check out are the Attempto project[5], the discussion in [SKC$^+$08], results with isiZulu [KK17a] or Afrikaans [STK16] in case you're in South Africa, or either of the review articles [BACW14, SD17].

---

[3] http://ceur-ws.org/Vol-1015/, and there have been subsequent editions of the ORE workshops.
[4] https://github.com/caesar0301/awesome-public-datasets
[5] http://attempto.ifi.uzh.ch/site/tools/

6. Create a decision diagram for BFO or GFO, alike the D3 of FORZA, and validate it (e.g., by checking whether extant ontologies linked to BFO or GFO were linked correctly).

7. There are many works on criteria to evaluate the quality of an ontology or an ontology module (e.g., [McD17, PVSFGP12, Vra09]). Provide an overview and apply it to several of your classmates' ontologies developed in the practical assignment and/or ontologies taken from online repositories. In a larger group, this may also include evaluating the evaluation strategies themselves.

8. Take a thesaurus represented in SKOS[6] and convert that into a real ontology (i.e., not simply only converting into OWL). There are manual and semi-automated approaches.

9. Compare and contrast tools for ontology visualization (i.e., their graphical renderings in, e.g., Ontograf, OWLGrEd, SOVA, and so on).

10. OWL (and DL) is claimed to provide a 'unifying paradigm' for several knowledge representation languages. Evaluate this claim, taking into consideration Common Logic as alternative ontology language that makes the same claim.

11. Conduct a literature review on, and, where possible, test, several so-called 'non-standard reasoning' reasoners. Among others, you could consult one of the least-common subsumer papers [PT11], and/or reasoner-mediated ontology authoring tools [FR12, Fer16], among others.

12. Write a plugin for Semantic MediaWiki such that an ontology can be used during the page editing stage; e.g., to have the hierarchy with terms (classes, object/data properties) on the left-hand side of the screen, and easily pick one of them, adding the annotation to the text automatically. Another idea for a semwiki plugin you may have may be considered (but check out first which ones are already there).

---

[6]see, e.g., the list at http://code.google.com/p/lucene-skos/wiki/SKOSThesauri, but there are others you may wish to consider

13. Compare and contrast the two OntoClean implementations [GRV10, Wel06], including experimental assessment.

14. Translational Research and the Semantic Web. Students should study and analyse the 'old' paper "Advancing translational research with the Semantic Web" [RCB+07]. For the report, you can envision yourself as a consultant to the authors (from W3C's HCLS IG[7]) and suggest them improvements to what they did, given that a lot of new material has been developed over the past 12 years.

15. Consider bottom-up ontology development starting from a conceptual data model (e.g., UML class diagrams, EER). Find a way to generate an OWL file from it such that it provides candidate classes, object properties, and constraints for an actual ontology. You may want to take one of the freely available conceptual modelling tools (e.g., ArgoUML) and use that serialisation for the transformations. There are a few tools around that try this already, but they have incomplete coverage (at best).

16. Compare and contrast ontology editors in a meaningful way; e.g., the Protégé stand-alone tool, WebProtégé, MoKI, NeON toolkit, etc.

17. Implement the RBox reasoning service and demonstrate correctness of implementation in the software.

18. OWL does not consider time and temporal aspects. To address this shortcoming, several 'workarounds' as well as temporal description logics have been proposed. Compare and contrast them on language features and modelling problems and reasoning.

19. Develop a Protégé plugin that will show in the interface not the Manchester syntax with "some" and "not" etc, but the DL axiom components (e.g., alike it was in its v3.x), or with the corresponding keywords in a natural language other than English.

20. Provide a state of the art on research into competency questions.

---

[7]http://www.w3.org/blog/hcls

21. Represent DOLCE—or another ontology that has indicated to be needing more than OWL expressiveness—in DOL on OntoHub; e.g., by adding those axioms in a module and link them to the OWL file into a network of ontologies.

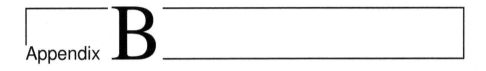

OWL 2 Profiles features list

OWL 2 EL

Supported class restrictions:
- existential quantification to a class expression or a data range
- existential quantification to an individual or a literal
- self-restriction
- enumerations involving a single individual or a single literal
- intersection of classes and data ranges

Supported axioms, restricted to allowed set of class expressions:
- class inclusion, equivalence, disjointness
- object property inclusion (w. or w.o. property chains), and data property inclusion
- property equivalence
- transitive object properties
- reflexive object properties
- domain and range restrictions
- assertions
- functional data properties
- keys

NOT supported in OWL 2 EL (with respect to OWL 2 DL):
- universal quantification to a class expression or a data range
- cardinality restrictions
- disjunction
- class negation

- enumerations involving more than one individual
- disjoint properties
- irreflexive, symmetric, and asymmetric object properties
- inverse object properties, functional and inverse-functional object properties

OWL 2 QL

The supported axioms in OWL 2 QL take into account what one can use on the left-hand side of the inclusion operator ($\sqsubseteq$, SubClassOf) and what can be asserted on the right-hand side:

- Subclass expressions restrictions:
  - a class
  - existential quantification (ObjectSomeValuesFrom) where the class is limited to owl:Thing
  - existential quantification to a data range (DataSomeValuesFrom)
- Super expressions restrictions:
  - a class
  - intersection (ObjectIntersectionOf)
  - negation (ObjectComplementOf)
  - existential quantification to a class (ObjectSomeValuesFrom)
  - existential quantification to a data range (DataSomeValuesFrom)

Supported Axioms in OWL 2 QL:

- Restrictions on class expressions, object and data properties occurring in functionality assertions cannot be specialized
- subclass axioms
- class expression equivalence (involving subClassExpression), disjointness
- inverse object properties
- property inclusion (not involving property chains and SubDataPropertyOf)
- property equivalence
- property domain and range
- disjoint properties
- symmetric, reflexive, irreflexive, asymmetric properties
- assertions other than individual equality assertions and negative

property assertions (DifferentIndividuals, ClassAssertion, Object-PropertyAssertion, and DataPropertyAssertion)

NOT supported in OWL 2 QL (with respect to OWL 2 DL):
- existential quantification to a class expression or a data range in the subclass position
- self-restriction
- existential quantification to an individual or a literal
- enumeration of individuals and literals
- universal quantification to a class expression or a data range
- cardinality restrictions
- disjunction
- property inclusions involving property chains
- functional and inverse-functional properties
- transitive properties
- keys
- individual equality assertions and negative property assertions

OWL 2 RL

Supported in OWL 2 RL:
- More restrictions on class expressions (see table 2 of [MGH+09]; e.g., no SomeValuesFrom on the right-hand side of a subclass axiom)
- All axioms in OWL 2 RL are constrained in a way that is compliant with the restrictions in Table 2.
- Thus, OWL 2 RL supports all axioms of OWL 2 apart from disjoint unions of classes and reflexive object property axioms.

A quick one-liner of the difference is: No $\forall$ and $\neg$ on the left-hand side, and $\exists$ and $\sqcup$ on right-hand side of $\sqsubseteq$.

Appendix C

Complexity recap

This appendix is expected to be relevant only to those who have no idea of, or too little recollection of, computational complexity, or who have come across it many years ago and may like a brief refresher.

Theory of computation concerns itself with, among other things, languages and its dual, problems. A problem is the question of deciding whether a given string is a member of some particular language; more precisely: if Σ is an alphabet, L is a language over Σ, then the problem L is "given a string $w \in \Sigma^*$, decide whether or not w is in L". The usage of 'problem' and 'language' is interchangeable. When we focus on strings for their own sake (e.g., in the set $\{o^n 1^n \mid n \geq 1\}$), then we tend to think of the set of strings as a language. When we focus on the 'thing' that is encoded as a string (e.g., a particular graph, a logical expression, satisfiability of a class), we tend to think of the set of strings as a problem. Within the context of ontologies, we typically talk of the representation languages and reasoning problems.

There are several classes of languages; see Figure C.1. The regular free languages have their counterpart with finite automata; the context-free languages with push-down automata; the recursive languages is the class of languages accepted by a Turing machine (TM) that always halts; the recursively enumerable languages is the class of languages defined by a TM; the non-recursively enumerable languages is the class of languages for which there is no TM (e.g., the diagonalization language). The recursive languages, and, to a lesser extent, the recursively enumerable languages, are by far the most interesting ones for ontologies.

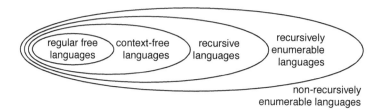

Figure C.1: Graphical depiction of the main categories of languages.

Turing machines are used as a convenient abstraction of actual computers for the notion of computation. *A TM that always halts = algorithm*, i.e., the TM halts on all inputs in finite time, either accepting or rejecting; hence, the recursive languages are *decidable* problems/languages. Problems/languages that are not recursive are called *undecidable*, and they do not have an algorithm; if they are in the class of recursively enumerable languages (but not recursive), then they have a *procedure that runs on an arbitrary TM* that may give you an answer but may very well never halt; see also Figure C.2. First order predicate logic in its full glory is undecidable. Description logics are decidable fragments of first order predicate logic[1], i.e., they are recursive languages and (can) have algorithms for the usual problems (standard reasoning services).

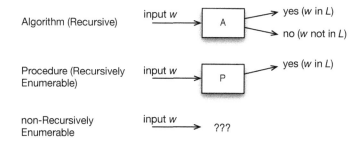

Figure C.2: Graphical depiction of the main categories of languages; the rectangle denotes a Turing Machine; w is a string and L is a language.

Not all algorithms are alike, however, and some take up more time (by the CPU) or space (in the form of memory size) to compute the answer than others. So, we want to know for a given problem, the answer

---

[1]More precisely: there is at least one that turned out to be undecidable ($\mathcal{DLR}_{\mathcal{US}}$), but this is an exception to the rule.

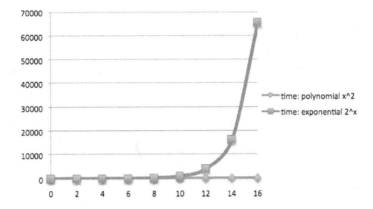

Figure C.3: General idea of time complexity of an algorithm, as function of the size of the input. e.g.: All basic arithmetic operations can be computed in polynomial time; evaluating a position in generalised chess and checkers on an $n \times n$ board costs exponential time.

to *"how much time [/space] does it take to compute the answer, as a function of the size of the input?"*. If the computation takes many years with the top-of-the-range hardware, then it is still not particularly interesting to implement (from a computer science viewpoint, that is). To structure these matters, we use the notion of a *complexity class*. There are very many of them, but we only refer to a few in the context of ontologies. For instance, it may take a polynomial amount of time to compute class subsumption for an OWL 2 EL-formalised ontology and exponential time to compute satisfiability of an EER diagram (represented in the DL $\mathcal{DLR}_{ifd}$) and the bigger the diagram (more precisely: the logical theory), correspondingly the longer it takes. The intuition is depicted in Figure C.3: for small ontologies, there is but a minor difference in performance, but one really starts to notice it with larger logical theories.

Looking ahead at the complexity classes relevant for OWL, we list here a description of the meaning of them (copied from the OWL 2 Profiles Standard page [MGH+09]):

- **Decidability open** means that it is not known whether this reasoning problem is decidable at all.
- **Decidable, but complexity open** means that decidability of this reasoning problem is known, but not its exact computational

complexity. If available, known lower bounds are given in paren-
thesis; for example, (NP-Hard) means that this problem is at least
as hard as any other problem in NP.

- **X-complete** for X one of the complexity classes explained below
  indicates that tight complexity bounds are known—that is, the
  problem is known to be both in the complexity class X (i.e., an
  algorithm is known that only uses time/space in X) and hard for
  X (i.e., it is at least as hard as any other problem in X). The
  following is a brief sketch of the classes used in Table 4.3, from the
  most complex one down to the simplest ones.

  - **2NEXPTIME** is the class of problems solvable by a nonde-
    terministic algorithm in time that is at most double exponen-
    tial in the size of the input (i.e., roughly 2^{2^n}, for n the size of
    the input).
  - **NEXPTIME** is the class of problems solvable by a nonde-
    terministic algorithm in time that is at most exponential in
    the size of the input (i.e., roughly 2^n, for n the size of the
    input).
  - **PSPACE** is the class of problems solvable by a deterministic
    algorithm using space that is at most polynomial in the size
    of the input (i.e., roughly n^c, for n the size of the input and
    c a constant).
  - **NP** is the class of problems solvable by a nondeterministic
    algorithm using time that is at most polynomial in the size
    of the input (i.e., roughly n^c, for n the size of the input and
    c a constant).
  - **PTIME** is the class of problems solvable by a deterministic
    algorithm using time that is at most polynomial in the size of
    the input (i.e., roughly n^c, for n the size of the input and c a
    constant). PTIME is often referred to as tractable, whereas
    the problems in the classes above are often referred to as
    intractable.
  - **LOGSPACE** is the class of problems solvable by a determin-
    istic algorithm using space that is at most logarithmic in the
    size of the input (i.e., roughly $log(n)$, for n the size of the in-
    put and c a constant). NLOGSPACE is the nondeterministic
    version of this class.
  - $\mathbf{AC^0}$ is a proper subclass of LOGSPACE and defined not via

Turing Machines, but via circuits: AC^0 is the class of problems definable using a family of circuits of constant depth and polynomial size, which can be generated by a deterministic Turing machine in logarithmic time (in the size of the input). Intuitively, AC^0 allows us to use polynomially many processors but the run-time must be constant. A typical example of an AC^0 problem is the evaluation of first-order queries over databases (or model checking of first-order sentences over finite models), where only the database (first-order model) is regarded as the input and the query (first-order sentence) is assumed to be fixed. The undirected graph reachability problem is known to be in LogSpace, but not in AC^0.

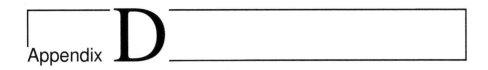

Appendix D

Answers of selected exercises

Answers Chapter 2

Answer Exercise 2.1. Indicative descriptions:
(a) All lions are mammals.
(b) Each PC has as part at least one CPU and at least one Monitor connected
(c) Proper part is asymmetric.

Answer Exercise 2.2.
(a) $\forall x(Car(x) \rightarrow Vehicle(x))$
(b) $\forall x(HumanParent(x) \rightarrow \exists y(haschild(x, y) \wedge Human(y)))$
(c) $\forall x, y(Person(x) \wedge Course(y) \rightarrow \neg(lecturerOf(x, y) \wedge studentOf(x, y)))$

Answer Exercise 2.3.
(b) There exists a node that does not participate in an instance of R, or: it does not relate to anything else: $\exists x \forall y. \neg R(x, y)$.
(c) $\mathcal{L} = \langle R \rangle$ as the binary relation between the vertices. Optionally, on can add the vertices as well. Properties:
R is symmetric: $\forall xy. R(x, y) \rightarrow R(y, x)$.
R is irreflexive: $\forall x. \neg R(x, x)$.
If you take into account the vertices explicitly, one could say that each note participates in at least two instances of R to different nodes.

Answer Exercise 2.4.
(a) R is reflexive (a thing relates to itself): $\forall x. R(x, x)$.
R is asymmetric (if a relates to b through relation R, then b does not relate back to a through R): $\forall xy. R(x, y) \rightarrow \neg R(y, x)$.
(b) See the example on p21 of the lecture notes.

Answers Chapter 3

Answer Exercise 3.1.

i. Rewrite (Eq. 3.25) into negation normal form:

$Person \sqcap \forall eats.Plant \sqcap (\neg Person \sqcup \neg \forall eats.(Plant \sqcup Dairy))$

$Person \sqcap \forall eats.Plant \sqcap (\neg Person \sqcup \exists \neg eats.(Plant \sqcup Dairy))$

$Person \sqcap \forall eats.Plant \sqcap (\neg Person \sqcup \exists eats.(\neg Plant \sqcap \neg Dairy))$

So our initial ABox is:

$S = \{(Person \sqcap \forall eats.Plant \sqcap (\neg Person \sqcup \exists eats.(\neg Plant \sqcap \neg Dairy))) (a)\}$

ii. Enter the tableau by applying the rules until either you find a completion or only clashes.

($\sqcap$-rule): $\{Person(a), \forall eats.Plant(a),$
    $(\neg Person \sqcup \exists eats.(\neg Plant \sqcap \neg Dairy))(a)\}$

($\sqcup$-rule): (i.e., it generates two branches)

  (1) $\{Person(a), \forall eats.Plant(a),$
      $(\neg Person \sqcup \exists eats.(\neg Plant \sqcap \neg Dairy))(a),$
      $\neg Person(a)\}$ ¡clash!

  (2) $\{Person(a), \forall eats.Plant(a),$
      $(\neg Person \sqcup \exists eats.(\neg Plant \sqcap \neg Dairy))(a),$
      $\exists eats.(\neg Plant \sqcap \neg Dairy)(a)\}$
      ($\exists$-rule): $\{Person(a), \forall eats.Plant(a),$
          $(\neg Person \sqcup \exists eats.(\neg Plant \sqcap \neg Dairy))(a),$
          $\exists eats.(\neg Plant \sqcap \neg Dairy)(a), eats(a,b),$
          $(\neg Plant \sqcap \neg Dairy)(b)\}$
      ($\sqcap$-rule): $\{Person(a), \forall eats.Plant(a),$
          $(\neg Person \sqcup \exists eats.(\neg Plant \sqcap \neg Dairy))(a),$
          $\exists eats.(\neg Plant \sqcap \neg Dairy)(a), eats(a,b),$
          $(\neg Plant \sqcap \neg Dairy)(b), \neg Plant(b), \neg Dairy(b)\}$
      ($\forall$-rule): $\{Person(a), \forall eats.Plant(a),$
          $(\neg Person \sqcup \exists eats.(\neg Plant \sqcap \neg Dairy))(a),$
          $\exists eats.(\neg Plant \sqcap \neg Dairy)(a), eats(a,b),$
          $(\neg Plant \sqcap \neg Dairy)(b), \neg Plant(b),$
          $\neg Dairy(b), Plant(b)\}$ ¡clash!

iii. $\mathcal{T} \vdash Vegan \sqsubseteq Vegetarian$? yes

Answers Chapter 4

Answer Exercise 4.2. Use a property chain.

Answer Exercise 4.4.
  (c) Expressivity: $\mathcal{ALN}$, in OWL DL. Not in OWL Lite and OWL 2 EL, QL, RL because of the minCardinality.
  (e) Expressivity: $\mathcal{ALQ}$, in OWL 2 DL. Not in OWL DL anymore because of the qualified number restriction.

Answer Exercise 4.7. As historical note: the original exercise came from SSSW 2005[1], which was at the time of OWL 1. The answers here and the next ones have been updated taking into account OWL 2.
  (a) The description is sufficiently vague that it may be either of
  JointHonsMathsComp ≡ ∃takes.MathsModule ⊓
                 ∃takes.ComputerScienceModule
  JointHonsMathsComp ≡ Student ⊓ ∃takes.MathsModule ⊓
                 ∃takes.ComputerScienceModule
  In any case, observe that it is not
  takes.(MathsModule ⊓ ComputerScienceModule); see Example 5.3 for further explanation.
  (b) SingleHonsMaths ≡ Student ⊓ ∃takes.MathsModule ⊓
                 ∀takes.ComputerScienceModule.
  This is also called 'closing' the axiom.
So: yes, this is possible. A possible solution is shown in `university1.owl`

Answer Exercise 4.8. Deductions: they are undergrad students, and students 2, 4, and 7 are JointHonsMathsComp. Student7 is one, because it is an instance of ∃takes.MathsModule and has a property assertion that s/he takes CS101.

No student is a SingleHonsMaths, despite that, e.g., Student3 has declared taking two math modules. This is due to the Open World Assumption: student3 may well take other courses that we don't know of as of yet, so it is not guaranteed in all possible worlds that student3 takes *only those two* math courses.

Answer Exercise 4.9. This can now be done with OWL 2, for it permits qualified number restrictions; see `university2.owl`
  (a) This poses no problem, because of the no unique name assumption: it will infer that CS101 and CS102 must be the same object, so then student 9 still takes 2 courses and all is well; see `university2.owl`.
  (b) This does pose a problem, because each of the three courses mentioned are member of their respective classes that are disjoint, so they must be distinct individuals, and thus we obtain a violation in cardinality restrictions (=2 vs =3), and therewith the ontology has become inconsistent.

---

[1]`http://owl.man.ac.uk/2005/07/sssw/university.html`

Answer Exercise 4.10. Let us first have a look randomly at a deduction and its explanation (click on the "?" right from the deduction in Protégé) as a first step toward figuring out why so many classes are unsatisfiable (i.e., equivalent to Nothing, or $\perp$). Take the explanation for CS_StudentTakingCourses:

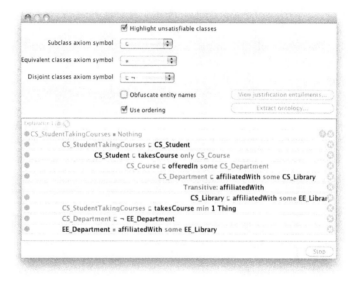

This CS_StudentTakingCourses has a long explanation of why it is unsatisfiable, and we see that some of the axioms that it uses to explain the unsatisfiability also have unsatisfiable classes. Hence, it is a good idea to set this aside for a while, as it is a knock-on effect of the others that are unsatisfiable.

Let us have a look at the unsatisfiability regarding departments.

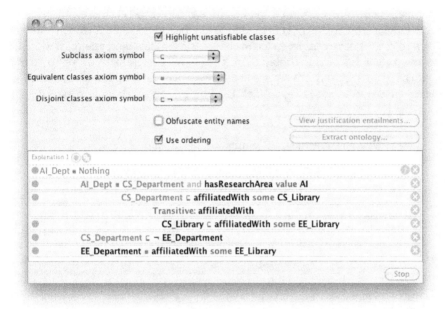

So, the AI_Dept is unsatisfiable because its superclass CS_Department is, i.e., it is a knock-on effect from CS_Department. Does this give sufficient information as to say why CS_Department is inconsistent? In fact, it does. See the next screenshot, which is the same as lines 3-7, above.

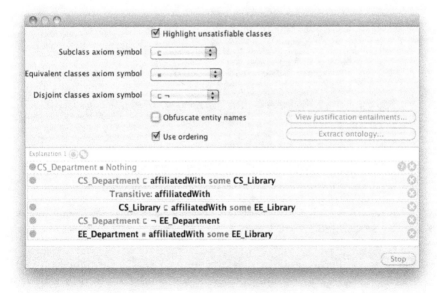

CS_Department is unsatisfiable, because it is affiliatedWith some CS_Library that, in turn (by transitivity), is affiliatedWith some EE_Library that belongs to the EE_Department, which is disjoint from CS_Department. Two 'easy' options to get rid of this problem are to remove the transitivity or to remove the disjointness. Alternatively, we could revisit the domain knowledge; e.g., CS library may not be affiliatedWith EE library, but is, adjacentTo or disjoint with the EE library.

Let us now consider why CS_course is unsatisfiable:

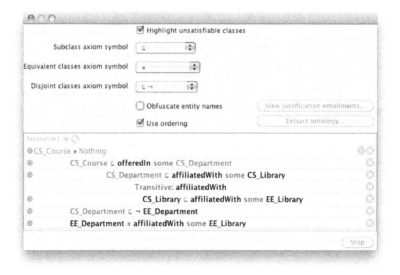

We have again that the real problem is CS_Department; fix that one, and CS_course is satisfiable, too.

There is a different issue with AIStudent. From the explanation in the next screenshot, we can see immediately it has something to do with the inconsistency of HCIStudent.

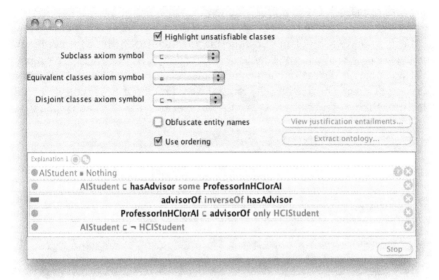

But looking at `HCIStudent` for a clue does not help us further in isolating the problem:

Considering the axioms in the explanation only, one can argue that the root of the problem is the disjointness between `AIStudent` and `HCIStudent`, and remove that axiom to fix it. However, does it really make sense to have the union `ProfessorInHCIorAI`? Not really, and therefore it would be a better fix to change that one into two separate classes, `ProfessorInHCI` and `ProfessorInAI` and have them participating in

`ProfessorInHCI ⊑ ∀advisorOf.HCIStudent` and

ProfessorInAI ⊑ ∀advisorOf.AIStudent,
respectively.

Last, we have a problem of conflicting cardinalities with LecturerTaking-4Courses: it is a subclass of TeachingFaculty, which is restricted to taking at most 3 courses, which is in conflict with the "exactly 4" of LecturerTaking4-Courses. This can be fixed by changing the cardinality of either one, or perhaps a lecturer taking 4 courses is not a sub- but a sister-class of TeachingFaculty.

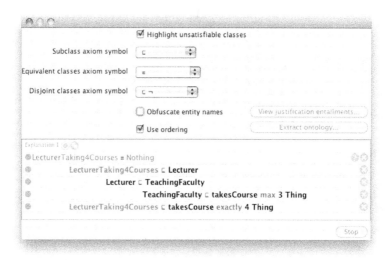

Answers Chapter 5

Answer Exercise 5.1. No, in that case, it is definitely not a good ontology. First, there are several CQs for which the ontology does not have an answer, such as not having any knowledge of monkeys represented. Second, it does contain knowledge that is not mentioned in any of the CQs, such as the carnivorous plant.

Answer Exercise 5.2. *Note:* Double-checking this answer, it turns out there are various versions of the pizza ontology. The answer given here is based on the output from the version I submitted in 2015; the output is available as "OOPS! - OntOlogy Pitfall Scanner! - Results pizza.pdf" in the PizzaOOPS.zip file from the book's website. The other two are: "OOPS! - OntOlogy Pitfall Scanner! - ResultsPizzaLocal.pdf" based on pizza.owl from Oct 2005 that was distributed with an old Protégé version and "OOPS! - OntOlogy Pitfall Scanner! - ResultsPizzaProtegeSite.pdf", who's output is based on having given OOPS! the URI https://protege.stanford.edu/ontologies/pizza/pizza.owl in July 2018.

There are 39 pitfalls detected and categorised as 'minor', and 4 as 'important'. (explore the other pitfalls to see which ones are minor, important, and critical).

The three "unconnected ontology elements" are used as a way to group things, so are not really unconnected, so that can stay.

ThinAndCripsyBase is detected as a "Merging different concepts in the same class" pitfall. Aside from the typo, one has to inspect the ontology to determine whether it can do with an improvement: what are its sibling, parent and child classes, what is its annotation? It is disjoint with DeepPanBase, but there is no other knowledge. It could just as well have been named ThinBase, but the original class was likely not intended as a real merging of classes, at least not like a class called, say, UndergradsAndPostgrads.

Then there are 31 missing annotations. Descriptions can be added to say what a DeepPanBase is, but for the toppings this seems less obvious to add.

The four object properties missing domain and range axioms was a choice by the modellers (see the tutorial) to not 'overcomplicate' the tutorial for novice modellers as they can have 'surprising' deductions, but it would be better to add them where possible.

Last, OOPS detected that the same four properties are missing inverses. This certainly can be added for isIngredientOf and hasIngredient. That said, in OWL 2, one also can use hasIngredient$^-$ to stand in for the notion of "isIngredientOf", so missing inverses is not necessarily a problem. (Ontologically, one easily could argue for 'non-directionality', but that is a separate line of debate; see e.g., [Fin00, KC16]).

Answer Exercise 5.3. No, A is unsatisfiable. Reason: A $\sqsubseteq$ ED (EnDurant), it has a property R (to B), which has declared as domain PD (PerDurant), but ED $\sqsubseteq$ ¬PD (endurant and perdurant are disjoint), hence, A cannot have any instances.

Answer Exercise 5.4. There are several slides with the same 'cleaning procedure' and one of them is uploaded on the book's webpage, which was from the Doctorate course on Formal Ontology for Knowledge Representation and Natural Language Processing 2004-2005, slide deck "Lesson3-OntoClean". Meanwhile, there is also a related paper that describes the steps in more detail, which appeared in the Handbook on Ontologies [GW09].

Answers Chapter 6

Answer Review question 6.3. Some of the differences are: descriptive, possibilism, and multiplicative for DOLCE versus prescriptive and realist, actualism, and reductionist for BFO. You can find more differences in Table 1 of [KK12] and online in the "comparison tables" tab at http://www.thezfiles.

co.za/ROMULUS/.

Answer Review question 6.4. There are several differences. The major differences are that DOLCE also has relationships and axioms among the categories using those relationships (i.e., richly formalised), whereas BFO v1 and v1.1 is a 'bare' taxonomy of universals (some work exist on merging it with the RO, but not yet officially). Others are the Abstract branch and the treatment of 'attributes'/quality properties in DOLCE that do not have an equivalent in BFO. The BFO-core has a more comprehensive inclusion of parthood and boundaries than DOLCE.

Answer Review question 6.5. The most often recurring relationships are parthood, participation, constitution, and inherence or dependence.

Answer Exercise 6.1. Informal alignments:
  (a) dolce:Endurant maps roughly to bfo:Continuant (though actually, more precisely to bfo:IndependentContinuant), dolce:Process as a sub-class of bfo:Process, and dolce:quality to bfo:quality.
  (b) Amount of Matter, Accomplishment, Agentive Physical Object, and Set do not have a mapping. An example of the possible reasons: Set is abstract, but not existing in nature (hence, by philosophical choice, not in BFO).
A more detailed comparison—or: the results of trying to align DOLCE, BFO, and GFO—is available at http://www.thezfiles.co.za/ROMULUS/.

Answer Exercise 6.2. Options may vary:
  (a) DOLCE or GFO
  (b) BFO or GFO
  (c) Depends on you chosen topic

Answer Exercise 6.4. The main 'trick' with such questions is to be able to detect key words and phrases, such as the description stating that there will be "concrete entities ... and ... abstract entities": this data provide answers to one of the questions in ONSET, and will affect the choice of the foundational ontology (BFO does have abstract entities, but GFO and DOLCE do), and likewise the sentence on mereology and the text mentioning OWL 2 DL. Three use case with sample answers can be found at http://www.meteck.org/files/onset/UseCasesExperiment.pdf.

Answer Exercise 6.6. I use the version with DOLCE in the following answers
  (a) To have RockDassie classified as a subclass of Herbivore (still both animals, and physical objects, and physical endurants, and endurants), it needs to have more, or more constrained properties than Herbivore. In

Protégé notation, each `Herbivore` is equivalent to:
`(eats only plant) or (eats only (is-part-of some plant))`.
Rockdassies eat grasses and broad-leafed plants. The easiest way to modify the ontology is to add that grasses are plants (already present), that broad-leafed plants are kinds of plants, and that rockdassies eat only grass or broad-leafed plant. This is not to say this is the best thing to do: there are probably also other animals that eat grasses and broad-leafed plants, which now unintentionally will be classified as rockdassies. This does not really need any of the foundational ontology content. One could align the parthood relations.

(b) The ontology does not contain any knowledge on 'residing in' and 'nature reserves', let alone sloppy word use of 'found on' (or, more precisely: in an area where a university campus is located). Nature reserves are administrative entities, but also can be considered only by their region-of-space aspect; for the sake of example, let's add NatureReserve ⊑ space-region. Trickier is the living, or living in: one could add it as an OWL object property livesIn or as a subclass of Process and add participation relations between that, the nature reserve, and the lions, impalas, and monkeys. The former is less cumbersome, the latter more precise and interoperable.

(c) Ranger is a role that a human plays for some time, with Human being a physical object, Ranger an agentive social object, and that the latter inheres in the former.

Answers Chapter 7

Answer Exercise 7.1. Phone points conceptual data model to ontology:
(a) A sample formalisation is available at the book's resources page as `phonepoints.owl`.
(b) Yes, all of it it can be represented.
(c) Yes, there are problems. See Figure D.1 for a graphical rendering that MobileCall and Cell are unsatisfiable; verify this with your version of the ontology. Observe that it also deduced that PhonePoint ≡ LandLine.

Answer Exercise 7.2. Integration issues:
a. See Figure D.2
b. Multiple answers are possible due to various design decisions. E.g.,:
- Did you represent Salary as a class and invented a new object property to relate it to the employees, or used it as a name for an OWL data property (preferably the former)? And when a data property, did you use different data types (preferably not)?
- Did you add RichEmployee, or, better, Employee that has some property of being rich?

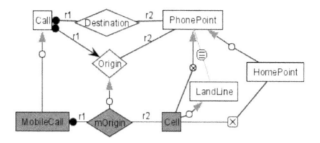

Figure D.1: Answer to Exercise 7.1-c: red: inconsistent class, green: 'positive' deduction

- Did you use a foundational ontology, or at least make a distinction between the role and its bearer (Employee and Person, respectively)?

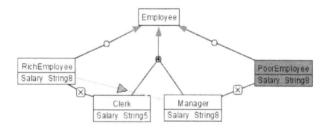

Figure D.2: Answer to Exercise 7.2-a.

Answer Exercise 7.3. Thesauri:
   a. Language: SKOS or OWL 2 EL. Why:
      - SKOS: was the purpose of it, to have a simple, but formal, language for 'smooth transition' and tagging along with the SW
      - OWL 2 EL: intended for large, simple, type-level ontologies, and then still some reasoning possible
   b. Regarding mass media, films and news media: not necessarily, but to be certain, check yourself what the definition of Mass Media is, when something can be called News Media, and then assess the differences in their properties.
      Propaganda has as broader term Information Dissemination, but a characteristic of propaganda is dissemination of *mis*information.

Answer Exercise 7.6. The description of the n-ary ODP can be found in the NeON deliverable D2.5.1 on pp67-68. Also, you may wish to inspect the draft ODPs that have been submitted to the ODP portal (at http://www.

ontologydesignpatterns.org).

Answer Exercise 7.7. One could make a Content ODP out of it: for each AssistiveDevice that is added to the ontology, one also has to record the Disability it ameliorates, it requires some Ability to use/operate the device, and performs a certain Function. With that combination, one even can create some sort of an 'input form' for domain experts and administrators, which can then hide all the logic entirely, yet as long as they follow the pattern, the information gets represented as intended.

Another one that may be useful is the Architectural OP: adolena.owl now contains some bits and pieces of both DOLCE (endurant, perdurant, and some of their subclasses) and some terms from BFO (realizable), neither of the two ontologies were imported. The architectural ODP can help cleaning this us and structuring it.

Answer Exercise 7.8. One could check the design against a foundational ontology and check whether the instantiations makes sense. There may be more options to evaluate it, as there has not been done much work on ODP quality.

Answer Exercise 7.10. Principally:
- expressive foundational ontology, such as DOLCE or GFO for improved ontology quality and interoperability
- bottom-up onto development from the thesaurus to OWL
- integration/import of existing bio-ontologies
- Domain ontology in OWL taking the classification of the chemicals, define domain & range and, ideally, defined concepts
- Add the instance data (the representation of the chemicals in stock) in the OWL ABox (there are only 100, so no real performance issues), and add a dummy class disjoint from DruTopiate destined for the 'wrong' chemicals
- Take some suitable reasoner for OWL 2 DL (either the 'standard' reasoners or names like Fact++)
- Then classify the instances availing of the available reasoning services (run Fact++ etc.): those chemical classified as instances of the 'ideal chemical' are the candidate for the lab experiments for the drug to treat blood infections.
- Alternatively: add DruTopiate as class, add the other chemicals as classes, and any classes subsumed by DruTopiate are the more likely chemicals, it's parents the less likely chemicals.
- Methods and methodologies that can be used: single, controlled ontology development, so something like METHONTOLOGY will do, and for the micro-level development something like OD101, ontospec, or DiDON.

Answers Chapter 8

Answer Exercise 8.1. Two of the reasons:
1. the ontology is specific to the application, hater than being application-independent. If it wouldn't be, then there will be mismatches (either too much/irrelevant content in the ontology, or data that should be queried but can't if there's no corresponding knowledge in the ontology)
2. the ontology contains implementation decisions, such as data properties, which will hamper any reuse, be that for another application or as a module of another ontology.

Answers Chapter 9

Answer Exercise 9.2. Possible templates are as follows, noting that one can choose other words as well, and choose between being as close to the structure of the axiom, or decide on a more 'colloquial' rendering
(a) "$< C >$ and $< D >$ are disjoint"
(a) "If there exists an outgoing arc from $< R >$ to $< C >$, then it originates in $< D >$", or, easier to read: "$< D >$ is the domain of $< R >$ (when $< R >$ relates to $< C >$)"
(a) "Each $< C > < R >$ only $< D >$"

Answer Exercise 9.3. There are clearly many possibilities. Some essential ingredients, however, are: some place where language annotations can be stored, where some rules for the sentence can be stored and used, templates or patterns to generate a sentence for the axioms and/or parts thereof, and possibly algorithms to finalise the sentence, and the ontology.

Answers Chapter 10

Answer Exercise 10.1. They do not fare well in case 2 (*for* ISs), at least not in theory. First, because of the reliance on concrete domains. Second, the numbers you and your classmate had chosen for 'old' was likely not the same—it certainly wasn't for the students in one of my classes and the cut-off point I had in mind!—which then raises the general question as to what to do with something like such a number difference when faced with choosing to reuse an ontology and when aligning ontologies or integrating system. Conversely, it thus may work well for a particular application scenario (case 1, *in* ISs), assuming all its users agree on the fuzzy membership functions.

Answer Exercise 10.2. Chronos and PROTON are relatively easy to find. Chronos uses constraint satisfaction for the temporal component, PROTON is based on Prolog. Chronos uses the 4d-fluents approach (i.e.: perdudantist [recall Chapter 6]) and implements a reasoner for the Allen relations. PROTON uses intervals and extends the situation calculus.

Answer Exercise 10.3. No. (this is basically the same as the previous review question). Consider also the scope, as state in the W3C standard, with emphasis added: "OWL-Time is an OWL-2 DL ontology of temporal concepts, for *describing* the temporal properties of resources in the world or described in Web pages. The ontology provides a *vocabulary for expressing facts* about topological (ordering) relations among instants and intervals, together with information about durations, and about temporal position including date-time information. Time positions and durations may be expressed using either the conventional (Gregorian) *calendar and clock, or using another temporal reference system such as Unix-time, geologic time, or different calendars.*". That is: for annotations, but not for reasoning with it.

About the author

Maria Keet (PhD, MSc, MA, BSc(hons)) is an Associate Professor with the Department of Computer Science, University of Cape Town, South Africa. She has taught multiple courses on ontology engineering at various universities yearly since 2009, as well as related courses, such as databases and theory of computation. Her research focus is on knowledge engineering with ontologies and Ontology, and their interaction with natural language and conceptual data modelling, which has resulted in over 100 peer-reviewed publications at venues including KR, FOIS, EKAW, K-CAP, ESWC, ER, CIKM, COLING, INLG, Applied Ontology, Data and Knowledge Engineering, and the Journal of Web Semantics, having received best paper awards at EKAW'12 and K-CAP'17. She has been a PI on NRF and DST funded projects, and she was involved in several EU projects (TONES, Net2, e-Lico). She has been (co-)PC chair of CNL'18, the ESWC'14 track on ontologies, OWLED'14, and ISAO'16, local chair of FOIS'18 and ISAO'18, and has served on many Program Committees and reviewed for numerous journals.

Before her employment at UCT, Maria was a (tenured) Senior Lecturer at the School of Mathematics, Statistics, and Computer Science at the University of KwaZulu-Natal, South Africa and before that, a non-tenured Assistant Professor at the KRDB Research Centre, Free University of Bozen-Bolzano, Italy. She obtained a PhD in Computer Science at the KRDB Research Centre in 2008, which was preceded by a BSc(honours) 1st class in IT & Computing from the Open University UK in 2004 and 3.5 years as systems engineer in the IT industry. She also obtained an MSc in Food Science (Microbiology) from Wageningen University, the Netherlands, in 1998, and an MA 1st class in Peace & Development Studies from the University of Limerick, Ireland, in 2003.

www.ingramcontent.com/pod-product-compliance
Lightning Source LLC
LaVergne TN
LVHW012327060326

832902LV00011B/1758